ESSENTIALS OF
PHYSICAL ANTHROPOLOGY

ESSENTIALS OF
PHYSICAL ANTHROPOLOGY

HARRY NELSON

Emeritus
Department of Anthropology
Foothill College
Los Altos, California

ROBERT JURMAIN

Department of Anthropology
San Jose State University
San Jose, California

LYNN KILGORE

Department of Anthropology
San Jose State University
San Jose, California

WEST PUBLISHING COMPANY

St. Paul   New York   Los Angeles   San Francisco

COPYRIGHT © 1992   By WEST PUBLISHING COMPANY
610 Opperman Drive
P.O. Box 64526
St. Paul, MN 55164–0526

99 98 97 96 95 94 93 92   8 7 6 5 4 3 2

Design: Janet Bollow
Copyediting: Stuart Kenter
Illustrations: Barbara Barnett, Brenda Booth,
                  Joseph Fay, Sue Sellars,
                  Evanell Towne,
                  Alexander Productions
Cover art: Edward Leonard
Composition: Alphatype
Production: Janet Bollow Associates

LIBRARY OF CONGRESS CATALOGING-IN-PUBLICATION DATA

Nelson, Harry.
    Essentials of physical anthropology/Harry Nelson, Robert
Jurmain, Lynn Kilgore
        p.   cm.
    Includes bibliographical references and index.
    ISBN 0–314–93440–5
    1. Physical anthropology.   I. Jurmain, Robert.
II. Kilgore, Lynn   III. Title.
GN60.N43 1992
573—dc20
                                92-72
                                CIP

CREDITS

CHAPTER 1
1-2 Harry Nelson. **1-3** Harry Nelson. **1-4** Public Relations, San Francisco State University. **1-5** Robert Jurmain. **1-7** Diana I. Davis, University of Oklahoma. **1-8** Wayne Fogle.

CHAPTER 2
2-1 The American Museum of Natural History. **2-5** Library, New York Academy of Medicine. **2-6** Bancroft Library, University of California, Berkeley. **2-7, 2-8, 2-9, 2-10, 2-11, 2-12** Library, New York Academy of Medicine.

CHAPTER 3
3-7 Courtesy, Wayne Savage; Photomicrograph by Mark Cunningham.

PHOTO ESSAY 1
1, 2, 3, 4, 5, 6, 7, 8, 9 Robert Jurmain. **10** X-ray by M. Binns; photo, Robert Jurmain. **11** C-T scan courtesy of Dr. A. Musladin; photo, Robert Jurmain. **12** Robert Jurmain. **13** Lynn Kilgore. **14** Scanning electron micrograph by M. Cunningham. **15** Scanning electron micrograph by M. Cunningham. **16, 17, 18** Courtesy, Diane France. **19, 20** Robert Jurmain. **21** Courtesy, Judy Reggensteiner/Michael Whitney. **22** Courtesy, Lorna Pierce/Judy Suchey.

CHAPTER 7
7-10 Robert Jurmain. **7-13** David Pilbeam and William Sacco.

CHAPTER 8
8-6, 8-7 Courtesy, Fred Jacobs. **8-8** Courtesy, San Francisco Zoo, Lisa Lecter. **8-9** Robert Jurmain. **8-11** San Diego Zoo. **8-12** Robert Jurmain. **8-13** Harry Nelson. **8-14** Courtesy, Bonnie Pederson/Arlene Kruse. **8-15** Hans Kummer. **8-16** Courtesy, Arlene Kruse/Bonnie Pederson. **8-17** Phyllis Dolhinow. **8-18** Lynn Kilgore. **8-19** Robert Jurmain; photo by Jill Matsumoto/Jim Anderson. **8-20(a)** Lynn Kilgore. **8-20(b)** Courtesy, Arlene Kruse/Bonnie Pederson. **8-21(a) and (b)** Robert Jurmain, photo by Jill Matsumoto/Jim Anderson. **8-22** Lynn Kilgore. **8-23** Arlene Kruse/Bonnie Pederson.

CHAPTER 9
9-1 Courtesy, Fred Jacobs. **9-2** Courtesy, Arlene Kruse/Bonnie Pederson. **9-3(a)** Harry Nelson. **9-3(b)** Jean DeRousseau.

(continued following Index)

CONTENTS

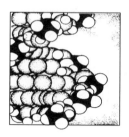

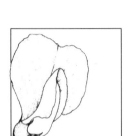

CHAPTER 6
CONTEMPORARY VIEWS
OF HUMAN VARIATION 87

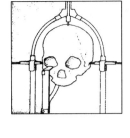

CHAPTER 7
MAMMALIAN/PRIMATE
EVOLUTIONARY HISTORY 105

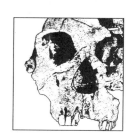

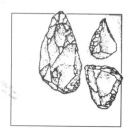

PHOTO ESSAY
PALEOPATHOLOGY: DISEASES AND INJURIES OF BONE   285

CHAPTER 14
LESSONS FROM THE PAST,
LESSONS FOR THE FUTURE   297

APPENDIX A: ATLAS OF PRIMATE SKELETAL ANATOMY   311

APPENDIX B: FORENSIC ANTHROPOLOGY   321

PREFACE

This text is designed as a reduced, essentials version of the larger text, *Introduction to Physical Anthropology* by Nelson and Jurmain, first published in 1979. Over the years, in response to suggestions made by instructors and students, the textbook has grown from its original 520 pages to the 640 pages of the fifth edition. As the full text expanded in length as well as in detail, the book may have begun to exclude part of its audience—indeed a most crucial segment in its original orientation. In particular, some instructors teaching courses designed for ten-week or twelve-week terms have found it difficult to complete a textbook of the dimensions now found in *Introduction to Physical Anthropology*. Also, for fifteen-week terms, some instructors may prefer a text that is shorter and less detailed. Moreover, using a shorter text provides the option to use other texts as well.

Consequently, our editors at West Publishing Company asked the two original authors to seriously consider ways to review and reformat the material of the introductory text in order to reach the varied audience of today. The result is *Essentials of Physical Anthropology*, which as the title suggests, is reduced to the basic essentials. Nevertheless, the text contains all the major topics necessary for an introductory physical anthropology course.

An additional author, Lynn Kilgore, was brought in and has supplied a fresh perspective throughout the text. The content has been selectively reorganized, and several topics formerly covered in two chapters have been combined into one chapter. For example, before Mendelian inheritance and polygenic inheritance were discussed in separate chapters; here they are discussed together (Chapter 4). Also, the subjects of general mammalian evolution and early primate evolution are combined in a single presentation (Chapter 7). To further reduce detail and produce a shorter book, we have deleted chapter opening Issues, as well as in-text boxes, some tables, and the annotated lists of suggested further readings at the end of each chapter. As a new feature, we have included three photo essays that vividly illustrate some of the research pursued by physical anthropologists. We hope the photo essay sections will convey the excitement and intriguing work our field of study has to offer.

Over the past twelve years we have been pleased by the response to our textbooks. From comments of our own students and from the letters of students at other universities, we have become increasingly aware of student needs. Because of these continual suggestions, we have been able to consistently improve and refine our text and also to become more effective instructors in physical anthropology.

We hope our current effort will bring our discipline to an expanded readership so that others are able to share our sense of wonder at the knowledge and inquiry of physical anthropology.

We wish to acknowledge all the helpful reviewers who have contributed their time and expertise to our texts, especially those who provided direct input for this book:

Clay Dillingham, Baylor University
David H. Dye, Memphis State University
Kenneth H. Fliess, University of Nevada, Reno
Roberta Lenkeit, Modesto Junior College
Cheryl Lee Puskarich, University of Arkansas, Little Rock
Jerome C. Rose, University of Arkansas, Fayetteville
David L. Schutzer, Los Angeles Pierce College

We also wish to thank Clyde Perlee, our editor, and Denise Simon, Executive Editor at West Educational Publishing; Janet Bollow, text designer; Stuart Kenter, copy editor; and Janet Hansen, compositor.

For her expertise and willingness to provide help with the photo essays, appendices, and other aspects of the book, we are deeply grateful to Diane France. In addition, for their assistance with the photo essays, we thank Margaret Binns, Martin Girouard, Viviana Sanchez-Chopitea, Leon Pappanostos, Brian Wesenberg, Carol Martinez, Arlene Christopherson, Ruby Tilley, and the staff of the Photo Department, Instructional Resource Center, San Jose State University. We are also most appreciative to those who have generously provided us with photographs: Phyllis Dolhinow, Fred Smith, Milford Wolpoff, Günter Bräuer, Lorna Pierce, Judy Suchey, Judith Reggensteiner, Virginia Landau, Julie Bittnoff, Patti Gibson, Carol Lofton, Bonnie Pederson, Arlene Kruse, Paul Sledzick, Wayne Savage, Fred Jacobs, Jean DeRousseau, Joyce Bizjack, and JoAnn Brisko.

Harry Nelson
Robert Jurmain
Lynn Kilgore

ESSENTIALS OF
PHYSICAL ANTHROPOLOGY

INTRODUCTION

CHAPTER 1

What Is Anthropology?
The Biocultural Approach
What Is Physical Anthropology?
What Is Human?
The Scientific Approach
Summary
Questions for Review

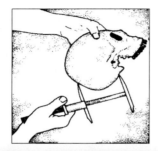

CHAPTER 1

WHAT IS ANTHROPOLOGY?

ANTHROPOLOGY anthropos: man
logos: science study of

Anthropology is a scientific approach to the study of human beings, both past and present. It encompasses the study of all human behavior—for example, the building of shelters, the care of children, farming, hunting, religious ritual, speech, and much more. The field of anthropology also incorporates concepts such as economics, kinship, relationships, and social status. Such activities and concepts are the concern of *cultural anthropology*. Another main component of anthropology is archeology. The focus of archeological research is the recovery, analysis, and interpretation of material culture from earlier populations. Archeologists use many of the same theoretical principles as cultural anthropologists in explaining patterns of human behavior. Moreover, they also work closely with physical anthropologists, especially in the excavation of archeological sites.

Physical anthropology, on the other hand, is concerned with the physical or biological aspects of human beings. Professionals in this field investigate such areas as our ancestry and ancestors, genes and their effect on humans, nonhuman **primates** and their relation to humans, and the evolutionary processes involved in our physical development.

PRIMATES (pry'-mates)
The order of mammals to which humans, apes, monkeys, and prosimians belong. All life forms are arranged in a number of divisions. These divisions (e.g., *class*, *order*, *family*, *species*) include groups of animals or plants.

HOLISM Viewing the whole in terms of an integrated system; cultural and ecological systems as wholes.

Anthropology, therefore, is a **holistic** science, with the entire gamut of humankind as the focus of study. Other disciplines that deal with people—sociology, psychology, economics, political science, history, and others—tend to specialize in single aspects of human activity. Economists, for example, study the production, distribution, and consumption of goods; market systems; and systems of exchange; but they would rarely consider the effect of religion or kinship on the economic system. Anthropology, however, takes a broader, holistic approach and considers the findings of all academic fields that pertain to humans; in fact, anything associated with humankind is considered within anthropology's range.

CULTURE The set of rules, standards, and norms shared by members of a society; transmitted by learning, and responsible for the behavior of those members.

The wide scope of anthropology is reflected in its two broad, basic categories: cultural (including archeology) and physical, which are further divided into subdisciplines, as shown in Fig. 1-1. The focus of cultural anthropology is **culture**, which refers to the way of life of a society, including behavior, ideas, values, principles, rituals, methods of organi-

ANTHROPOLOGY	

Physical Anthropology
  Human evolution (macroevolution)
    Paleoanthropology
      Comparative anatomy
    Primatology
  Human variation (microevolution)
    Human genetics
    Population genetics
      Human diversity (race)
    Human osteology
	Cultural Anthropology
	  Sociocultural anthropology
	  Archeology
	  Linguistics
	  or
	Behavioral Anthropology
	  Cultural anthropology
	  Archeology
	  Linguistics

FIGURE 1-1 The field of anthropology. This chart is a general guide to the field of anthropology and its many subdivisions. Other anthropologists may, according to their own views, add, subtract, or rearrange what is presented here.

zation, aims, goals, spiritual beliefs, subsistence methods, technologies, relationships of all sorts, and more—all are part of culture.

Culture is learned. It is transmitted socially as the older generation enculturates its succeeding generation by deliberate instruction or by the passive role it plays as a model. In many societies, especially in industrial countries, enculturation is brought about not merely by family and kin, but by the massive influence of modern communication, such as books, newspapers, movies, formal education, and television.

The concept of culture is twofold: on the one hand a culture, as noted above, is the totality of the learned behavior and ideas of a particular society. This information is gathered by cultural anthropologists, called **ethnographers**, who traditionally spend a year or so with a society usually not their own. In recent years, anthropologists have included urban and industrial areas in their ethnographic studies.

ETHNOGRAPHY The study of surviving nonliterate societies. (Literate societies may also be studied.)

Culture may also be approached as a theoretical construct. Material gathered by ethnographers from hundreds of diverse cultures form a data base for constructing hypotheses and theories about the nature of culture. For example, cultural anthropologists have developed theories pertaining to various aspects of culture change.

Another aspect of the broad anthropological approach is that these data come from so many different sources. The anthropological view of humans is not based on any particular culture. Anthropological field work covers the globe. Cultural anthropologists work on every continent, archaeologists dig wherever there are research problems to be addressed, and anthropological linguists do their field work in the areas where the language they are studying is spoken.

THE BIOCULTURAL APPROACH

In order to understand the human condition, anthropologists believe it is necessary to investigate human biology *and* cultural behavior. Since we are biological organisms that possess culture, such a broad perspective— what is known as a **biocultural** approach—makes sense. If we exclusively

BIOCULTURAL The interaction of biological and cultural factors. An approach to the study of human evolution and behavior that stresses the influence of each of these and their reciprocating effects on one another.

examine only our cultural behavior, we fail to consider our biological capabilities and limitations, and if we concentrate solely on our biology, we omit the single most important attribute of humans—culture.

It is both possible and desirable to view our evolutionary history bioculturally. When we ponder the origin of hominids (members of the Homindae, our zoological family), we can best understand it from the interaction of body form and behavior. There are two outstanding features of hominids that separate us from other animals: (1) a large complex brain and (2) **bipedalism**. It is probable that bipedalism initiated the hominid diversification from apes. One of the most important results of this development was the freeing of the hands for activities such as carrying (babies, stones, wood, food, weapons, etc.) and making tools. (Apes, especially chimpanzees, also make rudimentary tools, but tool use never became as significant a factor for apes as it has for humans.)

Freeing the hands spurred the development of culture; that is, behavior *not* genetically based. Carrying objects, making tools, and other manual activities opened up avenues of behavior that enhanced reproduction and survival. (We may assume that evolution selected for brains that encouraged successful cultural behavior.) Thus, we see that biology affected behavior and was in turn affected by culture. From the very start, human evolution was most likely a biocultural event, one that has continued up to the present.

Biology and culture continue to interact, but our culture has become so sophisticated, especially technologically, that major alterations in our body form are improbable. Should conditions arise that require adaptive body changes, we are more likely to resolve the problem technologically than by body modification, which again reflects the relationship of biology and culture. However, it is important to recall that, as biological organisms, we are still subject to the laws of evolution and natural selection, and major adaptive changes remain a possibility.

It is interesting, from a biocultural point of view, that humans have culturally created an environment that threatens our biological existence. Will we adapt biologically to increased exposure to electromagnetic forces and toxic substances? Or will we invent technologies that will avert the necessity to do so? Or, will we fail on both counts?

This biocultural approach to the study of human beings makes anthropology a unique discipline. As a social science, cultural anthropology is the study of culture—that broad area of learned behavior that humans have developed as their basic strategy for survival. As a biological science, physical anthropology is the study of the biological aspects of humans. Combining the biological and social aspects, we have a comprehensive view of the animal *Homo sapiens*, which we call human.

In order to understand the physical human being, we must of necessity consider the special way of life of this organism. Unlike all other creatures in the animal kingdom, we human beings have developed a strategy of adaptation (Fig. 1-2)—obtaining food, producing the next generation, protecting the group against enemies and the elements, developing concepts of life's meaning—that, again, we call culture, which serves as a mediator between society and the environment. In order to serve this function, culture must be learned by humans, as contrasted to the direct

BIPEDALISM (bipedality) (by-pee'-dal-ism)
bi: two
ped: feet
Walking on two feet as among hominids and some other animals.

comprehension of the environment by other animals. All animals, especially mammals, are capable of learning, and nonhuman primates excel at this. The learning ability of the great apes (gorillas, orangutans, and chimpanzees) is now well recognized; nevertheless, no other mammal depends on learning to anywhere near the extent that humans do.

While possessing a biologically based capacity for culture, humans must learn behavior anew every generation. We must learn what, when, where, and with whom to obtain food, eat, marry, and associate. We must learn what is right and wrong, what to wear and not to wear, what weapons and utensils to use and when, and how to relate to parents, cousins, and friends. All of this learning process comes under the heading of culture.

Culture, then, is an accumulation of knowledge, rules, standards, skills, and mental sets that humans utilize in order to survive; that is to say, adapt to the environments in which they live. One cannot imagine humans today surviving without culture. Indeed, such a case is virtually impossible. Obtaining and preparing food, coping with severe climatic conditions, trying to understand the world around us, cooperating with others—all of these normal and daily activities require cultural solutions. Our bodies alone are not adequate for the task of living. We must have material items (Fig. 1-3) to help us acquire what we need; we must have ideas to help us communicate with one another.

Cultural anthropology, as we have emphasized, is the comprehensive study of what humans have learned to do, and are doing, in order to survive and adapt. What is the connection between these learned processes and our biological constitution? Did our evolutionary development depend on culture? Or did the development of culture depend on our biological constitution?

FIGURE 1-2 Humans are biocultural animals who developed culture as an adaptive strategy for survival and thus became human. Note the many items of material culture and social behavior that make the human way possible.

FIGURE 1-3 Early humans possessed a small and simple tool kit. At a modern hardware store, an overwhelming variety of tools, utensils, and weapons is available.

In the biocultural view, culture and our biological structure are critically related. Had we not come from primate beginnings, culture would not have developed, and had our ancestors not developed culture, we would not have evolved our present physical form. The two are inextricably related, and if we wish to learn something of physical anthropology, we *must* understand the role culture has played in the process of human evolution.

The human biological structure today is not simply the result of genetic inheritance; the influence of cultural factors plays a large role in our biology. The shape of our bodies, as well as the function of most of our internal organs, have been impacted by culture. Our large brain did not come about by accident. It is capable of *producing* culture, but its evolutionary growth is a result of the culture it produced. There is a feedback mechanism at work here in which the brain generated the initial development of culture which, in turn, provoked and stimulated further expansion of the brain. We do not simply invent tools and language and conceive arts and sciences, we are also the product of these events.

WHAT IS PHYSICAL ANTHROPOLOGY?

With this introduction, utilizing a biocultural perspective, let us examine more closely the field of physical anthropology, the concern of this book. Although physical anthropologists are not in complete agreement on precisely what is to be included within their field, they do generally agree that two areas are fundamental: **human evolution** and **human variation**.

Human evolution, the subject of much of this text, especially Chapters 7 through 13, may in turn be divided into two areas: paleoanthropology and primatology.

HUMAN EVOLUTION Physical changes over time leading to anatomically modern human beings.

HUMAN VARIATION Physical differences among humans.

Paleoanthropology is the study of the fossil remains of our ancestors. Physical anthropologists, together with archaeologists, geologists, and other scientists, have unearthed fossil remains in many parts of the world. With their knowledge of **osteology**, paleoanthropologists examine, measure, and reconstruct these remains, often from mere fragments. Such analysis has enabled physical anthropologists to propose possible lines of descent from our ancient ancestors to our present form.

Primatology, as the word suggests, is the study of nonhuman primates, the group (*order* is the technical term) of the animal kingdom to which humans, apes, monkeys, and **prosimians** belong. The anatomy of nonhuman primates, especially monkeys and apes, has been studied to ascertain the similarities and differences between these primates and humans. This kind of study helps trace the evolutionary relationships of human and nonhuman primates.

Because of the remarkable similarities among monkeys, apes, and humans, researchers have been able, through laboratory experiments with monkeys and apes, to learn what effects certain diseases, stresses, and other conditions might have on humans. Work with the rhesus monkey, for example, led to the discovery of the Rh blood factor which, due to incompatibility between mother and fetus, may cause a disease fatal to human infants. Because of the similarity in blood types and physiological responses of chimpanzees and humans, chimpanzees are highly prized as laboratory "models" in biomedical studies, as in research on vaccines for hepatitis and AIDS.

A fascinating area of primate investigation concerns observing primates in their natural habitat as a means of understanding the organism-environment interaction. This type of investigation, often difficult and dangerous, has become much more common in the last three decades. Perhaps the best-known field study is Jane Goodall's work with the chimpanzees in East Africa, but a number of others have attracted attention: for example, Phyllis Dolhinow's work with langurs in India; the study of mountain gorillas in Rwanda (Africa), begun by Dian Fossey and now continued by her successors; Biruté Galdikas' work with orangutans in Borneo; the extensive research on baboons in Africa; and the long-term research on macaques at the Japanese Monkey Centers.

These studies have uncovered important patterns of social interactions, such as the relationships between dominant and subordinate males, mothers and offspring, and the young and old. In addition, tool-making and the ability to learn complex tasks (behaviors until recently hardly believed possible) have also been discovered with surprising frequency among certain species of primates. In light of these developments, physical anthropologists hope that such current and rapidly cumulating data will help in tracing human evolution from our primate ancestors, as well as aid in understanding the behavior of humans today.

We have discussed what might be termed *academic anthropology*. There are, however, physical anthropologists who pursue their work outside of (or in addition to) academic institutions in a branch called *applied anthropology*. In this field, the principles and data of anthropology are related to practical situations. Many years ago, for example, physical anthropologists were already applying their knowledge by developing

OSTEOLOGY (os-tee-ol'-o-jee)
osteon: bone
The study of bones.

PROSIMIANS (pro-sim'-ee-ens)
pro: before
simian: ape or monkey
Common form of Prosimii, a suborder of primates, composed of small primates such as lemurs and tarsiers.

standard sizes for the clothing industry and the military, and more comfortable seats for automobiles and airplanes. Space requirements for industrial workers were also analyzed, and mechanical problems associated with the body, such as the placement of foot pedals and hand controls for machine operators, were studied.

Some physical anthropologists sometimes also assist judicial and law enforcement agencies. Practitioners of **forensic anthropology** (Fig. 1-4), as the field is called, may be asked to ascertain the age and sex of a corpse, and how long it has been buried; they may, in some cases, assist the coroner in determining the cause of death. A recent development, part of the remarkable achievement of *biotechnology*, is the technique of DNA fingerprinting. The DNA of an individual can be compared with the DNA in a hair, or a drop of semen. If matched, the individual is positively identified by these bits of evidence; if not matched, he or she is thus excluded. Forensic anthropologists are now participating in this work.

For many years, physical anthropology has had considerable application in the field of medicine. The relationship between body build and disease, and the question of whether a particular disease is hereditary or culturally mediated have been among the subjects investigated by physical anthropologists. Data on diseases have been collected from many countries in an effort to determine what special social conditions might be involved in the causes and cures.

An area of physical anthropology that has been a central focus since the beginnings of the discipline in this country might be termed *skeletal biology*. Over the years, archaeologists have excavated thousands of human burials from sites around the world. As the most durable parts of the human organism, the hard tissues (bones and teeth) may endure for centuries and, if fossilized, millions of years. As experts in the anatomical structure of these hard tissues, physical anthropologists (here usually

FORENSIC (from forum) Pertaining to courts of law. In anthropology, the use of anthropology in questions of law.

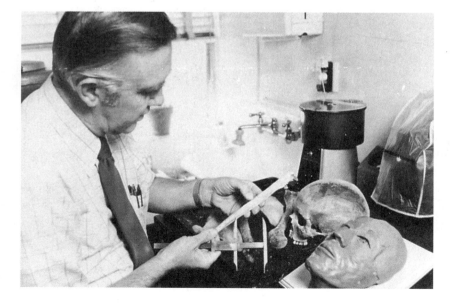

FIGURE 1-4 Physical anthropologist in his lab.

ls. Our social relationships are not only
iety to society. The family structure differs
called *osteologists*) can, by ʋ⸍ quite often within societies. Human social
anthropologists, often dete⸍ range from rigid caste systems to systems
ual from which the specin⸍l mobility.
aid of specialized instru⸍mbers of a particular category (such as sex or
mensions regarding si⸍milarly. Mammals exhibit more flexibility than
fully inspect the ske⸍n primates displaying the most of all. Recent obser-
tuberculosis, healed⸍y of behavior among chimpanzees in the wild have
called **paleopatholc**⸍s. Nevertheless, no chimpanzee community displays
of human disease, ty in behavior found in *any* human society.
certain diseases ⸍ɹost important factors that distinguishes humans from

Human var our ability to communicate symbolically and orally
anthropology, ʒe. This activity, as far as we know, is specific to humans.
populations. Ir⸍nans (mainly psychologists), chimpanzee achievements
world's popul⸍uage are truly remarkable (Fig. 1-7). However, even when
however, pre⸍ent apes sign to other chimps, such a display in no way com-
cent years, crucial reliance humans place on symbolic communication.
genetically ɔre, what chimpanzees or other animals achieve with *human*
Wit⸍ is quite different from what humans, as a species, have de-
variatic by themselves.
gans, a
and e⸍
tal ar
evol⸍

ᴜRE 1-7 Jesabel, a 6-year-old chimp
to ʒning "drink."

f⸍

T⸍

A
a usefui
superiorit⸍
include the
species, and ⸍
of), who emer⸍

*mya stands for m⸍

THE SCIENTIFIC APPROACH

EMPIRICAL (em-pir'-i-kal)
empirikos: experienced
Derived from or depending on experience or experiment.

HYPOTHESIS Unproved theory. A theory is a statement with some confirmation.

COSMOLOGY kosmos: world
The study of the creation of the universe and the laws that govern it.

WORLD VIEW A literal translation from the German *Weltanschauung* (Welt: world; anschauung: view). A personal or group philosophy explaining history; a way of looking at the world.

Physical anthropology is a scientific discipline and, more precisely, a *biological science*. Physical anthropologists, therefore, employ an **empirical**/scientific approach to understanding the universe.

What do we mean by "scientific"? The scientific approach is still largely misunderstood by the general public. First of all, scientists do *not* seek to disprove religious doctrine but, rather, they attempt to understand the universe through direct *observation* (Fig. 1-8), generating **hypotheses** to explain these observations, and then continually testing their results against further information. As new evidence accumulates, hypotheses are modified.

Strict theologians, on the other hand, understand the universe through faith, not through physical evidence. The written documents of the Eastern and Western religions reveal the universe through the direct word of an all-knowing spiritual power. Such a **cosmology** is intended to explain systematically and completely the nature of the universe, our planet, and ourselves. Since the Truth is known absolutely, there is little room for argument. The furthest extension of this world view holds that it is not even necessary or desirable to gather additional information about our universe.

In the last 400 to 500 years, however, a different **world view** has come to predominate in the Western world. This view entails what we

FIGURE 1-8 Observation is a scientific approach.

have called the empirical/scientific approach. Since theological and scientific approaches consist of entirely different ways of understanding the universe, no reasonable means exist for arguing one versus the other. We simply start with alternate assumptions: either we understand the universe by divine revelation, or we comprehend it by observation. In the former, we can find absolute Truth (large T); in the latter, we merely make the most reasonable hypotheses, and, in a sense, know only relative truth (small t). All of our understanding, religious and scientific, is based on *some* kind of theory.

Because scientists must theorize does not mean, however, that they cannot come to grips with the physical universe and the organisms within it. Scientific theories are only as good as their capacity to explain comprehensively natural and experimental observations, both those already gathered and those that may be made in the future. Some hypotheses, theories, or laws are powerful explanatory principles indeed. Consider these, for example: that the sun is the center of the solar system with the earth rotating around it; that our universe is not fixed but in constant motion; that heredity is transmitted from one generation to the next by cells, not blood. Organic evolution (discussed in the next chapter) is also a theory; but like those just noted, it has tremendous explanatory value, and has been *confirmed* by millions of independent observations.

Must science and religion conflict? Certainly not. It is possible for scientists to believe in some form of supernatural doctrine and, at the same time, accept evolution as a fact. Paradoxically, science in our society today has become a kind of religion for many people who "believe" in scientific principles as unalterable dogma. However, from an empirical point of view, our understanding of the universe is never absolute; it is gained by human beings slowly piecing together bits of evidence gathered through observations that explain the universe. We certainly do not know everything. But we do know enormously more than we did a century, a decade, or even a year ago. Every day our data increase, and, consequently, our understanding increases as well. This book adds to our body of knowledge by telling the dramatic and continually unfolding story of human evolution.

SUMMARY

Anthropology is the study of human beings and their primate ancestors. It is a holistic science divided into two main branches: cultural and physical. Cultural anthropology, including archeology, is the study of what humans have learned to do in order to adapt to their environment; physical anthropology, the study of humans as animals, is mainly concerned with human variation and human evolution.

Specialized fields within physical anthropology include comparative human genetics, growth and development, paleoanthropology, human osteology, and primatology. Some physical anthropologists have specialized in applied anthropology, forensic anthropology, and paleopathology.

Physical anthropologists, in order to understand the universe, employ an empirical/scientific approach, one based on observation and physical evidence. This method of understanding is contrasted to a religious approach, which is based on faith. Since these are alternative ways of comprehending the universe, there is no necessary conflict between them.

QUESTIONS FOR REVIEW

1. What is meant by *holistic*? Why is anthropology a holistic science?
2. Explain the biocultural approach in anthropology.
3. What are the two main branches of anthropology?
4. What are the two main areas of physical anthropology?
5. What are some of the fields of specialization within physical anthropology?
6. In what ways are humans unique from other animals?
7. Discuss the concept of culture.
8. What role does culture play in human uniqueness?
9. Explain why there is no necessary conflict between the scientific and religious approach to understanding the universe.
10. How do you think culture affects human evolution?

DARWIN AND NATURAL SELECTION

CHAPTER 2

INTRODUCTION

The major result of evolution—that is, the development of new species from already existing **species**—was not taken seriously by medieval philosophers. Literal reading of the Bible, especially Genesis, taught that all plants and animals had been created. Nothing in the Bible suggested the creation of new species; ergo, there were none. Furthermore, the universe was *fixed* at creation and forever remained unchanged. The idea of evolution, then, not only would have been considered heretical, but "common sense" would have labeled it ridiculous.

Nevertheless, scholars of the fifteenth, sixteenth, and seventeenth centuries demonstrated that the universe was *not* rigidly fixed. The belief that organic beings were also not fixed was being entertained, especially in the eighteenth century. Unfortunately, attempts to explain how the process of evolution worked failed until Charles Darwin, in the nineteenth century, succeeded with his theory of *natural selection*.

Our understanding of evolution today is based essentially on Darwin's work as well as contributions made in the twentieth century, mainly from the field of genetics. Although our focus throughout the text is *human evolution*, in this chapter we discuss general evolutionary principles applicable to all organisms.

We will examine the changes in intellectual thought that led to the theory of natural selection, acclaimed as the most important scientific contribution of the nineteenth century. First, though, let us take a brief look at the man most responsible for this theory: Charles Darwin.

DARWIN'S LIFE

FIGURE 2-1   Charles Darwin (at age 32).

Charles Darwin (1809–1882) was the son of Dr. Robert and Susannah Darwin and grandson of the eminent Dr. Erasmus Darwin. Charles, one of six children, was thought by his family and by himself to be a "very ordinary boy." As an ordinary boy, he did the usual things (collecting shells, stamps, coins) and, at school, displayed no special inclination for scholarship.

At his father's urging, Charles took up residence at Christ's College, Cambridge University, in 1828 at the age of 19. Although he was not enrolled in science, he became a constant companion of the Reverend John Stevens Henslow, professor of botany, and often joined his classes in their botanical excursions.

In the summer of 1831, following his graduation, Darwin received a letter from Professor Henslow informing him that he had recommended Darwin as the best qualified person he knew for the position of naturalist on a scientific expedition aboard the H.M.S. *Beagle*, a ship that would circle the globe. Darwin was eager to go, but his father objected, and it took some time before he was persuaded to give his consent.

Darwin went aboard the *Beagle* not as an evolutionist but as a believer in the fixity of species; that is, he believed that species remain as they were created and never change. His observations, however, quickly raised his suspicions that species may indeed change. He noted that a snake with rudimentary hind limbs might indicate a relationship with lizards. He came across fossils of ancient giant animals that looked, except for size, very much like living forms, and wondered whether the fossils were the ancestors of those forms. He observed that the Andean Mountain range constituted a natural barrier that produced different flora and fauna on each side of the mountains.

The stopover at the Galápagos Islands (see Fig. 2-2b) profoundly impressed Darwin. He noted that the flora and fauna of South America were very similar—yet dissimilar—to those of the Galápagos. Even more surprising, similar inhabitants of the various islands differed slightly. For example, the thirteen kinds of finches resembled one another in the structure of their beaks, body forms, and plumage, and yet each constituted a separate species (but only one species existed on the mainland, the original habitat of the finches) despite the fact that few geographic differences existed among the islands. What, he asked himself, could produce these patterns if physical geography and climate were not responsible? The questions raised caused Darwin to wonder whether the theory of fixity of species was a valid one after all.

This abbreviated account of Darwin and his research on the *Beagle* does not do justice to the significant role the voyage played in Darwin's intellectual growth. He returned to England on board the *Beagle* on October 2, 1836, just short of five years from the date he sailed, a more mature and serious scientist.

Settling down in the village of Downe with his bride in his newly built home he called Down, Darwin spent the rest of his life in writing and research. In 1842, he wrote a short summary of his views on natural selection and revised it in 1844. The 1844 sketch is surprisingly similar to the argument he presented fifteen years later in *On the Origin of Species*, but Darwin did not feel he yet had sufficient data to support his views, and he continued his research.

Time passed. In 1855, an article by Alfred Russel Wallace on the succession of species impressed Darwin, because it supported his own views on species' mutability. Darwin was not disturbed at this time by the possibility that the publication of his own theory might be anticipated. However, in June 1858, Darwin was shaken when he received a paper from Wallace on natural selection, a solution that Darwin himself had developed many years earlier.

FIGURE 2-2 Examples of some of Darwin's finches. Note the similarities and differences in beak structure.

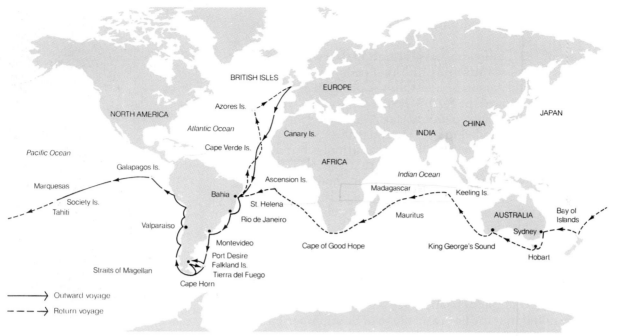

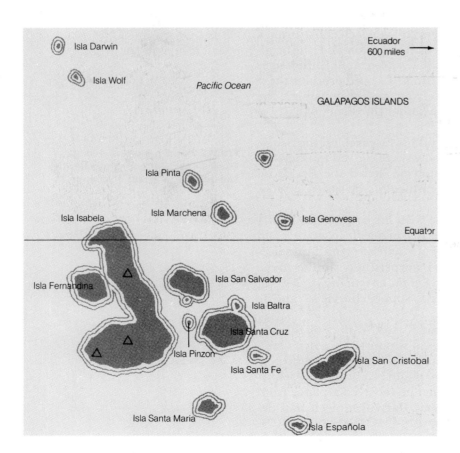

FIGURE 2-3a The route of the H.M.S. *Beagle.*

FIGURE 2-3b The Galápagos Islands. Finches (because of their variety) and tortoises (because each island was inhabited by its own variety) influenced Darwin's thinking about evolution.

FIGURE 2-4 Darwin's home in the village of Downe, where he wrote *The Origin of Species*.

Alfred Russel Wallace (1823–1913) was born in a small English village into a family of modest means. He went to work at 14 and, without any special talent, moved from one job to the next. He became interested in collecting, and joined an expedition to the Amazon in 1848, at the age of 25. In 1854, he sailed to the Malayan Archipelago to continue his study and collection of bird and insect specimens.

In 1858, while in bed suffering from one of his periodic attacks of fever, the solution to the problem he had so long sought flashed through his mind. He recalled the phrase, "the positive checks to increase," from an essay on population by Thomas Malthus, an English political scientist. Malthus had pointed out that human populations would double every generation if they were not checked by the *struggle for existence*. Wallace now realized that this phenomenon could apply to animals as well as to humans. If there were no checks, the earth would soon be overrun by the most prolific breeders.

When Darwin read Wallace's paper he was thoroughly depressed; he thought Wallace might be credited for a theory—natural selection—that Darwin believed he himself had formulated. He quickly wrote a paper expounding his ideas, and both the paper by Darwin and the one by Wallace were read before the Linnaean Society of London. Darwin was urged to publish, as speedily as possible, a full account of his theory. With exemplary energy, he returned to work and, within a year, in 1859, completed and published his great work, *The Origin of Species*.*

With publication, the storm broke and has not abated even to this day. While there was much praise for the book, the gist of opinion was

FIGURE 2-5 Alfred Russel Wallace.

---

*The full title of the book is *On the Origin of Species by Means of Natural Selection, or the Preservation of Favoured Races in the Struggle for Life*.

negative. Scientific opinion gradually came to Darwin's support, assisted especially by Darwin's able friend, Thomas Huxley (known as "Darwin's bulldog"), who for years wrote and spoke in favor of natural selection. The riddle of species was now explained: species were mutable, not fixed; they evolved from other species through the mechanism of natural selection. Science was never to be the same again.

DARWIN'S THEORY OF EVOLUTION

Darwin did not originate the idea of evolution, which had been suggested (or at least hinted at) 200 years earlier—and much longer, if we include Greek thought of 2000 years ago. Darwin's grandfather, Erasmus Darwin, had written in defense of evolution before Charles was born, and Lamarck, a French scientist, had drawn up a schema explaining, unsuccessfully, how new species were formed.

Nor were the basic ideas used by Darwin completely of his own invention. Struggle for existence, extinction of species, variation, adaptation—these were all known and discussed for years by many European scientists. Darwin's brilliant contribution was to bring these divergent ideas together and add the key: natural selection.

In his book, *The Origin of Species*, Darwin presented his concept of evolution:

1. All species are capable of producing offspring faster than the food supply increases
2. All living things show variations; no two individuals of a species are exactly alike
3. Because there are more individuals than can possibly survive, there is a fierce struggle for existence, and those with a favorable variation in size, strength, running ability, or whatever characteristics are necessary for survival, will possess an advantage over others
4. These favorable variations are inherited and passed on to the next generation; less favorable variations tend not to be passed on as frequently as favorable ones
5. Over long periods of geologic time, these successful variations produce great differences that result in new species

Darwin had now come full circle from his earlier view that species were fixed.

THE PATH TO NATURAL SELECTION

Darwin did not arrive at natural selection—his solution to the process of evolution—without assistance. When we look at the intellectual climate of Europe of the Middle Ages, we find that Christianity was associated with certain views of the universe. Since the time of Ptolemy, a Greco-Egyptian mathematician, geographer, and astronomer of the second century A.D., the earth was considered to be fixed at the center of a universe of spheres that revolved with perfect regularity around it. Not only was the inorganic world fixed and unchanging, but the organic world was believed to be equally static.

It was accepted that all species of the earth had been created (according to Genesis of the Old Testament) on a *progression* from the simplest living forms to the most complex—humans. This progression was not evolutionary; that is, one species did not lead to or evolve into the next. The forms and sequence were fixed, each creature forever linked to the next in a great chain of beings. No new ones had appeared since creation, and none had disappeared. This concept was known as the Great Chain of Being.

Originating from ideas of Plato and Aristotle, the Chain of Being was a world view widespread in Europe, especially during the seventeenth and eighteenth centuries. This philosophy held that the earth, even the universe, was "full"; that is, everything that *could* exist, already did exist. There was no space for anything more. Also, the universe was composed of an infinite and continuous series of forms, each one *grading* into the next, arranged in an hierarchical sequence from the simplest kind of existence to the perfection of God.

Thus, there were superior and inferior beings, and perhaps more important (for evolutionary concepts), a being's place in this linear sequence was *fixed* and could not be altered. And since the earth was "full," nothing new (such as species) could be added and nothing could be removed. Furthermore, a superior being did not evolve from the next lower one; rather, as mentioned, a being was created forever, set and unchangeable in its position in the chain. Since God created the chain, change was inconceivable, for this would challenge God's perfection.

The plan of the entire universe was seen as the Grand Design, that is, God's Design. The limbs of men and animals seemed designed to meet the purpose for which they were required. Wings, arms, eyes, and so forth, all of these structures were interpreted as neatly fitting the functions they performed. Nature was considered to be a deliberate plan of the Grand Designer, a concept supported by what is known as "argument from design." As John Ray, one of the leading naturalists of the sixteenth century, put it:

> If works of art, designed for a certain purpose, infer the existence of an intelligent Architect or Engineer, then why should not Nature, which transcends human art, infer the existence of an Omnipotent and Allwise Creator? (Quote rendered in more modern English.)

The date the Grand Designer had completed his work was relatively recent—4004 B.C.—according to Archbishop James Ussher (1581–1656), an Irish prelate and scholar, who worked out the date of creation by analyzing the "begat" chapter of Genesis.

Until these ideas of fixity and time were changed, it would be very unlikely that a concept such as natural selection could even be imagined. What, then, upset the medieval belief in a rigid universe of planets, stars, plants, and animals? What scientific philosophy would, within the following 150 years, strike a death blow to the whole medieval system of

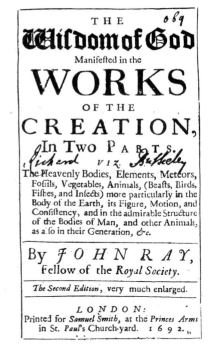

THE
Wisdom of God
Manifested in the
WORKS
OF THE
CREATION,
In Two PARTS.
Richard viz. *Berkeley*
The Heavenly Bodies, Elements, Meteors, Fossils, Vegetables, Animals, (Beasts, Birds, Fishes, and Insects) more particularly in the Body of the Earth, its Figure, Motion, and Consistency, and in the admirable Structure of the Bodies of Man, and other Animals, as also in their Generation, &c.

By *JOHN RAY,*
Fellow of the *Royal Society.*

The Second Edition, very much enlarged.

LONDON:
Printed for *Samuel Smith,* at the *Princes Arms* in St. *Paul's* Church-yard. 1 6 9 2.

FIGURE 2-6 An early (seventeenth-century) version of the Argument from Design.

thought? How would the scientific method as we know it today develop and, especially with Newton and Galileo in the seventeenth century, demonstrate a moving, not unchanging, universe?

THE SCIENTIFIC REVOLUTION

The change might be said to have begun in the sixteenth century when Copernicus, a Polish cleric and astronomer, noted that earth was not the center of the universe but, rotating on its axis, revolved around a fixed sun. This heresy attracted little attention at the time, but in the next century Galileo reintroduced Copernicus' heliocentric (sun-centered) theory. Although this brought him into conflict with the Church, most scientists no longer took seriously the notion that the sun revolved around a fixed earth.

Scientists of the sixteenth and seventeenth centuries developed methods and theories that revolutionized scientific thought. The seventeenth century, in particular, was a beehive of scientific activity that ended almost 2000 years of dependence on the Aristotelian view of the universe, and set on course the methodology of modern science. These early scientists gave the intellectual milieu of their era a definite naturalistic basis. While still a significant element in scientific thinking, God was increasingly viewed as an unnecessary factor in a more naturalistic view of the universe. It was becoming possible to investigate the stars, planets, animals, and plants without reference to the supernatural. Nature was seen as a mechanism, functioning according to certain physical laws, and it was these laws that scientists were to seek.

The work of naturalists of that period reflected a modern biological approach. They collected, classified, described; they upset ancient notions and exploded old fables. They adopted the mechanical model of nature to explain organic function. And yet, the notion lingered that a *vital* principle was necessary to understand the works of nature, which ultimately depended on God's design. God was not considered dead, and many scientists could believe in a mechanistic universe and still insist that a First Cause initiated the entire system. It was a confusing time in scientific thought; science was moving toward a secular approach, but not quite ready to move all the way.

Nevertheless, the erosion of the concept of God as the center of scientific and philosophic thought continued into the eighteenth century, which was a less religious time in Europe than the seventeenth century. The argument from design was still defended, and support for it continued well into the nineteenth century. The *watch*, signifying the order that reigned in the universe, argued the existence of the watch*maker*.

Also retained by many scientists was the insistence on stasis as it applied to life forms. The stars, the sun, the planets, and the earth might move, but life remained as it was created—no new species; no extinctions.

It is ironic that Christian belief—that the order and design of the universe could be interpreted by rational minds—led to Darwin and natural selection. We have remarked that in the seventeenth century there appeared to be an overwhelming thrust by philosopher/scientists toward examining nature in all its aspects. Studying natural relationships diligently was not an irreverant exercise, but a human duty. Such study would demonstrate the majesty and glory of God. This conviction continued through the next two centuries and drove many to search out the mysteries of nature. It was this same conviction and drive that not only led to Darwin, but to the modern concept of a secular science.

Linnaeus

The course toward evolution was not an easy one, however. The notion of the fixity of species held sway among the public, as well as with most scientists. One such scientist, and one of the leading naturalists of his day, was **Carolus Linnaeus** (1707–1778) of Sweden, best known for developing a classification system for plants and animals, first published in 1735. He used a binomial system for naming plants and animals, assigning two Latin words to each organism. The first word was the generic term (genus) and the second word the specific term (species); for example, *Homo* (genus) *sapiens* (species). Linnaeus also classified plants and animals by isolating particular physical traits that best characterized a group of organisms. In plants, for instance, he used blossoms; in insects, wings; and in fish, scales. This system still serves as the basis of modern taxonomy.

However, Linnaeus was a firm believer in the fixity of species,* that species living in his day were the same as those that had been originally created—there were no additions, no extinctions. He agreed with the "chain of being" view that all life forms were linked together in one great chain, and each species was permanently fixed in the chain, which was itself unalterable.

Nevertheless, there were other voices, especially in France, in favor of a universe based on change and, more to the point, of the relationship between similar forms based on descent from a common ancestor.

Buffon

Buffon (1707–1788), a famous French naturalist and Keeper of the King's Gardens, recognized the dynamic relationship between environment and living forms. He was convinced that different species could develop from a common ancestor, which gave rise to two or more groups through migration to different areas of the world. Each group was then influenced by local climatic conditions and, through adaptation, gradually changed form. This idea was very close to what Darwin was to say in the next century, but Buffon rejected transformism; that is, the change of one species into another.

Erasmus Darwin

A most interesting figure who saw clearly the force of evolutionary ideas was Erasmus Darwin (1731–1802), grandfather of Charles. He expressed

---

*He modified his views late in life.

FIGURE 2-7 Linnaeus.

TAXONOMY The science of the classification or organisms, including the principles, procedures, and rules of classification.

FIGURE 2-8 Buffon.

FIGURE 2-9 Erasmus Darwin.

FIGURE 2-10 Lamarck.

FIGURE 2-11 Cuvier.

such concepts as evolution by natural and sexual selection, inheritance of acquired characteristics, and even the evolution of humankind. However, Erasmus Darwin was unable to solve the riddle of the evolutionary process.

Neither Buffon nor Erasmus Darwin codified his beliefs into a comprehensive system. The first European scientist to do so was Jean Baptiste Pierre Antoine de Monet de Lamarck.

Lamarck

Lamarck (1744–1829) was the first major proponent of the idea of organic evolution who also organized his views into a system that attempted to explain how it all happened.

Lamarck postulated that if a race of four-legged animals lost their habit of climbing trees and grasping branches with their feet, and were forced, for a series of generations, to use their feet only for walking, there would be no doubt these four-legged animals would eventually be transformed into *two-legged* animals. In addition, the "thumbs" on their feet would no longer be separated from the other digits.

Furthermore, if these individuals found it desirable to look out over a broad and distant view, and stood erect to do so, generation after generation, again there would be no doubt that their feet would acquire a form fit to support them in an upright position.

According to Lamarck, then, when the environment changes, there is an alteration in the needs of animals that necessitates new activities. The animals are then required to use their organs more frequently or to make use of entirely new organs developed by body fluids. The altered, or new, organs would then be *passed on through heredity* to the next generation. Thus, offspring inherit characteristics acquired by their parents and, in time, a new and more complex species would evolve.

Unfortunately, Lamarck's theory of evolution—spontaneous generation, the action of body fluids, and acquired characteristics—cannot be supported by the evidence.

Although Lamarck developed a detailed system to account for the acquisition of new traits, and collected vast quantities of material to support his evolutionary ideas, his system was not acceptable. Today, we know that Darwin's *natural selection* explains evolution more systematically. We may credit Lamarck for popularizing the idea of evolution, but there remained vehement opposition to the view that species change and develop into new species. The outstanding opponent of evolution at this time was another Frenchman, and one of the best known scientists of his day, Georges Cuvier, who was to become famous as the "Pope of Bones," the father of zoology, paleontology, and comparative anatomy.

Cuvier

Cuvier (1769–1832) never grasped the dynamic concept of nature and insisted on the fixity of species. Like Linnaeus, he believed that naming, classifying, and describing were the alpha and omega of science. To explain the appearance of new forms, he proposed a theory of *catastrophism*. His theory was based on the assumption of a series of violent and sudden catastrophes (such as the formation of the Alps) that destroyed all creatures in the regions they struck. Then, after things settled down, the areas were restocked with new forms, which came from neighboring areas unaffected by the catastrophes, or by creations of new organisms of more modern form. Cuvier's representation thus avoided evolutionary theory to explain the appearance of new forms.

Cuvier's catastrophism was popular for a time, but it lost favor under attacks by Lyell and other scientists. Darwin, influenced by Lyell, rejected catastrophism early in his thinking.

Lyell

Charles Lyell (1797–1875) was a lawyer by training and geologist by choice. When Darwin returned to England in 1836, he became Lyell's close friend and confidant, a relationship that was to last a lifetime despite their differences concerning a number of intellectual points.

Lyell's important contribution to science was his popular three-volume work, *Principles of Geology* (1830–1833), in which he rejected the catastrophism of Cuvier. Lyell reaffirmed the principle of **uniformitarianism**; that is, no forces had been active in the past history of the earth that are not also working today—an idea introduced into European thought in 1785 by James Hutton.

From Lyell's work Darwin realized that the slow and gradual development of the earth's crust could provide the environmental conditions that, through the struggle for existence, could modify living forms. From Lyell he also learned of the immense age of the earth, far beyond Archbishop Ussher's 4004 B.C.

Two important points in Darwin's explanation of evolution are the struggle for existence and descent with modification. The principle of struggle for existence was basic to Darwin's evolutionary theory, and this he credits to Lyell, though the idea did not originate with Lyell. Descent with modification Darwin saw as a gradual process and, for this to work, time would be necessary. Lyell believed the earth was extremely old, on the order of hundreds or thousands of million years, thus giving a dimension of time that would have made the gradual process of evolution possible.

Soon after Darwin's return to England, he started working on his evolutionary ideas. He planned to collect evidence on the subject of the gradual modification of species. As the evidence accumulated, he came to realize that for success in improving the breeds of animals and plants, *selection* was the keystone. But how selection could be applied to organisms in a state of nature remained a mystery for some time. The mystery was solved for Darwin in October, 1838, fifteen months after he had begun his systematic inquiry, when he happened ("for amusement") to read Malthus' essay on population.

Malthus

In 1798, **Thomas Robert Malthus** (1766–1834) wrote *An Essay on the Principle of Population*, which inspired both Charles Darwin and Alfred Wallace in their separate discoveries of the principle of natural selection.

UNIFORMITARIANISM A concept maintaining that the ancient changes in the earth's surface were caused by the same physical principles acting today.

FIGURE 2-12 Lyell.

Great moments in evolution.

Malthus pointed out that human population growth is not restrained by natural causes and increases geometrically, possibly doubling every generation. On the other hand, food production increases only in a straight arithmetic progression. In nature, Malthus noted, the impulse to multiply was *checked by the struggle for existence*, but humans had to apply artificial restraints. Upon reading this, Darwin wrote:

> . . . it at once struck me that under these circumstances favourable variations would tend to be preserved, and unfavourable ones to be destroyed. The result of this would be the formation of a new species. *Here then I had at last got a theory by which to work* (F. Darwin, 1950, pp. 53–54). (Emphasis added.)

While Darwin had already realized that selection was the key to evolution, it was due to Malthus that he saw *how* selection in nature could be explained. In the struggle for existence, those *individuals* with favorable variations would survive; those with unfavorable variations would not. The significance here is that Darwin was thinking in terms of individuals (not species) that interact with one another.

Before Darwin, scientists thought of species as an entity that could not change. It was species solely that were at the basis of the discussions of plants and animals. Individuals within the species did not appear to be significant and, therefore, it was difficult for many scientists to imagine how change could occur. Darwin, as we have pointed out, saw that variation of individuals could explain how selection occurred. Favorable variations were "selected" by nature for survival; unfavorable ones eliminated.

This emphasis on the uniqueness of the individual (the variation that occurs in all populations—that a population is a group of interacting individuals and cannot be classified as a single type) led Darwin to natural selection as the mechanism that made evolution work. Natural selection *operates on individuals*, favorably or unfavorably, but it is *the population that evolves*. The unit of natural selection is the individual; the unit of evolution is the population.

NATURAL SELECTION IN ACTION

The best historically documented case of natural selection acting in a modern population concerns changes in pigmentation among peppered moths in various parts of Europe, especially well researched in parts of England. Before the nineteenth century, the common variety of moth was a mottled gray color that provided extremely effective camouflage against lichen-covered tree trunks. Also present, though in much lower frequency, was a dark variety of moth. While resting on such trees, the dark, uncamouflaged moths against the light tree trunks were more visible to birds, and were therefore eaten more often. Thus, in the end, they produced fewer offspring than the light, camouflaged moths. Yet, in fifty years, by the end of the nineteenth century, the common, gray form had been almost completely replaced by the black variety. What had brought about this rapid change?

The answer lies in the rapidly changing environment of industrialized nineteenth-century England. Pollutants released in the area settled on trees, killing the lichen and turning the bark a dark color. Moths living in the area continued to rest on trees, but the gray variety was increasingly conspicuous as the trees became darker. Consequently, they were preyed upon more frequently by birds and contributed fewer genes to the next generation. This process caused the gene influencing gray coloration in moths to decrease in frequency. On the other hand, the darker variety had greater reproductive success, and the gene influencing dark coloration increased from one generation to the next.

In the twentieth century, increasing control of pollutants has allowed some forested areas to return to their lighter, preindustrial conditions, with lichen growing again on the trees. As would be expected, in those areas the dark variety is now being supplanted by the gray.

The substance that produces pigmentation is called *melanin*, and the evolutionary shift in the peppered moth, as well as in many other moth species, is termed *industrial melanism*. Such an evolutionary shift in response to environmental change is called **adaptation**.

ADAPTATION An evolutionary shift in a population in response to environmental change; the result of natural selection.

This example provides numerous insights into the mechanism of evolutionary change by natural selection:

1. A trait must be inherited to have importance in natural selection. A characteristic that is not hereditary will not be passed on to succeeding generations. Therefore, frequencies of genes will not change, and evolution will not occur. In moths, pigmentation is a demonstrated hereditary trait.

2. Natural selection cannot occur without variation in inherited characteristics. If all the moths had initially been gray (you will recall some dark forms were present) and the trees became darker, the survival and reproduction of all moths may have been so low that the population would have become extinct. Such an event is not at all unusual in evolution and, without variation, would nearly always occur. *Selection can only work with variation already present.*

3. "Fitness" is a relative measure that will change as the environment changes. Fitness is simply reproductive success. In the initial stage, the gray moth was the most-fit variety, but as the environment changed, the darker moth became more fit, and a further change reversed the adaptive pattern. It should be obvious that statements regarding the "most fit" life forms are meaningless without reference to specific environments.

The example of peppered moths shows how different death rates influence natural selection, for moths that die early tend to leave fewer offspring. But mortality is not the entire picture. Another important aspect of natural selection is *fertility*, for an animal that gives birth to more young would pass its genes on at a faster rate than those who bear fewer offspring. However, fertility is not the whole picture either, since the crucial element is the *number of young raised successfully* to the point where they reproduce themselves. We may state this simply as *differential reproductive success*. The way this mechanism works can be demonstrated through another example.

In a common variety of small birds called swifts, data show that starting out with more offspring does not necessarily guarantee that more young will be successfully raised. The number of eggs hatched in a breeding season is a measure of fertility. The number of birds that mature and are eventually able to leave the nest is a measure of net reproductive success, or offspring successfully raised. The following tabulation shows the correlation between the number of eggs hatched (fertility) and the number of young that leave the nest (reproductive success) averaged over four breeding seasons (Lack, 1966).

NUMBER OF EGGS HATCHED (FERTILITY)	2 EGGS	3 EGGS	4 EGGS
Average number of young raised (reproductive success)	1.92	2.54	1.76
Sample size	72	20	16

As the tabulation shows, the most efficient fertility number is three eggs, for that yields the highest reproductive success. Raising two is less beneficial to the parents since the *end result* is not as successful as with three eggs. Trying to raise more than three young is actually detrimental, since the parents may not be able to provide adequate nourishment for any of the offspring. An offspring that dies before reaching reproductive age is, in evolutionary terms, an equivalent of never having been born in the first place. Selection will favor those genetic traits that yield the maximum net reproductive success. If the number of eggs laid is a genetically influenced trait in birds (and it seems to be), natural selection in swifts, assuming similar environmental pressures, should act to favor the laying of three eggs as opposed to two or four.

DARWIN'S FAILURES

Darwin argued eloquently for the notion of evolution in general and the role of natural selection in particular, but he did not entirely comprehend the exact mechanism of evolutionary change. As we have seen, natural selection acts on *variation* within species. Neither Darwin, nor anyone else in the nineteenth century, understood the source of all this variation. Consequently, Darwin speculated about variation arising from "use"— an idea similar to Lamarck's. Darwin, however, was not as dogmatic about his views as Lamarck, and most emphatically rejected the idea of inner "needs" or "effort." Nevertheless, when it came to explaining variation, Darwin had to confess he simply did not know.

> Our ignorance of the laws of variation is profound. Not in one case out of hundred can we pretend to assign any reason why this or that part differs, more or less, from the same part in the parents (Darwin, 1859, p. 167).

In addition to his inability to explain the origins of variation, Darwin also did not completely understand the mechanism by which parents transmitted traits to offspring. Almost without exception, nineteenth-century scholars were confused about the laws of heredity, and the popular consensus was that inheritance was *blending* by nature. In other words, offspring were expected to express intermediate traits as a result of a blending of their parents' contributions. Given this view, we can see why the actual nature of genes was unimaginable. Without any viable alternatives, Darwin accepted this popular misconception. As it turned out, a contemporary of Darwin had systematically worked out the rules of heredity. However, the work of this relatively obscure Augustinian monk, Gregor Mendel (discussed in Chapter 4), was not recognized until the beginning of the twentieth century.

SUMMARY

The concept of evolution as we know it today is directly traceable to developments in intellectual thought in Western Europe over the last 300 years. In particular, the contributions of Linnaeus, Lamarck, Buffon, Lyell, and Malthus all had significant impact on Darwin. The year 1859 marks a watershed in evolutionary theory for, in that year, the publication of Darwin's *The Origin of Species* crystallized the evolutionary process (particularly, the crucial role of natural selection) and, for the first time, thrust evolutionary theory into the consciousness of the common person. Debates both inside and outside the sciences continued for decades (and, in some corners, persist today), but the theory of evolution irrevocably changed the tide of intellectual thought. Gradually Darwin's formulation of the evolutionary process became accepted almost universally by scientists as the very foundation of all the biological sciences, physical anthropology included. In this century, contributions from genetics allow us to demonstrate the mechanics of evolution in a way unknown to Darwin and his contemporaries.

Natural selection is the central factor influencing the long-term direction of evolutionary change. How natural selection works can best be explained as differential reproductive success, meaning in other words, how successful individuals are in leaving offspring to succeeding generations.

QUESTIONS FOR REVIEW

1. Trace the history of ideas that led to evolutionary theory from Copernicus to Darwin.
2. Explain how Darwin became an evolutionist.
3. What evidence did Darwin use to support natural selection? How do finches figure in this?
4. How did "Principles of Population" authored by Thomas Malthus help Darwin?
5. Write a critique of the Grand Design.
6. What was Linnaeus' significant contribution to science? Why is it significant?
7. In what ways do Linnaeus and Buffon differ in their approach to the concept of evolution?

8. What are the bases of Lamarck's theory of acquired characteristics? Why is this theory unacceptable?
9. What is the theory of catastrophism? Do you think it has any validity? Why?
10. How was Lyell's *Principles of Geology* helpful to Darwin?
11. What is meant by adaptation? Illustrate through the example of industrial melanism.
12. Why have Darwin's views on the origin of species been accepted while Lamarck's have not?

THE BIOLOGICAL BASIS OF LIFE

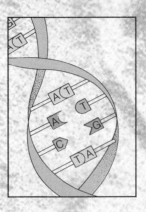

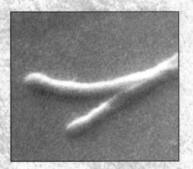

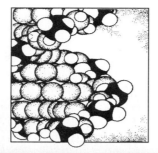

CHAPTER 3

INTRODUCTION

Because physical anthropologists attempt to explain human variation and the mechanisms of evolution, they are concerned with the field of **genetics**. Genetics is the study of the inheritance of traits, or how traits are transmitted from generation to generation. The discipline of genetics is largely a twentieth-century development, and much of the knowledge we now have has been acquired within the last 50 years. What follows is a brief summary of the prinicples of inheritance, which lie at the root of biological variation, adaptation, and evolution.

GENETICS The branch of science that deals with the inheritance of biological characteristics.

THE CELL

In order to discuss genetic and evolutionary principles, it is first necessary to have a basic understanding of cell function. Cells are the basic units of life in all living organisms. In some forms, such as bacteria, amoebae, and paramecia, a single cell constitutes the entire organism. However, more complex *multicellular* forms, such as plants, insects, birds, and mammals, are composed of billions of cells. Indeed, an adult human is made up of perhaps as many as 1000 billion (1000,000,000,000) cells, all functioning in complex ways to promote the survival of the individual.

Life first appeared on earth at least 3.7 billion years ago, in the form of *prokaryotic* cells. Prokaryotes are single-celled organisms, represented today by bacteria and blue-green algae. Structurally more complex cells appeared approximately 1.2 billion years ago and are referred to as *eukaryotic* cells. Because eukaryotic cells are found in all multicellular organisms, they are the focus of the remainder of this discussion. In spite of the numerous differences between various life forms and the cells that comprise them, it is important to understand that the cells of all living organisms share numerous similarities as a result of their common evolutionary past.

In general, a eukaryotic cell is a three-dimensional entity composed of *carbohydrates*, *lipids*, *nucleic acids*, and *proteins*. It contains a variety of structures called *organelles* within a surrounding membrane, the *cell*

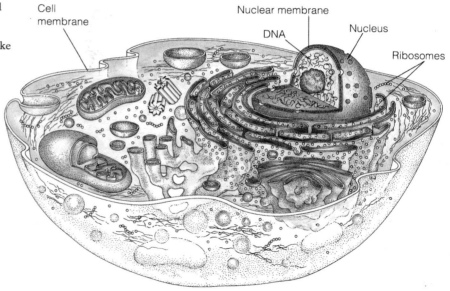

FIGURE 3-1 Structure of a generalized eukaryotic cell illustrating the cell's three-dimensional nature. Although various organelles are shown, for the sake of simplicity most are not labeled.

Cell membrane

Nuclear membrane

DNA

Nucleus

Ribosomes

membrane (see Fig. 3-1). One of these organelles is the **nucleus** (pl. nuclei), a discrete unit, surrounded by a thin nuclear membrane. Within the nucleus are two nucleic acids or molecules that contain the genetic information that controls the cell's functions. These two critically important molecules are **deoxyribonucleic acid (DNA)** and **ribonucleic acid (RNA)**. (In prokaryotic cells, genetic information is not contained within a walled nucleus.) Surrounding the nucleus is the **cytoplasm**, which contains numerous other types of organelles involved in various activities, such as breaking down nutrients and converting them to other substances (*metabolism*), storing and releasing energy, eliminating waste, and manufacturing proteins (**protein synthesis**).

There are basically two types of cells: *somatic cells* and *sex cells*. **Somatic** cells are the cellular components of bodily tissues, such as muscle, bone, skin, nerve, heart, brain, and so forth. Sex cells, or **gametes**, are specifically involved in reproduction and are not important as structural components of the body. There are two types of gametes: *ova*, or egg cells, produced in the ovaries in females; and *sperm*, which develop in male testes. The sole function of a sex cell is to unite with a gamete from another individual and transmit genetic information from parent to offspring.

DNA STRUCTURE

As mentioned above, cellular functions are directed by DNA. If we are to understand these functions, and how characteristics are inherited, we must first know something about the structure and function of DNA.

In 1944, published results of a 10-year study demonstrated that the DNA molecule was the material responsible for the transmission of in-

NUCLEUS A structure (organelle) found in all eukaryotic cells. The nucleus contains chromosomal DNA.

DEOXYRIBONUCLEIC ACID (DNA) The double-stranded molecule that contains the genetic code. DNA is a main component of chromosomes.

RIBONUCLEIC ACID (RNA) A single-stranded molecule, similar in structure to DNA. The three types of RNA are essential to protein synthesis.

CYTOPLASM The portion of the cell contained within the cell membrane, excluding the nucleus. The cytoplasm consists of a semifluid material and contains numerous structures involved with cell function.

PROTEIN SYNTHESIS The assembly of chains of amino acids into functional protein molecules. The process is directed by chromosomal DNA.

SOMATIC CELLS Basically, all the cells in the body except those involved with reproduction.

GAMETES Reproductive cells (eggs and sperm in animals) developed from precursor cells in ovaries and testes.

herited traits, at least in some bacteria (Avery, MacLeod, and McCarty, 1944). However, the exact physical and chemical properties of DNA were at that time still unknown. In 1953 at Cambridge University, an American researcher, James Watson, and three British scientists, Francis Crick, Maurice Wilkins, and Rosalind Franklin, developed a structural and functional model for DNA (Watson and Crick, 1953a, 1953b). For their discovery, Watson, Crick, and Wilkins were awarded the Nobel Prize in medicine and physiology in 1962. The importance of their achievement cannot be overstated, for it completely revolutionized the fields of biology and medicine and forever altered our understanding of biological and evolutionary mechanisms.

The DNA molecule is composed of two chains of even smaller molecules called **nucleotides**. A nucleotide, in turn, is made up of three components: a sugar molecule (deoxyribose); a phosphate; and one of four nitrogenous bases (see Fig. 3-2). In DNA, nucleotides are stacked upon one another to form a chain. This chain is bonded along its bases to another **complementary** nucleotide chain, and together the two twist to

NUCLEOTIDES Nucleotides are basic units of the DNA molecule composed of a sugar, a phosphate, and one of four DNA bases.

COMPLEMENTARY Refers to the specific manner in which DNA bases bond to one another. Complementary base pairing allows for accurate DNA replication.

FIGURE 3-2 Part of a DNA molecule. The illustration shows the two DNA strands with the sugar and phosphate backbone and the bases extending toward the center.

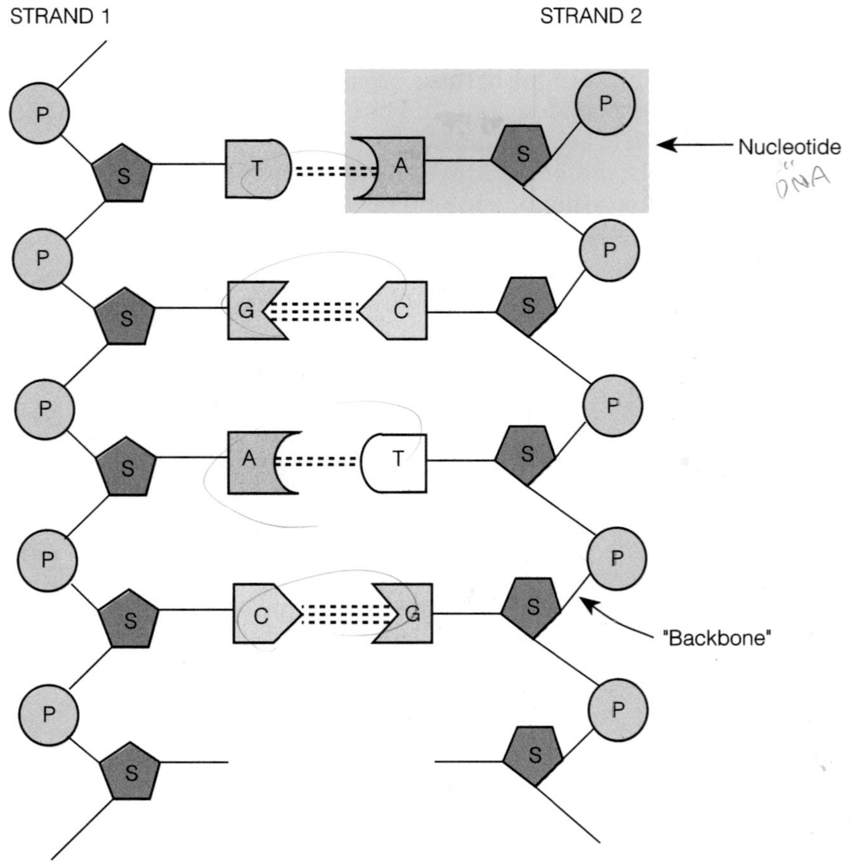

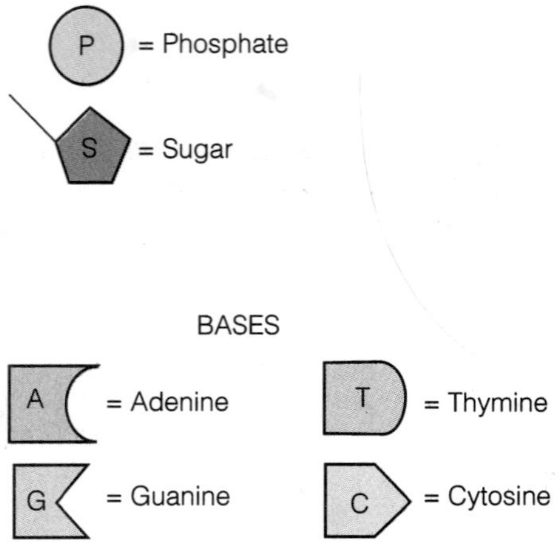

STRAND 1   STRAND 2

Nucleotide

DNA

"Backbone"

P = Phosphate

S = Sugar

BASES

A = Adenine   T = Thymine

G = Guanine   C = Cytosine

FIGURE 3-3 (*a*) DNA molecule resembles a ladder. (*b*) Ladder twisted into a helix.

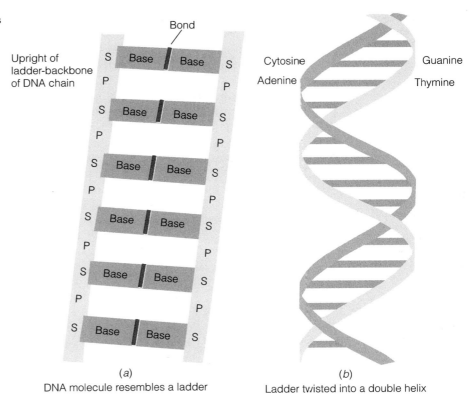

(*a*)
DNA molecule resembles a ladder

(*b*)
Ladder twisted into a double helix

form a spiral or helical shape. The resulting DNA molecule then, is two-stranded and is described as forming a *double helix* that resembles a twisted ladder (see Fig. 3-3). If one follows the twisted ladder analogy, it can be seen that the sugars and phosphates represent the two sides, and the nitrogeneous bases and the bonds that join them comprise the rungs.

The secret of how DNA functions lies within the four nitrogenous bases. These are called *adenine, guanine, thymine,* and *cytosine* and they are frequently referred to by their initial letters, A, G, T, and C. In the formation of the double helix, the joining of bases is done in a very specific manner. Chemically, it is possible for one type of base to pair or bond with only one other. Thus, base pairs can form only between adenine and thymine, and between guanine and cytosine (see Figs. 3-2 and 3-3). This specificity is essential to the DNA molecule's ability to **replicate**, or make an exact copy of itself. DNA is the only molecule known to have this capacity.

REPLICATE To duplicate. The DNA molecule is able to make copies of itself.

DNA REPLICATION

As will soon be shown, cells multiply by dividing, with the result that each new cell receives a full complement of genetic material. In order for such transmission of genetic information to occur, it is essential that the DNA replicate.

Prior to cell division, specialized **enzymes** break the bonds between bases in the DNA molecule, leaving the two previously joined strands of nucleotides with their bases exposed (see Fig. 3-4). The exposed bases attract unattached nucleotides, which are free-floating in the cell nucleus.

Since one base can be joined to only one other, the attraction between bases occurs in a complementary fashion. For example, if the exposed base in the original nucleotide chain is adenine, it will attract a nucleotide carrying thymine, and the two nucleotides will be joined at their bases. If the next exposed base in the chain is guanine, it will bond to a nucleotide bearing cytosine, and so on. In this manner, the two previously joined parental nucleotide chains serve as models or *templates* for the formation of a new strand of nucleotides.

As each new strand is formed, its bases are joined to the bases of an original strand. When the process is completed, there are two double-stranded DNA molecules exactly like the original one, and each newly formed molecule consists of one original nucleotide chain, joined to a newly formed one (see Fig. 3-4).

PROTEIN SYNTHESIS

One of the most important functions of DNA is that it directs protein synthesis within the cell. Proteins are complex, three-dimensional molecules that function through their ability to bind to other molecules. For example, the protein hemoglobin, found in red blood cells, is able to bind to oxygen and serves to transport oxygen to cells throughout the body.

Proteins function in a myriad of ways. Some are structural components of tissues. Collagen, for example, is the most common protein in the body and is a major component of all connective tissues. Aside from mineral components, it is the most abundant structural material in bone. Enzymes are also proteins, and their function is to initiate and enhance chemical reactions. An example of a digestive enzyme is *lactase*, which breaks down *lactose* or milk sugar into the two simple sugars that comprise it. Another class of proteins includes many types of **hormones**. Hormones are produced by specialized cells that release them into the bloodstream to circulate to other areas of the body, where they produce specific effects in tissues and organs. A good example of this type of protein is *insulin*, produced by cells in the pancreas. Insulin causes cells in the liver and certain types of muscle tissue to absorb glucose (sugar) from the blood.

Proteins are composed of linear chains of smaller molecules called **amino acids**. In all, there are 20 amino acids, which are combined in different amounts and sequences to produce potentially millions of proteins. What makes proteins different from one another is the number of amino acids involved and the *sequence* in which they are arranged. In order for a protein to function properly, if at all, its amino acids must be arranged in the proper sequence.

DNA serves as a recipe for making a protein, for it is the sequence of DNA bases that ultimately determines the order of amino acids in a protein molecule. In the DNA instructions, a *triplet*, or group of three bases, specifies a particular amino acid. For example, if a triplet includes the

FIGURE 3-4 DNA replication. During DNA replication, the two strands of the DNA molecule are separated and each strand serves as a template for the formation of a new strand. When replication is complete there are two DNA molecules. Each molecule consists of one new and one old DNA strand.

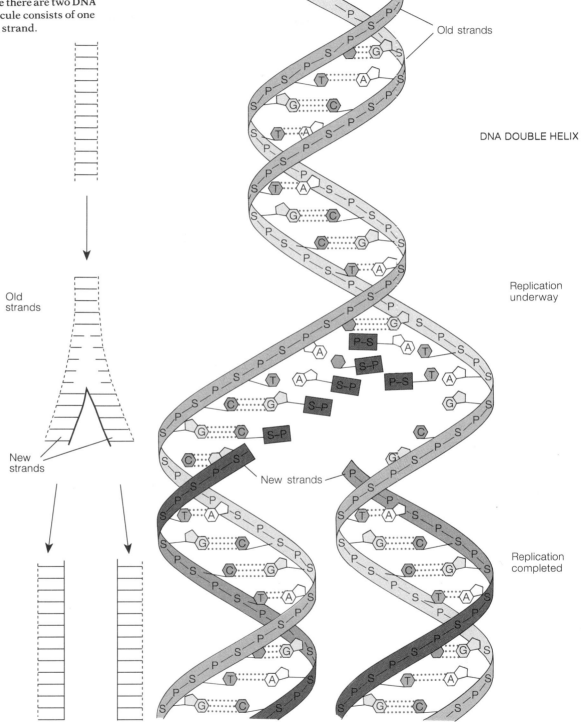

Old strands

DNA DOUBLE HELIX

Replication underway

New strands

Replication completed

Old strands

New strands

bases cytosine, guanine, and adenine (CGA), it specifies the amino acid alanine. If the next triplet in the chain contains guanine, thymine, and cytosine (GTC), it refers to another amino acid—glutamine. Therefore, a DNA recipe might look like this: AGA, CGA, ACA, ACC, TAC, TTT, TTC, CTT, AAG, GTC, etc., as it directs the cell in assembling proteins.

Protein synthesis is a little more complicated than the above few sentences would imply. For one thing, protein synthesis occurs outside the nucleus at specialized structures in the cytoplasm called **ribosomes**. A logistics problem arises because the DNA molecule is not capable of traveling outside the cell's nucleus. Thus, the first step in protein synthesis is to copy the DNA message into a form that can pass through the nuclear membrane into the cytoplasm. This process is accomplished through the formation of a molecule similar to DNA called RNA. RNA is different from DNA in that it:

1. is single-stranded
2. contains a different type of sugar
3. contains the base uracil as a substitute for the DNA base thymine (uracil is attracted to adenine, just as thymine is)

The RNA molecule forms on the DNA template in much the same manner as new strands of DNA are assembled during DNA replication. Again, DNA bases become exposed and, as this occurs, free-floating nucleotides are attracted to them. However, during protein synthesis, the free-floating nucleotides are RNA (not DNA) nucleotides. As the RNA bases arrive at the DNA template, their nucleotides attach to one another in linear fashion to produce a chain of RNA nucleotides that is complementary to the DNA strand it is reading (see Fig. 3-5).

The new RNA nucleotide chain (containing from 300 to 10,000 nucleotides) is a particular type of RNA called **messenger RNA** (mRNA). During its assembly on the DNA model, mRNA is transcribing the DNA code and, in fact, the formation of mRNA is called *transcription*. Once the appropriate DNA segment has been copied the mRNA strand peels away from the DNA model and travels through pores in the nuclear membrane to the ribosome. Meanwhile, the bonds between the DNA bases are reestablished and the DNA molecule is once more intact.

As the mRNA strand arrives at the ribosome, the message it contains is translated. (This stage of the process is called *translation* because, at this point, the genetic instructions are actually being decoded and implemented.) Just as each DNA triplet specifies one amino acid, mRNA triplets—called **codons**—also serve this function. Therefore, the mRNA strand is "read" in codons or groups of three bases taken together.

One other form of RNA—**transfer RNA** (tRNA)—is essential to the actual assembly of a protein. Each molecule of tRNA has the ability to bind to one specific amino acid. A particular tRNA molecule, carrying the amino acid matching the mRNA codon being translated, arrives at the ribosome, and deposits its amino acid (see Fig. 3-6). As a second amino acid is deposited, the two are joined in the order dictated by the sequence of mRNA codons. In this way, series of amino acids are linked together to form a strand of amino acids that will eventually function as a protein.

RIBOSOMES Structures composed of a specialized form of RNA and protein. Ribosomes are found in the cell's cytoplasm and they are essential to protein synthesis.

MESSENGER RNA A form of RNA that is assembled on one sequence (one strand) of DNA bases. It carries the DNA code to the ribosome during protein synthesis.

CODONS The triplets of messenger RNA bases that refer to a specific amino acid during protein synthesis.

TRANSFER RNA The type of RNA that binds to specific amino acids and transports them to the ribosome during protein synthesis.

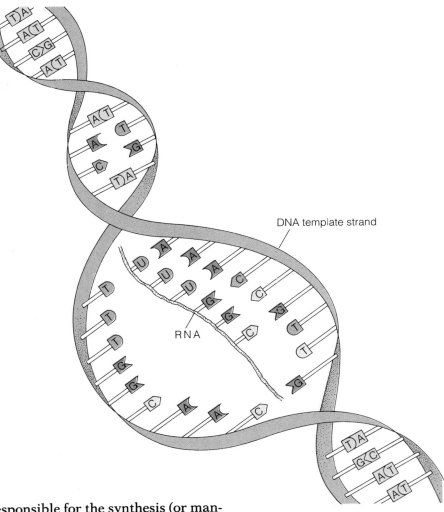

FIGURE 3-5 Transcription. The two DNA strands have partly separated. Free messenger RNA nucleotides have been drawn to the template strand and a strand of mRNA is being made. Note that the RNA strand will exactly complement the DNA template strand except that uracil (U) replaces thymine (T).

DNA template strand

RNA

The entire sequence of bases responsible for the synthesis (or manufacture) of a protein, or in some cases, a portion of a protein, is referred to as a **gene**. Or, put another way, a gene is a segment of DNA or sequence of DNA triplets that specifies the sequence of amino acids in a particular protein. A gene may comprise only a few hundred bases, or it may be composed of thousands. If the sequence of DNA bases is altered through **mutation** (a change in the DNA sequence), or it is somehow lost, the manufacture of some proteins may not occur, and the cell (or indeed the organism) may not function properly, if at all.

The genetic code is said to be universal in the sense that, at least on earth, DNA is the genetic material in all forms of life. Moreover, the DNA of all organisms, from bacteria to oak trees to human beings, is composed of the same molecules using the same kinds of instructions. These similarities imply biological relationships between, and an ultimate common ancestry for, all forms of life. What makes oak trees distinct from humans is not differences in the DNA material, but differences in how that material is arranged.

GENE A gene is a sequence of DNA bases that specifies the order of amino acids in an entire protein or, in some cases, a portion of a protein. A gene may be made up of hundreds of thousands of DNA bases.

MUTATION A change in DNA. Technically, "mutation" refers to changes in DNA bases as well as changes in chromosome number and/or structure.

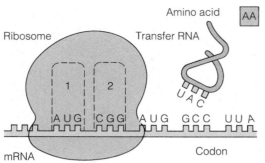

Amino acid   [AA]

Ribosome   Transfer RNA

(a)
As the ribosome binds to the mRNA, tRNA brings a particular amino acid, specified by the mRNA codon to the ribosome.

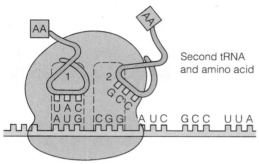

Second tRNA and amino acid

(b)
The tRNA binds to the first codon while a second tRNA — amino acid complex arrives at the ribosome.

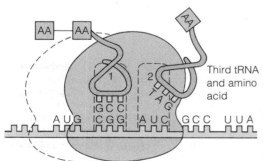

Third tRNA and amino acid

(c)
The ribosome moves down the mRNA, allowing a third amino acid to be brought into position by another tRNA molecule. Note that the first two amino acids are now joined together.

FIGURE 3-6 Assembly of an amino acid chain in protein synthesis.

CELL DIVISION: MITOSIS AND MEIOSIS

CHROMOSOMES Discrete structures composed of DNA and protein found only in the nuclei of cells. Chromosomes are only visible under magnification during certain stages of cell division. Each species is characterized by a specific number of chromosomes.

CENTROMERE The constricted portion of a chromosome. After replication, the two strands of a double-stranded chromosome are joined at the centromere.

Throughout much of a cell's life, its DNA exists as an uncoiled, filamentous substance. (Incredibly, there are an estimated six feet of DNA in the nucleus of every one of your somatic cells!) However, during cell division, the DNA becomes tightly coiled and is visible under a light microscope as a set of discrete, structures called **chromosomes** (Fig. 3-7).

A chromosome is composed of a DNA molecule and associated proteins. During normal cell function, if chromosomes were visible, they would appear as single-stranded structures. However, during the early stages of cell division, they are made up of two strands, or two DNA molecules, joined together at a constricted area called the **centromere**. There

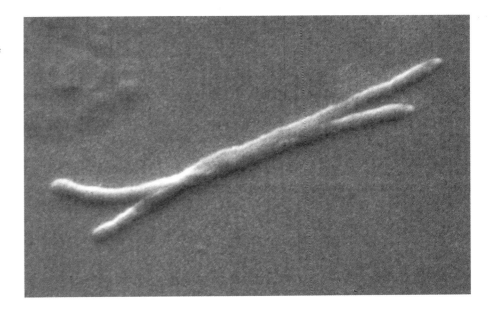

FIGURE 3-7 Scanning electron micrograph of a human chromosome during cell division. Note that this chromosome is composed of 2 strands, or, 2 DNA molecules.

are two strands because, as we have seen, the DNA molecules have *replicated*. Therefore, one strand of a chromosome is an exact copy of the other.

Every species is characterized by a specific number of chromosomes in somatic cells. In humans there are 46, organized into 23 pairs. One member of each pair is inherited from the father (paternal), and the other member of each pair is inherited from the mother (maternal). Members of chromosomal pairs are said to be **homologous** in that they are alike in size and position of the centromere, and they carry genetic information influencing the same traits (e.g., ABO blood type). This does not imply that partner (homologous) chromosomes are genetically identical, it simply means that the traits they govern are the same. (This topic will be discussed in more detail in Chapter 4.)

There are two basic types of chromosomes, **autosomes** and **sex chromosomes**. Autosomes carry genetic information that governs all physical characteristics except primary sex determination. The two sex chromosomes are the X and Y chromosomes. The Y chromosome carries genes that are directly involved with determining maleness. The X chromosome, however, is larger and functions more like an autosome. All genetically normal females have two X chromosomes and all genetically normal males have one X and one Y. Thus, normal human somatic cells have 22 pairs of autosomes and 1 pair of sex chromosomes. It should be noted that abnormal numbers of autosomes are usually fatal to the individual. Although abnormal numbers of sex chromosomes are not usually fatal, they usually result in sterility and frequently have other consequences as well. Therefore, in order to function normally, it is essential to possess both members of each chromosomal pair, or 46 chromosomes, no more, no less.

HOMOLOGOUS Refers to members of chromosome pairs. Homologous chromosomes carry genes that govern the same traits. During meiosis, homologous chromosomes pair and exchange segments of DNA. They are alike with regard to size and position of the centromere.

AUTOSOMES All chromosomes except the sex chromosomes.

SEX CHROMOSOMES The X and Y chromosomes.

Mitosis

Cell division in somatic cells is called **mitosis**. Mitosis occurs during growth of the individual; to promote healing of injured tissues; and to replace older cells with newer ones. In short, it is the way somatic cells reproduce.

In the early stages of mitosis, the cell possesses 46 double-stranded chromosomes, which line up in random order along the center of the cell (Fig. 3-8). As the cell wall begins to constrict at the center, the chromosomes split apart at the centromere. When the two strands are separate, they pull away from one another and move to opposite ends of the dividing cell. At this point, each strand is now a separate chromosome, *composed of one DNA molecule*. Once this separation occurs, the cell wall pinches in and becomes sealed so that two new cells are formed, each with a full complement of DNA, or 46 chromosomes (Fig. 3-8).

Mitosis is referred to as "simple cell division," because a somatic cell divides one time to produce two daughter cells (which are exactly like each other and exactly like the original). In mitosis, the original cell possesses 46 chromosomes, and each new daughter cell inherits an exact copy of all 46 (Fig. 3-9a). This precision is possible because of DNA replication.

Meiosis

While mitosis produces new cells, **meiosis** may lead to the development of new individuals, for meiosis produces reproductive cells or gametes. Although meiosis is another form of cell division and is in some ways similar to mitosis, it is a more complicated process.

During meiosis, specialized cells in male testes and female ovaries divide and develop, eventually to produce sperm or egg cells. Meiosis is characterized by *two divisions* that result in *four daughter cells*, each containing only 23 chromosomes, or half the original number (Fig. 3-9b).

Reduction of chromosome number is a critical feature of meiosis, for the resulting gamete, with its 23 chromosomes, may ultimately unite with another gamete that also carries 23 chromosomes. The product of this union is a **zygote** or fertilized egg, which (in humans) receives a total of 46 chromosomes. In other words, the zygote inherits the full complement of DNA (half from each parent) it needs in order to develop and function normally. If it were not for reduction division (the first division) in meiosis, it would not be possible to maintain the correct number of chromosomes from one generation to the next.

During the first meiotic division, chromosomes line up at the center of the cell as in mitosis, but there is a difference. In the first division, homologous chromosomes come together, forming pairs of double-stranded chromosomes. In this way, then, *pairs* of chromosomes line up along the cell's equator (Fig. 3-10).

Pairing of homologous chromosomes is highly significant, for while they are together, members of pairs exchange genetic information in a process called **recombination** or *crossing over*. Pairing is also important as it facilitates the accurate reduction of chromosome number, by ensur-

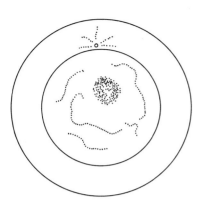

(a) Cell is involved in metabolic activities. DNA replication occurs, but chromosomes are not visible.

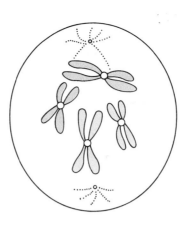

(b) Nuclear membrane disappears and double-stranded chromosomes are visible.

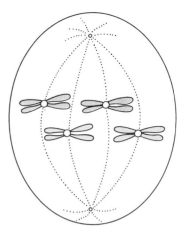

(c) Chromosomes align themselves at center of cell.

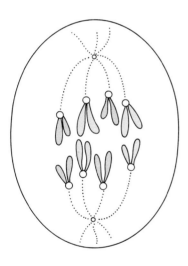

(d) The chromosomes split at the centromere and the strands separate and move to opposite ends of the dividing cell.

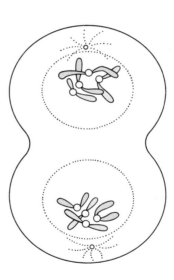

(e) The cell wall pinches in as the cell continues to divide.

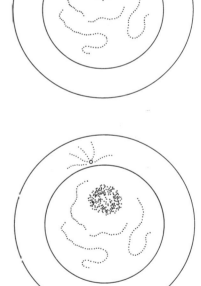

(f) After mitosis is complete, there are two identical daughter cells. The nuclear wall is present and chromosomes are no longer visible.

FIGURE 3-8 Mitosis.

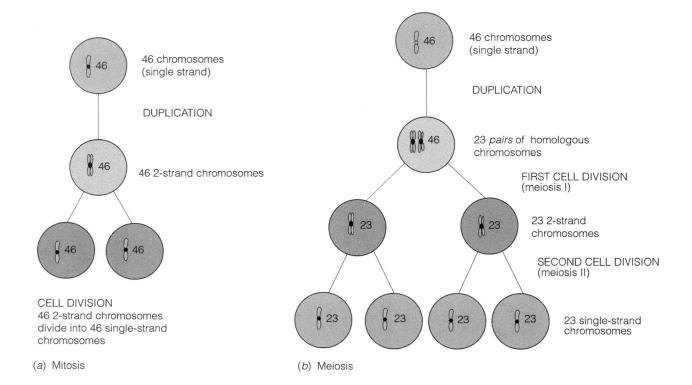

46 chromosomes
(single strand)

DUPLICATION

46 2-strand chromosomes

CELL DIVISION
46 2-strand chromosomes
divide into 46 single-strand
chromosomes

(a) Mitosis

46 chromosomes
(single strand)

DUPLICATION

23 *pairs* of homologous
chromosomes

FIRST CELL DIVISION
(meiosis I)

23 2-strand
chromosomes

SECOND CELL DIVISION
(meiosis II)

23 single-strand
chromosomes

(b) Meiosis

FIGURE 3-9 Mitosis and meiosis compared. In mitosis, one division produces two daughter cells, both of which contain 46 chromosomes. Meiosis is characterized by two divisions. After the first, there are two cells each containing only 23 chromosomes (one member of each original chromosome pair). Each daughter cell divides again so that the final result is four cells, each with only half the original number of chromosomes.

ing that each new daughter cell will receive only one member of each pair.

As the cell begins to divide, the chromosomes themselves remain intact, i.e., double-stranded, but members of pairs separate and migrate to opposite ends of the cell. After the first division, there are two new daughter cells, but they are not identical to each other or to the parental cell because each contains only one member of each chromosome pair, and therefore only 23 chromosomes (each double-stranded).

The second meiotic division proceeds in much the same way as in mitosis. In the two newly formed cells, the 23 double-stranded chromosomes align themselves at the cell's center and, as in mitosis, the strands of each chromosome separate from one another at the centromere and move apart. Once this second division is completed, there are four daughter cells, each with 23 single-stranded chromosomes (i.e., 23 DNA molecules).

Meiosis occurs in all sexually reproducing organisms and is an important evolutionary innovation, since it is believed to increase genetic variation in populations at a faster rate than *mutation* alone can in asexually reproducing species. Individual members of sexually reproducing species are not genetically identical clones of other individuals. Rather, they result from the contribution of genetic information from two parents. Therefore, each individual represents a combination of genes that, in all likelihood, has never occurred before and will never occur again.

The genetic uniqueness of individuals is enhanced by recombination between homologous chromosomes during meiosis, for recom-

FIGURE 3-10 Meiosis.

Chromosomes not visible as DNA replication occurs in cell that is preparing to divide.

Double-stranded chromosomes become visible and homologous chromosomes exchange genetic material in a process called "recombination" or "crossing over".

Chromosome pairs migrate to center of cell.

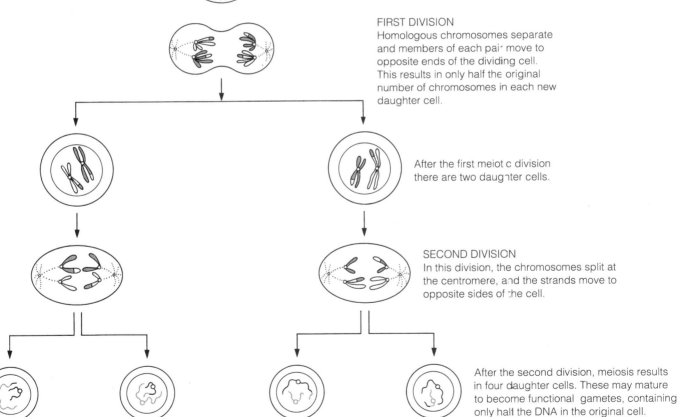

FIRST DIVISION
Homologous chromosomes separate and members of each pair move to opposite ends of the dividing cell. This results in only half the original number of chromosomes in each new daughter cell.

After the first meiotic division there are two daughter cells.

SECOND DIVISION
In this division, the chromosomes split at the centromere, and the strands move to opposite sides of the cell.

After the second division, meiosis results in four daughter cells. These may mature to become functional gametes, containing only half the DNA in the original cell.

bination ensures that chromosomes are not passed on intact from one generation to the next. Instead, in every generation, parental contributions are reshuffled in an almost infinite number of combinations, thus altering the genetic composition of chromosomes even before they are passed on.

Genetic diversity is therefore enhanced by meiosis. As was mentioned in Chapter 2, natural selection acts upon genetic variation in populations. If all individuals in a population are genetically identical over time, then natural selection (and evolution) cannot occur. Although there are other sources of variation (such as mutation), sexual reproduction and meiosis are of major evolutionary importance because they contribute to the role of natural selection in populations.

SUMMARY

This chapter has dealt with several concepts that are fundamental to understanding human variation, as well as the processes of biological evolution. These are topics that will be discussed in succeeding chapters.

It has been shown that cells are the fundamental units of life and that there are basically two types of cells. Somatic cells comprise body tissues, while gametes (eggs and sperm) are reproductive cells that transmit genetic information from parent to offspring.

Genetic information is contained in the DNA molecule, found in the nuclei of cells. The DNA molecule is capable of replication, or making copies of itself, and is the only molecule known to have this ability. Replication makes it possible for parent cells to retain a full complement of DNA while also passing on a full complement to daughter cells.

DNA also controls protein synthesis by directing the cell to arrange amino acids in the proper sequence for each particular type of protein. Also involved in the process of protein synthesis is another, similar molecule called RNA.

Cells multiply by dividing, and during cell division DNA is visible under a microscope in the form of chromosomes. In humans, there are 46 chromosomes, or 23 pairs.

Somatic cells divide during growth, tissue repair, or to replace old worn-out cells. Somatic cell division is called mitosis. During mitosis, a cell divides one time to produce two daughter cells, each possessing a full and identical set of chromosomes.

Sex cells are produced when specialized cells in the ovaries and testes divide in meiosis. Unlike mitosis, meiosis is characterized by two divisions, which produce four nonidentical daughter cells, each containing only half the amount of DNA (23 chromosomes) carried by the original cell.

QUESTIONS FOR REVIEW

1. Genetics is the study of what?
2. What components of a eukaryotic cell are discussed in this chapter?

3. What are the two major types of cells? Give an example of each.
4. What are nucleotides?
5. Name the four DNA bases. Which pairs with which?
6. What is DNA replication and why is it important?
7. What are enzymes?
8. What are the building blocks of protein? How many different kinds are there?
9. What is the function of DNA in protein synthesis?
10. What is the function of mRNA?
11. What is the function of tRNA?
12. Define *gene*.
13. Define *chromosome*.
14. What are homologous chromosomes?
15. How many cell divisions occur in mitosis and how many chromosomes does each new cell have?
16. How many cell divisions occur in meiosis? How many daughter cells are produced when meiosis is complete? How many chromosomes does each new cell contain?
17. Why is reduction division important?
18. What is recombination and why is it important? When does it occur?
19. Why is the genetic code said to be universal?
20. What are the two sex chromosomes? Which two do males have? Which two do females have?

PRINCIPLES OF INHERITANCE

CHAPTER 4

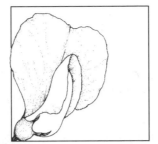

INTRODUCTION

In Chapter 3, we discussed the structure and function of DNA within the cell. In this chapter, we shift to a somewhat broader perspective and focus on the principles that guide how characteristics are passed from parent to offspring.

Since at least 10,000 years ago, when the domestication of plants and animals was a relatively new human enterprise, people have attempted to explain how traits were passed from parents to offspring. Although theories were far from accurate, farmers and herders have known for millennia they could enhance desirable attributes through selective breeding. However, exactly why desirable traits were often seen in offspring of carefully chosen breeding stock remained a mystery. It was equally curious when offspring did not show the traits their human owners had hoped for.

Since the time ancient Greek philosophers considered the problem until well into the nineteenth century, one predominant belief was that characteristics of offspring resulted from the *blending* of parental traits. Blending was supposedly accomplished by means of particles, called *pangenes*, which existed in every part of the body, and were miniatures of whatever body part (limbs, organs, etc.) they inhabited. These particles traveled through the blood to the reproductive organs, and blended with particles of another individual during reproduction. There were variations on the theme of *pangenesis*, and numerous scholars including Charles Darwin adhered to some aspects of the theory.

There were also questions as to which parent made the greater contribution to the sex and appearance of offspring. One widely accepted explanation, developed in the seventeenth and eighteenth centuries, proposed the existence of a miniature, preformed adult called a *homunculus* (Fig. 4-1). Controversy arose, however, over which parent (male or female) contributed the homunculus, and which primarily provided nutrition for its development.

GREGOR MENDEL'S EXPERIMENTS WITH GARDEN PEAS

It was not until an Augustinian monk, Father Johann Gregor Mendel (1822–1884), addressed the question of inheritance that the basic princi-

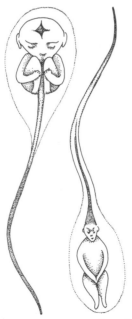

FIGURE 4-1 Depictions of two homunculi. Some early investigators thought that they could see tiny human embryos within the sperm.

ples of heredity were discovered (Fig. 4-2). Gregor Mendel grew up in a poor peasant family in what is now Czechoslovakia, and at the age of 21 he was accepted as a novice at the monastery at Brno, Czechoslovakia.

Mendel was attracted to monastic life, partly because of the security it offered, and because it presented opportunities for higher education. In fact, it was relatively common for young men with few other options to seek a life in the Church. Moreover, life in Brno did not fit the stereotype of cloistered monasticism, and Mendel was not isolated in some backwater village, denied contact with the rest of the world. Indeed, at the time, Brno was a center of scientific and cultural endeavor for much of southeastern Europe, and many of the monks there were involved in various areas of scientific research (Hartl, 1983).

After becoming established at Brno, Mendel left for two years to study at the University of Vienna, where he acquired scientific expertise from leading professors in botany, physics, and mathematics. Given this impressive background, perhaps it is not so surprising that an obscure monk was able to unravel the mysteries of inheritance and thus achieve one of the most important biological discoveries ever made.

When Mendel returned to Brno, he resumed his former occupation as a substitute teacher in a nearby town. He also returned to work in the monastery garden where he had been experimenting with the fertilization of flowers, hoping to develop new variations in colors. This activity eventually led him to attempt to elucidate the various ways in which physical traits (such as color or height) could be expressed in plant **hybrids.**

Mendel hoped that by making crosses between two strains of *purebred* plants and examining their progeny, he could determine (and predict) how many different forms of hybrids there were; arrange the forms according to generation; and evaluate the proportion in each generation of each type represented.

FIGURE 4-2 Gregor Mendel.

HYBRID Offspring of mixed ancestry; a heterozygote.

Crosses Between Plants: Single Traits

Mendel chose to work with the common garden pea and he wisely chose to consider one characteristic at a time, rather than do what other investigators had done—namely, to examine several simultaneously. In all, he focused on seven different traits, each of which could be expressed in two different ways (Table 4-1).

In 1856, Mendel began his experiments by making 287 crosses between 70 different purebred plants, which differed with regard to a specific trait. (In all, Mendel used over 28,000 pea plants before he completed his research.) The plants used in this first cross were designated the "parental generation" or P_1. Using pure lines meant that, for example, if the trait in question were height of the plant (tall or short) he made crosses between varieties that produced only tall plants with varieties that produced only short plants. If he was interested in seed color (yellow or green), he made crosses between plants that produced only yellow seeds and those with all green seeds.

The offspring of the parental generation were designated the F_1 (first filial) generation. As the F_1 plants matured, all were tall. Not one was short. According to blending theories, height in the F_1s should have

TABLE 4-1   The Seven Characteristics of the Garden Pea Mendel Selected

CHARACTERISTICS	DOMINANT TRAITS	RECESSIVE TRAITS
1. form of the ripe seed	smooth	wrinkled
2. color of seed albumen	yellow	green
3. color of seed coat	gray	white
4. form of ripe pods	inflated	constricted
5. color of unripe pods	green	yellow
6. position of flowers	axial	terminal
7. length of stem	tall	dwarf

been intermediate between the heights of the parent plants, but these theories were not confirmed by Mendel's results.

Next, since pea plants have both male and female parts, the F_1s were allowed to self-fertilize to produce a second hybrid generation (the F_2 generation). This time all the offspring were not uniformly tall. Instead, approximately ¾ were tall and the other ¼ were short (dwarf). In one experiment, there were 787 tall plants and 277 dwarfs. This produced an almost exact ratio of 3 tall plant seeds for every dwarf (3:1).

Regardless of the trait he examined, every time the experiment was done, Mendel obtained almost exactly the same results. One expression of the trait disappeared in the F_1 generation and reappeared in the F_2s. Moreover, the expression that was present in the F_1 generation was more common in the F_2s, occurring in a ratio of approximately 3:1 to the less common expression.

These results suggested at least two important facts. First, it appeared that the various expressions of a trait were controlled by discrete *units*, which occurred in pairs; and that offspring inherited one *unit* from each parent. Mendel correctly reasoned that the members of a pair of units controlling a trait somehow separated into different sex cells and were united with another member during fertilization of the egg. This is Mendel's *first principle of inheritance*, known as the **principle of segregation**.

Today we know that meiosis explains Mendel's principle of segregation. You will remember that during meiosis, homologous chromosomes (and thus the genes they carry) separate from one another and end up in different gametes. However, in the zygote, the full complement of chromosomes is restored and both members of each chromosome pair (homologous chromosomes) are present in the offspring.

Secondly, Mendel recognized that the expression that was absent in the F_1s had not actually disappeared at all. It had remained present, but somehow it was masked and could not be expressed. To describe the trait manifestation that seemed to be lost, Mendel used the term **recessive**; and the one that was expressed was said to be **dominant**. Thus, the important **principles of dominance** and **recessiveness** were formulated, and they remain as basic underlying concepts in the field of genetics.

PRINCIPLE OF SEGREGATION   Genes occur in pairs (because chromosomes occur in pairs). During gamete production, the members of each gene pair separate so that each gamete contains one member of each pair. During fertilization, the full number of chromosomes is restored and members of gene pairs are reunited.

RECESSIVE   A trait that is not phenotypically expressed in heterozygotes. Also refers to the allele that governs the trait. In order for the trait to be expressed there must be two copies of the allele (i.e., the individual must be homozygous).

DOMINANT   A trait governed by an allele that can be expressed in the presence of another, different allele (i.e., in heterozygotes). Dominant alleles prevent the expression of recessive alleles in heterozygotes.

As you already know, a *gene* is a segment of DNA that controls the production of a specific protein. Furthermore, the location of a gene on a chromosome is its *locus* (plural *loci*). At numerous genetic loci, however, there is more than one form of the gene, and these variations of genes at specific loci are called **alleles**. Therefore, an allele is an alternate form of a gene that can direct the cell to produce slightly different forms of the same protein and, ultimately, different expressions of traits.

As it turns out, plant height in garden peas is controlled by two different alleles at one genetic locus. The allele that determines that a plant will be tall is dominant to the allele for short or dwarf. (It is worth mentioning that height is not governed in this manner in all plants.)

In Mendel's experiments, all the parent plants (P_1s) had two copies of the same allele, either dominant or recessive, depending upon whether they were tall or short. When two copies of the same allele are present at the same locus on homologous chromosomes, the individual is said to be **homozygous**. Thus, all the tall P_1 plants were homozygous for the dominant allele and all the short P_1 plants were homozygous for the recessive allele. (This homozygosity explains why tall plants crossed with tall plants produced only tall offspring, and short plants crossed with short plants produced all short offspring; i.e., they were "pure lines" and lacked genetic variation at this locus.) However, all the F_1 plants (hybrids) had inherited one allele from each parent plant and, therefore, they all possessed two different alleles. Individuals who possess two different alleles at a locus are **heterozygous**.

Figure 4-3 illustrates the crosses Mendel initially performed. Geneticists use standard symbols to refer to alleles. Thus, uppercase letters refer to dominant alleles, (or dominant traits) and lowercase letters refer to recessive alleles (or recessive traits). As a matter of convention, the initial letter of the word for the recessive expression is used, and in the case of short pea plants, the term "dwarf" describes shortness. Therefore, we let:

> D = the allele for tallness
> d = the allele for shortness (dwarfism)

The same symbols are combined to describe an individual's actual genetic makeup, or **genotype**. The term *genotype* can be used to refer to the alleles at a genetic locus on homologous chromosomes. Thus, the genotypes of the plants in Mendel's experiments were:

> DD = homozygous tall plants
> Dd = heterozygous tall plants
> dd = homozygous short plants

Figure 4-4 is what is called a *Punnett square*, which diagrammatically represents the different ways the alleles can be combined when the F_1s are self-fertilized to produce an F_2 generation. In this way, the figure shows the *genotypes* that are possible in the F_2 generation, and it also demonstrates that approximately ¼ of the F_2s are *DD (homozygous dominant)*; ½ are heterozygous (*Dd*); and the remaining ¼ are *homozygous recessive (dd)*.

ALLELE An alternate form of a gene. Alleles occur at the same locus on homologous chromosomes and govern the same trait; however, their action results in different expressions of the trait.

HOMOZYGOUS Having the same allele at the same locus on both members of a pair of homologous chromosomes.

HETEROZYGOUS Having different alleles at the same locus on both members of a pair of homologous chromosomes.

GENOTYPE The genetic makeup of an individual. *Genotype* can refer to an organism's entire genetic makeup, or to the alleles at a particular locus.

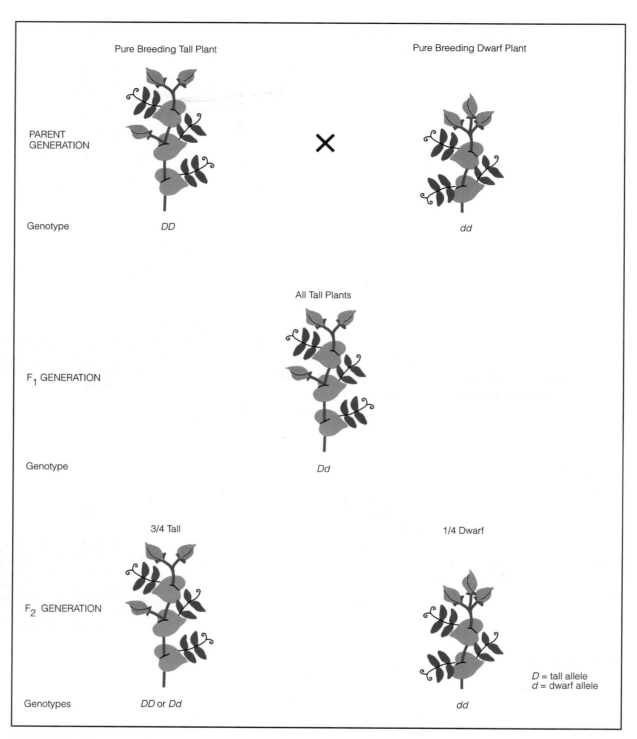

FIGURE 4-3 Diagrammatic representation of crosses considering only one trait at a time.

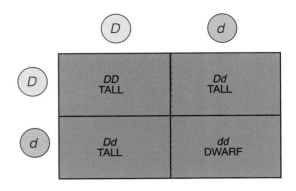

FIGURE 4-4 Punnett square representing possible genotypes and phenotypes and their proportions in the F_2 generation.

The circles across the top and at the left of the Punnett square represent the gametes of the F_1 parents. The four inner squares illustrate that 1/4 of the F_2s will be tall (*DD*); another 1/2 also will be tall but will be heterozygous (*Dd*); and the remaining 1/4 will be dwarf (*dd*). Thus, 3/4 can be expected to be tall, and 1/4 will be dwarf.

The Punnett square can also be used to show (and predict) the proportions of F_2 **phenotypes**, or the observed physical manifestations of genes. Moreover, the Punnett square also illustrates why Mendel observed three tall plants for every short plant in the F_2 generation. By examining the Punnett square, you can see that ¼ of the F_2s are tall because they have the *DD* genotype. Moreover, an additional ½, which are heterozygous (*Dd*), will also be tall because *D* is dominant to *d*, and will therefore be expressed in the phenotype. The remaining ¼ are homozygous recessive (*dd*), and they will be short because no dominant allele is present. It is important to note that the *only* way a recessive allele can be expressed is if it occurs with another recessive allele; that is, if the individual is homozygous recessive at the particular locus in question.

It is shown, therefore, that ¾ of the F_2 generation will express the dominant phenotype, and ¼ will show the recessive phenotype. This relationship is expressed as a **phenotypic ratio** of 3:1 and typifies all *Mendelian traits* (characteristics governed by only one genetic locus) when only two alleles are involved, one of which is completely dominant to the other.

PHENOTYPE The observable or detectable physical characteristics of an organism; the detectable expression of the genotype.

PHENOTYPIC RATIO The proportion of phenotype to other phenotypes in a population. For example, Mendel observed that there were approximately three tall plants for every short plant in the F_2 generation. This is expressed as a phenotypic ratio of 3:1.

Crosses Between Plants: Two Traits Together

Mendel then made crosses in which two characteristics were considered simultaneously to determine whether there was a relationship between them. Two such characteristics were plant height and seed color.

In peas, seeds are either yellow (dominant) or green (recessive). We use the symbols *G* to represent the dominant allele and *g* for the recessive allele.

In the P_1 generation, crosses were made between tall plants with yellow seeds and short plants with green seeds (Fig. 4-5). As expected, the recessive expression of each trait was not seen in the F_1 generation: All plants were tall and all produced yellow seeds. However, in the F_2 plants,

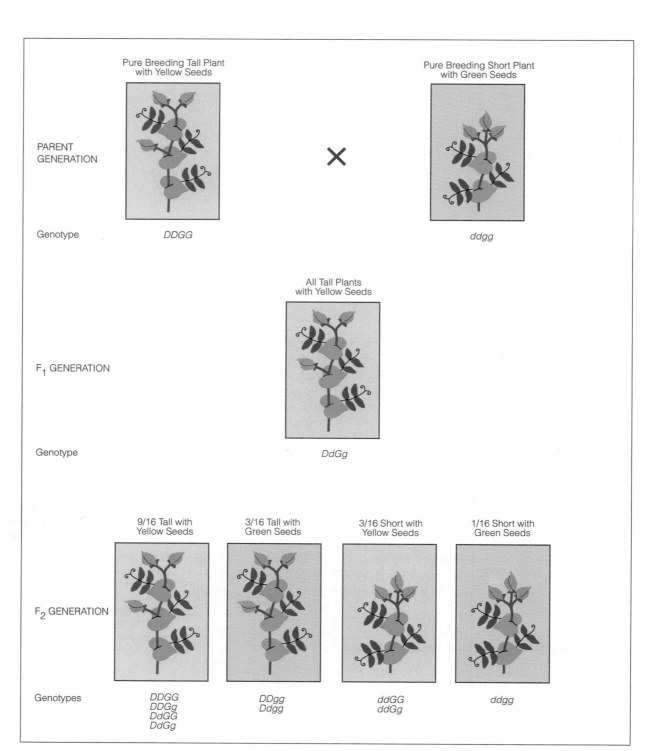

FIGURE 4-5 Results of crosses when two traits are considered simultaneously. It is shown that height of plant and seed color are independent of one another. Also shown are the genotypes associated with each phenotype.

both recessive traits reappeared in a small proportion of individuals. The phenotypic ratio for this type of cross is 9:3:3:1, meaning that: 9/16 will be tall with yellow seeds; 3/16 will be tall with green seeds; 3/16 will be short with yellow seeds; and 1/16 will show both recessive traits and be short with green seeds.

Although this may seem confusing, it serves to illustrate the point that there is no relationship between the two traits; that is, there is nothing to dictate that a tall plant must have yellow (or green) seeds. The expression of one trait is not influenced by the expression of the other trait. The allele for tallness (D) has equal probabilities (50-50) of ending up in a zygote with either G or g.

Mendel stated this principle as his second law of inheritance, the **principle of independent assortment**. The principle of independent assortment says that the units (genes) that code for different traits assort independently of each other during gamete formation. Today, we know this to be true because the genetic loci controlling these two characteristics are located on different, nonhomologous chromosomes, and during meiosis, chromosomes travel to newly forming cells independently of one another.

If Mendel had used just *any* two traits, the phenotypic ratios may well not have conformed to those expected by independent assortment (9:3:3:1). The ratios came out as he predicted because the loci governing most of the traits he chose were carried on different chromosomes. In a couple of cases, the situation was more complex and need not be dealt with here.

In 1865, Mendel presented his results at a meeting of the local Natural History Society. The following year, the society published his report but, unfortunately, the methodology and the statistical nature of the results were beyond the thinking of the time. Indeed, the scientific community was not at all prepared for what they considered to be Mendel's unusual approach, and consequently the significance of his work was unappreciated.

In the latter part of the nineteenth century, several investigators made important contributions to the understanding of chromosomes and cell division. Moreover, the discovery of reduction division in meiosis provided an explanation for Mendel's discoveries. However, Mendel's research remained unknown until 1900, when three different scientists, conducting similar experiments to Mendel's, came across his paper. Unfortunately, however, Mendel had died 16 years earlier and never saw his work vindicated.

MENDELIAN INHERITANCE IN HUMANS

Mendelian traits (also referred to as *discrete traits* or *traits of simple inheritance*) are controlled by alleles at *one* genetic locus. Currrently, more than 4000 human traits are known to be inherited according to simple Mendelian principles. Examples include several blood group systems, such as *ABO* and *Rh*.

The *ABO* system is governed by three alleles, *A*, *B*, and *O*, found at the *ABO* locus on the ninth chromosome. (It should be clear that although three alleles are present in populations, each individual can possess only two.) These alleles determine which *ABO* blood type an individual has by coding for the production of special substances, called *antigens*, on the surfaces of red blood cells. If only antigen *A* is present, the blood type (phenotype) is *A*; if only *B*, then the individual has *B* blood; if both are present, blood type is *AB*; and when neither is present, blood type is said to be *O*.

The principles of dominance and recessiveness, as well as a third, **codominance**, are clearly illustrated by the *ABO* system. The *O* allele is recessive to both *A* and *B*; therefore, if a person has type *O* blood, he or she must be homozygous for the *O* allele. Since both *A* and *B* are dominant to *O*, an individual with blood type *A* can have one of two genotypes: *AA* or *AO*. The same is true of type *B*, which results from the genotypes *BB* and *BO* (Table 4-2). However, type *AB* presents a slightly different situation and is an example of codominance.

Codominance is seen when two different alleles occur in heterozygous condition, but instead of one having the ability to mask the expression of the other, the products of *both* are seen in the phenotype. Therefore, when both *A* and *B* alleles are present, both *A* and *B* antigens can be detected on the surfaces of red blood cells.

A number of genetic disorders are inherited as dominant traits. This means that if a person inherits only one copy of a harmful, dominant allele, the condition it causes will be present (regardless of the existence of a different, recessive allele on the corresponding chromosome). Some conditions inherited as dominant characteristics are *achondroplasia*, *brachydactyly*, and *familial hypercholesterolemia* (Table 4-3).

Recessive conditions are commonly associated with the lack of a substance, usually an enzyme. In order for a person actually to have a recessive disorder, he or she must have *two* copies of the recessive allele that causes it. Heterozygotes who have only one copy of a harmful recessive allele are unaffected. Such individuals are called *carriers*.

Although carriers do not actually have the recessive condition they carry, they can pass the allele that causes it to their children. (Remember, half their gametes will carry the recessive allele.) If their mate is also a carrier, then it is possible for them to have a child who will be homozygous for the allele, and that child will be affected. In fact, in a mating between two carriers, the risk of having an affected child is 25 percent (refer

CODOMINANCE Refers to the expression of two alleles in heterozygotes. In this situation, neither is dominant nor recessive so that both influence the phenotype.

TABLE 4-2 ABO Genotypes and Associated Phenotypes

GENOTYPE	ANTIGENS ON RED BLOOD CELLS	ABO BLOOD TYPE (PHENOTYPE)
AA, AO	A	A
BB, BO	B	B
AB	A and B	AB
OO	none	O

back to Fig. 4-4). Some recessive disorders that affect humans are *cystic fibrosis*, *Tay-Sachs disease*, *sickle-cell anemia* (see Chapter 6), and *phenylketonuria* (PKU) (Table 4-4).

TABLE 4-3 Some Mendelian Disorders Inherited as Dominant Traits in Humans

CONDITION	MANIFESTATIONS
Achondroplasia	Dwarfism due to growth defects involving the long bones of the arms and legs. Trunk and head size usually normal.
Brachydactyly	Shortened fingers and toes.
Familial hyper-cholesterolemia	Elevated cholesterol levels and cholesterol plaque deposition. A leading cause of heart disease with death frequently occurring by middle age.
Neuro-fibromatosis	Symptoms range from the appearance of abnormal skin pigmentation, to large tumors resulting in gross deformities. This, so-called *elephant man disease* can lead to paralysis, blindness, and death.
Marfan syndrome	Affects the eyes, and cardiovascular and skeletal systems. Greater than average height, long arms and legs, eye problems, and enlargement of the aorta. Death due to rupture of the aorta is common. Abraham Lincoln may have had Marfan syndrome.

TABLE 4-4 Some Mendelian Disorders Inherited as Recessive Traits in Humans

CONDITION	MANIFESTATIONS
Cystic fibrosis	The most common genetic disease among whites in the United States. Abnormal secretions of the exocrine glands with pronounced involvement of the pancreas. Most patients develop obstructive lung disease and only about half live to early adulthood.
Tay-Sachs disease	Most common among Ashkenazy Jews. Degeneration of the nervous system beginning at about six months of age. Lethal by age two or three years.
Phenylketonuria (PKU)	Inability to metabolize the amino acid phenylalanine. Results in mental retardation if left untreated during childhood. Treatment involves strict dietary management and some supplementation.
Albinism	Inability to produce normal amounts of the pigment melanin. Results in very fair, untannable skin, light blond hair and light eyes. May also be associated with vision problems.

POLYGENIC INHERITANCE

Mendelian traits are said to be *discrete* or *discontinuous* because their phenotypic expressions do not overlap, but rather they fall into clearly defined categories. For example, Mendel's pea plants were either short or tall, but none was intermediate in height. In the *ABO* system, the four phenotypes are completely distinct from one another; that is, there is no intermediate form between type *A* and type *B* to represent a gradation between the two. In other words, Mendelian traits do not show *continuous* variation.

However, many traits do have a wide range of phenotypic expressions that overlap to form a graded series. These are called **polygenic** or *continuous* traits. While Mendelian traits are governed by only one genetic locus, polygenic characteristics are influenced by alleles at *several* loci, with *each* locus making a contribution to the phenotype.

Polygenic traits actually account for most of the phenotypic variation seen in humans, and they have traditionally served as a basis for racial classification (see Chapter 5). Skin color, hair color, eye color, weight, shape of face, fingerprints, and IQ are but a few examples of polygenic inheritance. Since they exhibit continuous variation, most polygenic traits can be measured on a scale composed of equal increments. For example, height (stature) is measured in feet and inches, or meters and centimeters. If one were to measure height in a large number of individuals, the distribution of measurements would continue uninterrupted from the shortest extreme to the tallest. This is what is meant by the term *continuous traits*.

Biologists, geneticists, and physical anthropologists treat polygenic characteristics statistically, and use such concepts as the *mean* (average), among others, to describe and compare populations. Such statistical manipulations are not possible with Mendelian traits, nor would such treatments be particularly desirable. After all, what we are after here is a characterization of the *genetic pattern*. This is exactly what can be achieved for Mendelian traits but is still methodologically impossible for polygenic features.

POLYGENIC Refers to traits that are influenced by genes at two or more loci. Examples of such traits are stature, skin color, and IQ. Many polygenic traits are also influenced by environmental factors.

GENETIC AND ENVIRONMENTAL FACTORS

From the preceding discussion it might appear that phenotype is solely the expression of the genotype, but this is not true. (Here we use the terms *genotype* and *phenotype* in a broader sense to refer to an individual's *entire* genetic makeup, and *all* observable characteristics.) The genotype sets limits and potentials for development, but it also interacts with the environment, and many aspects of phenotype are influenced by this genetic/environmental interaction. Scientists have developed statistical methods for calculating what proportion of phenotypic variation is due to genetic or environmental components. However, it is usually not possible to identify the *specific* environmental factors affecting the phenotype.

Many polygenic traits are influenced by environmental conditions. Adult stature is strongly affected by the individual's nutritional status during growth and development. One study showed that children of Japanese immigrants to Hawaii were, on average, three to four inches taller than their parents. This dramatic difference, seen in one generation, was attributed to environmental alteration, and specifically to a change in diet (Froelich, 1970).

Other important environmental factors include exposure to sunlight, altitude, temperature, and, unfortunately, increasing levels of exposure to toxic waste and airborne pollutants. All these and many more contribute in complex ways to the continuous phenotypic variation seen in characteristics governed by multiple genes.

Mendelian traits are less likely to be influenced by environmental factors. For example, *ABO* blood type is determined at fertilization and remains fixed throughout the individual's lifetime regardless of diet, exposure to ultraviolet radiation, temperature, and so forth.

Mendelian and polygenic inheritance produce different manifestations of phenotypic variation. In the former, variation occurs in discrete categories, while in the latter, it is continuous. However, it is important to understand that, regarding polygenic characteristics, Mendelian principles still apply at individual loci. In other words, if a trait is influenced by seven loci, each one of those loci may have two or more alleles with one perhaps being dominant to the other, or they may be codominant. It is the combined action of the alleles at all seven loci, interacting with the environment, that results in observable phenotypic expression.

SUMMARY

We have seen how Gregor Mendel discovered the principles of segregation, independent assortment, and dominance and recessiveness by conducting experiments on garden peas. Although the field of genetics has progressed dramatically in the twentieth century, the concepts first put forth by Gregor Mendel remain as the basis of our current knowledge of how traits are inherited.

Traits that are influenced by only one genetic locus are *Mendelian traits*. At many genetic loci, two or more alleles may interact in dominant/recessive or codominant fashion with one another. Examples of Mendelian traits in humans include *ABO* blood type, cystic fibrosis, and sickle-cell anemia. In contrast, many characteristics, such as stature and skin color, are said to be polygenic or continuous, because they are influenced by more than one genetic locus and show a continuous range of expression.

The expression of all traits is, to varying degrees, under genetic control. Genetics, then, can be said to set limits and potentials for human growth, development, and achievement. However, these limits and potentials are not written in stone so to speak, because many characteristics are also very much influenced by such environmental factors as temperature, diet, sunlight, and so on. Thus, ultimately it is the interaction between genetic and environmental factors that produces phenotypic variation in all species, including *Homo sapiens*.

QUESTIONS FOR REVIEW

1. What is Mendel's principle of segregation?
2. How does meiosis explain the principle of segregation?
3. What is Mendel's principle of independent assortment?
4. Explain dominance and recessiveness.
5. Define *allele*.
6. What is *phenotype* and what is its relationship to *genotype*?
7. Why were all of Mendel's F_1 pea plants phenotypically the same?
8. Explain what is meant by a phenotypic ratio of 3:1 in the F_2 generation.
9. What is codominance? Give an example.
10. If two people who have blood type *A* (with the *AO* genotype) have children, what proportion of their children would be expected to have *O* blood? Why?
11. Can the two parents in question 10 have a child with *AB* blood? Why?
12. In a hypothetical situation, a serious disorder is caused by a recessive allele (*a*). The dominant allele (*A*) produces the normal phenotype. What is the genotype of people who have the disorder? Can *unaffected* people have more than one genotype? What is/are the genotype(s) of unaffected people?
13. What are polygenic traits? Give two examples.
14. Why are polygenic traits said to be continuous?
15. What factors, other than genetic, contribute to phenotypic variation in populations?

Physical anthropologists are interested in the study of people, both living and dead. Except for some unusual circumstances, such as natural mummification (where some soft tissues are preserved; see photo essay, p. 285), what is left of earlier populations are the hard tissues (bones and teeth).

One very common approach in the study of these hard tissues is to take precise measurements of the cranium and other elements of the skeleton. Several standard tools have been developed for this purpose.

FIGURE 1 The osteometric board is used to measure lengths of long bones, such as a human femur shown here. The degree of accuracy is to 1 mm.

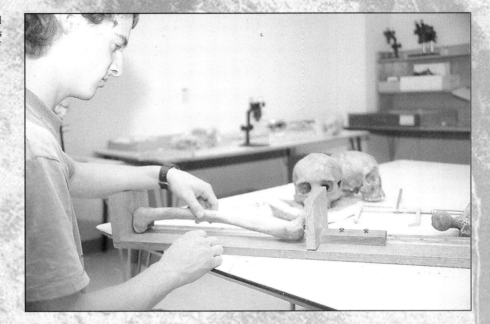

FIGURE 2 Sliding dial calipers are here shown determining upper facial height on a human cranium. The calipers are both pointed (those being used in this example) and blunt (projecting in opposite direction). The pointed ends, especially, are very useful for accurate placement when taking measurements of the face or dentition. The degree of accuracy is to .05 mm.

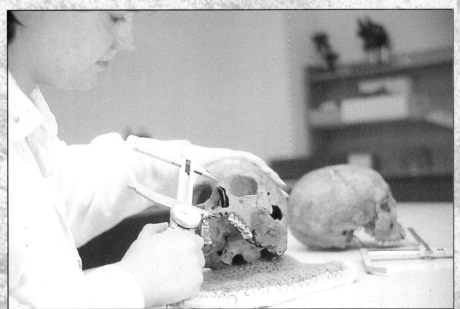

Carefully defined landmarks have been established on the cranium, as well as on many of the long bones, to facilitate standardization of measurements. Practitioners of osteometric techniques can then make sure that the measurement device (calipers) are placed in exactly the proper location.

FIGURE 3 (right) Another kind of sliding calipers: digitally calibrated ones, which are easy to read. Here, they are shown measuring a human mandible. Such an instrument can also be connected to a personal computer (through a digitizer), so the results are directly recorded (obviously saving time and greatly reducing the potential for error). Degree of accuracy of the readout here is to .01 mm; however, because the points of the calipers themselves are not as sharp as in the dial version (Figure 2), they are not as accurate for very precise measurements.

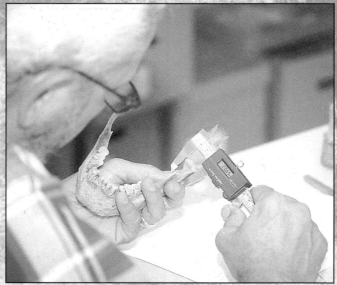

FIGURE 4 (below) While sliding calipers are used for measurement across relatively flat surfaces, spreading calipers are used for the three dimensional surfaces of the cranial vault. Spreading calipers are being used here to measure cranial length. Degree of accuracy is to 1 mm.

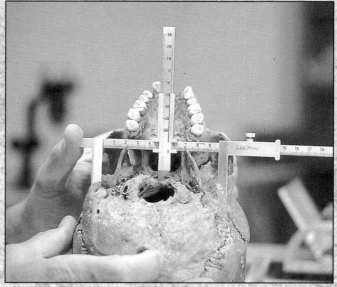

FIGURE 5 Coordinate calipers are used to measure the height or depth of surfaces relative to another surface (plane). Here the height (19 mm) is shown at a defined point on the base of the skull (basion) relative to a plane defined by the two external ear openings (porion). Degree of accuracy is to 1 mm.

Physical anthropologists (osteologists) can observe many useful characteristics using simple tools. (This approach is called gross analysis.) However, other specialized equipment can also be utilized to provide data for variables that cannot be observed directly. Standard X-rays are most helpful in revealing subsurface bone modifications, such as those resulting from healed fractures. The techniques used for taking, as well as reading, the X-rays are exactly analogous to those developed for living patients. Indeed, skeletal biologists often work closely with medical colleagues in analyzing and interpreting human skeletal anatomy and diseases seen in bone (see photo essay, pp. 285–295).

FIGURE 6 A standard X-ray machine at a university student health center being used to radiograph two human long bones (femur and tibia).

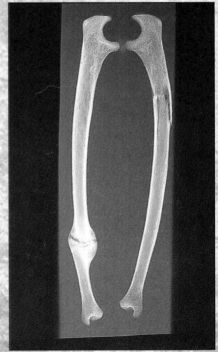

FIGURE 7 (left) Left and right forearm bones (ulnae) from an adult female chimpanzee killed by other chimpanzees at Gombe National Park. The right ulna (on right) has a partially healed fracture. The left side is shown for comparison. This animal (Madam Bee) was attacked several times, and it appears that an earlier injury (as evidenced by thickened portion of the shaft) was fractured again, presumably during the fatal attack.

FIGURE 8 (right) X-ray of same two elements shown in Figure 7. The partially healed fracture is clearly visible. The breakage of the left side probably occurred after death, but it also might have occurred at death.

A more sophisticated application of X-ray technique makes use of C-T (computed tomography) scans. This type of equipment, available at major medical facilities, allows much sharper images that are determined at precisely defined cross-sectional levels within the bone.

FIGURE 9 A C-T machine shown here being prepared to do a scan of adolescent human bones from a 500–1000 year-old American Indian site. Data from the scan provide information regarding bone development.

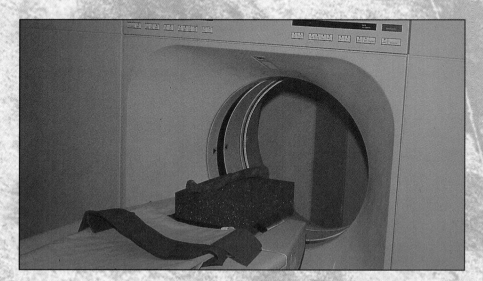

FIGURE 10 A fifth lumbar vertebra (of a young adult female) from a 500–100-year-old Indian site. Embedded in the bone, is an obsidian projectile point (presumably an arrow point).

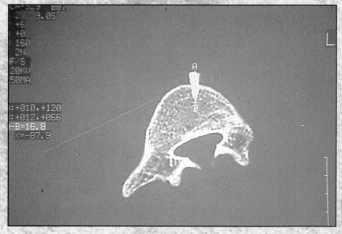

FIGURE 11 A C-T scan of the same element as shown in Figure 10. It is possible to see the projectile point clearly, even the portion embedded within the bone. From this view, it is obvious that no bony reaction (such as healing) occurred, suggesting that the wound (through the abdomen and penetrating into the spine) was fatal.

Another application of sophisticated technology utilizes the scanning electron microscope (SEM). This technique provides very high-quality resolution at either low or high magnification.

FIGURE 12 A scanning electron microscope.

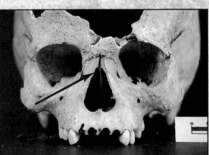

FIGURE 13 A human cranium from North Africa (Carthage, c. 600–700 A.D.) showing unusual indentations above the nose (arrow).

FIGURE 14 Scanning electron micrograph of area indicated in Figure 13 (magnification: 70X).

FIGURE 15 Scanning electron micrograph of same area at higher magnification (700X). The form of the edges of the depression, as seen at high resolution and magnified, suggests it was caused not by a tooth of a carnivore, but more likely by a sharp implement (i.e., a knife?). Speculation, thus has been made that this individual was subjected to ancient surgery (there is a large active bony reaction of the right orbit and surrounding sinuses, caused by an infection or, perhaps, a tumor).

Making exact replicas (casts) of specimens is another useful technique. By this method, it is possible to preserve precise three-dimensional models of rare specimens (e.g., fossils) or those of unusual diseases (pathologies). In addition, for forensic (legal) cases, where the human remains are eventually buried, the casts allow preservation of evidence. Finally, in cases where Native American remains are scheduled for reburial, retaining the replicas will serve as the best record of these individuals.

FIGURE 16 Dr. Diane France in her laboratory pours casting mixture into a rubber mold. The mold for this casting was formed earlier around a human cranium.

FIGURE 17 After a casting mixture sets up, the mold is peeled away from cast. The cast will then be finished by hand. The same mold can be used several times to make further identical replicas.

FIGURE 18 A completed cast of a siamang skull is shown at left in this photograph. The original skull is on the right. The cast is accurate to within the degree of accuracy of standard osteometric tools—to 1 mm or less.

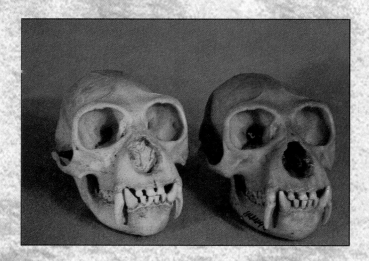

Physical anthropologists also focus on variation seen in living populations. A common technique used on human populations worldwide is blood typing. The best known, and most widely reported, manifestation of blood type is the ABO system

(note: there are many other "blood types" under genetic control of different loci). For each blood type (actually, antigens on the surface of cells) specific antisera have been developed. The reaction with the antisera indicates which antigens are present.

From data on blood type, the frequency of the genes (alleles) responsible for each antigen can be calculated. These data then become the baseline for measuring and interpreting human microevolution.

FIGURE 19
Blood sample is drawn from the end of a finger.

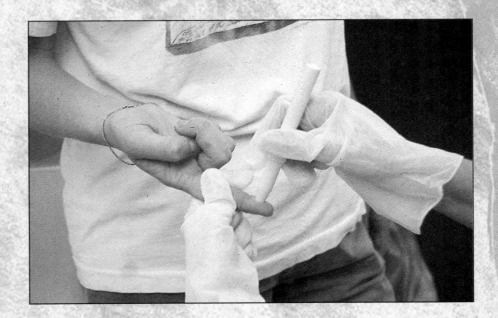

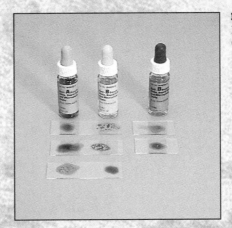

FIGURE 20   Presence of A or B as well as Rh (D) antigens is indicated by reaction (clumping) with commercially available antisera. The slides on left show reactions for ABO; the top is AB, the middle, B, and the bottom slide, A. On right the top slide is Rh$^-$, and the bottom is Rh$^+$.

Physical anthropologists, working with other biomedical scientists, are also concerned with measuring physiological response to environmental stress. Techniques include use of such tools as treadmill tests, bicycle ergometer tests, and questionnaires. These techniques are useful in measuring functional capacity in healthy and diseased persons. In addition, they can be used to assess human biological adaptation to different environments (e.g., high altitude) or to disease (e.g., coronary artery disease).

Physical anthropologists also work with law enforcement agencies and the military as forensic anthropological experts. They participate in locating, removing, and analyzing human remains, especially those that are skeletonized, burned, or fragmented.

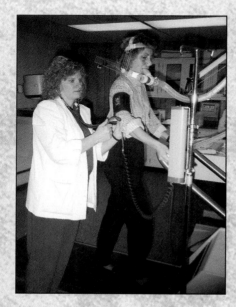

FIGURE 21 A treadmill test is one direct method of assessing functional capacity. A person walks on the treadmill while measurements are collected to determine heart rate, blood pressure, and oxygen consumption.

FIGURE 22 Physical anthropologists Lorna Pierce (on left) and Judy Suchey are seen here working as forensics experts in a training session with a scent-detection dog and a law enforcement officer. The dog has just located a concealed human cranium.

HUMAN DIVERSITY: THE CONCEPT OF RACE

CHAPTER 5

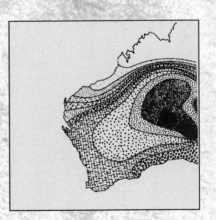

INTRODUCTION

In Chapters 3 and 4 we saw how physical characteristics are influenced by the DNA in our cells. Furthermore, we discussed how individuals inherit genes from parents and how variations in genes (alleles) can cause different expressions of traits. In this chapter, we will broaden our perspective somewhat and focus on phenotypic variability as it is expressed both within and between entire *populations* of humans.

THE CONCEPT OF RACE

In discussions of human variation, people typically clump together various attributes such as skin color, shape of face, shape of nose, hair color, hair form, and eye color. They then place particular combinations of these traits into categories called *races*.

Although we all think we know what we mean by the term "race," in reality the term is often misused, for the concept of race is a very elusive one. First of all, the term *race* is frequently misapplied to groups that differ with regard to various cultural attributes.

One often hears references to, for example, the "English race" or the "German race." In these cases, people are really referring to nationality, not biological differences between groups. Another often heard phrase is the "Jewish race." What the speaker is really talking about here is a particular ethnic and religious identity. One even occasionally hears references to the "male" or "female race." Undeniably, gender differences do exist; however, it is hardly justifiable to categorize males and females within the same groups as racially distinct.

When anthropologists, geneticists, and other researchers use the term *race* they are referring specifically to populations that differ with regard to biological (i.e., inherited) characteristics. However, placing biological limitations upon the concept offers little clarification, and defining race is still an enormously difficult task, as we shall see.

All humans are members of the same **polytypic** species, *Homo sapiens*. A polytypic species is one composed of local populations that differ from one another with regard to one or several traits. Moreover, within

POLYTYPIC Refers to species composed of several populations that differ from each other with regard to certain physical traits.

local populations there is a great deal of phenotypic variability among individuals. Most species are polytypic, and, thus, there is no species type to which all members exactly conform.

Geographically localized human populations that share a cluster of *biological* traits not shared by other such populations are called races. Actually, there are probably as many definitions of the term *race* as there are people who write about it. While most definitions repeat a basic theme, there is, nevertheless, no general consensus as to what a precise definition is.

E. A. Hooten of Harvard University defined race:

> A race is a great division of mankind, the members of which, though individually varying, are characterized as a group by a certain combination of morphological and metrical features, principally non-adaptive, which have been derived from their common descent (Hooten, 1926).

Here is a more modern definition:

> . . . a division of a species which differs from other divisions by the frequency with which certain hereditary traits appear among its members (Brues, 1990).

One of the most recent modifications of the definition of race adds the concept of a *breeding* (or Mendelian) population (Garn, 1965). Objections to this approach are based on the idea that the concept of breeding populations may be difficult to apply (Livingstone, 1964). For example, Stanley Garn (1965) applies the term *Mediterranean* to a local race (see Table 5-1) that ranges from Tangier to the Dardanelles and includes the Arabian Peninsula. However, this is a very unlikely breeding population, containing as it does a number of different nationalities and ethnic and religious groupings. Very few Christians interbreed with Muslims, or Arab Beduins with, say, Italian farmers.

The foregoing comments are not intended to discourage or confuse. However, the fact is that there exists a great deal of confusion about race among anthropologists, geneticists, and others concerned with this concept. Obviously, there *are* physical differences among human beings. No one will mistake an indigenous resident of China for a European or African. However, the matter cannot rest with this statement, for the issue is not that simple.

To understand the difficulties the concept of race presents, it may help to summarize briefly the process of *speciation*, or the appearance of a new species. A species is defined as a *group of interbreeding organisms that is reproductively isolated from other such groups*. As populations within a species diverge geographically, differences between them arise as each population makes biological adjustments to its own local environment. When the differences become detectable, taxonomists may classify these populations as races or subspecies. Eventually, they may become sufficiently distinct that breeding between the two is no longer possible. At that point they are considered two separate species. (See Chapter 7 for more detail.)

Populations of humans are not on their way to becoming separate species. Although human groups have been distributed throughout the

TABLE 5-1 Racial Classifications

LINNAEUS, 1758

Homo europaeus
Homo asiaticus
Homo afer
Homo americanus

BLUMENBACH, 1781

Caucasian
Mongolian
Malay
Ethiopian
American

E. A. HOOTEN, 1926

Primary Race	Primary Subrace	Composite Race*	Composite Subrace*	Residual Mixed Types*
White	Mediterranean	Australian	Armenoid	Nordic-Alpine
	Ainu	Indo-Dravidian	Dinaric	Nordic-Mediterranean
	Keltic	Polynesian		
	Nordic			
	Alpine			
	East Baltic			
Negroid	African Negro	Bushman-Hottentot		
	Nilotic Negro			
	Negrito			
Mongoloid	Classic Mongoloid	Indonesian-Mongoloid		
	Arctic Mongoloid	American Indian		
	Secondary Subrace			
	Malay-Mongoloid Indonesian			

STANLEY M. GARN, 1965

Geographical Races: "A collection of race populations, separated from other such collections by major geographical barriers."

Amerindian	Melanesian-Papuan	Indian
Polynesian	Australian	European
Micronesian	Asiatic	African

Local Races: "A breeding population adapted to local selection pressures and maintained by either natural or social barriers to gene interchange."

These are examples of local races; there are many, many more.

Northwest European	East African	North Chinese
Northeast European	Bantu	Extreme Mongoloid
Alpine	Tibetan	Hindu
Mediterranean		

Micro-Races: Not well defined but apparently refers to neighborhoods within a city or a city itself since "marriage or mating, is a mathematical function of distance. With millions of potential mates, the male ordinarily chooses one near at hand."

*Example of categories, not to be read across.

Old World long enough for regional variations to appear, we do not know exactly when the process began. More importantly, by the time humans dispersed out of Africa to Europe and Asia, they were, to some extent, adapting to the natural environment by cultural means. Since that time, we have increasingly used culture to buffer the effects of the environment. Consequently, biological adaptation has, to varying degrees, been shaped by cultural evolution.

HISTORICAL VIEWS TOWARD HUMAN VARIATION

The first step toward human understanding of natural phenomena is the ordering of variation into categories that can then be named, discussed, and perhaps studied. Historically, when different groups came into contact with one another, they offered explanations for the phenotypic variations they saw. Because skin color was so noticeable, it was one of the more frequently explained traits, and most systems of racial classification were based upon it.

The ancient Egyptians may have been the first to classify humans on the basis of skin color. Because of their military and trading successes (including the slave trade), the Egyptians were familiar with black Africans to the south and many peoples to the east. As early as 1350 B.C., they had classified groups on the basis of skin color: red for Egyptian, yellow for people to the east, white for those to the north, and black for Africans from the south (Gossett, 1963, p. 4).

The ancient Greeks referred to all black Africans as "Ethiopians," meaning "scorched ones" (Brues, 1990), implying a response to exposure to the sun. Ovid, a first century A.D. Roman poet, presents us with a Greek myth that offers an environmental explanation for the dark skin color of sub-Saharan Africans (Book Two of Ovid's *Metamorphoses*).

The sun god, Apollo, ill-advisedly allowed his adolescent son Phaeton to drive the chariot of the sun through its daily round across the sky. Feeling an unfamiliar hand upon the reins, the fiery chariot horses bolted, and in their frenzy, they plummeted toward the earth. In the end, Apollo was forced to kill Phaeton in order to keep the earth from burning and, as Ovid tells us:

> . . . that was when, or so men think, the people
> Of Africa turned black, since the blood was driven
> By that fierce heat to the surface of their bodies . . .
> (Humphries, 1973, p. 35).

Until the late fifteenth century, most Europeans were unfamiliar with people from other parts of the world. From the fall of Rome (A.D. 455) until the Renaissance, most Europeans were pretty much isolated from the mainstream of people and events in the rest of the world.

The Arabs, who by the seventh century A.D. had expanded throughout the Mediterranean, were not so isolated. Through extensive trade routes and because they controlled the slave trade out of what is now the Sudan, the Arabs had knowledge of many peoples. Not surprisingly, they had their own explanations for how humans came to differ from area to area. Skin color was seen as a function of a type of embryonic cooking process. In northern climates, infants were pale and blond because the womb never warmed up properly, so they were not quite "done." By contrast, in hot southern areas, the contents of the womb were overdone to the point that people had their skin burned black and their hair scorched and frizzled (Lewis, 1971, *in*: Brues, 1990). The Arabs considered themselves to be intermediate between these extremes and, "To their way of thinking, only they themselves were 'done' just right" (Brues, 1990, p. 13).

In the sixteenth century, after the discovery of the New World, Europe embarked upon a period of intense exploration and colonization in both the New and Old Worlds. Resulting from this contact was an increased awareness of racial diversity.

The discovery of the New World was of major importance in shaking the complacency of Europeans, who viewed the world as static and non-changing. In the Americas, early explorers found numerous species of previously unknown (to them) plants and animals. But the most important discovery was that these new lands were inhabited by groups of dark-skinned people who were not Christian, spoke strange languages, and by all appearances, were not "civilized." Native Americans were, at first, thought to be Asian, and since Columbus believed he had discovered a new route to India, he called them "Indians." (This term was later applied to indigenous, dark-skinned populations of Australia as well.)

By the late eighteenth century, Europeans and Americans were asking questions that posed challenges to traditional Christian beliefs and standards of morality. They wanted to know if other groups belonged to the same species as themselves; that is, were they indeed human? Were they descendants of Adam and Eve or had there been later creations of non-Europeans? If the latter were true, then they had to represent different species or else the Genesis account of creation could not be taken literally.

Europeans also wondered if it were possible for themselves and non-Europeans to interbreed and produce fertile offspring. Was mental capacity in Native Americans and the peoples of Africa, India, and elsewhere comparable to that of Europeans? Did traits such as skin color and shape of face and head contribute to character and morality?

MONOGENISM The theory that all human races are descendants of one pair (Adam and Eve).

POLYGENISM The theory that human races are not all descended from Adam and Eve and therefore are not all members of the same species.

Two schools of thought, known as **monogenism** and **polygenism**, devised responses. In the monogenist view, all races were descended from a single, original pair (Adam and Eve). Insisting on the plasticity of the human physical structure, monogenists contended that climate, environment, and local conditions modified the original form, resulting in separate races. Monogenist views were initially attractive to many, for they did not conflict with the Genesis version of creation.

The polygenist view, on the other hand, argued that races did not descend from a single, original pair, but from a number of pairs. Also, they saw such a wide gap in the physical, mental, and moral attributes between themselves and other races, that they were sure that outsiders belonged to different species.

Other polygenists were dissatisfied with the concept of species and resorted to using the word *type* instead. However, they believed there had been "pure" races in the past, which through intermixture, migration, and conquest, had become modified to their present condition. Nor did polygenists accept the monogenist notion of plasticity of physical traits, and they rejected the proposition that climate and environment were modifying instruments.

The first scientific attempt to describe the newly discovered variation, including human, was Linnaeus' taxonomic classification, which ordered humans into four separate categories (Linnaeus, 1758). (See Table 5-1.) Linnaeus assigned behavioral and intellectual qualities to each group, with the least complimentary descriptions going to African blacks. This ranking was typical of the period and reflected the almost universal European view that they were superior to all other peoples.

Johann Friedrich Blumenbach (1752–1840), a German anatomist, classified humans into five races: Caucasoid, Mongoloid, American, Ethiopian, and Malayan. Although Blumenbach's categories came to be described simply as White, Yellow, Red, Black, and Brown, he also used other criteria than skin color. Moreover, Blumenbach emphasized that racial categories based upon skin color were arbitrary and that many traits, including skin color, were not discrete phenomena. Rather, what we now call polygenic traits existed on a continuum and showed a wide range of expression. He pointed out that to attempt to classify all humans using such a system would be to omit altogether all those who did not neatly fall into a specific category.

Although most scientists were monogenists in the early nineteenth century, by 1850 polygenism was gaining favor. Some scientists, taking the polygenist view that certain physical traits were stable (i.e., nonadaptive), began measuring the skull. (The skull was regarded as unchanging and in order to determine racial differences fully, it was necessary to use a trait that, in their view, did not change.) Also, the skull was selected because it housed the brain, and conventional wisdom of the time erroneously held that there was a direct correlation between size and shape of the brain and intelligence and morality. There is certainly a relationship between the brain and intelligence. However, there is a wide range of normal variation regarding brain size in humans, and within that range, we now know that size is not an indicator of cognitive ability.

In 1842, Anders Retzius, a Swedish anatomist, developed the *cephalic index* as a method for describing the shape of the head. The cephalic index illustrates the ratio of head breadth to length, and Retzius used it to divide Europeans into two types: **dolichocephalics**, or those with long, narrow heads; and those with broad heads, or **brachycephalics**. Northern Europeans tended to be dolichocephalic while southern Europeans (including the French and many Germans) were brachycephalic. Not surprisingly, these results led to some heated and nationalistic debate over whether one group was superior to the other.

By the mid-nineteenth century, monogenists were beginning to reject their somewhat egalitarian concept of race in favor of a more hierarchical view. Therefore, they came to accept what was obvious to most Europeans; namely, that Europeans were superior to all other peoples. Races were ranked essentially on a scale based on color (along with size and shape of the head), with Africans at the bottom. Moreover, Europeans themselves were ranked so that northern, light-skinned popula-

DOLICOCEPHALIC Having a long, narrow head. A skull in which the width is less than 75 percent of the length.

BRACHYCEPHALIC Having a broad head or a skull in which the width is 80 percent or more of the length.

BIOLOGICAL DETERMINISM The concept that various aspects of behavior (e.g., intelligence, values, morals) are governed by biological factors (genes). The inaccurate association of various behavioral attributes with certain biological traits, such as skin color.

tions were considered superior to their southern, more olive-skinned neighbors.

Many non-Europeans were not Christian and were seen as "uncivilized," which implied an inferiority of character and intellect. This view was based upon a concept known as **biological determinism**, which holds that there is an association between physical characteristics and such attributes as intelligence, morals, values, abilities, and even social and economic differences between groups. In other words, cultural variations are inherited in the same manner as are biological variations. It follows then that there are inherent behavioral and cognitive differences between groups (racism), or between sexes (sexism); and, therefore, some groups are *by nature* superior to others. Following this logic, it is a simple matter to justify the persecution and enslavement of other peoples, simply because their appearance differs from what is familiar.

After 1850, biological determinism was a constant theme underlying common thinking as well as scientific research in Europe and the United States. Moreover, deterministic views (and, indeed, what we today would call racist views) were held to some extent by such notable figures as Thomas Jefferson, Georges Cuvier, Benjamin Franklin, Charles Lyell, Abraham Lincoln, Charles Darwin, and Oliver Wendell Holmes. Commenting upon this usually deemphasized characteristic of notable historical figures, Stephen J. Gould (1981, p. 32) of Harvard University emphasizes that, "All American culture heroes embraced racial attitudes that would embarrass public-school mythmakers."

At the same time, some scientists were becoming frustrated over their inability to define racial groups. Many shared the opinion that race was merely a hypothetical concept because it was rare that an individual possessed all the traits characteristic of his or her race. However, in spite of these sentiments, the predominant view was that races existed and culturally determined characteristics were inherited.

Francis Galton (1822–1911), a cousin of Charles Darwin, shared an increasingly common fear among Europeans that civilized society was being weakened by the failure of natural selection to eliminate unfit and inferior members (Greene, 1981, p. 107).* Galton wrote and lectured on the necessity of race improvement and suggested governmental regulation of marriage and family size, an approach he called **eugenics**.

Galton's writings attracted a considerable following both in Europe and the United States, and a number of eugenics societies were formed. The eugenics movement had a great deal of snob appeal, for fitness was deemed to be embodied in the upper classes, while the lower classes were associated with criminality, illness, and mental retardation. Moreover, many eugenics societies sought to rid society of crime, as well as such perceived ills as insanity and homosexuality, through mandatory sterilization programs.

EUGENICS The science of race improvement through forced sterilization of members of some groups and encouraged reproduction among others. An overly simplified, often racist view—now discredited.

Although eugenics had its share of critics, its popularity flourished on both sides of the Atlantic until the 1930s. After World War I, the movement was increasingly popular in Europe, but nowhere was it more

---

*Greene suggests that Darwin also held this belief. Scholars, however, are divided about whether or not Darwin himself held this view.

popular than in Germany, where the movement took a disastrous turn. The idea of a pure race was extolled as a means of reestablishing a strong and prosperous state, and eugenics was seen as scientific justification for purging Germany of her "unfit." Many of Germany's scientists accepted this interpretation (known as *Rassenhygiene* or racial hygiene) and continued to support it during the Nazi period (Proctor, 1988, p. 143), when it served as justification for condemning millions of people to death.

After World War I, some physical anthropologists turned away from racial classification as the validity of racial concepts, and the goals of the eugenics movement increasingly came into question. Moreover, the synthesis of Mendelian genetics and Darwin's theories of natural selection in the 1930s (see Modern Synthesis, p. 89) influenced all the biological sciences, and physical anthropologists began to apply evolutionary principles to the study of human variation (as illustrated in the next chapter).

Racial classification was not dead, however. Carleton S. Coon (1962) proposed a taxonomy also composed of five groups, based upon a somewhat earlier one developed by R. R. Gates (1948). The nomenclature used in these two systems was the same: Caucasoid, Negroid, Mongoloid, Australoid, and Capoid. Today three large racial groups are sometimes recognized by anthropologists: Caucasoid, Negroid, and Mongoloid.

THE PROBLEMS OF TYPOLOGICAL APPROACHES TO RACIAL TAXONOMY

There are numerous problems inherent in racial taxonomies. Classification schemes are *typological* in nature, meaning that categories are discrete and based upon a concept or ideal that comprises a specific set of traits. Typologies may be useful in certain situations. However, racial typologies are misleading, for there are always individuals in any grouping who do not fit a particular type.

In any so-called racial group there will be individuals who fall into the normal range of variation for another group, with regard to one or even several traits. Although, it is unlikely that anyone is going to mistake a person whose background is Danish for someone whose ancestry is Nigerian, these two individuals could share any number of traits, such as height, body build, or ABO blood type. In fact, they could easily share more genetic similarities with one another than they do with some individuals in their own population—in spite of the fact they differ regarding certain highly noticeable attributes, such as skin color.

Today, human biologists emphasize differences *within* populations as well as *between* them. A good example of this approach is a study by Harvard population geneticist, R. D. Lewontin (1972). Lewontin demonstrated that the vast majority of human variation is explained by differences between individuals in the same groups (or even in the same family), rather than differences between large, geographically distributed populations. These results are understandable in light of the genetic mechanisms we discussed in Chapters 3 and 4. Physical anthropologists focus upon such genetic/evolutionary factors in explaining human diversity (see Chapter 6).

THE ADAPTIVE SIGNIFICANCE OF HUMAN VARIATION

Today, physical anthropologists view human variation as the result of adaptations to environmental conditions, both past and present. Although cultural adaptations have certainly played an important role in the evolution of *Homo sapiens*, in this discussion we are primarily concerned with biological factors.

Physiological adaptation is under genetic control and operates at two levels. At one level are characteristics that are present regardless of environmental conditions. Examples of such traits are head shape and eye color. The term *acclimatization* is used to refer to traits that can alter *in the individual* to meet changing environmental demands. An example of acclimatization is the very rapid increase in hemoglobin production that occurs when individuals travel to higher elevations. This increase provides the individual with enhanced oxygen transport capabilities in an environment where available oxygen is less abundant. The fact that football teams sometimes travel to Colorado a few days before a game reflects the necessity of allowing athletes time to acclimatize to the change in elevation.

Solar Radiation, Vitamin D, and Skin Color

Skin color is an often cited example of adaptation and natural selection in human populations. In general, skin color in populations, prior to European contact, follows a particular geographic distribution, especially in the Old World. Figure 5-1 illustrates that populations with the greatest amount of pigmentation are found in the tropics, while lighter skin color is associated with more northern latitudes.

Skin color is influenced by three substances: hemoglobin, carotene, and most importantly, the pigment *melanin*. Melanin is a granular substance produced by specialized cells in the epidermis called *melanocytes*. All humans appear to have approximately the same number of melanocytes; however, they vary in the amount of melanin they produce.

Melanin has the capacity to absorb ultraviolet rays present (although not visible) in sunlight. Therefore, melanin provides protection from overexposure to ultraviolet radiation, which can cause mutations in skin cells. These mutations may ultimately lead to skin cancer which, if left untreated, can eventually spread to other organs and result in death.

Exposure to sunlight triggers a protective mechanism or adaptive response in the form of temporary increased melanin production. (The visible manifestation of this temporary increase is a tan.) This protective response is absent in albinos who carry a genetic mutation that prevents their melanocytes from producing melanin. Tanning is also limited in some individuals of northern European descent who do produce some melanin, but have a reduced capacity for temporary increases in melanin production.

Natural selection appears to favor dark skin in areas where exposure to ultraviolet light is pronounced. However, as hominids migrated out of Africa into Europe and Asia, selective pressures changed. Not only were these populations moving away from the tropics, where ultraviolet

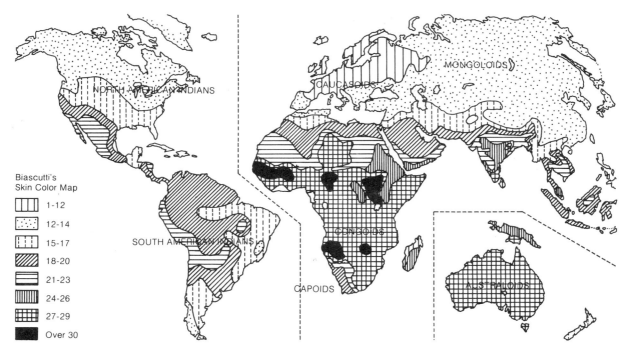

FIGURE 5-1 Distribution of skin color among the indigenous populations of the world. (After Coon and Hunt, 1965.)

Biascutti's
Skin Color Map

⊞	1–12
⠿	12–14
⊞	15–17
⧄	18–20
≡	21–23
⫴	24–26
⊞	27–29
■	Over 30

rays were most direct, but they were moving into areas where it was cold and cloudy during winter. Bear in mind also that physiological adaptations were not sufficient to meet the demands of living in colder climates. Therefore, we must assume that these populations had adopted certain cultural practices, such as the wearing of animal skins or other types of clothing. Although clothing would have added necessary warmth, it also would have effectively blocked exposure to sunlight. Consequently, the advantages provided by deeply pigmented skin in the tropics were no longer important, and selection for melanin production may have been relaxed (Brace and Montagu, 1977).

However, relaxed selection favoring dark skin may not be adequate to explain the very depigmented skin seen especially in some northern Europeans. Perhaps another factor, the need for adequate amounts of Vitamin D, was also critical. The theory concerning the possible role of Vitamin D is known as the *Vitamin D hypothesis* and offers the following explanation.

Vitamin D is synthesized in the body partly as a result of the interaction of ultraviolet radiation and a substance similar to cholesterol. Vitamin D is necessary for normal bone growth and mineralization, and some exposure to ultraviolet radiation is therefore essential. Insufficient amounts of Vitamin D during childhood result in *rickets*, which often leads to bowing of the long bones of the lower extremity and deformation of the pelvis.

Reduced exposure to sunlight due to climate and increased use of clothing could have been detrimental to dark-skinned individuals in more northern latitudes. In these individuals, melanin would have blocked absorption of the already reduced amounts of ultraviolet radiation required for Vitamin D synthesis. Therefore, selection pressures would have shifted over time to favor individuals with lighter skin. There is evidence in recent and current populations to support this theory.

During the latter decades of the nineteenth century in the United States, black inhabitants of northern cities suffered a higher incidence of rickets than whites. Northern blacks were also more commonly affected than blacks living in the south where exposure to sunlight is greater. (The supplementation of milk with Vitamin D was initiated to alleviate this problem.) Another example is seen in Britain, where darker-skinned East Indians and Pakistanis show a higher incidence of rickets than whites (Molnar, 1983).

At the same time, Vitamin D may have played a different role in the tropics, where perhaps it enhanced the selective advantage of deeply pigmented skin. Excessive levels of Vitamin D are known to be toxic to humans. Therefore, it is possible that deeply pigmented skin not only afforded protection from ultraviolet radiation, but also—by blocking ultraviolet light—it prevented the overproduction of Vitamin B to potentially dangerous levels (Molnar, 1983).

CLINAL DISTRIBUTION OF TRAITS

A relatively recent* approach to the study of human variation is to examine the *clinal distribution* of traits. In using this approach, we consider one trait at a time, examining its geographic distribution or how its frequency changes from one population to another. Just as temperature is plotted on a weather map by means of lines that connect points with the same temperature, so also may frequencies of alleles or some other measurement of physical traits be plotted (Fig. 5-2).

A clinal description simply reveals the variation of a trait over a geographic area, but it neither explains it nor does it lead to a racial typology. Clinal distribution does, however, call for an evolutionary explanation of variation (for further discussion see Chapter 6).

Human variation is perceived quite differently when approached from a clinal point of view. No attempt is made to construct a typology of traits, but rather to apply the principles of evolution. Is variation in frequency of a trait due to natural selection and adaptation in local areas? Or does it result from migration into or out of the clinal area?

An example of an evolutionary clinal approach may be seen in Dr. Joseph Birdsell's discussion of the distribution of tawny hair among children in dark-skinned aboriginal populations of Australia. Blond hair has its highest incidence among tribal groups in the Australian western desert (Fig. 5-2), and the frequency then declines on a gradient outward

---

*J. S. Huxley introduced the clinal concept, as it applied to plants, in 1938.

FIGURE 5-2 Phenotypic distribution, tawny hair in Australia. Note the concentration of tawny hair in the center of distribution which can be traced by clines in a decreasing gradient.

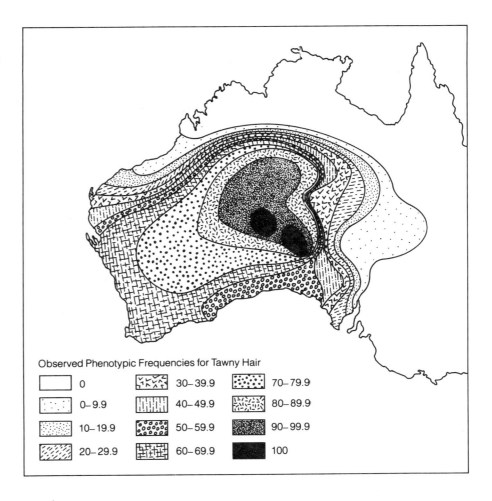

Observed Phenotypic Frequencies for Tawny Hair

0	30–39.9	70–79.9	
0–9.9	40–49.9	80–89.9	
10–19.9	50–59.9	90–99.9	
20–29.9	60–69.9	100	

from this center, although not uniformly in all directions. Professor Birdsell writes (1981, pp. 352–353):

> The evolutionary significance of this clinal distribution seems apparent, even though the exact genetic basis for its inheritance has not yet been unraveled. The trait acts as though it was determined by a single codominant gene. It would appear that somewhere in the central region of high frequency, mutations, and probably repeated mutations, occurred from normal dark brown hair to this depigmented variety. The pattern of distribution indicates that it was favored by selection in some totally unknown fashion. Over considerable periods of time, through gene exchange between adjacent tribes, the new mutant gene prospered and spread outward. It seems unlikely that lightly pigmented hair in childhood should in itself have any selective advantage. Rather, it is much more probable that certain effects of this mutant gene have somehow biochemically heightened the fitness of these Aborigines in their generally desert environment.

Professor Birdsell goes on to point out that one character cannot define a subspecies or a race, and that "this example illustrates why races are scientifically undefinable" (Birdsell, 1981, p. 352).

RACE AND BEHAVIOR

CULTURAL RELATIVISM The view that differences in attitudes, values, and other social attributes that exist between populations are due to cultural variations not biological variation.

We have dealt with biological determinism from a historical perspective, but not from a contemporary one. Lest we be too complacent about our own enlightened **cultural relativism**, we should remind ourselves that the belief in the inheritance of personality traits is widely held today. Moreover, although there is general consensus among scholars that there is no evidence that any aspect of culture (i.e., religion, values, technology) is genetically controlled, there is still some controversy over intelligence.

Early psychologists believed that IQ tests accurately measured an innate factor known as intelligence. That blacks repeatedly scored lower than whites on such tests was indicative of what many already held to be true: namely, that blacks were, by nature, mentally inferior to whites.

However, there are long-standing questions as to what IQ tests actually do measure. There is no IQ test that is entirely *culture free*; that is to say, no test exclusively measures innate ability uninfluenced by experience (including education). Moreover, it appears to be impossible to design an IQ test that does not to some extent reflect the cultural norms of the designer and/or those for whom the test is designed (i.e., an unbiased test). Therefore, IQ tests are said to be *culture bound*, and a test that is bound to one culture cannot accurately be used to assess the innate abilities of individuals from another culture.

Children growing up in United States suburbs have very different experiences from those who grow up, for example, in urban ghettos. Indeed, the two groups differ with regard to economic status, values, expectations, all types of childhood experiences, and even vocabulary. Therefore, it is to be expected that children from these two backgrounds will not score equally well on an IQ test that reflects the norms for only one group.

In the 1930s, Otto Klineberg, a psychologist, reexamined IQ test questions and identified numerous examples where either the language or the actual premise of the question was culture bound and presented problems for nonwhites (Klineberg, 1935).

Klineberg also examined results of United States Army intelligence tests and determined that regional variation was important. He showed that men from the north scored higher than those from the south, regardless of race. Moreover, and more revealing, northern blacks scored higher than southern whites. These findings strongly indicated not only that whites were not inherently superior to blacks intellectually, but that access to education was of major importance in influencing IQ test scores.

Today, there are still scientists who believe in the relationship between race and intelligence. Arthur R. Jensen, professor of educational psychology at the University of California at Berkeley, estimates the heritability of intelligence at about 75 percent (Jensen, 1980, p. 244). Jensen believes that intelligence is a correlate of race, which is inherited. It follows, then, that the lower average IQ scores of blacks (about 15 points) are a function of biology.

Jensen's views have been criticized by scientists from various disciplines, and numerous studies (including Klineberg's) have shown environment to be a vital factor. Currently, there is no consensus as to the extent of environmental influence, or how to factor in the many environmental components that affect IQ scores. Nevertheless, anthropologists Loring Brace and Frank Livingstone (1971, p. 67) suggest that *all* measured differences among major groups of humans may be explained primarily by environmental factors.

Innate factors set limits and define potentials for behavior and cognitive ability in any species. In humans, the limits are broad and the potentials are not fully known. Individual abilities result from complex interactions between genetic and environmental factors. One product of this interaction is learning, and the ability to learn has genetic or biological components. Undeniably, individuals vary regarding these biological components. However, elucidating what proportion of the variation in test scores is due to biological factors probably is not possible. Moreover, innate differences in abilities reflect individual variation *within* populations, not inherent differences *between* groups. Comparing populations on the basis of IQ test results is a misuse of testing procedures.

With the bulk of scientific opinion opposed to inheritance as the sole explanation for intelligence, we agree with Professor William Howells' (1971, p. 8) statement that, "In all honesty, therefore, scientists must decline to see the existence of racial variation in mental ability at this stage."

In conclusion, what we really observe when we see biological variations between populations (and individuals) are the traces of our evolutionary past. Different expressions of traits such as skin color, eye color, and shape of face are the results of biological adaptations our ancestors made to local environmental conditions, in a process that began perhaps several hundred thousand years ago. Instead of using these differences as a basis for prejudice and persecution, we should praise them. We should recognize them for what they are, a preserved record of how natural selection shaped our species to meet the varied environmental challenges it faced while expanding to become the dominant form of life on our planet.

SUMMARY

We have discussed how humans have attempted to explain and classify human variation. Classification schemes have usually focused primarily upon skin color, while secondarily relying upon other characters to define racial groupings.

Racial taxonomies are based upon typologies, and are not a particularly useful method of either categorizing or explaining phenotypic variation. In any typologically defined human group, there are always individuals who do not conform in all respects to that particular type. Moreover, such groupings tend to overlap with others regarding some traits. Lastly, it has been shown that there exists more genetic/phenotypic variation *within* racial groups than *between* them.

We have also illustrated how *biological determinism* has widely influenced scientific thinking, indeed up to the present day, and has served as a basis for racist views and policies. Numerous studies have amply demonstrated that there is no correlation between race, behavior, and cognitive abilities. Moreover, culture bound IQ tests have been identified as the cause of unequal performance on IQ tests among whites, blacks, and other groups earlier in this century.

Lastly, we have shown that today, anthropologists approach the question of race and human variation as results of adaptation through natural selection. Such traits as skin color vary from one area to another because of the need to meet various, interacting environmental demands. The fact that humans have met these demands so successfully stands as testimony to the plasticity of our remarkable species.

QUESTIONS FOR REVIEW

1. What are typologies? Why are racial typologies not adequate to explain human variation?
2. Why is *race* such a difficult term to define?
3. What is biological determinism?
4. When anthropologists use racial categories today, what are the three large groupings they refer to?
5. What was the eugenics movement, and what was its underlying premise?
6. How can it be said that human variation results from adaptation to local environmental conditions?
7. Discuss the current theories regarding differences in skin pigmentation in humans.
8. What are clinal populations?
9. What are some of the problems associated with comparing different groups on the basis of I.Q. test scores? What are the factors that influence I.Q. test results?

CONTEMPORARY VIEWS OF HUMAN VARIATION

CHAPTER 6

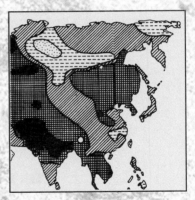

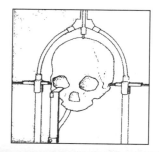

INTRODUCTION

In Chapter 4, we discussed the principles underlying heredity, and in Chapter 5, we reviewed the history of concepts that have attempted to account for human racial variation. In addition, you were introduced to the more contemporary view of explaining racial variation in terms of evolutionary/adaptive processes.

    In the previous chapter, variation was discussed using *complex* traits influenced by several genetic loci. Here, we will concentrate on those traits with a more clearly understood genetic basis—that is, Mendelian traits governed by a single genetic locus. We also continue in this chapter with the modern perspective of evolutionary explanations of biological variation. In this century, a *synthetic* view of evolutionary change has become the major cornerstone of modern biology. As with all other organisms, the variation exhibited by *Homo sapiens* can be understood within this contemporary evolutionary framework. Evolutionary change has not only characterized the human past but is a major feature shaping human beings today.

VARIATION Inherited differences among individuals.

THE MODERN THEORY OF EVOLUTION

At the beginning of this century, Mendel's principles were rediscovered. As a result, the two essential foundations of modern evolutionary theory were in place. Darwin and Wallace had articulated the crucial role of natural selection 40 years earlier, and in 1900 Mendel's pioneering work was rediscovered simultaneously by three different scholars, thus clearly establishing the mechanism for inheritance.

    We might expect that the two basic contributions would have been joined rather quickly into one consistent theory of evolution. However, such was not to be. For over 30 years, following 1900, rival "camps" advocated what seemed to be opposing viewpoints. One, supported by experimental biologists working with such organisms as fruit flies, emphasized the central role of mutation. The other school of thought continued with the more traditional Darwinian view, and pointed to the key role of natural selection.

A synthesis of these two views was not achieved until the mid-1930s, and we owe much of our current understanding of evolutionary change to this important intellectual breakthrough. Biologists working primarily on mathematical models came to realize that mutation and selection processes were not opposing themes, but that a comprehensive explanation of organic evolution required *both*. Small changes in the genetic material (i.e., mutations) are transmitted from parent to child according to the rules first discovered by Mendel. Such changes do not themselves produce evolutionary change, but are selected for (or against) in particular environments. Indeed, the mutational origin of variation is the only original source of "fuel" for natural selection.

Using such a perspective, evolution can be described as a two-stage process:

1. Production and redistribution of **variation** (inherited differences between individuals)
2. **Natural selection** results, as genetic differences in some individuals lead to their higher reproductive success

NATURAL SELECTION The differential reproductive success of some genotypes compared to others (relative to specific environments).

DEFINITION OF EVOLUTION

Darwin saw evolution as the gradual emergence of new life forms derived from earlier ones. Such a depiction is in accordance with the common understanding of evolutionary change and, indeed, is the end result of the evolutionary process. However, such long-term effects—called **macroevolution**—can only come about by the accumulation of many small evolutionary changes—called **microevolution**—which unfold every generation. In order to understand how the process of evolution works, we necessarily must study these short-term events. Using such a modern *population genetics* perspective, we define evolution as a **change in allele frequency** from one generation to the next. This concept is really very simple. As we have seen, *alleles* are alternative forms of genes that occur at the same locus. For example, the ABO blood type in humans is governed by a single locus on chromosome number 9. As such, it is a good example of a *Mendelian* trait in humans. As we have seen in Chapter 4, this locus has three alternative forms (alleles), A, B, or O.

The allele frequency is simply the proportion of alleles in a population. If 70% of all alleles are O, its allele frequency is .70. If A and B constitute respectively 10% and 20% of alleles, the frequencies are .10 and .20. In any genetic system, the total of allele frequencies must equal 1.0 (100%).

Evolution, then, is a *change* in these proportions. For example, if the allele frequencies noted above were to shift, over a few generations, to O = .50, A = .30, and B = .20, then we would say evolution had occurred (O had decreased in frequency, A had increased, and B had stayed the same).

How does such a process occur in human populations? In other words, what causes allele frequencies to change in human populations? First, we must define what we mean by "population."

MACROEVOLUTION Large-scale evolutionary changes that require many hundreds of generations and are usually only detectable palentologically (in the fossil record).

MICROEVOLUTION Small-scale evolutionary changes that occur over the span of a few generations, and, therefore, can be seen in living populations.

CHANGE IN ALLELE FREQUENCY The microevolutionary definition of evolution.

The Population

POPULATION Within a species, the community of individuals where mates are usually found.

GENE POOL The total complement of genes in a population.

A **population** is a group of interbreeding individuals. More precisely, a population is the group within which one is most likely to find a mate. As such, a population is marked by a degree of genetic relatedness and shares a common **gene pool**.

In theory, this is a straightforward concept. In every generation the genes (alleles) are mixed by recombination and rejoined through mating. What emerges in the next generation is a direct product of the genes going into the pool, which in turn is a product of who is mating with whom.

In practice, however, isolating and describing human populations is most difficult. The largest population of *Homo sapiens* that could be described is the entire species. All members of a species are *potentially* capable of interbreeding, but are incapable of fertile interbreeding with members of other species. Our species is thus a *genetically closed system*. The problem arises not in describing who potentially can interbreed, but in isolating exactly the pattern of those individuals who are doing so.

Factors that determine mate choice are geographical, ecological, and social. If individuals are isolated on a remote island in the middle of the Pacific, there is not much chance of finding a mate outside the immediate vicinity. Such **breeding isolates** are fairly easily defined and are a favorite target of microevolutionary studies. Geography plays a dominant role in producing these isolates by rather strictly determining the range of available mates. But even within these limits cultural rules can easily play a deciding role by prescribing who is most "proper" among those who are potentially available.

BREEDING ISOLATES Populations that are clearly isolated either geographically and/or socially from other groups.

ENDOGAMY Mating within the population.

Human population segments within the species are defined as groups with relative degrees of **endogamy** (marrying/mating within the group). These are, however, not totally closed systems. Migration often occurs between groups, and individuals may choose mates from distant localities. With the modern advent of rapid transportation, greatly accelerated rates of **exogamy** (marrying/mating outside the group) have emerged.

EXOGAMY Mating outside the population.

It is obvious that most humans today are not clearly members of particular populations as they would be if they belonged to a breeding isolate. Inhabitants of large cities may appear to be members of a single population, but actually within the city borders social, ethnic, and religious boundaries crosscut in a complex fashion to form smaller population segments. In addition to being members of these highly open local population groupings, we are simultaneously members of overlapping gradations of larger populations—the immediate geographical region (a metropolitan area or perhaps an entire state), a region of the country, the whole nation, the Western World, and ultimately again, the whole species.

EVOLUTION IN ACTION— MODERN HUMAN POPULATIONS

GENETIC EQUILIBRIUM The mathematical relationship expressing—under ideal conditions—the predicted distribution of genes in a population; the central theorem of population genetics.

Once a population has been defined, a population geneticist will ascertain whether allele frequencies are stable (that is, in **genetic equilibrium**) or whether they are changing. A mathematical model (called the Hardy-

Weinberg equilibrium) provides the tool to establish whether allele frequencies are indeed changing. What factors initiate changes in allele frequencies? There are a number, including those that:

1. produce new variation (that is, mutation)
2. redistribute variation through *migration* or *genetic drift*
3. select "advantageous" allele combinations that promote reproductive success—that is, natural selection

As can be seen, (a) and (b) above are the first stage of the evolutionary process, and (c) is the second stage as described on page 89.

Mutation

Mutation is the only way totally *new* variation can be produced. Effects on any one gene should be minor, however, since mutation rates for any given locus are quite low (estimated at about 1 per 10,000 gametes per generation). In fact, because mutation occurs so infrequently at any particular locus, it would rarely have any significant effect on allele frequencies. Certainly, mutation occurs every generation, but unless we sample a huge number of subjects, we are unlikely to detect any noticeable effect.

However, because we each have many loci (estimated at about 100,000), we all possess numerous mutations that have accumulated over recent generations. Most of these are not expressed in the phenotype, but are "hidden" as recessive alleles (see Chapter 4 for a discussion of recessive inheritance). An example of such a recessive mutation is the allele for PKU (phenylketonuria). About 1 in 12,000 babies are born in the United States every year who carry this allele in double dose—and thus are affected phenotypically. Without early detection and treatment, this condition leads to catastrophic mental retardation (see p. 59).

Several dominant alleles that produce human disease are also well known. An example of such a condition is a type of dwarfism called achondroplasia. Individuals with the responsible mutant allele in single dose are very short in limb length, but have a normally sized heads and trunk. The incidence of achondroplasia among newborns in the United States is about 1 in 10,000.

Migration

Migration, also known as gene flow, is the movement of alleles between populations. In the last 500 years especially, population movements have reached enormous proportions, and few breeding isolates remain. It should not, however, be assumed that significant population movements did not occur prior to modern times. Our hunting and gathering ancestors probably lived in small groups, which were mobile as well as flexible in membership. Early farmers may well have been fairly mobile, moving from area to area as the land wore out. Intensive, highly sedentary agricultural communities came later, but even then significant migration was still possible. From the Near East, one of the early farming centers, populations spread gradually in a "creeping occupation of Europe, India, and northern and eastern Africa" (Bodmer and Cavalli-Sforza, 1976, p. 563).

MIGRATION The exchange of alleles between populations (also called gene flow).

An interesting application of how migration influences microevolutionary change in modern human populations is seen in the admixture of parental groups among American blacks over the last three centuries. Blacks in the United States are of largely West African descent, but there has also been considerable influx of alleles from European populations. By measuring allele frequencies for specific genetic loci, we can estimate the amount of migration: European alleles into an Afro-American gene pool. By using different methods, the migration rate (the percentage of gene flow from one population to another) has been estimated, and with strikingly varied results. One of the most comprehensive studies, conducted in Oakland, California, determined a migration rate of 22% (the proportion of *non*-African genes in the black Oakland population), and this may be reasonably characteristic of northern cities; however, studies in the deep South (Charleston, South Carolina) found a rate of just 4%, while in rural Georgia, the migration rate was 11%.

It would be a misconception to conclude that human migration can occur only through large-scale movements of whole groups. In fact, significant alterations in allele frequencies can come about through long-term patterns of mate selection. If exchange of mates were consistently in one direction over a long period of time, ultimately allele frequencies would be altered. Due to demographic, social, or economic pressures, an individual may choose a mate from outside the immediate vicinity. For example, exogamy rates (percent marrying outside village or parish) for English villages were 40% in the seventeenth century, but has increased to 64% in the last fifty years.

Transportation factors play an obvious role in influencing the manageable geographic distance for finding available mates. Limited to walking or use of the horse, transportation ranges were typically limited to about a 10-mile radius. With the spread of affordable railway transportation through rural England in the nineteenth century, a dramatic increase in the mean marital distance* to 20–30 miles was seen. Today, with even more efficient means of transportation, the potential range has become worldwide. Actual patterns are, however, obviously somewhat more restricted. For example data from Ann Arbor, Michigan, indicate a mean marital distance of close to 160 miles—not worldwide by any means, but still including a tremendous number of potential marriage partners.

Genetic Drift

RANDOM GENETIC DRIFT Shifts in allele frequency due to chance factors in small populations.

Random genetic drift is the chance factor in evolution and is tied directly to population size. An example of a particular kind of drift seen in modern populations is called *founder effect*. Founder effect operates when an unusually small number of individuals contributes genes to the next generation, making for a kind of genetic bottleneck. This phenomenon can occur when a small migrant band of "founders" colonizes a new and separate area away from the parent group. Small founding populations may

*The average distance between husband's and wife's birthplace.

also be left as remnants when famine, plague, or war ravage a normally larger group. Actually, each generation is the founder of all succeeding generations in any population.

The cases of founder effect producing evolutionary change in human populations are necessarily seen in small groups. For example, an island in the South Atlantic, Tristan da Cunha, has unusually high frequencies of an hereditary eye disorder. First settled in 1817 by one Scottish family, this isolated island's indigenous inhabitants include only descendants of this one family and a few other individuals. All in all, only about two dozen founders established this population. A fortuitous opportunity to study the dscendants occurred in 1961 when, owing to an imminent volcanic eruption, all 264 residents were evacuated to England. There, extensive medical tests were performed that revealed four individuals with the rare recessive disease retinitis pigmentosa. The allele frequency for the mutant allele was unusually high in this population and, no doubt, a high proportion of individuals were carriers.

How did this circumstance come about? Apparently, just by chance one of the initial founders carried the allele in single dose and later passed it on to descendants who, with some inbreeding, occasionally produced affected offspring. Since so few individuals founded this population, the fact that one carried the allele for this disease made a disproportionate contribution to succeeding generations.

Genetic drift has most probably played an important role in human evolution, influencing genetic changes in small groups. From studies of recent hunter-gatherers in Australia, we know that the range of available mates was restricted to within the linguistic tribe, usually consisting of about 500 individuals. In groups of this size, drift can have significant effects, particularly if drought, disease, and so on should temporarily reduce the population still further.

While drift has been a factor over the long term, the effects have been irregular and nondirectional (for drift is *random* in nature). Certainly, the pace of evolutionary change could have been accelerated if many small populations were isolated and thus subject to drift. However, by modifying such populations, drift only provides fodder for the truly directional force in evolution—natural selection.

Natural Selection

Over the long run of evolution in humans or any other organism, the most important factor influencing the direction of evolutionary change is natural selection. Controlled observations of laboratory animals or natural populations of quickly reproducing organisms, such as moths (see Chapter 2), have demonstrated how differential reproductive success eventually leads to adaptive shifts within populations.

Human beings are neither quickly reproducing nor amenable to controlled laboratory manipulations. Therefore, unambiguous examples of natural selection in action among contemporary humans are extremely difficult to demonstrate.

The best documented case deals with the *sickle-cell allele*, which is the result of a single substitution in the protein sequence in the hemoglobin molecule. If inherited in double dose, this gene causes severe anemia and frequently early death. Even with aggressive medical treatment, life expectancy in the United States today is less than 25 years for victims of this severe recessive disease, sickle-cell anemia. Worldwide, sickle-cell anemia is estimated to cause 100,000 deaths each year.

With such obviously harmful effects, it is surprising to find the sickle-cell allele so frequent in some populations. The highest allele frequencies are found in western and central African populations, reaching levels close to 20%; values are also moderately high in some Greek and Asiatic Indian populations. How do we explain such a phenomenon? Obviously, the allele originated from a simple mutation, but why did it ever increase in frequency?

The answer lies in yet another kind of disease, one which exerts enormous selective pressure. In those areas of the world where the sickle-cell allele is found in highest frequency, *malaria* is also found (Fig. 6-2). Caused by a single-cell parasite, this debilitating infectious disease is transmitted to humans by mosquitoes. In areas that are endemically infected, many individuals suffer sharply lower reproductive success owing to high infant mortality rates or to lowered vitality as adults.

Such a geographic correlation between malarial incidence and distribution of the sickle-cell allele is indirect evidence of a biological corre-

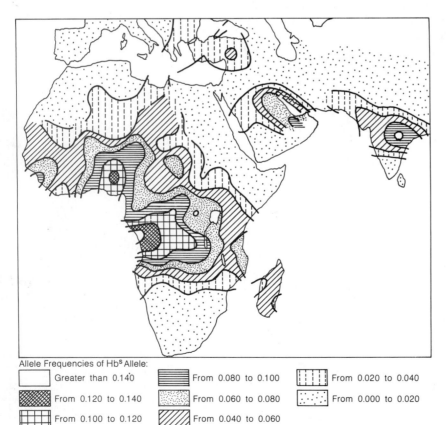

FIGURE 6-1 A clinal map of the sickle-cell allele distribution in the Old World.

Allele Frequencies of Hb^S Allele:

Greater than 0.140	From 0.080 to 0.100	From 0.020 to 0.040
From 0.120 to 0.140	From 0.060 to 0.080	From 0.000 to 0.020
From 0.100 to 0.120	From 0.040 to 0.060	

lation. Further confirmation was provided by the British biologist A. C. Allison. Volunteers from the Luo tribe of eastern Africa with known genotypes were injected with the malarial parasite. After a short time, results showed that carriers with the sickle-cell allele in single dose (called the *sickle-cell trait*) were much more resistant to malarial infection than the homozygous "normals." Apparently, carriers resist infection because their red blood cells provide a less conducive environment for the malarial parasite to reproduce itself. As a result, the parasite apparently often expires before widely infecting the body of a carrier. Conversely, for the homozygous normals, the infection usually persists lifelong.

Recent advances in recombinant DNA technology have provided evidence suggesting that the sickle-cell mutation arose independently in different parts of the world. The appearance of the sickle-cell mutation in West Africa was apparently of different origin from that in other parts of Africa or in Asia (Kan and Dozy, 1980).

A genetic trait such as sickle-cell that provides a reproductive advantage in certain environments is a clear example of natural selection in action among human populations. The precise evolutionary mechanism in the sickle-cell example is termed a **balanced polymorphism**.

A genetic trait is called a polymorphism "when two or more alleles at a given genetic locus occur with appreciable frequencies in a population" (Bodmer and Cavalli-Sforza, 1976, p. 308). How much is "appreciable" is a fairly arbitrary judgment, but is usually placed at 1%. In other words, if a population is sampled for a particular trait, and frequencies for more than one allele are higher than 1%, the trait (more precisely, the locus that governs the trait) is polymorphic.

The limit of 1% is an attempt to control for mutation effects, which normally adds new alleles at rates far below our 1% level. So when an allele like that for sickle-cell is found in a population in frequencies approaching 10%, this is clearly polymorphic. It is higher than can be accounted for by mutation *alone*, and thus demands a fuller evolutionary explanation. In this case, the additional mechanism is natural selection.

BALANCED POLYMORPHISM The maintenance of two or more alleles in a population due to the selective advantage of the heterozygote.

FIGURE 6-2 Malaria distribution in the Old World.

This brings us back to the other part of the term "balanced polymorphism." By "balanced," we are referring to the interaction of selective pressures operating in a malarial environment. Some individuals (mainly homozygous normals) will be removed by the infectious disease malaria and some (homozygous recessives) will die of the inherited disease sickle-cell anemia. Those with the highest reproductive success are the heterozygous carriers. But what alleles do they carry? Clearly, they are passing *both* the "normal" allele as well as the sickle-cell allele to offspring, thus maintaining both alleles at fairly high frequencies (*above* the minimum level for polymorphism). This situation will reach a balance and persist, at least as long as malaria continues to be a selective factor.

HUMAN BIOCULTURAL EVOLUTION

We have defined culture as "the human strategy of adaptation." Human beings live in cultural environments that are continually modified by human activity; thus, evolutionary processes are understandable only within this *cultural* context. You will recall that natural selection pressures operate within specific environmental settings. For humans, and many of our hominid ancestors, this situation means an environment dominated by culture. For example, the sickle-cell allele has not always been an important genetic factor in human populations. In fact, human cultural modification of environments apparently provided the initial stimulus. Before the development of agriculture, humans rarely, if ever, lived close to mosquito breeding areas. With the development and spread to Africa of slash-and-burn agriculture, perhaps in just the last 2000 years, penetration and clearing of tropical rain forests occurred. As a result of deforestation, open, stagnant pools provided prime mosquito breeding areas in close proximity to human settlements.

Malaria, for the first time, now struck human populations with its full impact, and as a selective force it was powerful indeed. No doubt, humans attempted to adjust culturally to these circumstances, and numerous biological adaptations also probably came into play. The sickle-cell trait is one of these. However, there is a definite cost involved with such

FIGURE 6-3 Evolutionary interactions affecting the frequency of sickle-cell.

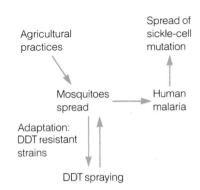

an adaptation. While carriers have more malarial resistance and presumably higher reproductive success, some of their offspring will be lost through the genetic disease sickle-cell anemia. So there is a counterbalancing of selective forces with an advantage for carriers *only* in malarial environments.

Following World War II, extensive DDT spraying by the World Health Organization began systematically to wipe out mosquito breeding areas in the tropics. As would be expected, malaria decreased sharply, and also as would be expected, the frequency of the sickle-cell allele also seemed on the decline. The intertwined story of human cultural practices, mosquitoes, malarial parasites, and the sickle-cell allele is still not finished. Forty years of DDT spraying killed many mosquitoes, but natural selection is also acting on these insect populations. Due to the tremendous amount of genetic diversity among insects, as well as their short generation span, several DDT-resistant strains have arisen and spread in the last few years. Accordingly, malaria is again on the rise, with several hundred thousand new cases reported in India, Africa, and Central America.

Another example of human biocultural evolution is seen in the remarkable variation among humans in their ability to digest milk. In all human populations, infants and young children can digest milk, an obvious necessity for any young mammal. A major ingredient of milk is the sugar *lactose,* which is broken down by humans and other mammals by the enzyme *lactase.* In most mammals, including humans, the gene coding for lactase production "switches off" by adolescence. If too much milk is then ingested, it ferments in the large intestine leading to diarrhea and severe gastrointestinal upset. Among many African and Asian populations—a majority of humankind today—most individuals are intolerant of milk (Table 6-1).

Quite apparently, lactose intolerance is an hereditary trait, but the pattern of inheritance is not clearly established. Some familial data suggest the trait operates as a simple dominant or, perhaps, is more complicated with three alleles.

The environment also plays a role in expression of the trait—that is, whether a person will be lactose intolerant—since intestinal bacteria can somewhat buffer the adverse effects. Because these bacteria will increase with previous exposure, some tolerance can be acquired, even in individuals who genetically have become lactase-deficient.

Why do we see such variation in lactose tolerance among human populations? Throughout most of hominid evolution, no milk was available after weaning. Perhaps, in such circumstances, continued action of an unnecessary enzyme might inhibit digestion of other foods. Therefore, there *may* be a selective advantage for the gene coding for lactose production to switch off. The question can then be asked: Why can some adults (the majority in some populations) tolerate milk? The distribution of lactose-tolerant populations is very interesting, revealing the probable influence of cultural factors on this trait.

European groups, who are generally lactose-tolerant, are partially descended from groups of the Middle East. Often economically depen-

TABLE 6-1   Frequencies of Lactose Intolerance

POPULATION GROUP	PERCENT
U.S. whites	2–19
Finnish	18
Swiss	12
Swedish	4
U.S. blacks	70–77
Ibos	99
Bantu	90
Fulani	22
Thais	99
U.S. Orientals	95–100
Australian Aborigines	85

Source: Lerner and Libby, 1976, p. 327.

dent on pastoralism, these groups raised cows and/or goats, and no doubt drank considerable milk. Strong selection pressures would act in such a *cultural* environment to shift allele frequencies in the direction of more lactose tolerance. Modern European descendants of these populations apparently retain this ancient ability.

Even more informative is the distribution of lactose tolerance in Africa. For example, groups such as the Fulani and Tutsi, who have been pastoralists probably for thousands of years, have much higher rates of lactose tolerance than non-pastoralists.

As we have seen, the geographic distribution of lactose tolerance is related to a history of cultural dependence on milk products. There are, however, some populations that culturally rely on dairying, but are not characterized by high rates of lactose tolerance. It has been suggested that such populations traditionally have consumed their milk produce as cheese and other derivatives in which the lactose has been broken down by bacterial action (Durham, 1981).

The interaction of human cultural environments and changes in lactose tolerance among human populations is another example of biocultural evolution. In the last few thousand years, cultural factors have initiated specific evolutionary changes in human groups. Such cultural factors have most probably influenced the course of human evolution for at least three million years, and today they are of paramount importance.

HUMAN POLYMORPHISMS

The sickle-cell trait and the production of the enzyme lactase are both examples of *Mendelian* traits. That is, the phenotype of each of these traits can unambiguously be linked to the action of a single locus. These more simple genetic mechanisms are much more straightforward than the polygenic traits usually associated with studies of human racial variation (discussed in Chapter 5). In fact, the difficulty in tracing the genetic influence on such characteristics as skin color or face shape has led some human biologists to avoid altogether investigations of such polygenic traits. Although physical anthropologists, by tradition, have been keenly interested in explaining such variation, we have seen a trend toward greater concentration on those traits with a clearly demonstrated genetic mechanism (i.e., Mendelian characteristics).

Of greatest use in contemporary studies of human variation are those traits that can be used to document genetic differences among various populations. Such genetic traits are what we have defined as polymorphisms and, as we noted above, must have more than one allele in appreciable frequency. In order to explain this pattern of variation, beyond mutation, some *additional* evolutionary factor (migration, drift, natural selection) must also have been at work.

Clearly, then, the understanding of human genetic polymorphisms demands evolutionary explanations. As students of human evolution, physical anthropologists use these polymorphisms as their principle tool to understand the dynamics of evolution in modern populations. Moreover, by utilizing these simple polymorphisms, and comparing allele frequencies in different populations, we can begin to reconstruct the evolutionary events that link human populations with one another.

ABO In addition to hemoglobin, there are many other polymorphisms known in human blood. Because samples can be easily obtained and transported, blood has long been a favorite tissue for studying human polymorphisms. Consequently, we know a great deal regarding genetic traits found in red blood cells, white blood cells, and in the blood serum. The first of these to be described, and certainly the best known, is the ABO blood group system. As we have seen, ABO is expressed phenotypically in individuals as protein molecules called antigens on the surface of red blood cells. One's blood group (that is, what antigens are on their red blood cells) is directly determined by his/her genotype at the ABO locus. The complications that result from mismatched blood transfusions are the result of antigen-antibody reactions. The body has a finely tuned capacity to recognize foreign antigens and to produce antibodies to them. Such an immune response is normally beneficial (indeed, indispensable), as it allows the body to fight infections—especially those caused by viruses and bacteria.

Usually antibodies are produced "on the spot" only after foreign antigens have been introduced and recognized. However, in the case of ABO, naturally occurring antibodies are already present in the blood serum at birth. Actually, no antibodies are probably "natural," although they may be (as in ABO) stimulated in fetal life. The genotypes, phenotypes, and antibody reactions in the ABO system are shown in Table 6-2.

TABLE 6-2 The ABO Blood Group System			
INDIVIDUAL'S GENOTYPE	PHENOTYPE (BLOOD GROUP)	ANTIBODIES IN SERUM	CLUMPING WILL OCCUR WHEN EXPOSED (E.G., THROUGH TRANSFUSION) TO THE FOLLOWING KINDS OF BLOOD:
OO	O	anti-A and anti-B	A, B, AB
AA AO }	A	anti-B	B, AB
BB BO }	B	anti-A	A, AB
AB	AB	neither	none

*In ABO antigen-antibody reactions, clumping, or agglutination, of cells occurs with some destruction of cells. In other immune responses, such as Rh, more complete destruction of cells takes place.

The ABO system is most interesting from an anthropological perspective because the frequencies of the three alleles (A, B, O) vary tremendously among human populations. In most groups, A or B are only rarely found in frequencies greater than 50%; usually, frequencies for these two alleles are considerably below this figure (Fig. 6-4). Most human groups, however, are polymorphic for all three alleles. Occasionally, as in native South American Indians, frequencies of O reach 100%, and this allele is said to be "fixed" in this population. Indeed, in most native New World populations, O is at least 80% and is usually considerably higher. Unusually high frequencies of O are also found in northern Australia, and some islands off the coast show frequencies exceeding 90%. Since these figures are higher than presumably closely related mainland populations, founder effect is most probably the evolutionary factor responsible.

HLA Another important polymorphic system, is found on the surface of certain white blood cells. Called HLA, this genetic system influences histocompatability (i.e., "tissue type") and is the reason that organ transplants are usually rejected if not properly matched. Genetically, the HLA system is exceedingly complex, and researchers are still discovering more details about it. There are at least seven closely linked loci on chro-

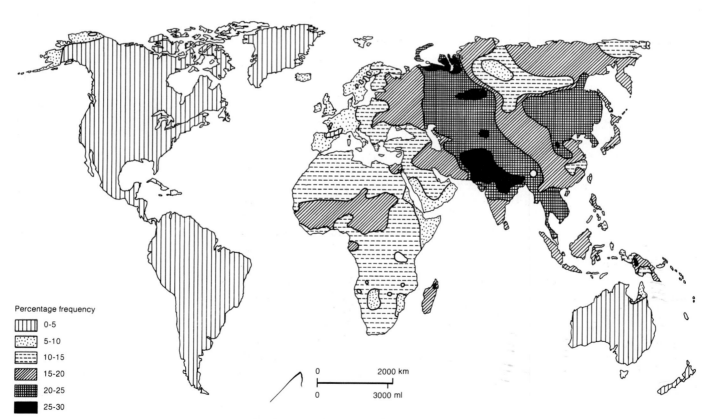

Percentage frequency

0-5
5-10
10-15
15-20
20-25
25-30

0   2000 km

0   3000 mi

FIGURE 6-4 (*a*) ABO blood group system. Distribution of the A allele in the indigenous populations of the world. (*b*) ABO blood group system. Distribution of the B allele in the indigenous populations of the world. (After Mourant et al., 1976.)

mosome 6 which make up the HLA system. Taken together, there are already well over 100 antigens known within the system, with a potential of at least 30,000,000 different genotypes (Williams, 1985). By far, this is the most polymorphic of any known human genetic system.

The component loci of the HLA system function together as a kind of "supergene." In addition to the components of the HLA system itself, there are several other loci located nearby on chromosome 6. Altogether, the entire region has been designated the *major histocompatibility complex* (MHC).

Since the system has only fairly recently been discovered, the geographic distribution of many of the alleles is still not well known. Some interesting patterns, however, are apparent. For example, Lapps, Sardinians, and Basques show differences in frequencies of some HLA alleles from that seen in other European populations, paralleling evidence from ABO. In addition, many areas of New Guinea and Australia are quite divergent, possibly resulting from past effects of genetic drift. It is imperative, however, that care be taken in postulating genetic relatedness on the basis of very restricted polymorphic data; otherwise, such ridiculous links as some proposed for HLA (e.g., Tibetans with Australian Aborigines; Eskimos with some New Guineans) would confound our attempts to understand human microevolution (Livingstone, 1980). Since HLA is involved in the superfine detection of foreign antigens, selection relative to infectious disease, especially viruses, may also play a significant role in the distribution (and past evolution) of HLA alleles. Further understanding of these processes is among the most exciting frontiers of medical and evolutionary biology.

Miscellaneous Polymorphisms An interesting genetically controlled variation in human populations was discovered by accident in 1931. When the artificially synthesized chemical phenylthiocarbamide (PTC) was dropped in a laboratory, some researchers were able to smell it, while others could not. It was later established that there is a dichotomy among humans regarding those who can versus those who cannot taste PTC. Although tasters vary considerably in sensitivity, most report a very bitter, unpleasant sensation. The pattern of inheritance follows a Mendelian model, with the inability to taste behaving as a simple recessive. In most populations, a majority of individuals are tasters, but the frequency of nontasters varies dramatically—from as low as 5% in Africa to as high as 40% in India.

The evolutionary function of this polymorphism is not known, although the fact that it is also seen in some other primates argues it has a long history. Obviously, evolution has not acted to produce discrimination for an artificial substance recently concocted by humans. The variation seen *may* reflect selection for taste discrimination of other, more significant, substances. Indeed, taste discrimination, to allow the avoidance of many toxic plants (which frequently are bitter), may well be an important evolutionary consideration.

Another puzzling human polymorphism is the genetic variability seen in earwax, or cerumen. Earwax is found in human groups in two basic varieties: (1) yellow, sticky with a good deal of lipids (fats and fatlike substances); and (2) gray, dry, with less lipids.

Cerumen variation appears also to be inherited as a simple Mendelian trait with two alleles (sticky is dominant; dry is homozygous recessive). Interestingly, frequencies of the two varieties of earwax vary considerably among human populations. In European populations, about 90% of the individuals typically have the sticky variety, while in northern China, only about 4% are of this type.

How do we explain these differences? Even very large groups show consistent differences in cerumen type, arguing that drift is an unlikely causal mechanism. However, it is difficult to imagine what kind of selective pressure would act directly on earwax. Perhaps, like that previously suggested for PTC discrimination, earwax variation is an incidental expression of a gene controlling something more adaptively significant. Suggestions along these lines have pointed to the relation of cerumen to other body secretions, especially those affecting odor. Certainly, other mammals, including nonhuman primates, pay considerable attention to smell stimuli. Although the sense of smell is not as well developed as in other mammals, humans still process and utilize olfactory (smell) stimuli. Thus, it is not impossible that during the course of human evolution genes affecting body secretions (including earwax) came under selective influence.

MULTIVARIATE POPULATION GENETICS

As mentioned, physical anthropologists and other human biologists utilize the fairly straightforward genetic data provided by population studies of simple genetic polymorphisms. However, as discussed for HLA, single traits when used *by themselves* often can yield conflicting interpretations regarding likely population relationships. What is needed, then, is a method to analyze a larger, more consistent body of data; that is, to look at several traits simultaneously. Such an approach can be termed *multivariate* and makes ready use of digital computers.

An excellent example of this kind of approach to human diversity was undertaken by Harvard population geneticist R. D. Lewontin (1972), and his results are most informative. Lewontin calculated population differences in allele frequency for 17 polymorphic traits. In his analysis, Lewontin immediately faced the dilemma: Which groups (populations) should he contrast and how should they be weighted? That is, should larger population segments such as Arabs carry the same weight in the analysis as small populations such as the one from the island Tristan da Cunha? After considerable deliberation, Lewontin decided to break down his sample into seven geographical areas and included several, all equally weighted, population samples within each (Table 6-3). He then calculated how much of the total genetic variability within our species could be accounted for by these population subdivisions.

The results are surprising. Only 6.3% of the total genetic variation is explained by differences among major races (Lewontin's seven geographic units). In other words, close to 94% of human genetic diversity occurs *within* these very large groups. The larger population subdivisions, local races, within the geographic clusters (e.g., within Caucasians,

TABLE 6-3   Population Groupings Used by Lewontin in Population Genetics Study (1971)

GEOGRAPHIC GROUPING	EXAMPLES OF POPULATIONS INCLUDED*
Caucasians	Arabs, Armenians, Tristan da Cunhans
Black Africans	Bantu, San, U.S. blacks
Mongoloids	Ainu, Chinese, Turks
South Asian Aborigines	Andamanese, Tamils
Amerinds	Aleuts, Navaho, Yanomama
Oceanians	Easter Islanders, "Micronesians"
Australian Aborigines	All treated as a single group

*Not inclusive

Arabs, Basques, Welsh) account for another 8.3%. Amazingly, the traditional concept of geographic and local race together explain just 15% of all human genetic variation, leaving the remaining 85% unaccounted for.

The vast majority of genetic differences among human beings is thus explicable in terms of differences from one village to another, one family to another, and to a very significant degree, from one person to another—even within the same family. Of course, when you recall the high degree of genetic polymorphism discussed in this chapter combined with the vast number of combinations resulting from recombination during meiosis (discussed in Chapter 3), all this individual variation should not be that surprising.

Our superficial visual perceptions tell us race does exist. But the visible phenotypic traits most frequently used to make racial distinctions (skin color, hair form, nose shape, etc.) may very well produce a highly biased sample, not giving an accurate picture of the actual pattern of *genetic variation*. The simple polymorphic traits discussed in this chapter (many of the same used by Lewontin) are a more objective basis for accurate biological comparisons of human groups, and they indicate that the traditional concept of race is very limited. Indeed, Lewontin concludes his analysis with a ringing condemnation of traditional studies:

> Human racial classification is of no social value and is positively destructive of social and human relations. Since such racial classification is now seen to be of virtually no genetic or taxonomic significance either, no justification can be offered for its continuance (Lewontin, 1972, p. 397).

However, not all population geneticists are this critical. After all, Lewontin did find that about 6% of human variation is accounted for by the large geographic population segments traditionally called major races. Whereas this is certainly a minority of all human genetic variation, it is not necessarily biologically insignificant.

If one feels compelled to continue to classify humankind into large geographic segments, population genetics offers some aid in isolating consistent patterns of genetic variation. One such classification suggests our species can be partitioned into three major geographic groups: Africans, Caucasians, and a heterogeneous group of Easterners, including all aboriginal populations of the Pacific area (Bodmer and Cavalli-Sforza, 1976). You should recall, however, that while these large groupings form contrasting genetic units, the total amount of genetic variation *within* them is far greater than exists *between* them.

SUMMARY

In this chapter, we have discussed human variation from an evolutionary perspective. Modern evolutionary theory views evolutionary change as a two-stage process specified in what has come to be known as "the modern synthesis." In this theory, *interaction* of the factors of (1) mutation, migration, genetic drift, and (2) natural selection come together to produce evolutionary change.

In the previous chapter, more complex, polygenic, types of human variation were described and put in the context of traditional racial studies. Here, we focus on the contemporary emphasis on description of those simple genetic polymorphisms that can be measured for allele frequencies.

Data on such traits as ABO and HLA can then be used to understand aspects of human microevolution. For humans, of course, culture also plays a crucial evolutionary role, and the sickle-cell trait and lactose intolerance are thus discussed from an explicit biocultural perspective.

Finally, data derived from population genetics analysis of several simple genetic polymorphisms are employed to measure human population diversity. From such studies, the traditional concept of race is shown to be of limited utility, but may be used from a population genetics perspective—if these limitations are recognized.

QUESTIONS FOR REVIEW

1. How is a population defined? Discuss why, in human groups, defining particular populations can be very difficult.
2. What are the two stages of the evolutionary process as postulated by the modern synthesis?
3. What role does variation play in natural selection?
4. Give a concise *genetic* definition of evolution. Discuss an example in human populations.
5. What is meant by migration? Discuss an example derived from human population studies.
6. How has the sickle-cell allele come to be common in some parts of the world? Why is it thought to be a good example of natural selection?
7. What biocultural interactions have occurred that help explain the distribution of lactose intolerance?
8. Discuss how genetic drift may have influenced the geographic distribution of the A, B, and O alleles.
9. Discuss how population genetics data can be used to assess the genetic diversity among geographic races. What do you think of this approach compared to traditional studies?

MAMMALIAN/PRIMATE EVOLUTIONARY HISTORY

CHAPTER 7

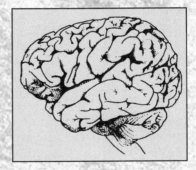

INTRODUCTION

In the preceding chapters we have surveyed the genetic mechanisms that are the foundation of the evolutionary process. Moreover, Chapter 6 shows in detail how *microevolutionary* changes are investigated in contemporary human populations. In this chapter, we turn to the *macroevolutionary* process. We thus will review aspects of vertebrate (and specifically mammalian) evolution over the great time depth of these major groups. Even more to the point, we will characterize and discuss that group of mammals to which humans and our closest relatives belong—the primate order. The fundamental perspectives reviewed here concerning geological history, principles of classification, and modes of evolutionary change will serve as a basis for topics covered throughout the remainder of this text.

THE HUMAN PLACE IN THE ORGANIC WORLD

There are millions of life forms living today. If we were to include microorganisms, the total would surely exceed tens of millions. And to this, when you further add all the vast multitudes of life forms that are now *extinct*, the total is staggering—perhaps hundreds of millions!

How do biologists cope with all this diversity? As is typical for *Homo sapiens*, scientists approach complexity through simplification. Thus, biologists group life forms together, or in other words, they construct a **classification**. For example, today there are probably more than 15 million species of animals, mostly including the insects. No one knows exactly how many species there are, as more than 90% have yet to be scientifically described or named.

Nevertheless, even with the tens of thousands of species that biologists do know something about, there is still too much diversity to handle conveniently, indeed, too many names for the human brain to remember. Thus, the solution is to organize the diversity into groupings in order to (1) reduce the complexity and (2) indicate evolutionary relationships.

Organisms that move about and ingest food (but do not photosynthesize, as in plants) we call animals. More precisely, the multicelled ani-

CLASSIFICATION The ordering of organisms into categories, such as phyla, orders, families, to show evolutionary relationship.

mals are placed within the group called the **Metazoa**. Within the Metazoa there are more than 20 major groups termed *phyla* (sing., *phylum*). One of these phyla is the **Chordata**, animals with a nerve cord, gill slits (at some stage of development), and a stiff supporting cord along the back called a *notochord*. Most chordates today are **vertebrates**, in which the notochord has become a vertebral column (which gives its name to the group); in addition, vertebrates also have a developed brain and paired sensory structures for sight, smell, and balance.

The vertebrates themselves are subdivided into six classes: bony fishes, cartilaginous fishes, amphibians, reptiles, birds, and mammals. We will discuss mammal classification below.

METAZOA Multicellular animals. A major division of the Animal Kingdom.

CHORDATA (Chordates) The phylum of the Animal Kingdom that includes vertebrates.

VERTEBRATES Animals with bony backbones. Includes fishes, amphibians, reptiles, birds, and mammals.

TAXONOMY

Before we go further, however, it will be useful to discuss the bases of animal classification. The field that specializes in delineating the rules of classification is called *taxonomy*. Organisms are classified firstly, and most traditionally, on the basis of physical similarities. Such was the basis of the first systematic classification devised by Linnaeus in the eighteenth century (see Chapter 2). Still today, basic physical similarities are considered a good starting point in postulating schemes of organic relationships. In order for similarities to be useful, however, they *must* reflect evolutionary descent. For example, the bones of the forelimb of all terrestrial air-breathing vertebrates (tetrapods) are so similar in number and form (Fig. 7-1) that the obvious explanation for the striking resemblances is that all four kinds of air-breathing vertebrates ultimately derived their forelimb structure from a common ancestor.

Such structures that are shared by descendants on the basis of descent from a common ancestor are called **homologies**. Homologies alone are the reliable indicators of evolutionary relationship. But we must be

HOMOLOGIES Similarities between organisms based on descent from a common ancestor.

FIGURE 7-1 Homologies. The similarities in the bones of these animals can be most easily explained by descent from a common ancestor.

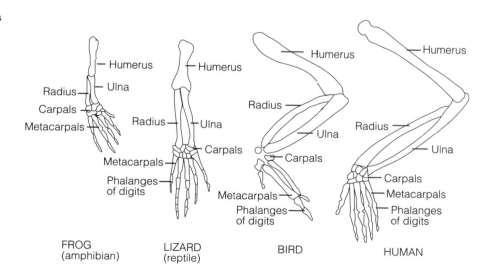

FROG (amphibian) LIZARD (reptile) BIRD HUMAN

ANALOGIES Similarities between organisms based strictly on common function with no assumed common evolutionary descent.

careful not to draw hasty conclusions from superficial similarities. For example, both bats and birds have wings, but should not be grouped together on this basis alone. In many other respects (e.g., only birds have feathers; only mammals have fur), bats and birds clearly are *not* closely related. Such structural features as the wing of a bird and the wing of a bat that superficially appear to be similar and have evolved through common function are called **analogies**. The separate development of analogous structures comes about in evolution through a process called *parallelism*. In making consistent evolutionary interpretations and devising classifications that reflect these interpretations, evolutionary biologists must concentrate on the homologies and treat the analogies as extraneous "noise."

Nor is it sufficient simply to isolate the homologies. For certain purposes, some structural homologies are much more informative than others. To return to our example above, the forelimbs of air-breathing vertebrates are all similar in overall structure. Some may be adapted into wings, others into legs. If we were to group birds and bats on the basis of a functional (derived) modification into a wing, we would be assuming the common ancestor of both already possessed wings. From fossil evidence, this clearly was *not* the case. Nor can we sort birds from bats or frogs from lizards on the basis of the number of bones in the forelimb. They all possess *generally* similar structures (presumably which they all *did* inherit from a common vertebrate ancestor). We would say, therefore, that the basic forelimb structure for all tetrapods is **primitive**.

PRIMITIVE Relating to a character state that reflects an ancestral condition, and thus not diagnostic of those derived lineages usually branching later.

DERIVED Relating to a character state that reflects a more specific evolutionary line, and thus more informative of precise evolutionary relationships.

On the other hand, as we noted, *only* birds have feathers and *only* mammals have fur. In comparing mammals with other vertebrates, presence of fur is a **derived** characteristic. Similarly, in describing birds, feathers are derived only in this group.

So, how do we know what kinds of characters to use? The answer is determined by which group one is describing and with what it is being compared. For the most part, it is usually best to use those character states that reflect more specific evolutionary adaptations; in other words, derived character states usually are the more informative. Moreover, when grouping two forms together (say, a bat with a mouse, both as mammals), this should be done *only* when they show **shared derived** characteristics (here, both possessing fur).

SHARED DERIVED Relating to specific character states shared in common between two forms and considered the *most* useful for making evolutionary interpretations.

TIME SCALE

In addition to the staggering array of living and extinct life forms, biologists must also contend with the vast amount of time that life has been evolving on earth. Scientists have also devised simplified schemes—but in this case to organize *time*, not organic diversity.

Geologists, in particular, have formulated the **Geological Time Scale** (Fig. 7-2). Very large time spans are here organized into eras and periods. Periods, in turn, can be broken down into epochs (as we will do later in this chapter for the most recent part of geological history so as to organize the discussion of primate evolution).

GEOLOGICAL TIME SCALE The organization of earth history into eras, epochs, and periods. Commonly used by geologists and paleoanthropologists.

FIGURE 7-2 Geological time scale.

ERA	PERIOD	(Began mya)	EPOCH	(Began mya)
CENOZOIC	Quaternary	1.8	Holocene Pleistocene	.01 1.8
CENOZOIC	Tertiary	65	Pliocene Miocene Oligocene Eocene Paleocene	5 22.5 37 53 65
MESOZOIC	Cretaceous	136		
MESOZOIC	Jurassic	190		
MESOZOIC	Triassic	225		
PALEOZOIC	Permian	280		
PALEOZOIC	Carboniferous	345		
PALEOZOIC	Devonian	395		
PALEOZOIC	Silurian	430		
PALEOZOIC	Ordovician	500		
PALEOZOIC	Cambrian	570		
PRE-CAMBRIAN				

VERTEBRATE EVOLUTIONARY HISTORY—A BRIEF SUMMARY

In broad outline, there are three eras: the Paleozoic, the Mesozoic, and the Cenozoic. For a breakdown of the major divisions of the Paleozoic and Mesozoic, the student should refer to Figure 7-2. The first vertebrates are on the scene early in the Paleozoic by 500 million years ago (mya) and probably go back considerably further. It is the vertebrate capacity to form bone that accounts for their more complete fossil record *after* 500 mya.

During the Paleozoic, several varieties of fishes (including the ancestors of modern sharks and bony fishes), amphibians, and reptiles all appeared. In addition, at the end of the Paleozoic, close to 250 mya, several varieties of mammal-like reptiles were also diversifying. It is widely thought that some of these gave rise to the mammals.

During most of the Mesozoic, reptiles were the dominant land vertebrates and exhibited a broad expansion into a variety of **ecological niches**, which included flying and swimming forms. Such a fairly rapid expansion marked by diversification of many new species is called an **adaptive radiation**. No doubt, the most famous of these highly successful Mesozoic reptiles are the dinosaurs, which themselves evolved into a wide array of sizes and lifestyles. Dinosaur paleontology, never a boring field, has advanced several startling notions in recent years: that many dinosaurs were warm-blooded; that some varieties were quite social and probably also showed considerable parental care; that many forms went extinct as the result of major climatic changes to the earth's atmosphere from collisions with comets or asteroids; and, finally, that not all dinosaurs went entirely extinct, with many descendants still living and doing remarkably well (i.e., all modern birds).

The first mammals are known from fossil traces fairly early in the Mesozoic, but the first *placental* mammals cannot be positively identified until quite late in the Mesozoic, *circa* 70 mya. This highly successful mammalian adaptive radiation is thus almost entirely within the most recent era of geological history, the Cenozoic.

The Cenozoic is divided into two periods, the Tertiary (about 63 million years duration) and the Quaternary, from about 1.8 mya up to and including the present. Because the above division is rather imprecise, paleontologists more frequently refer to the next level of subdivision within the Cenozoic, the **epochs**. There are seven epochs within the Cenozoic, the Paleocene, Eocene, Oligocene, Miocene, Pliocene, Pleistocene, and Holocene (the last often referred to as, "the Recent") (Fig. 7-2).

MAMMALIAN EVOLUTION

Following the extinction of dinosaurs and many other Mesozoic forms (at the beginning of the Cenozoic), there was a wide array of ecological niches open for rapid expansion and diversification of mammals. And, indeed, in the Cenozoic, conditions were nearly ideal for mammals. Their resulting adaptive radiation was so rapid and so successful that the Cenozoic is known as the Age of Mammals. Mesozoic mammals were small animals, about the size of mice, which they resembled superficially. Romer (1959) suggests the Mesozoic may be seen as a training period during which mammalian characters were being perfected. The mammalian adaptive radiation of the Cenozoic saw the rise of the major lineages of all modern mammals. Mammals, along with birds, replaced reptiles as the dominant terrestrial vertebrate.

How do we account for the rapid success of mammals? Several characteristics relating to learning and general flexibility of behavior are of prime importance. In order to process more information, mammals were selected for larger brains than those typically found in reptiles. In particular, the **cerebrum** became generally enlarged, especially the outer

FIGURE 7-3 Lateral view of brain. The illustration shows the increase in the cerebral cortex of the brain. The cerebral cortex integrates sensory information and selects responses.

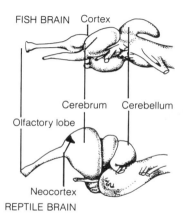

FISH BRAIN Cortex

Cerebrum Cerebellum

Olfactory lobe

Neocortex

REPTILE BRAIN

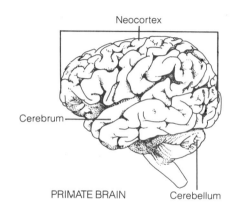

Neocortex

Cerebrum

PRIMATE BRAIN Cerebellum

covering called the **neocortex**, which controls higher brain functions. In mammals, the cerebrum has expanded so much in size that it came to comprise the majority of brain volume; moreover, greater surface convolutions evolved, creating more surface area, and thus providing space for even more nerve cells (neurons).

For an animal to develop such a large and complex organ as the mammalian brain, a longer, more intense period of growth is required. This slower development can occur internally (*in utero*) as well as after birth. While internal fertilization, and especially internal development, are not unique to mammals, the latter is a major innovation among terrestrial vertebrates. Other forms (some reptiles, birds) incubate their young externally (oviparous), while mammals give birth to live young and are thus called **viviparous**. Even among mammals, however, there is considerable variation among the major groups in how mature the young are at birth. As we will see below, it is in mammals like us, the *placental* forms, where development *in utero* goes the furthest.

NEOCORTEX The outer (cellular) portion of the cerebrum, which has expanded through evolution, particularly in primates, and most especially in humans. The neocortex is associated with higher mental function.

VIVIPAROUS Giving birth to live young.

MAJOR MAMMALIAN GROUPS

There are three major subgroups of living mammals: the egg-laying mammals (monotremes); the pouched mammals (marsupials); and the placentals. The monotremes are extremely primitive and are considered more distinct from marsupials or placentals than these latter are from each other.

The most notable distinction differentiating the marsupials from the placentals is the form and intensity of fetal development. In marsupials, the young are born extremely immature and must complete development in an external pouch. It has been suggested (Carrol, 1988) that such a reproductive strategy is more energetically costly than retaining the young for a longer period *in utero*. In fact, this is exactly what placental mammals have done, through a more advanced placental connection (from which the group gets its popular name). But perhaps even more basic than fetal nourishment, was the means to allow the mother to *tolerate* her young internally over an extended period. Marsupial young are born so quickly after conception that there is little chance for the mother's system to recognize and have an immune rejection of the fetal "foreign" tissue. But in placental mammals, such an immune response would occur were it not for the development of a specialized tissue that isolates fetal tissue from the mother's immune detection, and thus prevents tissue rejection. Quite possibly, this innovation is the central factor in the origin and initial rapid success of placental mammals (Carrol, 1988).

In any case, with a longer gestation period, the brain and central nervous system could develop more completely in the fetus. Moreover, after birth, the "bond of milk" between mother and young also would allow more time for complex neural structures to form. It should also be emphasized from a *biosocial* perspective that this dependency period not only allows for adequate physiological development, but also provides greater learning stimuli. That is, the young mammal brain, exposed through observation of the mother's behavior as well as perhaps other adults, and through play with age mates, is a receptacle for a vast amount of learning stimuli. It is not sufficient to have evolved a brain capable of learning. Collateral evolution of mammalian social systems has ensured that young mammal brains are provided with ample learning opportunities and are thus put to good use.

PRIMATES

This text focuses on human evolution. Thus, we are most interested in those mammals to whom we are most closely related. Placental mammals today are distributed over most of the world in a wide variety of forms. In fact, there are more than 20 orders of mammals recognized by biologists that include flying, swimming, and burrowing varieties, and a host of other adaptations as well. Sizes range from the tiny (just a few grams) up to the whales, the largest animals ever to inhabit the earth.

The order of placental mammals to which humans and our closest relatives belong is the **Primates**. As placental mammals, all primates possess numerous *primitive* characteristics, shared in common with other placentals. These include fur, relatively long gestation and live birth, expanded neocortex, varied (heterodont) dentition, and considerable capacity for learning and behavioral flexibility. Yet, what is it that makes primates different from other placental mammals? Which group of characteristics defines the Primate order?

These are not particularly simple questions to answer, for among mammals, primates have remained quite *generalized*. That is, primates maintain many primitive mammalian characteristics and are able to respond usually even more flexibly to environmental challenges than is typical of other placentals. Many other mammals in response to particular selection pressures have evolved distinctive **specialized**, derived characteristics. Thus, rodents all have enlarged front teeth; horses and their cousins (tapirs, rhinos) have hooves with an odd number of toes (one or three); and bats have evolved wings and sonar.

PRIMATES The order of placental mammals including prosimians, monkeys, apes, and humans.

SPECIALIZED A trait evolved for a specific function.

Primates, precisely because they are *not* so specialized, cannot be simply defined by one or even two common character states. As a result, biologists (LeGros Clark, 1971; Napier and Napier, 1967) have pointed to a group of **evolutionary trends** that, to a greater or lesser degree, characterize the entire order. Keep in mind, these are a set of *general* tendencies and are not all equally expressed in all primates. Indeed, this situation is one we would expect in a diverse group of generalized animals.

Moreover, while some of the trends listed below are derived features found in primates, many others are retained primitive mammalian characteristics. These latter are useful in contrasting the generalized primates with the more specialized varieties (for the most part typical of other placentals). Those evolutionary biologists who practice cladistic methods (called "cladists") would take exception to the use of retained primitive traits in classification of primates—or of any other groups, for that matter. They believe it would be more straightforward to isolate *only* shared derived features to characterize primates. But the problem is, that with the exception of some details of cranial bone configuration, there are *no* derived features that completely and adequately define the primate order.

Thus, the list below is assembled to give an overall structural and behavioral picture of that kind of animal we call "primate." Using primitive traits along with derived ones to accomplish this task has been the traditional approach of **primatologists**. Such an approach emphasizes "grade" level grouping instead of the strictly defined methods favored by the cladists. Nevertheless, some contemporary primatologists (Fleagle, 1988) feel that it is still highly useful to enumerate all these features in order to better illustrate primate adaptations.

Following is a list of those evolutionary trends that tend to set primates apart from other mammals. A common evolutionary history with similar adaptations to common environmental challenges is reflected in the limbs and locomotion, teeth and diet, and in the senses, brain, and behaviors of those animals that make up the primate order.

A. Limbs and Locomotion
1. *Retention of five digits* in the hands and feet—*pentadactyly*. A retention from primitive mammals, this characteristic is found in all primates, though some show marked reduction of the thumb or the second digit.
2. *Nails instead of claws*. A consistent characteristic on at least some digits of all contemporary primates. Unlike rodents or cats, primates must climb by wrapping their hands and feet around branches and holding by grasping. This grasping function is further aided by the presence of tactile pads at the ends of digits.
3. *Flexible hands and feet* with a good deal of **prehensility** (grasping ability). This feature is associated directly with the lack of claws and retention of five digits.
4. *A tendency toward erectness* (particularly in the upper body). Shown to some degree in all primates, this tendency is variously associated with sitting, leaping, standing, and, occasionally, walking.

FIGURE 7-4 Primate (macaque) hand.

5. *Retention of the clavicle* (collarbone). Another primitive retention and seen in all primates. Conversely, in many other quadrupedal mammals, the clavicle has been lost. In primates, the clavicle allows for flexibility of the shoulder joint and aids upper limb mobility.

B. Teeth and Diet

6. *A generalized dental pattern*, particularly in the back teeth (molars). Another primitive mammalian trait characteristic of primates. Such a pattern contrasts with the highly specialized molars of many other mammals (such as herbivores).

7. *A lack of specialization of diet.* This attribute is usually correlated with lack of specialization in teeth. In other words, primates can generally be described as *omnivorous*, that is, exploiting a varied diet consisting of both animal and vegetable products.

C. Senses, Brain, and Behavior

8. *A reduction of the snout* and the proportionate reduction of the smell (olfactory) area of the brain.

9. *An increased emphasis on vision* with elaboration of visual areas of the brain, a trend related to the decreased dependence on smell. **Binocular** and **stereoscopic vision** is a further elaboration wherein visual fields of the two eyes overlap, transmitting both

BINOCULAR STEREOSCOPIC VISION
Vision where visual fields overlaps and sensory input is sent from each eye to both sides of the brain. Seen typically in primates.

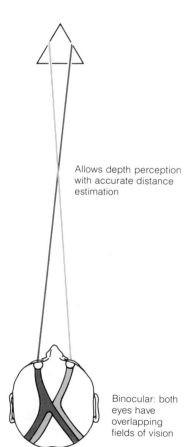

FIGURE 7-5 Binocular, stereoscopic vision. Fields of vision overlap and sensory information from each eye is relayed to both sides of the brain.

Allows depth perception with accurate distance estimation

Binocular: both eyes have overlapping fields of vision

images to the brain, thus allowing for depth perception. Except for some specialized nocturnal forms, color vision is most likely present in all primates.

10. *Expansion and increased complexity of the brain.* A general trend among placental mammals and one further elaborated in primates. The expansion is most evident in the visual and association areas of the neocortex.

11. *A more efficient means of fetal nourishment,* as well as *longer periods of gestation, infancy,* and extension of the whole life span.

12. *A greater dependence on highly flexible learned behavior* is correlated with the longer periods of infant and child dependency. As a result of both these trends, parental investment in each offspring is increased so that, although fewer young are born, they receive more efficient rearing.

13. *Adult males often associate long-term with the group.* A behavioral trait rarely seen in other mammals, but widespread among primates.

MAJOR PRIMATE GROUPS

When we apply the set of evolutionary trends discussed above, we are able to classify a remarkable array of living forms as members of the same mammalian order, the Primates. For purposes of discussion in this chapter, you need refer only to those large groupings of primates shown in Table 7-1. A more detailed primate classification is discussed in the next chapter.

TABLE 7-1   Major Primate Groups

Prosimians
    Lemurs
    Lorises
    Tarsiers
Anthropoids
    New World Anthropoids (New World monkeys)
    Old World Anthropoids
    Old World monkeys
    Hominoids (apes and humans)
        Small-bodied hominoids (gibbons and siamangs)
        Large-bodied hominoids
            Asian form (orangutan)
            African forms
                Gorilla
                Chimpanzee
                Human (hominids)

THE ARBOREAL ADAPTATION

ARBOREAL Tree-living.

ADAPTIVE NICHE The whole way of life of an organism: where it lives, what it eats, how it gets food, and so forth.

The single most important factor influencing the evolutionary divergence of primates was the adaptation to **arboreal** living. While other placental mammals were adapting to grasslands, subterranean, or even marine environments, primates found their **adaptive niche** in the trees. Indeed, some other mammals also were adapting to arboreal living, but primates found their home (and food) mainly in the treetops and the ends of terminal branches. This environment—with its myriad challenges and opportunities—was the one in which our ancestors established themselves as a unique kind of animal.

Primates became primates *because* of their adaptation to aboreal living. We can see this process at work in their reliance upon vision for survival. In a complex, three-dimensional environment with uncertain footholds, acute vision with depth perception is a necessity. Climbing can be accomplished by either digging in with claws or grasping around branches with prehensile hands and feet. Primates adopted this latter strategy, which allowed a means of progressing on the most tenuous of **substrates**. Thus, in primates we also see pentadactyly, prehensility, and flattened nails. In addition, the varied foods found in a tropical arboreal environment (such as fruit, leaves, berries, insects, and small mammals) led to the primate omnivorous adaptation and, hence, to retention of a generalized dentition.

SUBSTRATES The surfaces over which an animal locomotes (e.g., ground, small branch, etc.).

Finally, the elongated life span, increased intelligence, and a more elaborated social system are primate solutions to coping with the manifold complexities of their arboreal habitat; in such an environment, there are varied and seasonal food resources, and predators can appear from above (eagles), in the trees (snakes), or from below (e.g., leopards, wild dogs). This crucial development of increased behavioral flexibility may have been further stimulated by a shift from **nocturnal** (nighttime) to **diurnal** (daytime) activity patterns (Jerison, 1973).

NOCTURNAL Active at night.

DIURNAL Active during the day.

ARBOREAL HYPOTHESIS The traditional view that primate characteristics can be explained as a consequence of primate diversification into arboreal habitats.

A critique of this traditional **arboreal hypothesis** for the origin of primate structure has been proposed by Matt Cartmill (1972; 1974) of Duke University. Cartmill points out that the most significant primate trends—forward-facing eyes, grasping extremities, and reduced claws—may *not* have arisen from adaptive advantages in a purely arboreal environment. According to this alternative theory, called the *visual predation hypothesis*, primates may first have adapted to the bushy forest undergrowth and only the lowest tiers of the forest canopy. Here, early primates could have exploited insects, which they may have preyed upon primarily by stealth. Thus we could envision a small, primitive, largely insectivorous primate ancestor clinging to small branches with its prehensile appendages and snatching prey with a forelimb while judging the distance with its close-set eyes.

The visual predation ("bug snatching") hypothesis and the arboreal theory are not mutually exclusive explanations. The complex of primate characteristics might have begun in nonarboreal settings, but could have become even more adaptive once bug snatching was done *in the trees*.

At some point, the primates did take to the trees in earnest, and that is where the vast majority still live today. Whereas the basic primate structural complexes may have been adapted for visual predation, they became ideally suited for the arboreal adaptation that followed. We would say, then, that primates were "preadapted" for arboreal living. When did these early primates appear? How and when did they begin their adaptation to arboreal environments? It is to these questions that we now turn.

EARLY PRIMATE EVOLUTION

The roots of the primate order go back to the beginnings of the placental mammal radiation *circa* 65 mya (discussed earlier in this chapter). Thus, the earliest primates were diverging from quite early, primitive placental mammals. We have seen that strictly defining living primates using clear-cut derived features is not an easy task. The further back we go in the fossil record, the more primitive and, in many cases, the more generalized the fossil primates become. Such a situation makes classifying them all the more difficult.

As a case in point, the earliest identifiable primates were long thought to be a Paleocene group known as the plesiadapiforms (for time scale, see p. 109). You must remember, however, that much of our understanding, especially of early primates, is based upon quite fragmentary evidence, mostly jaws and teeth. In just the last two years much more complete remains of plesiadapiforms from Wyoming have been discovered, including a nearly complete skull and elements of the hand and wrist.

As a result of this more complete information, the plesidapiforms have been removed from the primate order altogether. From distinctive features (shared derived characteristics) of the skull and hands, these Paleocene mammals are now thought to be closely related to the colugo. The colugo is sometimes called a "flying lemur," a name that is actually a misnomer, as it is not a lemur nor does it fly (it glides). This group of unusual mammals is probably closely linked to the roots of primates, but apparently was already diverged by Paleocene times.

Given these new and major reinterpretations, we are left with extremely scarce traces of the beginnings of primates. Scholars have suggested that some other recently discovered bits and pieces from North Africa *may* be that of a primitive, very small primate. Until more evidence is found, and remembering the lesson of the plesiadapiforms, we will just have to wait and see.

In the Eocene (53–37 mya), a large array of fossil primates, which now display distinctive primate features, have been identified. Indeed, primatologist Elwyn Simons has called them, "the first primates of modern aspect." These animals have been found in sites primarily in North America and Europe (which were then still connected). It is important to recall that the continents are not fixed, but "float" on huge plates. As a result of this continental drift, the position of the continents has shifted dramatically over the last several million years (Fig. 7-6). Either the land masses that connect continents, or the water boundaries that separate

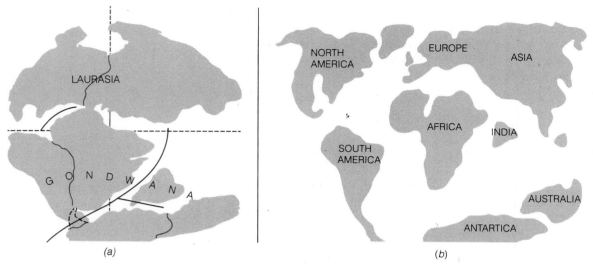

FIGURE 7-6 Continental drift. Changes in position of the continental plates from Late Paleozoic to Late Eocene. (*a*) The position of the continents during the Mesozoic (*c.* 125 mya). Pangea is breaking up into a northern land mass (Laurasia) and a southern land mass (Gondwanaland). (*b*) The position of the continents during much of the Paleocene and Eocene (up to *c.* 45 mya).

ANTHROPOID The suborder of primates including New World monkeys, Old World monkeys, apes, and humans.

OLD WORLD ANTHROPOID Anthropoids native to the Old World, including Old World monkeys, apes, and humans.

them, have obvious impact on the geographic distribution of such terrestrially bound animals as primates.

Some interesting late Eocene forms have also been found in Asia, which was joined to Europe by the end of the Eocene epoch. Looking at the whole array of Eocene primates, it is certain they (1) were primates, (2) were widely distributed, and (3) mostly were extinct by the end of the Eocene. What is less certain is how any of them might be related to the living primates. Some of these forms are probably ancestors of the *prosimians*—the lemurs and lorises. Others are probably related to the tarsier. Faint glimmers of **anthropoid** origins are also hinted in some of the late Eocene fossils. But for clear anthropoid affinities, we will have to wait for the next epoch, the Oligocene.

The Oligocene (37–22.5 mya) has yielded numerous fossil remains of several different species of early anthropoids. Most of these forms are **Old World anthropoids**, all discovered at a single locality in Egypt, the Fayum. In addition, from North and South America, there are a few known bits that relate only to the ancestry of New World monkeys. By the early Oligocene, continental drift had separated the New World (i.e., the Americas) from the Old World (Africa and Eurasia). Some of the earliest Fayum forms, nevertheless, *may* potentially be close to the ancestry of both Old and New World anthropoids. It has been suggested that late in the Eocene or very early in the Oligocene (40–35 mya) the first anthropoids (primitive "monkeys") arose in Africa and later reached South America by "rafting" over the water separation on drifting chunks of vegetation. What we call "monkey" then may have a *common* Old World origin, but the ancestry of New World and Old World varieties remain separate after about 35 mya. Our closest evolutionary affinities after this time are with other Old World anthropoids, Old World monkeys, and apes.

The possible roots of anthropoid evolution are illustrated by different forms from the Fayum. One is the **genus** *Apidium*. By genus (pl. genera), we are referring to a group of species that are closely related. In Chapter 2, we discussed Linnaeus' binomial system for designating different organisms; (e.g., *Equus callabus* for the horse, *Pan troglodytes* for the chimp, and *Homo sapiens* for humans). The first term (always capitalized—*Equus*, *Pan*, *Homo*) is the genus term. In paleontological contexts, when remains are fragmentary and usually separated by long time spans, often the best that can be achieved is to make genus-level distinctions (see section at end of chapter for further discussion).

Apidium, well known at the Fayum, is represented by 80 jaws or partial dentitions and more than 100 specimens from the limb and trunk skeleton. Because of its primitive dental arrangement, some paleontologists have suggested that *Apidium* may lie near or even *before* the evolutionary divergence of Old and New World anthropoids. As so much fossil material of teeth and limb bones of *Apidium* have been found, some informed speculation regarding diet and locomotory behavior is possible. It is thought this small, squirrel-sized primate ate mostly fruits and some seeds and was most likely an arboreal quadruped, adept at leaping and springing.

The other genus of importance from the Fayum is *Aegyptopithecus*. This genus, also well known, is represented by several well-preserved crania and abundant jaws and teeth. The largest of the Fayum anthropoids, *Aegyptopithecus* is roughly the size of a modern howler monkey, 13 to 18 pounds (Fleagle, 1983) and is thought to have been a short-limbed, slow-moving arboreal quadruped. *Aegyptopithecus* is important, because better than any other known form, it bridges the gap between the Eocene fossils on the one hand and the succeeding Miocene **hominoids** on the other.

GENUS A group of closely related species (e.g., *Homo*, *Pan*).

FIGURE 7-7 Location of the Fayum, an Oligocene primate site in Egypt.

HOMINOID Apes and humans and all extinct forms, back to the time of divergence from Old World monkeys.

TABLE 7-2 Inferred General Paleobiological Aspects of Oligocene Primates

	WEIGHT RANGE	SUBSTRATUM	LOCOMOTION	DIET
Apidium	850–1,600 gm (2–3 lb)	arboreal	quadruped	fruit, seeds
Aegyptopithecus	6,700 gm (15 lb)	arboreal	quadruped	fruit, some leaves?
(After Fleagle, 1988)				

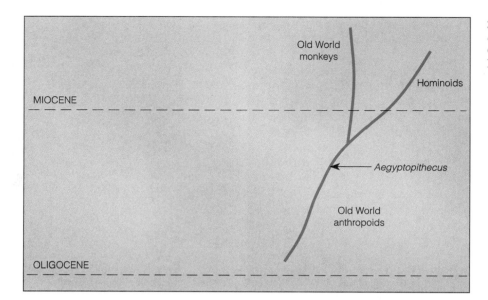

FIGURE 7-8 *Aegyptopithecus* placed evolutionarily as a common ancestor for Old World anthropoids, *prior* to origin of hominoids.

Nevertheless, *Aegyptopithecus* is a very primitive Old World anthropoid, with a small brain and long snout, and not showing any derived features of either Old World monkeys or hominoids. Thus, it may be close to the ancestry of *both* major groups of living Old World anthropoids.

Aegyptopithecus is found in geological beds dating to 35–33 mya. A further inference from its proposed evolutionary status is that the crucial evolutionary divergence of hominoids from other Old World anthropoids occurred *after* this time (Fig. 7-8).

MIOCENE FOSSIL HOMINOIDS

During the approximately 17 million years of the Miocene (22.5–5 mya) a great deal of evolutionary activity took place. In particular in Africa, Asia, and Europe a diverse and highly successful group of hominoids emerged. Indeed, there were many more forms of hominoids from the Miocene than are found today (now represented by the highly restricted groups of apes and one species of humans). In fact, the Miocene could be called, "the golden age of hominoids." Many thousands of fossils have been found from dozens of sites scattered in East Africa, Southwest Asia, into Western and Southern Europe, and extending into South Asia and east to China.

A problem arises in any attempt to simplify this complex evolutionary situation. For example, for many years paleontologists tended to think of these fossil forms as either "ape-like" or "human-like" and used modern examples as models. But, as we have just noted, there are only very few hominoids remaining. We thus should not rashly generalize from the living forms to the much more diverse fossil forms. Otherwise, we obscure the evolutionary uniqueness of these animals. In addition, we should not expect all fossil forms to be directly or even particularly

FIGURE 7-9 Miocene hominoid
distribution—fossils thus far discovered.

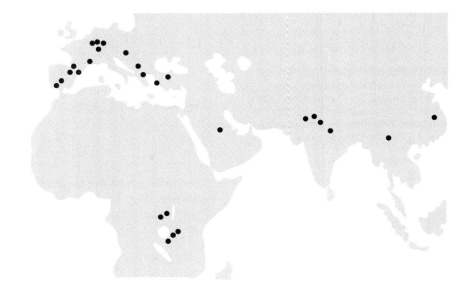

closely related to living varieties. Indeed, we should expect the opposite—that is, most lines vanish without descendants.

Over the last two decades, the Miocene hominoid assemblage has
been interpreted and reinterpreted. As more fossils are found, the evolutionary picture grows more complicated. The vast array of fossil forms
has not yet been completely studied, so conclusions remain tenuous.
Given this uncertainty, it is probably best, for the present, to group
Miocene hominoids geographically:

1. *East African forms (23–14 mya)* Known especially from western
   Kenya, these include quite generalized, in many ways primitive,
   hominoids. The best-known genus is *Proconsul*.
2. *European forms (13–11 mya)* Known from widely scattered
   localities in France, Spain, Italy, Greece, Austria, and Hungary, most
   of these forms are quite derived. However, this is a varied and not
   well-understood lot. The best known of the forms are placed in the
   genus *Dryopithecus*; the Hungarian and Greek fossils are usually assigned to other genera.
3. *Asian forms (16–7 mya)* The largest and most varied group from the
   Miocene fossil hominoid assemblage, geographically dispersed from
   Turkey through India/Pakistan and east to the highly prolific site
   Lufeng, from Yunnan Province, southern China. Most of these forms
   are *highly* derived. The best known genus is *Sivapithecus* (known from
   Turkey and Pakistan). The Lufeng material (now totaling more than
   1000 specimens) is apparently not *Sivapithecus*. However, exactly
   where to place these important fossils still remains uncertain.

Four points are certain concerning Miocene hominoid fossils:
(1) they are widespread geographically; (2) they are numerous; (3) they
span a considerable portion of the Miocene with *known* remains dated between 23–7 mya; and (4) at present, they are poorly understood.

FIGURE 7-10 *Proconsul africanus* skull.
Discovered by Mary Leakey in 1948.
(From early Miocene deposits on Rusinga
Island, Kenya.)

However, some of the conclusions we can reasonably draw include:

LARGE-BODIED HOMINOID Those hominoids including "great" apes (orang, chimp, gorilla) and hominids, as well as all ancestral forms back to the time of divergence from small-bodied hominoids (i.e., the gibbon lineage).

HOMINIDS Popular form of Hominidae, the family to which modern humans belong. Includes all bipedal hominoids back to the divergence from African great apes.

SPECIATION The process by which new species are produced from earlier ones. The most important mechanism of macroevolutionary change.

1. These are hominoids—more closely related to the ape-human lineage than to Old World monkeys.
2. Moreover, they are mostly **large-bodied hominoids**; that is, more akin to the lineages of orangs, gorillas, chimps, and humans than to smaller-bodied apes (i.e., gibbons).
3. Most of the Miocene forms thus far discovered are so derived as to be improbable ancestors of *any* living form.
4. One lineage that appears well established relates to *Sivapithecus* from Turkey and Pakistan. This form shows some highly derived facial features similar to the modern orang, suggesting a fairly close evolutionary link (Fig. 7-11).
5. There are no definite **hominids** yet discerned from any Miocene-dated locale. All the confirmed members of our family come from Pliocene beds and later. (The detailed story of hominid evolution will encompass much of the remainder of this text.)

MODES OF EVOLUTIONARY CHANGE

We have discussed evolution from both a *microevolutionary* perspective in the previous chapter and from a *macroevolutionary* one in this chapter. The major evolutionary factor underlying macroevolutionary change is **speciation**, the process whereby new species first arise. As you will recall, we have defined a species as a group of *reproductively isolated* organisms, a characterization that follows the biological species concept (Mayr, 1970). According to this same view, the way new species are first produced involves some form of isolation. Picture a single species of some organisms (baboons, for example) composed of several populations distributed over a wide geographic area. Gene exchange (migration) will be limited, if a geographic barrier such as an ocean or mountain range effectively separates these populations. This extremely important form of isolating mechanism is termed *geographic isolation*.

Now if one population (A) is separated from another population (B) (Fig. 7-12) by a mountain range, individual baboons of population A will not be able to mate with individuals from B. As time passes (several gen-

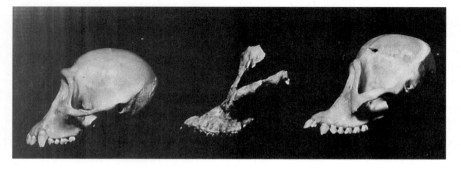

FIGURE 7-11 Comparison of *Sivapithecus* cranium (center) with modern chimpanzee (left) and orangutan (right). The *Sivapithecus* fossil is specimen GSP 15000 from the Potwar Plateau, Pakistan, *circa* 8 mya.

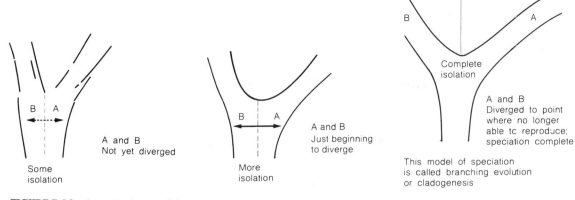

FIGURE 7-12 A speciation model.

erations), genetic differences will accumulate in both populations. If population size is small, we can predict that genetic drift will cause allele frequencies to change in both populations. Moreover, since drift is *random* in nature, we would not expect the effects to be the same. Consequently, the two populations will begin to diverge.

As long as gene exchange is limited, the populations can only become more genetically different with time. Moreover, further difference would be expected if the baboon groups are occupying slightly different habitats. These additional genetic differences would be incorporated through the process of natural selection. Certain individuals in population A may be most reproductively fit in their own environment, but would show less reproductive success in the environment occupied by population B. Thus, allele frequencies will shift further, and the results will be divergent in the two groups.

With the cumulative effects of genetic drift and natural selection acting over many generations, the result will be two populations that—even if they were to come back into geographic contact—could no longer interbreed fertilely.

More than just geographic isolation might now apply. There may, for instance, be behavioral differences interfering with courtship—what we call *behavioral isolation*. Using our *biological* definition of species, we now would recognize two distinct species, where initially only one existed.

Until recently, the general consensus among evolutionary biologists was that microevolutionary mechanisms could be translated directly into the larger-scale macroevolutionary changes, most especially, speciation (also called *transspecific evolution*). A smooth gradation of change was assumed to run directly from microevolution into macroevolution. A representative view was expressed by a leading synthesist, Ernst Mayr:

> The proponents of the synthetic theory maintain that all evolution is due to accumulation of small genetic changes, guided by natural selection, and that transspecific evolution is nothing but an extrapolation and magnification of events that take place within populations and species (Mayr, 1970, p. 351).

In the last decade, this view has been seriously challenged. Many theorists now believe that macroevolution cannot be explained *solely* in terms of accumulated microevolutionary changes. Many current researchers are convinced that macroevolution is only partly understandable through microevolutionary models.

Gradualism vs. Punctuationalism The traditional view of evolution has emphasized that change accumulates gradually in evolving lineages—the idea of "phyletic gradualism." Accordingly, the complete fossil record of an evolving group (if it could be recovered) would display a series of forms with finely graded transitional differences between each ancestor and its descendant. The fact that such transitional forms are only rarely found is attributed to the incompleteness of the fossil record, or, as Darwin called it, "a history of the world, imperfectly kept, and written in changing dialect."

For more than a century, this perspective dominated evolutionary biology, but in the last 15 years some biologists have called this notion into serious question. The evolutionary mechanisms operating on species over the long run are often not continuously gradual. In some cases, species persist for thousands of generations basically unchanged. Then, rather suddenly, at least in evolutionary terms, a "spurt" of speciation occurs. This uneven, nongradual process of long stasis and quick spurts has been termed **punctuated equilibrium** (Gould and Eldredge, 1977).

What the punctuationalists are disputing concerns the "tempo" and "mode" of evolutionary change commonly understood since Darwin's time. Rather than a slow, steady tempo, this alternate view postulates long periods of no change punctuated only occasionally by sudden bursts. From this observation, punctuationalists concluded that the mode of evolution, too, must be different from that suggested by classical Darwinists. Rather than gradual accumulation of small changes in a single lineage, advocates of punctuated equilibrium believe an *additional* evolutionary mechanism is required to push the process along. They thus postulate *speciation* as the major influence in bringing about rapid evolutionary change.

How well does the paleontological record agree with the predictions of punctuated equilibrium? Indeed, considerable fossil data show long periods of stasis punctuated by occasional quite rapid changes (on the order of 10,000 to 50,000 years). Intermediate forms are rare, not so much because the fossil record is poor, but because the speciation events and longevity of these transitional species were so short we should not expect to find them very often.

The best supporting evidence for punctuated equilibrium has come from the fossilized remains of marine invertebrates. How well, then, does the primate fossil record fit the punctuationalist model? In studies of Eocene primates, rates of evolutionary change were shown to be quite gradual (Gingerich, 1985; Brown and Rose, 1987; Rose, 1991). In another study, here of Paleocene plesiadapiforms, evolutionary changes were also quite gradual. Although no longer considered primates, these forms show a gradual tempo of change in another, closely related, group of

PUNCTUATED EQUILIBRIUM The concept that evolutionary change proceeds through long periods of stasis, punctuated by rapid periods of change.

mammals. The predictions postulated by punctuationalists have thus far not been substantiated in those evolving lineages of primates for which we have adequate data to test the theory.

It would, however, be a fallacy to assume that evolutionary change in primates or in any other group must therefore be of a completely gradual tempo. Such is clearly not the case. In all lineages, the pace assuredly speeds up and slows down due to factors that influence the size and relative isolation of populations. In addition, environmental changes as they influence the pace and direction of natural selection must obviously also be considered. In conclusion, then, as postulated by the modern synthesis, microevolution and macroevolution need not be "decoupled" as some evolutionary biologists have recently suggested.

THE MEANING OF GENUS AND SPECIES

Our discussion of fossil primates has introduced a variety of taxonomic names. We should pause at this point and ask: Why use so many names like *Aegyptopithecus*, *Apidium*, and *Sivapithecus*? What do such names mean in evolutionary terms?

Our goal when applying genus, species, or other taxonomic labels to groups of organisms is to make meaningful biological statements about the variation that is present. When looking at populations of living or long extinct animals, we are assuredly going to see variation. The situation is true of *any* sexually reproducing organism due to the factors of recombination (see Chapter 3). As a result of recombination, each individual organism is a unique combination of genetic material, and the uniqueness is usually reflected to some extent in the phenotype.

In addition to such *individual variation*, we see other kinds of systematic variation in all biological populations. *Age changes* certainly act to alter overall body size as well as shape in many mammals. One pertinent example for fossil hominoid studies is the great change in number, size, and shape of teeth from deciduous (milk) teeth (only 20 present) to the permanent dentition (32 present). It would be an obvious error to differentiate fossil forms *solely* on the basis of such age-dependent criteria. If one individual were represented just by milk teeth and another (seemingly very different) individual was represented just by adult teeth, they easily could be differently aged individuals from the *same* population. Variation due to sex also plays an important role in influencing differences among individuals observed in biological populations. Differences in structural traits between males and females of the same population are called **sexual dimorphism** and can result in marked variance in body size and proportion in adults of the same species.

Keeping in mind all the types of variation present within interbreeding groups of organisms, the minimum biological category we would like to define in fossil primate samples is the **species**. A species is biologically defined as a group of interbreeding or potentially interbreeding organisms that is reproductively isolated from other such groups. For example, lions reproduce only with lions and chimpanzees only with

SEXUAL DIMORPHISM Differences in size or shape between males and females of the same species.

SPECIES A group of interbreeding organisms reproductively isolated from other such groups.

chimpanzees. Monkeys of one species cannot mate and produce offspring with members of another species due to genetic and behavioral differences. In modern organisms this concept is theoretically testable by observations of reproductive behavior. In animals long dead, such observations are obviously impossible. Therefore, in order to get a handle on the interpretation of variation seen in fossil groups, we must refer to living animals.

We know without doubt that variation is present. The question is: What is its biological significance? Two immediate choices occur: either the variation is accounted for by individual, age, and sex differences seen within every biological species—**intraspecific**—or the variation present represents differences between reproductively isolated groups—**interspecific**. How do we judge between the alternatives, intra- or interspecific? We clearly must refer to already defined groups where we can observe reproductive behavior; in other words, contemporary species.

If the amount of morphological variation observed in fossil samples is comparable to that seen today *within species of closely related forms*, then we should not "split" our sample into more than one species. We must, however, be careful in choosing modern analogs, for rates of morphological evolution vary widely among different groups of mammals. In interpreting past primates, we do best when comparing them with well-known species of modern primates.

Nevertheless, studies of such living groups have shown that isolating exactly where species boundaries begin and end is oftentimes difficult. In contexts dealing with extinct species, the uncertainties are even greater. In addition to the overlapping patterns of variation *over space*, variation also occurs *through time*. In other words, even more variation will be seen in such **paleospecies**, since individuals may be separated by thousands or even millions of years. Applying strict Linnaean taxonomy to such a situation presents an unavoidable dilemma. Standard Linnaean classification, designed to take account of variation present at any given time, describes a static situation. However, when dealing with paleospecies, the time frame is expanded, and the situation may be dynamic (that is, later forms may be different from earlier ones). In such a dynamic situation, taxonomic decisions (where to draw species boundaries) are ultimately going to be somewhat arbitrary.

The next level of formal taxonomic classification, the *genus*, presents another problem. In order to have more than one genus, we obviously must have at least two species (reproductively isolated groups), and, in addition, the species must differ in a basic way. A genus is therefore defined as a group of species composed of members more closely related to each other than they are to species from any other genus.

Grouping species together into genera is a largely subjective procedure wherein the degree of relatedness becomes a strictly relative judgment. One possible test for contemporary animals is to check for results of hybridization between individuals of different species—rare in nature but quite common in captivity. If two normally separate species interbreed and produce live, though not necessarily fertile, offspring, they probably are not too different genetically and, therefore, should probably be grouped together in the same genus. A well-known example of such a

INTRASPECIFIC Within-species. Refers to variation seen within the same species.

INTERSPECIFIC Between-species. Refers to variation *beyond* that seen within the same species to include additional aspects seen between two different species.

PALEOSPECIES A species defined from fossil evidence, often covering a long time span.

cross is horses with donkeys (*Equus callabus* × *Equus asinus*), which normally produces live, sterile offspring (mules).

As previously mentioned, we cannot perform breeding experiments with extinct animals, but another definition of genus becomes highly relevant. Species that are members of the same genus share the same broad adaptive zone. What this represents is a general ecological lifestyle more basic than the narrower ecological niches characteristic of individual species. This ecological definition of genus can be an immense aid in interpreting fossil primates. Teeth are the most frequently preserved parts, and they often can provide excellent general ecological inferences.

As a final comment, we should point out that classification by genus is also not always a straightforward decision. Indeed, the argument among primatologists over whether the chimp and gorilla represent one genus (*Pan troglodytes*, *Pan gorilla*) or two different genera (*Pan troglodytes*, *Gorilla gorilla*) demonstrates that even with living, breathing animals the choices are not always clear. Or, for that matter, many current researchers—pointing to the very close genetic similarities between humans and chimps—would place these in the same genus (*Homo sapiens*, *Homo troglodytes*). When it gets this close to home, it is even more difficult to maintain objectivity!

SUMMARY

This chapter has surveyed the basic background information concerning mammalian/primate evolution. Two basic perspectives regarding organic diversity and the time scale of vertebrate evolution were discussed. Early vertebrate evolution was briefly reviewed; specifically, placental mammal adaptations were highlighted. Even more specifically, the evolutionary trends that characterize the primate order were reviewed.

Primate evolution during the early Cenozoic was then briefly surveyed, with more attention focused on the evolutionary radiation of hominoids in the Miocene.

Finally, critical aspects of evolutionary theory were discussed, emphasizing (1) the mode of evolutionary change (i.e., the gradualism/punctuationalism debate) and (2) the principles of classification (i.e., the biological significance of genus and species).

QUESTIONS FOR REVIEW

1. What are the two primary goals of organic classification?
2. What are the major groups of vertebrates?
3. What are the major eras of geological time over which vertebrates have evolved?
4. What primary features distinguish mammals—especially placental mammals—from other vertebrates?
5. What is meant by a homology? Contrast with analogy, using examples.

6. Why do evolutionary biologists concentrate on derived features rather than primitive ones? Give an example of each.
7. What are the seven epochs of the Cenozoic?
8. Discuss why primates are said to be "generalized mammals."
9. Summarize the major evolutionary trends that characterize the primate order.
10. How does adaptation to an arboreal environment help explain primate adaptations?
11. Why is it difficult to identify clearly very early primates from other primitive placental mammals?
12. How diversified and geographically widespread were hominoids in the Miocene?
13. Humans are Old World anthropoids. What other groups are also Old World anthropoids?
14. Contrast the gradualist view of evolutionary change with a punctuationalist view. Give an example from primate evolution that supports one view or the other.

AN OVERVIEW OF THE LIVING PRIMATES

CHAPTER 8

INTRODUCTION

In the last chapter, we briefly traced the evolutionary history of the primates and described the set of evolutionary trends that, taken together, set primates apart from other mammals. In this chapter, we introduce you to the approximately 190 nonhuman primate species still living today. We will discuss the three major groupings—prosimians, monkeys, and apes—in terms of geographic distribution, locomotion, and diet. Tragically, most of the species that comprise this diverse and fascinating order are either threatened or highly endangered, and many, if not most, will vanish completely from the wild before we are able to learn much more about them.

CHARACTERISTICS OF PRIMATES

With just a couple of exceptions, primates are found in tropical or semi-tropical areas of the New and Old Worlds. In the New World, these areas include southern Mexico, Central America, and parts of South America. Old World primates are found in Africa, India, Southeast Asia (including numerous islands), and Japan (Fig. 8-1).

The majority of primates are, as we have seen, mostly arboreal and live in forest or woodland habitats. However, some Old World monkeys (e.g., baboons) have, to varying degrees, adapted to life on the ground in areas where trees are sparsely distributed. Moreover, among the apes, gorillas and chimpanzees spend a considerable amount of time on the ground in forested and wooded habitats. However, no nonhuman primate is adapted to a fully terrestrial lifestyle, and all spend some time in the trees.

In general, primates are *omnivorous*. Indeed, the tendency toward omnivory is an example of the overall lack of specialization in primates. The fact that primates are not restricted to one or a few dietary items is important and has contributed to their enormous success during the last 50 million years.

In Chapter 7, you learned that most primates possess fairly generalized teeth. For example, the cheek teeth have low, rounded **cusps**.

CUSPS The elevated portions (bumps) on the chewing surfaces of premolar and molar teeth.

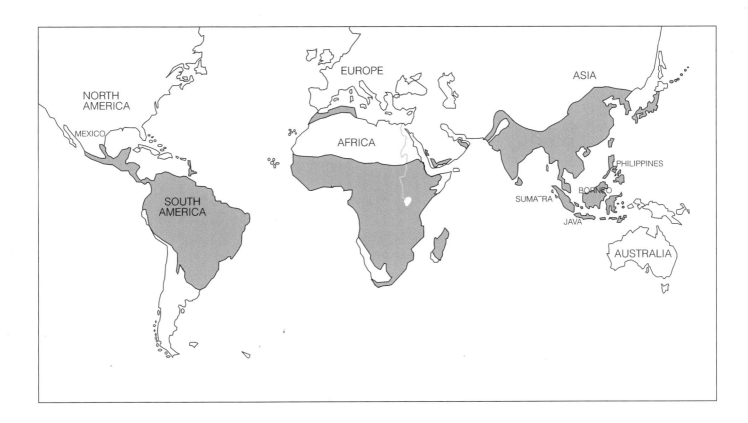

Equipped with this type of premolar and molar morphology, most primates are capable of processing a wide variety of foods ranging from tough or hard items, such as leaves and seeds, to more easily processed fruits, insects, and even meat. Such an array of choices is highly beneficial for species survival. Species with narrow dietary preferences frequently cannot exploit alternative resources if climate change or other factors reduce the availability of resources. Commonly, the end result of such an inability to adapt is extinction.

The number of teeth varies within the primate order. Most prosimians have 36, while most anthropoids have 32 (although some New World monkeys have 36). Biologists describe the number of each type of tooth that characterizes a species in terms of the *dental formula*. The dental formula refers to the number of each tooth type in each quadrant of the mouth (Fig. 8-2). Like all land mammals, primates possess four different kinds of teeth: incisors, canines, premolars, and molars. All Old World anthropoids have 2 incisors, 1 canine, 2 premolars, and 3 molars on each side of the **midline** in both the upper and lower jaws. This is represented as a dental formula of

$$\frac{2.1.2.3.}{2.1.2.3.}$$

Although the majority of primate species tend to emphasize some food items over others, most eat a combination of fruit, leaves, and in-

FIGURE 8-1 Geographic distribution of living nonhuman primates.

MIDLINE An anatomical term referring to a hypothetical line that divides the body into right and left halves.

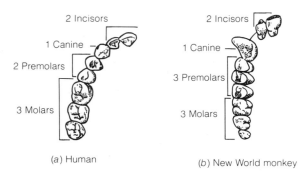

2 Incisors
1 Canine
2 Premolars
3 Molars

(a) Human

2 Incisors
1 Canine
3 Premolars
3 Molars

(b) New World monkey

FIGURE 8-2 Dental formulae. The number of each kind of tooth is given for one-quarter of the mouth.

sects. Many obtain animal protein from birds and amphibians as well. Some (baboons and, especially, chimpanzees) occasionally kill and eat small mammals, including other primates. Others, such as African colobus monkeys and the leaf eating monkeys (langurs) of southeast Asia have become more specialized and subsist primarily on leaves.

Almost all primates are, at least to some degree, **quadrupedal**, meaning they use all four limbs to support the body during locomotion. However, to describe most primate species in terms of only one or even two forms of locomotion would be to overlook the wide variety of methods many may use to get about. Many primates employ more than one form of locomotion, and they owe this ability to their generalized structure.

By retaining basic mammalian limb morphology, which includes five digits on hands and feet, primates do not show the specializations seen in many mammals. For example, through the course of evolution, horses and cattle have undergone a reduction of the number of digits from the primitive pattern of five, to one and two, respectively. Moreover, they have developed hard, protective coverings in the form of hooves. While these structures are adaptive in prey species whose survival depends upon speed and stability, they restrict the animal to only one type of locomotor pattern. Moreover, limb function is limited entirely to support and locomotion, while the ability to manipulate objects is completely lost.

Although the majority of quadrupedal primates are arboreal, terrestrial quadrupedalism is fairly common (e.g., some lemurs, baboons, and **macaques**). Typically, the limbs of terrestrial quadrupeds are approximately of equal length, with forelimbs being 90 percent (or more) as long as hind limbs (Fig. 8-3a). In arboreal quadrupeds, forelimbs are shorter and may be only 70 to 80 percent as long as hindlimbs (Fig. 8-3b).

Quadrupeds are also characterized by a relatively long and flexible *lumbar spine* (the portion of the spine between the ribs and the pelvis; i.e., the lower back). This lumbar flexibility permits the animal to bend the body during running, thus positioning the hindlimbs and feet well forward under the body and enhancing their ability to propel the animal forward. (Watch for this the next time you see slow motion footage of cheetahs or lions on television.)

QUADRUPEDAL (*quadrupedalism*) Using all four limbs to support the body during locomotion. The basic mammalian (and primate) form of locomotion.

MACAQUE (muh-kak′)

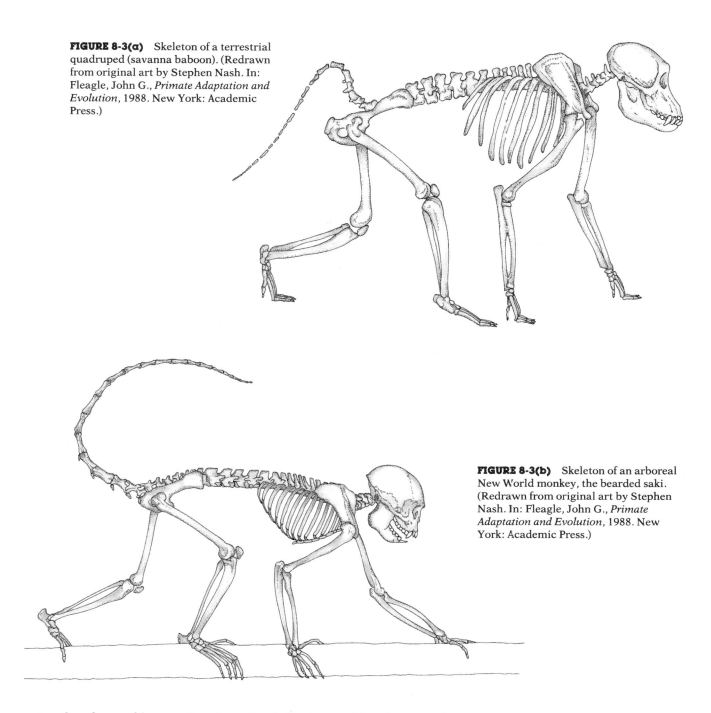

FIGURE 8-3(a) Skeleton of a terrestrial quadruped (savanna baboon). (Redrawn from original art by Stephen Nash. In: Fleagle, John G., *Primate Adaptation and Evolution*, 1988. New York: Academic Press.)

FIGURE 8-3(b) Skeleton of an arboreal New World monkey, the bearded saki. (Redrawn from original art by Stephen Nash. In: Fleagle, John G., *Primate Adaptation and Evolution*, 1988. New York: Academic Press.)

Another form of locomotion is *vertical clinging and leaping,* seen in many prosimians. As the term implies, vertical clingers and leapers support themselves vertically by grasping onto trunks of trees while their knees and ankles are tightly flexed (Fig. 8-3c). Forceful extension of their long hindlimbs allows them to spring powerfully away in either a forward or backward direction. Once in midair, the body rotates so the animal lands feet first on the next vertical support.

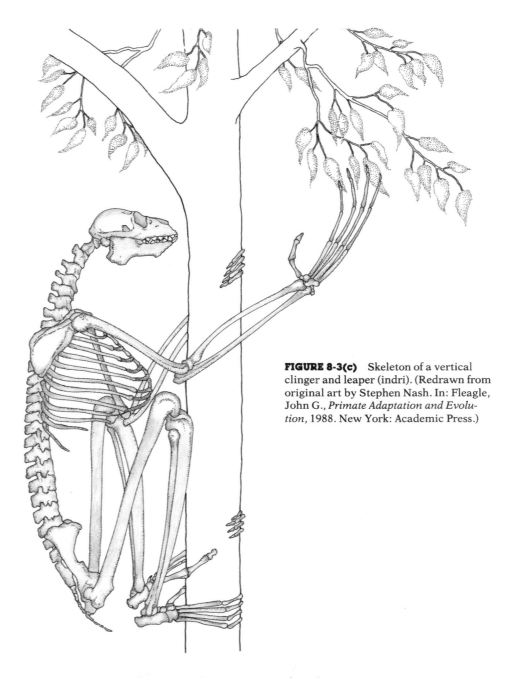

FIGURE 8-3(c) Skeleton of a vertical clinger and leaper (indri). (Redrawn from original art by Stephen Nash. In: Fleagle, John G., *Primate Adaptation and Evolution*, 1988. New York: Academic Press.)

A third type of primate locomotion is *brachiation* or arm-swinging, where the body is alternatively supported under either forelimb. Because of anatomical modifications at the shoulder joint, all the apes (and humans) are capable of true brachiation. However, only the small gibbons and siamangs of southeast Asia use this form of locomotion almost exclusively.

Brachiation is seen in species characterized by arms longer than legs, a short stable lumbar spine, long curved fingers, and reduced

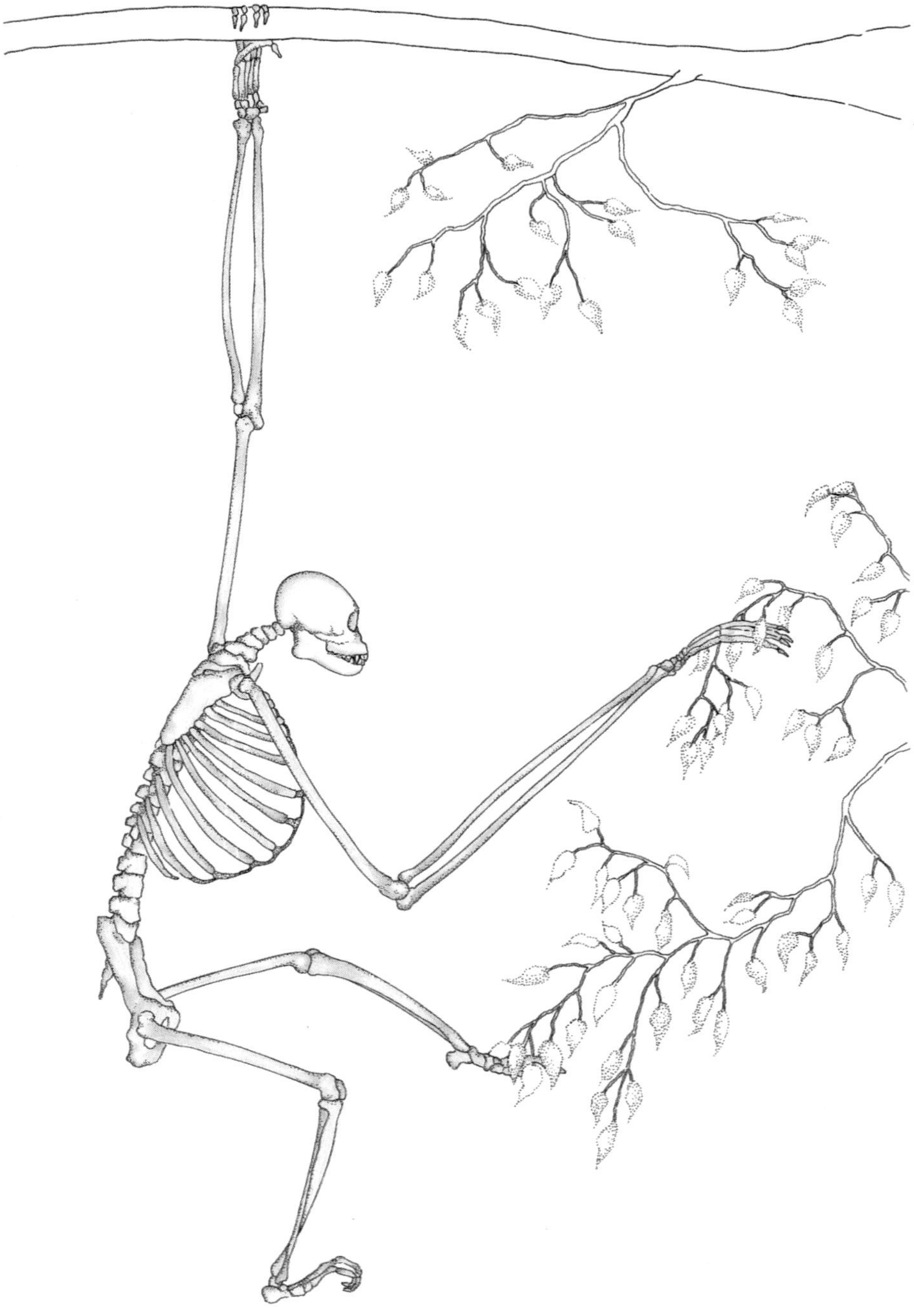

FIGURE 8-3(d) Skeleton of a brachiator (gibbon). (Redrawn from original art by Stephen Nash. In: Fleagle, John G., *Primate Adaptation and Evolution*, 1988. New York: Academic Press.)

thumbs (Fig. 8-3d). Because these are traits seen in all the apes, it is believed that, although none of the great apes (orangutan, gorilla, and chimpanzee) habitually brachiates today, they most likely inherited these characteristics from brachiating or perhaps climbing ancestors.

Some monkeys, particularly New World monkeys, are termed *semibrachiators*, as they practice a combination of leaping, with some arm-swinging. In some New World species, arm-swinging and other suspensory behaviors are enhanced by use of a *prehensile tail* which, in effect, serves as a marvelously effective grasping fifth "hand." It should be noted that prehensile tails are strictly a New World phenomenon and are not seen in any Old World primate species.

PRIMATE CLASSIFICATION

The living primates are commonly categorized into their respective sub-groupings as shown in Fig. 8-4. This taxonomy is based upon the system originally established by Linneaus. (Remember that the primate order includes a diverse array of approximately 190 species that, in turn, belong to a larger grouping, the class *Mammalia*).

In any taxonomic system, organisms are organized into increasingly specific categories. For example, the order *Primates* includes *all* primates. However, at the next level down—the *suborder*—the primates have traditionally been divided into two large categories, **Prosimii** (all the prosimians: lemurs, lorises, and tarsiers) and *Anthropoidea* (all the monkeys, apes, and humans). Therefore, the suborder distinction is more specific and more precise than is the order.

At the level of the suborder what we are saying is that the prosimians are distinct as a group from all the other primates. In other words, the prosimians are more closely related to each other than they are to any of the anthropoids. Likewise, all anthropoid species are more closely related to each other than any is to the prosimians.

At each succeeding level (infraorder, superfamily, family, genus, and species) finer distinctions are made between categories until, at the species level, only those animals that can interbreed and produce viable offspring are included. In this manner, taxonomies not only serve to organize diversity into categories, but also they illustrate evolutionary and genetic relationships between species and groups of species.

The taxonomy presented in Fig. 8-4 employs the traditional approach of looking for homologies in morphological traits. However, this technique can be problematic. For example, two primate species that superficially resemble one another (e.g., some New and Old World monkeys) may in fact not be closely related at all. Using external morphology alone may be confusing because of unknown effects of parallel evolution. But such evidence as biochemical data avoids these pitfalls, and indeed shows Old and New World monkeys as genetically and evolutionarily quite distinct.

This relatively new perspective has enormous potential for clarifying taxonomic problems by making between-species comparisons of chromosomes and amino acid sequences in proteins. Direct comparisons of proteins (products of DNA) are excellent indicators of homologies. If two primate species are systematically similar with regard to protein structure, we know their DNA sequences are also similar. It also follows that if two species share similar DNA, it is highly probable that both inherited the same blueprint (with some revisions) from a common ancestor.

Detailed protein structures can be compared by isolating the amino acid sequences. Comparisons between humans and the African great

PROSIMII (pro-sim-ee-eye')

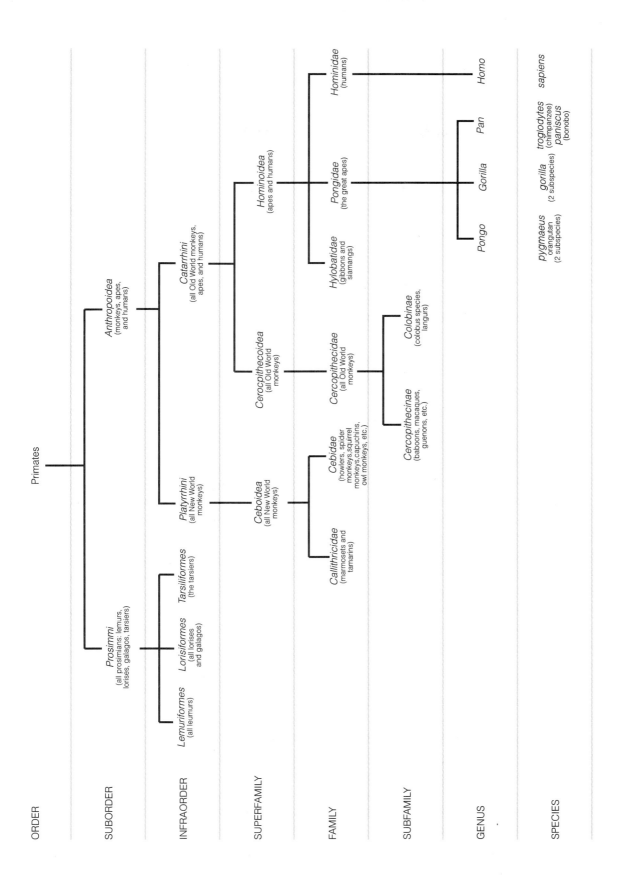

FIGURE 8-4 Primate taxonomic classification. This abbreviated taxonomy illustrates how primates are grouped into increasingly specific categories. Only the more general categories are shown, except for the great apes and humans.

apes for the approximately half dozen proteins analyzed in this manner show striking similarities: They are either identical or show a difference of only one or two amino acids in the entire sequence.

Another technique called DNA hybridization matches DNA strands from two species to determine what percentage of bases match. The higher the percentage, the closer is the genetic relationship between the two. The results of this technique show that human and chimpanzee DNA base sequences are 98.4 percent identical.

These techniques (amino acid sequencing and DNA hybridization) and others, have reaffirmed the basic tenets of primate classification. Moreover, they have shown how close genetically we and the African great apes are. A recent systematic application of DNA hybridization (Sibley and Ahlquist, 1984) demonstrated that humans and chimpanzees are closer genetically than either is to the gorilla and, in fact, even closer than two similar species of gibbons. For that matter, chimps and humans share more genetic similarities than do zebras and horses or goats and sheep. On the basis of these results, it would be entirely consistent to classify humans and chimps (perhaps gorillas as well) within the *same* genus. Humans would continue to be called *Homo sapiens* whereas chimpanzees would be classed as *Homo troglodytes*. Certainly, not everyone is prepared to accept this terminology; nevertheless, it underlies the basic genetic/evolutionary facts.

Prosimians

The most primitive, or least derived, of the primates are the true prosimians, the lemurs and lorises. By "least derived" we mean that these prosimians, taken as a group, are more similar anatomically to their earlier mammalian ancestors than are the other primates (monkeys and apes). Therefore, they tend to exhibit certain more primitive characteristics, such as a more pronounced reliance on *olfaction* (sense of smell). Their increased olfactory capabilities (compared to other primates) are reflected in the presence of a moist, fleshy pad (**rhinarium**) at the end of the nose and in the relatively long snout, which gives prosimians a somewhat doglike appearance. Moreover, prosimians mark territories with scent in a manner not seen in many other primates.

There are numerous other distinctions that set prosimians apart from the anthropoids, including somewhat more laterally placed eyes, differences in reproductive physiology, and shorter gestation and maturation periods. Prosimians also possess a dental specialization known as the "dental comb." The dental comb is formed by forward-projecting lower incisors and canines, and together these modified teeth are used in grooming and feeding (Fig. 8-5).

Lemurs and Lorises   There are two groupings of prosimians: lemurs and lorises. Lemurs are found only on the island of Madagascar and adjacent islands off the east coast of Africa. As the only primates on Madagascar, which comprises some 227,000 square miles, lemurs diversified into numerous and varied ecological niches without competition from the higher primates (i.e., monkeys and apes). Thus, while lemurs became ex-

RHINARIUM   (rine-air'-ee-um) The moist, hairless pad at the end of the nose seen in most mammalian species. The rhinarium functions to enhance an animal's ability to smell.

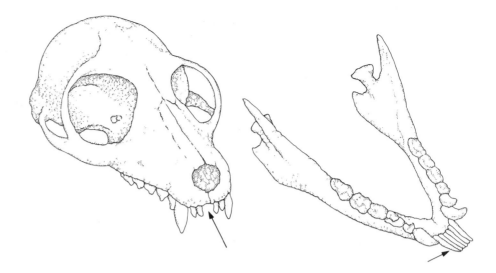

FIGURE 8-5 Prosimian dental comb, formed by forward projecting incisors and canines.

tinct elsewhere, the 22 surviving species of Madagascar represent a kind of "living fossil," preserving an evolutionary grade that has long since vanished elsewhere.

Lemurs range in size from the small mouse lemur, with a body length (head and trunk) of only 5 inches, to the indri, with a body length of a little over 2 feet (Napier and Napier, 1985). While the larger lemurs are diurnal and exploit a wide variety of dietary food items such as leaves, fruit, buds, bark, and shoots, the smaller forms (mouse and dwarf lemurs) are nocturnal and are insectivorous.

Lemurs display considerable variation regarding numerous other aspects of behavior. While many are primarily arboreal, others, such as the ring-tailed lemur (Fig. 8-6), are more terrestrial. Some arboreal species are quadrupeds, and others (sifaka and indri) are vertical clingers and leapers (Fig. 8-7). Socially, several species are gregarious and live in groups of 10 to 25 animals composed of males and females of all ages (ring-tailed lemur and sifaka). Others (the indri) live in monogamous family units, and several nocturnal forms are mostly solitary.

Lorises, which are very similar in appearance to lemurs (Fig. 8-8), were able to survive in continental areas by adopting a nocturnal activity pattern at a time when most other prosimians became extinct. In this way, they were (and are) able to avoid competition with more recently evolved primates (the diurnal monkeys).

The five loris species (loris, in the strict sense) are found in tropical forest and woodland habitats of India, Sri Lanka, southeast Asia, and Africa. Also included in the same general category are 6 to 9 species (Bearder, 1987) of galago, which are widely distributed throughout most of the forested and woodland savanna areas of sub-Saharan Africa (Fig. 8-9).

Locomotion in lorises is a slow, cautious climbing form of quadrupedalism, and flexible hip joints permit suspension by hind limbs while the hands are used in feeding. All galagos, however, are highly agile and active vertical clingers and leapers. Some lorises and galagos are al-

FIGURE 8-6 Ring-tailed lemur.

FIGURE 8-7 Sifakas in native habitat in Madagascar.

FIGURE 8-8 Slow loris.

FIGURE 8-9 Galago or "bushbaby."

most entirely insectivorous; others supplement their diet with various combinations of fruit, leaves, gums, and slugs. Lorises and galagos frequently forage for food alone (females leave infants behind in nests until they are older). However, ranges overlap and two or more females occasionally forage together or share the same sleeping nest.

Both lemurs and lorises represent the same general adaptive level. They both have good grasping and climbing abilities and a fairly well-developed visual apparatus, although vision is not completely stereoscopic, and color vision may not be as well developed as in higher primates. Most retain a claw, commonly called a "grooming claw," only on the second toe. Lemurs and lorises also have prolonged life spans as compared to most other small-bodied mammals, averaging about 14 years for lorises and 19 years for lemurs.

The Tarsier   Today there are three recognized species of tarsier, all restricted to island areas in Southeast Asia where they inhabit a wide range of forest types, from tropical forest to backyard gardens (Fig. 8-10). Tarsiers are nocturnal insectivores, leaping onto prey (which may also include small vertebrates) from lower branches and shrubs. They appear to form stable pair bonds, and the basic tarsier social unit is a mated pair and their young offspring (MacKinnon and MacKinnon, 1980).

Anatomically, the tarsier presents a rare and puzzling blend of characteristics not seen in other primates. It is unique in that its enormous eyes, which dominate much of the face, are immobile within their sockets. To compensate for its inability to move the eyes, the tarsier is able to rotate its head 180 degrees in a decidedly owl-like manner.

Like lemurs and lorises, tarsiers are traditionally classified as prosimians because of their small body size, large ears, unfused mandible (lower jaw) and grooming claws. However, they also share several derived physical characteristics with anthropoids, such as lack of a rhinarium. Moreover, biochemically, tarsiers are more closely related to anthropoids than to lemurs or lorises (Dene et al., 1976). However, with regard to chromosomes, tarsiers are set apart from either group.

Today, many primatologists classify tarsiers closer to anthropoids than to prosimians. One alternate scheme places lemurs and lorises in a relatively new suborder, *Strepsirhini* (moist nosed); and tarsiers are included along with monkeys, apes, and humans in another suborder, the *Haplorhini* (dry nosed) (Szalay and Delson, 1979). Other systems have also been proposed but, at this point, none has been agreed upon, and the tarsier remains a taxonomic problem.

FIGURE 8-10 Tarsier.

The Anthropoids

Several features distinguish the anthropoids from the prosimians. These include:

1. Generally larger body size
2. Larger brain (in absolute terms and relative to body weight)
3. More rounded skull
4. Complete rotation of eyes to front of face to permit full stereoscopic vision
5. Back wall of eye orbit completed
6. No rhinarium (implying reduced reliance upon the sense of smell)
7. More complex social systems
8. More parental care
9. Increased gestation and maturation periods
10. More mutual grooming

The monkey grade of evolution is today the most varied group of primates. Approximately 70 percent of all primates (about 130 species) are monkeys. (It is frequently impossible to give precise numbers of species as the taxonomic status of some primates remains in doubt. Also, primatologists are still making new discoveries.) Monkeys are divided into two groups separated by geographical area (New World and Old World), as well as by several million years of separate evolutionary history.

New World Monkeys The New World monkeys exhibit a wide range of size, diet, and ecological adaptation. In size, they vary from the tiny marmosets (about 12 ounces) to the 20-pound howler monkey (Figs. 8-11 and 8-12). New World monkeys are almost exclusively arboreal, and some never come to the ground. Like Old World monkeys, all except one species (the douroucouli or owl monkey) are diurnal. Although confined to the trees, New World monkeys can be found in a wide range of arboreal environments throughout most forested areas in southern Mexico, Central and South America.

One of the characteristics distinguishing New World monkeys from those found in the Old World is shape of the nose. New World forms have broad, widely flaring noses with outward facing nostrils. Conversely, Old World monkeys have narrower noses with downward facing nostrils. This difference in nose form has given rise to the terms *platyrrhine* (flat-

FIGURE 8-11 A pair of golden marmosets.

FIGURE 8-12 Howler monkey with infant.

CALLITRICHIDAE (kal-eh-trick'-eh-dee)

CEBIDAE (see'-bid-ee)

nosed) and *catarrhine* (downward-facing nose) to refer to New and Old World anthropoids respectively.

New World monkeys are divided into two families, **Callitrichidae** and **Cebidae**. The callitrichids (marmosets and tamarins) are the most primitive of monkeys, retaining claws instead of nails and usually giving birth to twins instead of one infant.

Marmosets and tamarins are mostly insectivorous, although marmoset diet includes gums from trees, and tamarins also rely heavily upon fruits. Locomotion is quadrupedal, and their claws aid in climbing vertical tree trunks, much in the manner of squirrels. Moreover, some tamarins employ vertical clinging and leaping as a form of travel.

Socially, callitrichids live in extended family groupings composed usually of a mated pair, or a female and two adult males, and their offspring. Indeed, marmosets and tamarins are among the few primate species in which males are heavily involved in infant care.

There are at least 30 cebid species ranging in size from the squirrel monkey (body length: 12 inches) to the howler (body length: 24 inches). Diet varies, with most relying on a combination of fruit and leaves supplemented to varying degrees by insects.

Most cebids are quadrupedal but some, for example, the spider monkey (Fig. 8-13), are semibrachiators. Some cebids, including the spider and howler, also possess powerful prehensile tails that are used not only in locomotion but also for suspension under branches while feeding on leaves and fruit. Socially, most cebids are found in either groupings of both sexes and all age categories, or in monogamous pairs with subadult offspring.

Old World Monkeys The monkeys of the Old World display much more morphological and behavioral diversity than is seen in New World monkeys. After humans, Old World monkeys are the most widely distributed

FIGURE 8-13 A New World monkey prehensile tail. Shown here in a spider monkey.

of all living primates. They are found throughout sub-Saharan Africa and southern Asia, ranging from tropical jungle habitats to semiarid desert and even to seasonally snow-covered areas in northern Japan.

Most Old World monkeys are quadrupedal and mostly arboreal, but some (e.g., baboons) are also adapted to life on the ground. Whether in trees or on the ground, these monkeys spend a good deal of time sleeping, feeding, and grooming while sitting with their upper bodies held erect. Usually associated with this universal sitting posture are areas of hardened skin on the rear end (**ischial callosities**) that serve as sitting pads. Old World monkeys also have a good deal of manual dexterity, and most have well-developed tails that serve in communication and balance.

Within the entire group of Old World monkeys there is only one taxonomically recognized family: **Cercopithecidae**. This family, in turn, is divided into two subfamilies: the **cercopithecines** and **colobines**.

The cercopithecines are the more generalized of the two groups, showing a more omnivorous dietary adaptation and distinctive cheek pouches for storing food. As a group, the cercopithecines eat almost anything, including fruits, seeds, leaves, grasses, tubers, roots, nuts, insects, birds' eggs, amphibians, small reptiles, and small mammals (the last seen in baboons).

The majority of cercopithecine species, such as the arboreal and colorful guenons and more terrestrial savanna (Fig. 8-14) and hamadryas baboons (Fig. 8-15) are found in Africa. However, the several species of macaque, which include the well known rhesus monkey, are widely distributed in southern Asia and India.

Colobine species are more limited dietarily, specializing more on mature leaves, a behavior that has led to their designation as "leaf-eating monkeys." The colobines are found mainly in Asia, but both the red colobus and black and white colobus are exclusively African (Fig. 8-16). Other colobines include several species of Asian langur (Fig. 8-17) and the proboscis monkey of Borneo.

Locomotory behavior among Old World monkeys includes arboreal quadrupedalism (guenons, macaques, and langurs); terrestrial quad-

ISCHIAL CALLOSITIES Patches of tough, hard skin on the rear ends of Old World monkeys and chimpanzees.

CERCOPITHECIDAE (serk-oh-pith'-eh-sid-ee)

CERCOPITHECINES (serk-oh-pith'-eh-seens)

COLOBINES (kole'-uh-beans)

(a)

(b)

FIGURE 8-14 Savanna baboons. (a) Male; (b) Female.

FIGURE 8-15 Hamadryas one-male groups. Note difference in size between large-bodied males and smaller females. Note also presence of infants.

rupedalism in baboons, patas, and macaques; and semibrachiation and acrobatic leaping in colobus.

Marked differences in body size or shape between the sexes, referred to as *sexual dimorphism*, is typical of some terrestrial species and is particularly pronounced in baboons and patas. In these species, male body weight (up to 80 pounds in baboons) may be twice that of females.

FIGURE 8-16 Free ranging black and white colobus monkeys.

FIGURE 8-17 Langur group in India.

Females of several species (especially baboons and some macaques) exhibit pronounced cyclical changes of the external genitalia. These changes, including swelling and redness, are associated with **estrus**, a hormonally initiated period of sexual receptivity in female mammals correlated with ovulation.

ESTRUS (ess'-truss)

Several types of social organization characterize Old World monkeys, and there are uncertainties among primatologists regarding some species. In general, colobines tend to live in small groups, with only one or two adult males. Savanna baboons and most macaque species are found in large social units comprising several adults of both sexes and offspring of all ages. Monogamous pairing is not common in Old World monkeys, but is seen in a few langurs and possibly one or two guenon species.

The Apes

The superfamily Hominoidea includes the "lesser" apes placed in the family **Hylobatidae** (gibbons and siamangs); the great apes in the family **Pongidae** (orangutans, gorillas, bonobos, and chimpanzees); and humans (family: **Hominidae**).

HYLOBATIDAE (high-lo-baht'-id-ee)
PONGIDAE (Ponj'-id-ee)
HOMINIDAE (Hom-in'-id-ee)

Apes differ from monkeys in numerous ways including:

1. generally larger body size, except for the lesser apes
2. absence of a tail
3. shortened trunk (lumbar area relatively shorter and more stable)
4. differences in position and musculature of the shoulder joint (adapted for suspensory locomotion)

5. more complex behavior
6. more complex brain and enhanced cognitive abilities
7. increased period of infant development and dependency

Gibbons and Siamangs The eight gibbon species and the closely related siamang are today found in the southeastern tropical areas of Asia. These animals are the smallest of the apes, with a long, slender body weighing 13 pounds in the gibbon and 25 pounds in the larger siamang (Fig. 8-18).

The most distinctive structural feature of gibbons and siamangs is related to their functional adaptation for brachiation. Consequently, they have extremely long arms, long, permanently curved fingers and short thumbs, and powerful shoulder muscles. This highly specialized locomotory adaptations may be related to feeding behavior while hanging beneath branches.

The diet of both species is largely composed of fruit. Both (especially the siamang) also eat a variety of leaves, flowers, and insects.

The basic social unit of gibbons and siamangs is the monogamous pair with dependent offspring. As in marmosets and tamarins, male gibbons and siamangs are very much involved in rearing their young. Both males and females are highly territorial and protect their territories with very elaborate and ear-splitting whoops and sirenlike "songs."

The Orangutan The orangutan (*Pongo pyqmaeus*) (Fig. 8-19) is represented by two subspecies found today only in heavily forested areas on the Indonesian islands of Borneo and Sumatra. Due to poaching by humans and continuing habitat loss on both islands, the orangutan faces imminent extinction in the wild.

FIGURE 8-18 White handed gibbon, Oakland Zoo.

FIGURE 8-19 Female orangutan.

Orangutans are slow, cautious climbers whose locomotory behavior can best be described as "four-handed," referring to the tendency to use all four limbs for grasping and support. Although they are almost completely arboreal, orangutans do sometimes travel quadrupedally on the ground. Orangutans are also very large animals with pronounced sexual dimorphism (males may weigh 200 pounds or more and females less than half that amount).

In the wild, orangutans lead largely solitary lives, although adult females are usually accompanied by one or two dependent offspring. Diet is primarily **frugivorous**, but bark, leaves, insects, and meat (on rare occasions) may also be eaten.

FRUGIVOROUS (fru-give'-or-us) Having a diet composed primarily of fruit.

The Gorilla The largest of all living primates, the gorilla (*Gorilla gorilla*) is today confined to forested areas in west Africa (the lowland gorilla) and the mountainous areas of East and central Africa (the mountain gorilla) (Fig. 8-20). Gorillas exhibit marked sexual dimorphism, with males weighing up to 400 pounds and females around 200 pounds. Due to their weight, adult gorillas are almost completely terrestrial, adopting a semiquadrupedal (knuckle-walking) posture on the ground.

Gorillas live in family groups consisting of one large *silverback male*, a few adult females, and their subadult offspring. The term "silverback" refers to the saddle of white hair across the back of fully adult (at least 12 or 13 years of age) male gorillas. Additionally, the silverback may tolerate the presence of a younger adult—*blackback male*—probably one of his sons.

Although gorillas have long been considered ferocious wild beasts, in reality they are shy and gentle vegetarians (Schaller, 1963; Fossey, 1983). When threatened, males can be provoked to attack and certainly they

(b)

FIGURE 8-20 (a) Male lowland gorilla, Woodland Park Zoo, Seattle; (b) Female mountain gorilla, Rwanda.

(a)

will defend their group, but the reputation gorillas have among humans is little more than myth. Sadly, because of their fierce reputation, the clearing of habitat for farms, and big game hunting by Europeans, gorillas have been hunted to extinction in many areas. Moreover, although there are perhaps 40,000 lowland gorillas remaining in parts of West Africa today, they are endangered, and the mountain gorilla (probably never very numerous) numbers only about 400.

The Chimpanzee Probably the best known and most loved of all nonhuman primates is the chimpanzee (Fig. 8-21). Often misunderstood because of their displays in zoos, circus acts, and sideshows, the chimpanzee's true nature did not become known until long hours of field work in their natural environments provided a reliable picture. Today, chimpanzees are found in equatorial Africa, stretching in a broad belt from the

FIGURE 8-21 Chimpanzees: (a) male; (b) female.

(a)

(b)

Atlantic Ocean in the west to Lake Tanganyika in the east. Their range, however, is patchy within this large geographic area, and with further habitat destruction, it is becoming even more so.

Actually there are two species of chimpanzee: the "common" chimpanzee (*Pan troglodytes*) and the bonobo (*Pan paniscus*). Because the bonobo is smaller than some (but not all) chimpanzees, it has often been called the "pygmy chimpanzee." However, the differences in body size are not great enough to warrant such a distinction. Bonobos do, however, exhibit several intriguing anatomical and behavioral differences from chimpanzees. These differences include a more linear body build, dark face from birth, and tufts of hair at the side of the face (Fig. 8-22). Behaviorally, bonobos appear to be somewhat less aggressive and excitable, and male-female bonding is more important than in *troglodytes*.

Unfortunately, bonobos have not been well-studied in the wild, although several research projects are currently in progress. This is indeed fortunate, as the bonobo's range is limited to a portion of central Zaire where, due to continuing habitat loss, it is in grave danger of extinction.

Chimpanzees (*troglodytes* more so than *paniscus*) are in many ways structurally similar to gorillas, with corresponding limb proportions and upper-body shape. This similarity is due to commonalities in locomotion when on the ground (quadrupedal knuckle walking). Indeed, many authorities (for example, Tuttle, 1990) consider chimps and gorillas as members of a single genus. However, the ecological adaptations of the chimp and gorilla differ, with chimps spending more time in the trees. Moreover, whereas gorillas are typically placid and quiet, chimpanzees are highly excitable, active, and noisy.

Chimpanzees and bonobos are smaller than the other great apes and, while they are sexually dimorphic, sex differences are not as pronounced

FIGURE 8-22 Female bonobo with infant, San Diego Zoo.

as in orangutans and gorillas. While male chimpanzees may weigh over 100 pounds, females may weigh at least 80.

In addition to quadrupedal knuckle walking, chimpanzees (particularly youngsters) may brachiate while in the trees. When on the ground, they frequently walk bipedally for short distances when carrying food or other objects. Indeed, one adult male at Jane Goodall's study area in Tanzania frequently walked bipedally due to an arm paralyzed by polio (Goodall, 1986).

Chimpanzees eat an amazing variety of items, including fruits, leaves, insects, nuts, bird eggs, berries, caterpillars, and small mammals. Moreover, both males and females occasionally take part in cooperative hunting efforts to kill such small mammals as red colobus, and young baboons, bushpigs, and antelope. When hunts are successful, the prey is shared by the group members.

Chimpanzees live in large, fluid communities of as many as 50 individuals or more. At the core of a chimpanzee community is a group of bonded males. Although relationships between these males are not always peaceful or stable, nevertheless they act as a group to defend territory and are highly intolerant of unfamiliar chimpanzees, especially nongroup males.

Although chimpanzees are said to live in communities, there are few times, if any, when all members are together. Indeed, it is the nature of chimpanzees to come and go so that the individuals they encounter vary from day to day. Moreover, adult females tend to forage either alone or in the company of their offspring (Fig. 8-23). The latter foraging group could comprise several chimps, as females with infants often accompany their own mothers and their younger siblings. A female may also leave her

FIGURE 8-23 Female chimpanzee with infant and subadult offspring.

community either permanently to join another, or temporarily while she is in estrus. This behavioral pattern may serve to reduce the risk of mating with close male relatives, for males apparently never leave the group in which they were born.

Chimpanzee social behavior is very complex, and individuals form lifelong attachments with friends and relatives. Indeed, the bond between mothers and infants often remains strong until one or the other dies. This may be a considerable period, as it is not unusual for some chimpanzees to live into their midthirties while others continue into their forties.

Humans Humans represent the only living species belonging to the family Hominidae (genus: *Homo*; species: *sapiens*). Our primate heritage is shown again and again in the structure of our body. Our dependence on vision, our lack of reliance on olfactory cues, and our flexible limbs and grasping hands are all long rooted in our primate, arboreal past. Indeed, among the primates, we show in many ways the most developed set of primate characteristics. For example, the development of our cerebral cortex and reliance on learned behavior (with resulting complexity in social behavior) are but elaborations of long-established primate trends.

As we will discuss in Chapter 10, there are several features of humans and our most immediate ancestors that distinguish us from other primates. However, probably the most distinctive, and certainly the most clearly observable difference seen in our earliest (hominid) ancestors is our unique manner of locomotion. The striding bipedal gait, with alternating support placed on one hindlimb at a time, has required significant structural modification in the pelvis and lower limb. By isolating similar structural modifications in the remains of fossil animals, we are able to distinguish our closely related or direct ancestors.

SUMMARY

In this chapter, we have briefly introduced you to the primates, the mammalian order that includes humans. As a group, the primates are generalized in terms of diet and locomotor patterns, and these behavioral generalizations are reflected in the morphology of the teeth and limbs.

We have also discussed some of the anatomical similarities and differences between the major groupings of primates: prosimians, monkeys (New and Old World), and apes. In the next chapter, we will turn our attention to primate social behavior and cognitive abilities. These are extremely important topics, for it is through better understanding of nonhuman primate behavior that we can make more general statements about human behavior. Moreover, increasing our knowledge is essential if we are to prevent many of these uniquely adapted and marvelous relatives of ours from being lost forever.

QUESTIONS FOR REVIEW

1. What is the geographical distribution of the nonhuman primates?
2. What are the two major subdivisions of the order *Primates*?
3. Which major groupings of primates are anthropoids?
4. What is a dental formula? What is the dental formula of all the Old World anthropoids?
5. What are *quadrupedalism*, *vertical clinging and leaping*, and *brachiation*? Name at least one primate species that is characterized by each of these.
6. What are the major differences between prosimians and anthropoids?
7. What are at least three anatomical differences between monkeys and apes?
8. Name the two major categories (subfamilies) of Old World monkeys. In general, what is the geographical distribution of each?
9. Explain how a taxonomic classification scheme reflects biological relationships.
10. Where are lemurs and lorises found today?
11. In general, which primates have prehensile tails?
12. What are the two family divisions of New World monkeys? Name at least one species for each.
13. In which taxonomic family are the great apes placed?
14. Define *estrus*.
15. Describe the type of social organization for chimpanzees (*Pan troglodytes*) and gorillas.

PRIMATE BEHAVIOR

INTRODUCTION

In Chapter 8, you were given a brief overview of the living nonhuman primates. You learned about the variety of primates, where they live and, in general, what they eat. In this chapter, then, discussion shifts to various aspects of nonhuman primate behavior.

Because primates live in highly complex natural and social environments, they have evolved increasingly complex neurological structures. That is to say, there is a *feedback mechanism* between the biosocial environment and neurological complexity, so that over time, complex lifestyles select for increased neurological complexity or intelligence. Intelligence, in turn, permits increasingly complex lifestyles. We know that all primates, including many prosimians, are extremely clever when compared to most other mammals. Herein, we will examine some of the evidence that illustrates just how complex and intelligent are the other members of the order to which we ourselves belong.

THE IMPORTANCE OF PRIMATE STUDIES

Modern African apes and humans last shared a common ancestor between 8 and 5 million years ago. Researchers believe that, although ape behavior has changed since that time, the behavior of hominids, who developed culture as an adaptive strategy, has changed much more dramatically. Accordingly, if we want to know what hominid behavior was like before culture became a factor, and if we wish to speculate as to which behaviors may have led to culture, we must look for clues in nonhuman primate behavior.

One approach is to correlate specific aspects of social structure with elements of primate habitats, since all living organisms must adapt to their environment. Because there are limits to the ways in which adaptation can occur, it follows that all organisms are to some degree governed by the same principles. By elucidating the various environmental pressures involved, and understanding how they have influenced nonhuman primate behavior, we can better comprehend the factors that led to human emergence.

In addition to studying primates to learn more about ourselves, it is just as important to learn more about them in their own right. The late twentieth century is indeed a critical time for much of life on our planet. If we hope to save even some of the many threatened and endangered species from extinction, we must understand their needs (e.g., space, diet, group organization, etc.) in the wild. Without this knowledge, we can neither preserve sufficient natural habitat for their survival in the wild, nor can we recreate it in captivity.

Studies of nonhuman primate behavior and intelligence actually began in the 1920s, but primatology remained in its infancy until the 1960s. Japanese scientists began their pioneering work with Japanese macaques in 1948 (see Sugiyama, 1965). In 1960, Dr. Jane Goodall began her now famous field study of chimpanzees at Gombe National Park, Tanzania. This remarkable project continues today and it, along with several others, has provided us with a wealth of information regarding the natural behavior of these remarkable animals. By the early 1960s field research was in full swing, and since that time researchers have painstakingly studied many species, including savanna baboons (DeVore and Washburn, 1963), mountain gorillas (Schaller, 1963; Fossey, 1981, 1983), langurs (Dolhinow, 1977), and orangutans (Galdikas, 1979).

PRIMATE SOCIOECOLOGY

Scientists who study behavior in free-ranging primates do so within an **ecological** framework, focusing upon the relationship between aspects of social behavior and the natural environment. One underlying assumption of such an ecological approach is that the various components of ecological systems have evolved together. Therefore, in order to understand the functioning of one particular component, such as the social organization of a given species, it is necessary to determine its relationships with numerous environmental factors, including:

ECOLOGICAL Pertaining to the relationship between organisms and all aspects of their environment.

1. Quantity and quality of different kinds of foods (caloric value), digestive energy required, net value to the animal)
2. Distribution of food resources (dense, scattered, clumps, and seasonal availability)
3. Distribution of water
4. Distribution and types of predators
5. Distribution of sleeping sites
6. Activity patterns (nocturnal, diurnal)
7. Relationship with other (nonpredator) species, both primate and nonprimate
8. Impact of human activities

Unfortunately, the relationships among ecological variables, social organization, and behavior have not been thoroughly worked out, but numerous factors certainly suggest a relationship between, for example, group size and the problems of obtaining food and avoiding predators. Indeed, average group size and group composition can be viewed as adaptive responses to these problems (Pulliam and Caraco, 1984).

For example, groups composed of several adult males and females (multimale, multifemale groups) have traditionally been viewed as advantageous in areas where predation pressure is high, particularly in mixed woodlands and on open savannas, where there are a number of large predators (e.g., hyenas, cheetahs, and lions). Where members of prey species occur in larger groups (versus smaller ones), there is increased likelihood of early predator detection, and thus avoidance. Moreover, large-bodied males in such groups are capable of joining forces to chase and even attack predators.

Savanna baboons (Fig. 9-1) have long been used as an example of these principles. They are found in semi-arid grassland and broken woodland habitats throughout sub-Saharan Africa. To avoid nocturnal predators, savanna baboons sleep in trees; however, they spend much of the day on the ground foraging for food.

In the presence of nonhuman predators, baboons flee to the safety of trees. (Frequently, they abandon trees at the approach of humans, for they have learned that humans shoot them from the ground.) However, if they are at some distance from safety, or if a predator is nearby, adult males may join forces to chase an intruder away. The effectiveness of male baboons in this regard should not be underestimated, for baboons have been known to kill domestic dogs and even to attack leopards and lions (Altmann and Altmann, 1970).

As you have already learned, not all primates are found in large groups. Solitary foraging is seen in many species and may be related to diet and distribution of resources. In the case of the slow moving, insectivorous loris, solitary feeding reduces competition, thus allowing for less distance traveled (and thus less expenditure of energy) in the search

FIGURE 9-1 Female savanna baboons.

for prey. Moreover, because insects usually do not occur in dense patches but are scattered, they are more efficiently exploited by widely dispersed individuals rather than by groups. Solitary foraging is also related to predator avoidance, and it is particularly effective in species that rely chiefly upon concealment rather than escape. Again, the less-than-agile loris serves as a good example.

Foraging alone or with offspring is also seen in females of some diurnal anthropoid species (e.g., orangutans, chimpanzees, and spider monkeys). These females, being relatively large-bodied, have little to fear from predators, but by feeding alone or with only one or two youngsters, they maximize their access to food, free from competition with others. In the case of the orangutan, this may be particularly important, as the female is effectively removing herself from competition with males who may be twice her size.

Although the exact relationships between group size and structure and the environment are not well known at this time, it is clear that certain environmental factors, such as resource availability and predation, exert strong influence. The various solutions primate species have developed to deal with the problems of survival differ in complicated ways. Indeed, closely related species living in proximity to one another and exploiting many of the same resources can have very different types of social structure. It is only with continued research that primatologists will be able to sort out the intricate relationships between society and the natural environment.

SOCIOBIOLOGY

The sociobiological perspective is an important **paradigm** in primatology today. In the last decade, this approach has been applied to a wide variety of animals. Indeed, for primatological interpretations, sociobiology holds a central position as a theoretical framework for a majority of current researchers.

PARADIGM A cognitive construct or framework within which we explain phenomena. Paradigms shape our world view. They can change as the result of technological and intellectual innovation.

Beyond the suppositions concerning nonhuman primates, some contemporary scholars even go so far as to extend this field to the interpretation of *human* primates as well.* Naturally, not all primatologists, and certainly not all anthropologists, are sociobiologists. Indeed, sociobiology has created and continues to generate a great deal of controversy.

Sociobiologists are basically classical Darwinists, postulating the *evolution of behavior through the operation of natural selection*. That is, natural selection is seen to act upon behavior in the same way it acts upon physical characteristics. However, in order for a behavior to be shaped by natural selection, it must be influenced by genetic factors; and if a given behavior has a genetic basis, then its evolutionary impact will be directly measured by its effect on *reproductive success*. Therefore, individuals

---

*Some recent publications reflect this trend. See *Child Abuse and Neglect*, Gelles and Lancaster, 1987; *Parenting across the Life Span*, Lancaster et al., 1987; *The Biology of Moral Systems*, Alexander, 1987; *Homocide*, Daly and Wilson, 1987; and *Depostism and Differential Reproduction*, Betzig, 1987.

whose genotypes code for behaviors that lead to higher reproductive success than others, will be more fit. Consequently, these individuals should pass on their genes at a faster rate.

Superficially, such an explanation implies the existence of genes that code for specific behaviors (e.g., a gene for aggression; another gene for cooperation, and so on). Such conclusions have caused a great deal of concern, and rightly so, especially when these principles are applied to humans. If specific human behaviors can be explained in terms of genes, and populations and sexes vary regarding the frequencies of these genes, then such theories could readily be used to support both racism and sexism.

It is true that much behavior in social insects and other invertebrates, as well as lower vertebrates, is under genetic control. In other words, most behavioral patterns in these forms are *innate*, not learned. In fact, recent research with marine snails has identified a family of genes that produces specific proteins whose actions govern egg-laying behavior (Scheller and Axel, 1984). This finding is of note because, for the first time, a given behavior has been traced to a specific genetic mechanism.

However, in higher vertebrates, particularly birds and mammals, the proportion of behavior due to *learning* is increased. Accordingly, the proportion that is under genetic influence is reduced. This phenomenon is especially true of primates, and most researchers agree that in humans, who are so much a product of culture, most behavior results from learning.

What sociobiologists are proposing then, is this: In higher organisms, some behaviors are influenced, at least in part, by certain gene products (such as hormones, for example). Currently, more is known about the behavioral effects of testosterone than any other hormone. Numerous studies have shown that increased levels of testosterone increase aggressive behavior and sexual arousal in many nonhuman species. However, there is current debate about whether this is also true for humans.

A major dispute arises when trying to postulate the actual mechanics of behavioral evolution in complex social animals with flexible neurological responses such as those seen in primates. Therefore, we need to determine which primate behaviors have a genetic basis, and how these behaviors influence reproductive success. In order to accomplish these goals, we must learn considerably more about genotype/phenotype interactions in complex traits, and such an understanding is probably decades away. We also need accurate data on reproductive success in primate groups, and, as of yet, such data are almost completely lacking. Thus, rather than offering precise explanations, sociobiology provides us with a set of hypotheses for explaining primate behavior, and it remains for these hypotheses to be tested.

Obtaining conclusive data for primates and other mammals is no easy matter. A good starting point, however, is framing hypotheses concerning behavioral evolution on the basis of the evidence that does exist. A good example of such a perspective is Sarah Blaffer Hrdy's (1977) explanation of infanticide among Hanuman langur monkeys of India.

Hanuman langurs typically live in social groups composed of one adult male, several females, and their offspring. Other males without mates associate in bachelor groups. These peripheral males occasionally attack a one-male group, violently overthrow the reproductive male, and take over the females. Sometimes, following such takeovers, the group's infants (fathered by the previous male) are attacked and killed by the new male.

It would certainly seem that such behavior is counterproductive, especially from the species' perspective. However, natural selection theory, as clarified by sociobiological explanations, teaches that individuals act to maximize their *own* reproductive success, no matter what its effect may be on the population, or ultimately, the species.

Ostensibly, that is exactly what the male langur is doing, albeit unknowingly. While a female is **lactating**, she does not come into estrus and therefore she is not sexually available. However, when an infant dies, its mother ceases to lactate and within two or three months she resumes cycling and becomes sexually receptive. Therefore, by killing the infants, the male avoids a two-to-three year wait until they are weaned. This could be especially advantageous to him as chances are quite good that his tenure in the group will not even last two or three years. Moreover, he does not expend energy and put himself at risk defending infants who do not carry his genes.

Hanuman langurs are not the only primates that engage in infanticide. Indeed, infanticide is not at all uncommon among primates and other mammals and has been observed (or surmised) in redtail monkeys, red colobus, blue monkeys, savanna baboons, howler monkeys, orangutans, gorillas, and chimpanzees (Struhsaker and Leyland, 1987), and humans. It also occurs among numerous nonprimate species, including rodents and cats.

Significantly, in the majority of nonhuman cases, infanticide occurs in conjunction with the transfer of a new male into a group or, as in chimpanzees, an encounter with an unfamiliar female and infant. *In no case* have primatologists shown that a male attacked an infant either known or presumed to be his own offspring.

Reproductive Strategies The **reproductive strategies** of primates, especially how they differ between the sexes, have been a primary focus of sociobiological research. The goal of such strategies is simply that the individual produce and successfully rear to adulthood as many offspring as possible.

Primates are among the most **K-selected** of mammal species. By this term, we mean that individuals produce but a few young, in whom they invest a tremendous amount of parental care. Contrast this pattern with **r-selected** species, where individuals produce large numbers of offspring but invest little or no energy in parental care. Good examples of r-selection include insects, most fish, and, among mammals, mice and rabbits.

When we consider the tremendous degree of care required by young, growing primate offspring, it is clear that enormous investment by at least one parent is necessary, and it is usually the mother who carries most of the burden both before and after birth (Fig. 9-2). Primates are totally helpless at birth. They develop slowly, and are thus exposed to expanded learning opportunities within a *social* environment. This trend has been elaborated most dramatically in the large-bodied hominoids

LACTATING (LACTATION) The production and secretion of milk by the mammary glands.

REPRODUCTIVE STRATEGIES The complex of behavioral patterns that contributes to individual reproductive success. The behaviors need not be deliberate, and they often vary considerably between male and female.

K-SELECTED (K-SELECTION) Adaptive strategy whereby individuals produce relatively few offspring in whom they invest increased parental care. Although only a few infants are born, chances of survival are increased for each individual because of parental investments in time and energy. Examples of nonprimate k-selected species are birds and wild canids (e.g., wolves, coyotes, and wild dogs).

R-SELECTED (R-SELECTION) Adaptive strategy that emphasizes relatively large numbers of offspring and reduced parental care (compared to K-selected species). (The terms *K-selection and r-selection* are relative terms; i.e., mice are r-selected compared to primates, but compared to many fish species, they are K-selected.)

FIGURE 9-2 Female chimpanzee inspects infant.

(great apes and humans) and most especially in the hominids, eventually producing the distinctively human primate. Thus, what we see in ourselves and our close primate kin (and presumably in our more recent ancestors as well) is a strategy wherein a few "high quality," slowly maturing offspring are produced through extraordinary investment by the parents, usually the mother.

Finding food and mates, avoiding predators, and caring for and protecting dependent young represent difficult challenges for nonhuman primates. Moreover, in most species, males and females employ different strategies to meet these challenges.

Female primates spend almost all of their adult lives either pregnant, lactating, and/or caring for offspring, and the resulting metabolic demands are enormous. A pregnant or lactating female, although perhaps only half the size of her male counterpart, may require about the same number of calories per day. Even then, her physical resources may be drained. For example, analysis of chimpanzee skeletons from Jane Goodall's population at Gombe shows significant loss of bone and bone mineral in older females (Sumner et al., 1989).

Given these physiological costs, a female's best strategy is to maximize the amount of resources available to her and her offspring. Indeed, females of many primate species (e.g., gibbons, marmosets, macaques, to name a few) are viciously competitive with other females and aggressively protect resources and territories. In other species, as we have seen, females distance themselves from others in order to avoid competition.

Males, however, face a separate set of challenges. Having little investment in the rearing of offspring (except those that live in monogamous pairs), it is to the male's advantage to secure as many mates as possible. By so doing he is effectively increasing his genetic contribution to the next generation relative to other males in the group. Therefore, sociobiological theory suggests that the male's best strategy is to compete aggressively with other males for mates.

As we have said before, there is no simple relationship between biology, ecology, and behavior among primates. Nor, obviously, can simplistic evolutionary scenarios adequately account for the diversity of behavior among primates. What makes sociobiology (and its ecological correlates) so important, however, is that it provides a framework to ask *relevant* questions, thus helping to shape future research. Nevertheless, sociobiological interpretation has been subject to considerable criticism by biologists and social scientists. For example, Richard and Schulman (1982, pp. 243–244), in a review of primate sociobiological research, list the following central problems for those attempting to apply this approach:

1. The lack of long-term data on the demography and social behavior of large groups of individually known animals.
2. The lack of long-term, fine-grained data on the distribution of resources in time and space.
3. The nearly complete absence of information on genetic relatedness through the male line.
4. The difficulty in assigning reproductive and other costs and benefits to particular behaviors.
5. Our almost total ignorance of how genes affect social behavior.
6. The untestable nature, even under the best of conditions, of many sociobiological models.

Some critics have gone even further to question the basic validity of sociobiology as a perspective. Eminent Harvard biologists Stephen Jay Gould and Richard Lewontin (1979) have portrayed sociobiology as a teleological (circular-reasoned) pursuit. In making this point, Gould and Lewontin see sociobiologists devising their scenarios to create highly simplistic, perfectly adaptive situations—a condition rarely (if ever) found in nature.

PRIMATE SOCIAL BEHAVIOR

Dominance Most primate societies are organized into **dominance hierarchies**. Dominance hierarchies impose a certain degree of order within groups by establishing parameters of individual behavior. Although aggression is frequently a means of increasing one's status, in general, dominance serves to reduce the amount of actual physical violence. Not only are lower-ranking animals unlikely to attack or even threaten a higher-ranking one, but dominant animals are frequently able to exert control by merely a threatening gesture.

DOMINANCE HIERARCHIES Systems of social organization whereby individuals within a group are ranked relative to one another. Higher-ranking individuals have greater access to preferred food items and mating partners than lower-ranking individuals. Dominance hierarchies are frequently referred to as "pecking orders."

Individual rank or status may be measured by priority access to resources, including food items and mating partners. Dominant individuals are given priority by others, and they usually do not give way in confrontations.

Many (but not all) primatologists believe that the primary benefit of dominance is the increased reproductive success of the individual. This observation would be true if, as many scientists postulate, dominant males compete more successfully for mates than do subordinate males. However, there is also good evidence that lower-ranking males of some species successfully mate; they just do so surreptitiously. Likewise, increased reproductive success can be postulated for high-ranking females who have greater access to food than subordinate females. Therefore, they are provided with more energy for offspring production and care (Fedigan, 1983), and their reproductive success consequently is greater.

An individual's rank is not permanent and changes throughout life. It is influenced by many factors, including sex, age, level of aggression, amount of time spent in the group, intelligence, perhaps motivation, and, sometimes, the mother's social position (particularly true of macaques). In females, the presence of a newborn infant enhances rank for a short time in some species. Females in estrus also experience a brief period of elevated status by virtue of their (albeit short-term) association with high-ranking males.

In species organized into groups containing a number of females associated with one or several adult males, the males are generally dominant to females. Within such groups, males and females have separate hierarchies, although very high-ranking females can dominate the lowest-ranking males (particularly young males). There are exceptions to this pattern of male dominance. Among all Madagascar lemurs studied, females are the dominant sex. Moreover, among species found in monogamous pairs, males and females seem to be codominant.

All primates *learn* their position in the hierarchy. From birth, an infant is carried by its mother, and it observes how she responds to every member of the group. Just as important, it sees how others react to her. Dominance and subordinance are indicated by gestures and behaviors, some of which are universal throughout the primate order (including humans), and this gestural repertoire is part of every youngster's learning experience.

Young primates also acquire social rank through play with age peers. As they spend more time with play groups, their social interactions widen. Competition and rough-and-tumble play allow them to learn the strengths and weaknesses of peers, and they carry this knowledge with them throughout their lives. Thus, through early contact with the mother and subsequent exposure to peers, young primates learn to negotiate their way through the complex web of social interactions that make up their daily lives. In so doing, they move through the hierarchy as they mature and age.

GROOMING Picking through fur to remove dirt, parasites, and other materials that may be present. Social grooming is common among primates and reinforces social relationships.

Grooming Grooming is seen in most primate species. Although grooming occurs in other animal species, social grooming is mostly a primate activity, and it plays an important role in day-to-day life (Fig. 9-3). Be-

FIGURE 9-3 Grooming primates.
(a) patas monkey; female grooming male;
(b) female rhesus macaque grooming
adolescent; (c) savanna baboons;
(d) chimpanzees.

cause grooming involves using the fingers to pick through the fur of another individual (or one's own) and removing insects, dirt, and other materials, it serves hygienic functions. But it is much more than that, for it is an immensely pleasurable activity that individuals of some species (especially chimpanzees) engage in for considerable periods of time.

Grooming occurs in a variety of contexts. Mothers groom infants. Males groom sexually receptive females. Subordinate animals groom dominant ones, sometimes to gain favor. Friends groom friends. In general, grooming is comforting. It restores peaceful relationships between animals who have quarreled and provides reassurance during tense situations. In short, grooming reinforces bonds and helps to maintain and strengthen the structure of the group. For this reason, it has been called "the social cement of primates from lemur to chimpanzee" (Jolly, 1984, p. 207).

Primate Communication *Communication* is universal among animals and includes scents and unintentional, **autonomic** responses and behaviors that convey meaning. Such attributes as body posture convey information about an animal's emotional state. For example, a crouched position indicates a certain degree of insecurity or fear, while a purposeful striding gait implies confidence. Moreover, autonomic responses to threatening or novel stimuli, such as raised body hair (most species) or enhanced body odor (gorillas), indicate excitement.

Many intentional behaviors also serve as communication. In primates, these include a wide variety of gestures, facial expressions, and vocalizations, some of which we humans share. Among many primates, a mild threat is indicated by an intense stare (indeed, we humans find prolonged eye contact with strangers very uncomfortable). For this reason, people should avoid eye contact with captive primates. Other threat gestures are a quick yawn to expose canine teeth (baboons, macaques) (Fig. 9-4); bobbing back and forth in a crouched position (patas monkeys); and branch shaking (many monkey species). High-ranking baboons *mount* the hindquarters of subordinates to express dominance (Fig. 9-5). Mounting may also serve to defuse potentially tense situations by indicating something like, "It's OK, I accept your apology, I know you don't intend to offend me."

There are also a variety of behaviors to indicate submission, reassurance, or amicable intentions. Submission is indicated by a crouched position (most primates); or presenting the hindquarters (baboons). Reassur-

AUTONOMIC Physiological responses that are not under voluntary control of the individual. The release of adrenaline when frightened is an example of an autonomic response.

FIGURE 9-4 Male savanna baboon reacts to possible threat (from a source not seen in the photo) with a characteristic threat gesture—the "yawn," which exposes his large canines.

FIGURE 9-5 Mounting behavior in rhesus macaques. (Redrawn from Napier & Napier, 1986)

Brian

Jason

ance takes the form of touching, patting, and, in chimpanzees, hugging and holding hands. As already mentioned, grooming also serves in a number of situations to indicate submission or reassurance.

A wide variety of facial expressions is seen in chimpanzees and bonobos that indicate emotional states (Fig. 9-6). These include the well-known play face (also seen in several other species) associated with play behavior; and the fear grin (seen in all primates) to indicate fear and submission.

Primates also use a wide array of vocalizations for communication. Some, such as the bark of a baboon that has just spotted a leopard, are un-intentional startled reactions. Others, such as the chimpanzee food

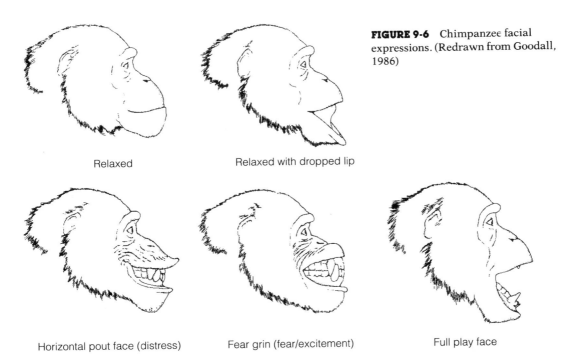

FIGURE 9-6 Chimpanzee facial expressions. (Redrawn from Goodall, 1986)

Relaxed

Relaxed with dropped lip

Horizontal pout face (distress)

Fear grin (fear/excitement)

Full play face

DISPLAYS Stereotyped behaviors that serve to communicate emotional states. Displays are most often associated with reproductive or agonistic behavior.

RITUALIZED Behaviors that are exaggerated and removed from their original context to communicate meaning. Mounting in macaques and baboons to express dominance is removed from its original context of reproduction.

grunt, are heard only in specific contexts. Nevertheless, both serve the same function: They inform others, although not necessarily deliberately, as to the presence of, for example, predators or food.

Primates (and other animals) also use **displays** or more complicated, frequently elaborate combinations of behaviors in communication. For example, the exaggerated, **ritualized** courtship dances of many male birds, often enhanced by colorful plumage, are displays. Common gorilla displays are chest slapping and the tearing of vegetation to indicate threat. Likewise, an angry chimpanzee may charge an opponent with hair bristling, while screaming, waving arms, and tearing vegetation (Fig. 9-7).

Many nonhuman animals employ various vocalizations, body postures, and—to some degree—facial expressions, to transmit information relating to their emotional state or—again to some degree—the external environment (e.g., presence of predators). However, the array of communicative devices is much richer among primates, even though they do not use language in the manner of humans. Communication is important, for it truly is what makes social living possible. Through submissive gestures, aggression is reduced and physical violence is less likely. Likewise, friendly intentions and relationships are reinforced through physical contact and grooming. Indeed, it is in the so familiar methods of nonverbal communication that we humans can see ourselves in other primate species most clearly.

Reproduction In most primate species, sexual behavior is tied to the female's reproductive cycle, so that females are sexually receptive to males only when they are in estrus. Estrus is characterized by behavioral

FIGURE 9-7 Great ape displays. (*a*) gorilla at right is engaged in a chest slapping display; (*b*) male chimpanzee displays at public at San Francisco Zoo.

(a)

(b)

Jason

FIGURE 9-8 Estrous swelling of genital tissues in a female chimpanzee.

changes that indicate a female is receptive. In addition in many species, estrus is accompanied by swelling and changes in color of the skin around the genital area. These changes serve as visual cues of a female's readiness to mate (Fig. 9-8).

Bonding between males and females is not common among nonhuman primates. However, male and female savanna baboons sometimes form mating *consortships*. These temporary relationships last while the female is in estrus, and the two spend most of the time together, mating frequently. Moreover, lower-ranking baboon males frequently form "friendships" with females and occasionally may mate with them, although they are usually driven away by higher-ranking males when the female is receptive.

Mating consortships are sometimes seen in chimpanzees and are particularly common among bonobos. In fact, a male and female bonobo may spend several weeks primarily in the company of one another. During this time, they mate often, even when the female is not in estrus. These relationships of longer duration are not typical of chimpanzee (*troglodytes*) males and females.

Such a male-female bond may result in increased reproductive success for both sexes. For the male, there is the increased likelihood that he will be the father of any infant the female conceives. At the same time, the female potentially gains protection from predators or others of her group, and perhaps assistance in caring for offspring she may already have.

Mothers and Infants The basic social unit among all primates is the female and her infants (Fig. 9-9). Except in those species in which

(a)

(b)

FIGURE 9-9 Primate mothers with young. (*a*) patas monkey; (*b*) orangutan; (*c*) chimpanzee mother with infant and adolescent offspring.

(c)

monogamy or **polyandry** occurs, males do not participate as members of the mother-infant social unit. Observations both in the field and in captivity suggest that the mother-offspring core provides the overall social grouping with its stability.

The mother-infant bond, one of the most basic themes running throughout primate social relations, begins at birth. Although the exact nature of the bonding process is not fully known, there appear to be very powerful innate factors that strongly attract the female to her infant, if she herself has had sufficiently normal experiences with her own mother. This does not mean that primate mothers (especially anthropoids) possess innate knowledge of how to care for an infant. Indeed, they do not. Monkeys and apes raised in captivity without contact with their own mothers not only do not know how to care for a newborn, they may be afraid of it and attack and kill it. Even if they do not directly attack the infant, they may kill it indirectly through mishandling or improper nursing.

The crucial role played by primate mothers was clearly demonstrated by the Harlows (1959), who raised some infant monkeys with surrogate mothers fashioned from wire or a combination of wire and cloth. Other monkeys were raised in isolation with no mothers at all. In one experiment, infants retained an attachment to their cloth-covered surrogate mother (Fig. 9-10). But those raised with no mother were incapable of forming lasting affectional ties. These deprived monkeys sat passively in their cages and stared vacantly into space. None of the motherless males ever successfully copulated, and those females who were (somewhat artificially) impregnated, either paid little attention to offspring or reacted aggressively toward them (Harlow and Harlow, 1961). The point is, monkeys reared in isolation were denied opportunities to *learn* the

POLYANDRY A mating system wherein a female continuously associates with more than one male (usually two or three) with whom she mates. Among nonhuman primates, this type of pattern is seen only in marmosets and tamarins.

FIGURE 9-10 An infant rhesus macaque clings to the cloth mother, ignoring the wire mother.

rules of social behavior. Moreover, and just as important, they were denied the all important physical contact so necessary for normal primate psychological and emotional development.

The importance of a normal relationship with the mother is demonstrated by field studies as well. From birth, infant primates are able to cling to their mother's fur, and they are in more or less constant physical contact with her for several months. During this critical period, the infant develops a closeness with the mother that, as we saw in Chapter 8, does not always end with weaning. This closeness is often maintained throughout life (especially among some Old World monkeys and chimpanzees). It is reflected in grooming behavior that continues between mother and offspring even after the children reach adulthood and have infants of their own.

Aggressive and Affiliative Behaviors   In primate societies, there is a constant interplay between aggression, which can lead to group disruption, and **affiliative** behaviors that promote group cohesion. As we have already discussed, both males and females engage in aggressive behaviors in competitive situations. Although aggressive behavior ranges from threatening gestures to the outright killing of an individual, the latter is relatively rare. This is because the use of various displays and the presence of dominance hierarchies serve to regulate behavior in ways that frequently prevent actual violence from occurring.

Between groups, aggression occurs in the defense of **territories**. Primate groups are associated with a *home range*. Within the home range is a portion called the **core area**, which contains the highest concentration of predictable resources, and where the group may most frequently be found. Although portions of the home range may overlap with the home range of one or more other groups, core areas of adjacent groups do not overlap. The core area can also be said to be a group's territory, and it is the portion of the home range that is usually defended against intrusion by others. However, in some species, such as chimpanzees, other areas of the home range may also be defended. Whatever area is defended, this portion is termed the *territory*.

Beginning in 1974, Jane Goodall and her colleagues witnessed at least five unprovoked and brutal attacks by groups of chimpanzees (usually males) upon lone individuals. To explain these attacks, it is necessary to point out that by 1973 the original Gombe community had divided into two distinct groups. The larger group was located in the north of the original home range. The smaller offshoot group established itself in the southern portion, effectively denying the others access to part of their former territory.

By 1977, all seven males and an older female of the splinter group were either known or suspected to have been killed. All observed incidents involved several animals who brutally attacked lone individuals. Although it is not possible to know exactly what were the motives of the attackers, it was clear that they intended to incapacitate their victims (Goodall, 1986). It is also likely that these attacks were territorially motivated.

AFFILIATIVE   Pertaining to associations between individuals. Affiliative behaviors—such as grooming—reinforce bonds between individuals.

TERRITORIES   A group's or individual's territory is the area that will be aggressively protected against intrusion, particularly by other members of the same species.

CORE AREA   The portion of a home range containing the highest concentration of resources.

Goodall has suggested that these attacks strongly imply that, although chimpanzees do not possess language and do not wage war as we know it, they do exhibit behaviors that could be considered precursors to war.

> The chimpanzee, as a result of a unique combination of strong affiliative bonds between adult males on the one hand and an unusually hostile and violently aggressive attitude toward nongroup individuals on the other, has clearly reached a stage where he stands at the very threshold of human achievement in destruction, cruelty, and planned intergroup conflict. If ever he develops the power of language—and, as we have seen, he stands close to that threshold, too—might he not push open the door and wage war with the best of us? (Goodall, 1986, p. 534.)

While it is undeniably true that some primates are capable of extreme violence, we must not overlook the *affiliative* behaviors seen in all species. Although aggression is useful in maintaining order within the group and protecting either individuals or group resources, it is also enormously destructive and can lead to death. Affiliative behaviors serve then to reduce levels of aggression—by defusing potentially dangerous situations, by reinforcing bonds between individuals, and by promoting group cohesion.

Behaviors that promote bonding and group cohesion are seen in numerous contexts, such as reconciliation, consolation, and simple amicable interactions between friends and relatives. Most such behaviors involve physical contact, and indeed, as we have already discussed, physical contact is one of the most important factors in primate development, and it is crucial in promoting peaceful relationships in primate social groupings (Fig. 9-11).

Following a conflict, chimpanzee opponents frequently move, within minutes, to reconcile (de Waal, 1982). Reconciliation takes many forms, including hugging, kissing, and grooming. Even uninvolved chimps may take part, grooming one or both participants, or forming their own

FIGURE 9-11 Male chimpanzee (at left) touches outstretched hand of crouching female in a gesture of reassurance. Note infant clinging to female's chest.

grooming parties. Indeed, grooming is a crucial component of reconciliatory behavior. In addition, bonobos use sex to promote group cohesion, restore peace after conflicts, and relieve tension within the group (de Waal, 1987; 1989).

Interpersonal relationships are crucial to nonhuman primates, and the bonds between individuals can last a lifetime. These relationships serve a variety of functions. For one thing, individuals of many species form alliances in which one supports another against a third. Alliances, or *coalitions* as they are also called, can be used to enhance the status of members. At Gombe, the male chimpanzee Figan achieved *alpha* status because of support from his brother (Goodall, 1986, p. 424). In fact, chimpanzees rely so heavily upon coalitions and are so skillful politically that an entire book, appropriately entitled *Chimpanzee Politics* (de Waal, 1982), is devoted to the topic.

Altruism, or behavior that benefits another but involves some risk or sacrifice to the performer, is seen in many primates species. Adoption of orphans is seen as altruistic behavior and is known to exist at least in macaques and baboons, and it is common in chimpanzees.

Primate Cultural Behavior　One important trait that makes primates, and especially chimpanzees and bonobos, attractive as models for behavior in early hominids may be called *cultural behavior*. Although many cultural anthropologists and others prefer to use the term *culture* to refer specifically to human activities, most biological anthropologists feel it is appropriate to use the term in discussion of nonhuman primates as well.

Undeniably, there are many aspects of culture that are uniquely human, and one must be cautious in interpreting nonhuman animal behavior. But, at the same time, we feel it is important to recognize that humans are products of the same evolutionary forces that have produced other species. As such, humans can be expected to exhibit some of the same *behavioral patterns*. However, due to increased brain size and learning capacities, humans express many characteristics to greater degree. We would argue that the *aptitude for culture*, as a means of adapting to the natural environment, is one such characteristic.

Cultural behavior is *learned* behavior, and it is passed from generation to generation—not biologically, but through learning. While humans *teach* their young, free-ranging nonhuman primates do not appear to do so, at least not deliberately. However, all mammals are capable of learning, and primates as a group possess this capacity to a greater degree than other mammals. We have already mentioned that primate infants, through observing their mothers and others, learn about appropriate behaviors as well as food items and so on. They also learn to use and modify objects to achieve certain ends in the same way. In turn, their own offspring observe their activities and what emerges is a *cultural tradition*, which may eventually come to typify an entire group or even a species.

Two famous examples of cultural behavior were seen in a *provisioned* group of Japanese macaques on Koshima Island. In 1952, Japanese researchers began provisioning the 22-member troop with sweet potatoes. The following year, a young female named Imo began washing her potatoes in a freshwater stream prior to eating them. Within three years, sev-

FIGURE 9-12 Macaque washing potatoes.

eral others had adopted the practice, but had switched from using fresh water to taking their potatoes to the ocean nearby. Perhaps they liked the salt seasoning (Fig. 9-12).

In 1956, the Koshima primatologists began scattering wheat grains onto the sandy beach, and again Imo introduced a novel behavior. Instead of picking out the wheat grains one at a time (as the researchers had expected), Imo picked up handfuls of grain and sand and dropped them together into the water. The sand sank, the wheat kernels floated, and ingenious Imo simply scooped them off the water and ate them. Just as with potato washing, others imitated Imo's technique until the new behavior eventually became common throughout the troop.

The Japanese researchers proposed that dietary habits and food preferences are learned, and that the potato washing and wheat floating were examples of nonhuman culture. Because these practices arose as innovative solutions to problems and were imitated by others until they became traditions, they were seen as containing elements of human culture.

Among chimpanzees, we see more elaborate examples of cultural behavior in the form of *tool use*. This point is very important, for traditionally, tool use and language were both said to be traits that set humans apart from other animals.

Chimpanzees insert stems and grass blades into termite mounds in a practice primatologists call "termite fishing" (Fig. 9-13). When the termites seize the stem, the chimpanzee withdraws it and eats the attached insects. Chimpanzees modify some of their stems by stripping the leaves (in effect, manufacturing a tool from the natural material). Chimpanzees, to some extent, can alter objects to a "regular and set pattern" and have been observed preparing objects for later use at an out-of-sight location (Goodall, 1986). For example, a chimp will very carefully select a piece of vine, bark, twig, or palm frond and modify it by removing leaves or other

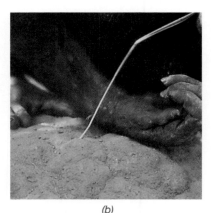

FIGURE 9-13 (*a*) Chimp termiting; (*b*) closeup of chimp hands while termiting.

extraneous material, then break off portions until it is the proper length. Chimps have also been seen making these tools even before the termite mound is in sight.

All this preparation has several implications. Firstly, the chimpanzees are engaged in an activity that prepares them for a future (not immediate) task at a location spatially removed, which implies planning and forethought. Secondly, attention to shape and size of raw material indicates that chimpanzee toolmakers have a preconceived idea of what the finished product needs to be in order to be useful. To produce a tool, even a simple tool, based upon a concept, is an extremely complex behavior. Such behavior was previously believed by scientists to be the exclusive domain of humans but now we must question this very basic assumption.

Chimps also crumple and chew handfuls of leaves that they dip into the hollow of a tree where water has accumulated. Then they suck the water from their "leaf sponge," water that otherwise would have been inaccessible to them. Leaves are also used to wipe substances from fur, twigs are sometimes used as toothpicks, stones may be used as weapons, and various objects, such as branches and stones, may be dragged or rolled to enhance displays. Indeed, chimpanzees show the greatest frequency and diversity of tool-using behavior of any nonhuman animal.

At Bossou, Guinea (Africa), observers Sugiyama and Koman (1979) watched chimpanzees crack nuts between two stones. The authors believe this nut-cracking behavior "is highly suggestive of early man's stone-tool culture," and perhaps it is. However, it is important to note that neither the hammer stone nor the platform stone was deliberately manufactured.*

Nut cracking with stones has not been observed in East African chimpanzees, which is very interesting in itself for it suggests regional cultural variation much the same as that seen in human groups.

PRIMATE COGNITIVE ABILITIES

As we have already seen, primates are extremely intelligent as demonstrated by their complicated social interactions and problem-solving abilities. Indeed, the use of tools represents solutions to such problems as how to get termites out of their earthen mounds, or how to gain access to water in difficult places.

Although numerous studies have demonstrated the problem-solving abilities of nonhuman primates, probably no research has had the impact, certainly on the general public, that the language acquisition studies have had. As already shown, all animals communicate through a variety of modalities including scent, vocal-auditory, touch, and visual (gestures, facial expressions, and body posture). However, the amount and kinds of information they are able to convey is limited.

---

*Observers of nonhuman primates rarely distinguish *natural objects used as tools* from *modified objects deliberately manufactured* for specific purposes. The term "tool" is usually employed in both cases.

In most cases, nonhuman communication deals with the emotional state of the animal (anger, fear, and so on). Nonhuman animals do not convey information regarding events, objects, or other animals that are removed in space or time. They usually have a limited repertoire of signals, which are repeatedly used in a variety of contexts. For example, when a startled baboon barks, its fellow baboons know only that it is startled. What they don't know is what startled it, and they can only ascertain this by looking around. In other words, the bark does not specifically refer to whatever elicited it. Although some nonhuman primates (e.g., vervets) appear to have specific vocalizations for particular categories of predator (e.g., snake, bird of prey), in general nonhuman primate communication is said to be a *closed system* of communication.

Human communication, on the other hand, is said to be an *open system*. Humans use *language*, a set of either written or spoken symbols that refer to concepts, other humans, objects, and so on. This set of symbols is said to be arbitrary in that the symbol itself has no relationship with whatever it represents. For example, the English word *tree* when written or spoken neither looks nor sounds like the thing it represents. Moreover, humans can recombine their linguistic symbols in an infinite number of ways to create new meanings, and we can use language to refer to events, places, objects, and people far removed in both space and time. For these reasons, humans are said to use an open system of communication, which in turn is based upon the human ability to think symbolically.

Language, as distinct from other forms of communication, has been considered a uniquely human achievement, but work with captive apes has raised doubts about that supposition. While many people were skeptical about the capacity of nonhuman primates to use language, reports from psychologists who work with apes, especially chimpanzees, leave little doubt that these apes learn to read signs and use them to communicate with their trainers, with companions in their own group, and even to sign to themselves. Most notable is their ability to pass the signs on to other members of their species.

We should point out that no mammal, other than humans, has the ability to speak. The fact that apes cannot acquire this skill seems to have little to do with intelligence. Rather, researchers have pointed to anatomical differences in the vocal apparatus to explain why humans speak and apes do not.

Because of failed attempts at teaching young chimpanzees to speak, psychologists Beatrice and Allen Gardner designed a study to test language capabilities in chimpanzees by teaching an infant female named Washoe to use ASL (American sign language for the deaf). Beginning in 1966, the Gardners began teaching Washoe signs in the same way parents would teach a deaf infant (Fig. 9-14). In just over three years, Washoe had acquired at least 132 signs. "She asked for goods and services, and she also asked questions about the world of objects and events around her" (Gardner, et al., 1989, p. 6).

Years later, an infant chimpanzee named Loulis, was placed in Washoe's care. Researchers wanted to know if Loulis would acquire signing skills from Washoe and other chimpanzees in the study group. Within just eight days Loulis began to imitate the signs of others. Moreover,

FIGURE 9-14 Washoe signing "hat" when being questioned about a woolen hat.

Washoe also deliberately taught Loulis some signs. For example, teaching him to sit "... Washoe placed a small plastic chair in front of Loulis, and then signed CHAIR/SIT to him several times in succession, watching him closely throughout" (Fouts, 1989, p. 290).

There have been other chimpanzee training experiments. The chimp, Sara, for instance, was taught by Professor David Premack to recognize plastic chips as symbols for various objects. The chips did not resemble the objects they represented. For example, the chip that represented an apple was neither round nor red. Another chimp, Lana, worked with a specially designed computer keyboard with chips attached to keys. After six months, Lana recognized symbols for 30 words and was able to ask for food and answer questions through the machine (Rumbaugh, 1977).

Dr. Francine Patterson, who taught ASL to Koko, a female gorilla, claims that Koko uses more than 500 signs. Furthermore, Michael, an adult male also involved in the gorilla study, has a considerable sign vocabulary, and the two gorillas communicate with each other via signs.

Questions have been raised about this type of experimental work. Do the apes really understand the signs they learn? Are they merely imitating their trainers? Do they learn that a symbol is a name for an object, or simply that executing a symbol will produce a desired object? There are also questions about their use of grammar, especially when they combine more than just a few "words" to communicate.

In any event, psychologists in charge of these projects are now convinced that apes are capable of employing signs to communicate with their companions and with humans. From an evolutionary point of view, these experiments may suggest clues to the origins of human language. In any event, there is now abundant evidence to suggest that humans are not the only species capable of some degree of symbolic thought, and it seems clear that the distinctions between humans and other species are not as clear-cut as most have previously thought (and hoped).

THE PRIMATE CONTINUUM

For decades, behavioral psychology taught that animal behavior represents nothing more than a series of conditioned responses to specific stimuli. (This perspective is very convenient for those who wish to use nonhuman animals, for whatever purposes, and remain free of guilt.) Fortunately, this attitude has begun to change in recent years to reflect a growing awareness that humans, although in many ways unquestionably unique, are nevertheless part of a **biological continuum**.

Where do humans fit, then, in this biological continuum? Are we at the top? The answer depends upon the criteria used, and we must also bear in mind that evolution is not a goal-directed process. Certainly, we are the most intelligent species, if we define intelligence in terms of problem-solving abilities and abstract thought. However, if we look more closely, we recognize that the differences between ourselves and our primate relatives, especially chimpanzees, are quantitative not qualitative.

Although human brains are absolutely and relatively larger, neurological processes are functionally the same. The necessity of close bonding with at least one parent, and the need for physical contact are the same. Developmental stages and dependence on learning are strikingly similar. Indeed, even in the capacity for cruelty and aggression combined with compassion, tenderness, and altruism exhibited by chimpanzees, we see a close parallel to the dichotomy between "good" and "evil" so long recognized in ourselves. The main difference between how chimpanzees and humans express these qualities, (and therefore the dichotomy) is one of degree. Humans are much more adept at both, and humans can reflect upon their behavior in ways chimpanzees cannot. While chimpanzees do not understand the suffering they inflict upon others, humans do. Likewise, while an adult chimpanzee may sit next to and protect a dying relative or friend, it does not appear to feel the intense grief and sense of loss to the extent a human normally does.

In order to arrive at any understanding of "human nature," then, it is vastly important to recognize that many of our behaviors are but elaborate extensions of those of our hominid ancestors and close primate relatives. We share 98 percent of our DNA with chimpanzees. The fact that so many of us prefer to bask in the warmth of the "sun belt" with literally millions of others reflects our heritage as social animals adapted to life in the tropics. Likewise, it is no mistake that industry has invested millions of dollars in the development of low calorie, artificial sweeteners. The "sweet tooth" so many humans are afflicted with is a direct result of our earlier primate ancestors' predilection for high-energy sugar contained in desirably sweet, ripe fruit.

BIOLOGICAL CONTINUUM When expressions of phenomenon continuously grade into one another so that there are no discrete categories, they are said to exist on a continuum. Color is such a phenomenon. The term *biological continuum* refers to the fact that biological organisms are related through common ancestry and that behaviors and traits seen in one species are also seen in others to varying degrees.

The fact that humans are part of an evolutionary continuum is the entire basis for animal research aimed at benefiting our species. Yet, even with our growing awareness of the similarities we share, we continue to cage nonhuman primates with little regard for the very needs they share with us. In fact, many officials of the National Institutes of Health (NIH) and others in the biomedical community strongly argue that the psychological needs of nonhuman animals (including primates) cannot be determined by human keepers. Indeed, some have argued that nonhuman primates do not have psychological needs.

Clearly, humans have benefited from biomedical research using primates and other animals. It is just as clear that such research will continue. However, we would argue that nonhuman primates should be maintained in social groupings and that habitat enrichment programs should be introduced. It would seem the very least we can do for our close relatives, from whom we continue to derive so many benefits.

PRIMATE CONSERVATION

Probably the greatest challenge facing primatologists today is the urgent need to preserve in the wild what remains of free-ranging primate species. Without massive changes in public opinion and in the economics of countries with surviving rainforests, it will not be long before there are only few nonhuman primates left in the world. Indeed, over half of all living nonhuman primates are now in jeopardy and some are facing almost immediate extinction in the wild.

Population estimates of free-ranging primates are difficult to obtain, but some species (hapalemur, diadem sifaka, aye-aye, lion tamarin, muriqui, red colobus subspecies, lion-tailed macaque, and mountain gorilla) now number only in the few hundreds. Others are believed to be represented in the wild by a few thousand (agile mangabey, mentawi langur, red colobus subspecies, moloch gibbon, Kloss' gibbon, orangutan, lowland gorilla, chimpanzee, and bonobo) (Mittermeier and Cheney, 1987).

There are three basic reasons for the worldwide depletion of nonhuman primates: habitat destruction, hunting, and live capture either for export or local trade. Actually, underlying all three causes is one major factor: unprecedented human population growth (see Chapter 14), which is occurring at a faster rate in developing countries than in the developed world.

Approximately 90 percent of all primates live in the tropical forests of Africa, Asia, and Central and South America, the same areas where many of the world's developing countries are found. Currently, these countries are cutting their forests at a rate of 25 to 50 million acres per year (Mittermeier, 1982). Put another way: Worldwide we lose one acre every second! In Brazil alone, only between 1 and 5 percent of the original Atlantic forest remains, the rest having been destroyed mostly within the last 20 to 30 years (Mittermeier and Cheney, 1987).

Because the rainforests are viewed as natural resources to be developed, the destruction will undoubtedly continue. Moreover, we must point out that it is partly the demand for tropical hardwoods (e.g., mahogany, teak, and rosewood) in the United States, Europe, and Japan that creates the market for rainforest products.

Hunting of primates occurs for numerous reasons, but chiefly they serve as an important source of food for peoples in parts of West and Central Africa and South America. In these areas, thousands of primates are killed annually to feed growing human populations. Primates are also killed for commercial products, such as skins, skulls, and other body parts. Although it is illegal for tourists from the United States and several other countries to return home with such products, the trade flourishes.

Primates have also been captured live for zoos, biomedical research, and the exotic pet trade. This practice peaked in the mid-twentieth century and much of it involved the rhesus macaque for use in medical research. Live capture has declined dramatically since the implementation of the Convention on Trade in Endangered Species of Wild Flora and Fauna (CITES) in 1973. Currently, 87 countries have signed this treaty, agreeing not to allow trade in species listed by CITES as being endangered. However, even some countries that are CITES members are still occasionally involved in the illegal primate trade (e.g., Japan and Belgium, among others).

Fortunately, steps are being taken to ensure the survival of some species. Many developing countries, such as Costa Rica and the Malagasy Republic (Madagascar), are designating national parks and other reserves for the protection of natural resources, including primates. It is only through such practices as these, and through educational programs, that many primate species have a chance of escaping extinction, at least in the immediate future.

If you are in your twenties or thirties, you will probably live to hear of the extinction of some of our marvelously unique and clever cousins. Many more will undoubtedly slip away unnoticed. Tragically, this will occur, in most cases, before we have even had the opportunity to get to know them.

Each species on earth is the current result of a unique set of evolutionary events that, over millions of years, have produced a finely adapted component of a diverse ecosystem. When it becomes extinct, that adaptation and that part of biodiversity is lost forever. What a tragedy indeed it will be if, through our own mismanagement and greed, we awake to a world without chimpanzees, mountain gorillas, or the tiny, exquisite lion tamarin. If and when this day comes, we truly will have lost a part of ourselves and we surely will be the poorer for it.

SUMMARY

We have discussed many aspects of nonhuman primate behavior, such as social organization and dominance hierarchies, communication, reproduction, intergroup relationships (including mothers and infants), aggression, friendship, culture (in the form of tool use), and intelligence. These behaviors have been treated, to considerable extent, from an ecological perspective; specifically, we have attempted to show what features of the environment are most likely to be important in shaping primate social behavior.

Group size and composition are influenced by such environmental components as diet, resource availability, predators, and so on. Moreover, many behavioral elements are seen as the results of natural selection; that is, they act to promote increased likelihood of survival and reproduction. Therefore, individuals, ideally, should behave in ways that will maximize their own reproductive success relative to others. Although this does not imply that in mammals and especially primates, there are genes for specific behaviors, it does suggest that genes may have mediating effects upon behavior—perhaps through such products as hormones.

We have emphasized that humans are part of a biological continuum that includes all the primates. It is this evolutionary relationship, then, that accounts for many of the behaviors we have in common with prosimians, monkeys, and apes. Lastly, we briefly discussed the problems facing nonhuman primates today and some of the steps being taken to protect those populations remaining in the wild.

QUESTIONS FOR REVIEW

1. What factors should be considered if one approaches the study of nonhuman primate behavior from an ecological perspective?
2. What are some of the environmental factors believed to influence group size and social organization? Give two examples.
3. How could multimale, multifemale groupings be advantageous to species living in areas where predation pressure is high?
4. How may solitary foraging be advantageous to primates? Discuss two examples.
5. Define *sociobiology*. What is the main premise of this theory?
6. List two objections to sociobiological theories.
7. How may genetic factors influence behavior?
8. Discuss a primate behavior that has traditionally been used as an example of sociobiological theory.
9. What are reproductive strategies and what is their basic goal?
10. Primates are said to be *K-selected*. What is meant by this? What is *r-selection*? Give an example of r-selection.
11. Explain male and female differences with regard to parental investment.
12. What are *dominance hierarchies*? What is their function in primate groups?
13. What is believed to be the primary benefit of being high-ranking? What are three factors that influence an individual's rank in a group?
14. What is grooming? Why is it so important in many primate species; that is, what functions does it serve?
15. Discuss three ways nonhuman primates can communicate information to other group members. Name at least two "threat gestures."
16. Name two ways in which nonhuman primates communicate reassurance.

17. What is meant by an *open system of communication*? How does it differ from a *closed system*?
18. What is seen as the basic social unit among all primates? Why is it so important?
19. Discuss an example of between-group aggression. What is thought to have motivated the violence between two groups of chimpanzees at Gombe?
20. Discuss two examples of nonhuman primate cultural behavior. Why is our discovery of these behaviors important to studies of early human evolution?
21. Discuss the language acquisition studies using chimpanzees and gorillas. What are the implications of this research?
22. What do we mean when we state that humans are a part of a biological continuum? How does the view expressed in this statement differ from traditional views expressed by most people?
23. Discuss the major problems facing wild populations of nonhuman primates today.

The study of primate social behavior, as a primary component of *primatology* in the United States, has been largely the domain of physical anthropologists. Indeed, primatology is one of the major subdisciplines of physical anthropology.

While anthropologists occasionally have studied primate behavior in *captive* situations, their primary focus has been collection of behavioral data in natural, free-ranging, habitats. Specialized studies in a laboratory setting (such as the language studies discussed in Chapter 9) or sometimes in zoo environments are usually undertaken by psychologists. Increasingly, in the last few years, interdisciplinary research has been originated in which methodologies developed in free-ranging contexts are applied to studies of captive animals. Moreover, such research holds the promise of comparing behaviors seen in the wild with those obtained in captivity—so to draw more general conclusions.

FIGURE 1
Dr. Jane Goodall records a chimpanzee interaction at Gombe National Park, Tanzania.

FIGURE 2
Yahaya Alamasi, a member of the senior field staff at Gombe National Park. Dr. Goodall and other primatologists rely heavily upon trained observers from neighboring villages and towns. This practice not only promotes good relations with neighboring communities but also increases interest and awareness of wildlife in African localities.

FIGURE 3
Dian Fossey relaxes with habituated group of mountain gorillas.

FIGURE 4
Shirley Strum, shown doing research in Kenya, observing a group of savanna baboons.

Captive Primate Studies— ChimpanZoo

The ChimpanZoo project was initiated by Dr. Jane Goodall and the Jane Goodall Institute in 1984. The initial goals were numerous, but chief among them was to establish a collaborative effort between zoo personnel and university faculty and students aimed at learning more about chimpanzee behavior in captivity.

Originally, Dr. Goodall developed the plan in response to numerous student inquiries regarding student research at Gombe. Because such studies were largely impossible, ChimpanZoo was seen as a way to involve students, while at the same time providing much needed information regarding captive chimpanzee behavior as well as their psychological and emotional needs.

Currently 14 zoos and the Friends of Washoe project at Central Washington University are active ChimpanZoo members. Participation involves cooperation between zoo personnel (keepers, docents, and research staff) and local university faculty and students. Zoo researchers and university faculty train students, keepers, and docents to collect and analyze behavioral data. Zoo personnel provide critical information regarding each animal, its history, personality, and any other relevant information.

The success of ChimpanZoo can be measured in the opportunities for students and zoo observers to participate in primate research, as well as to get to know their study subjects as individuals. The sense of reward is heightened when observers realize for the first time that their subjects recognize them, and in time, they often come to greet them as they arrive. Moreover, zoo personnel often report an increased familiarity with their animals, and they continuously report new findings revealing novel facets of their chimpanzees' personalities.

Of course, this increased knowledge has had numerous positive benefits for the chimpanzees themselves. As these captive chimps have become better known to their human caretakers, their needs are also better understood and are more likely to be met. Moreover, these chimpanzees are helping to give an even more complete picture of chimpanzee behavior than that already derived from their free-ranging counterparts.

There are numerous ways to study nonhuman animals. One method is to observe a *group* and describe (either by taking notes or speaking into a tape recorder) as completely as possible, everything that occurs. Another technique is to "follow" one animal, the "focal" animal, describing everything it does. Still another frequently used method involves taking observations of a focal animal at precise intervals, usually on the minute. This last procedure is attractive, for it allows the data to be quantified, facilitating statistical analysis. ChimpanZoo observers follow a focal animal for fifteen minutes, using a series of behavior codes to record whatever the animal does at precisely one-minute intervals.

FIGURE 5
ChimpanZoo student observer in discussion with primate supervisor at San Francisco Zoo.

In order to do this type of research, observers must know the animal well. Such familiarity facilitates interpreting sometimes difficult-to-assess behaviors. Moreover, this approach requires the development of an *ethogram*, or detailed list and description of behaviors. Many animal researchers devise a list of codes to refer to specific behaviors. These codes can be written or keyed directly into a laptop computer.

In the ChimpanZoo project, overall observations are coded within general contexts such as public orientation, agonistic, and submissive behavior. Within each context, there are more specific behavioral codes. For example, within the agonistic context, aggressive display, approach, arm threat, bite, and copulation/mount are all possible. For the submissive context, arm stretch/extend hand, appease, bob, and avoidance are among the appropriate responses.

FIGURE 6
Student observer coding chimpanzee behavior on a ChimpanZoo coding sheet, San Francisco Zoo.

FIGURE 7
Oakland Zoo docent records behavioral data using a specially designed software package.

FIGURE 8
Laptop computer used for ChimpanZoo data collection. Data are automatically stored, facilitating later analysis.

Habitat enrichment has become the goal of most zoos in recent years. Partly, this is done to create more attractive and interesting exhibits to encourage public interest. Even more important, however, has been the changing role of zoos in the past decade. In the past, zoo animals were kept in bare cages designed for easy viewing by the public and easy cleaning for keepers. Today, zoos are more and more seen as repositories for many endangered species, whose only hope for survival—at least in the short term—is captive breeding programs. As zoos become part of species survival plans, it is incumbent upon them to provide naturalistic habitats in which their animals can and will breed. This approach has served not only to provide the viewing public with more interesting and attractive exhibits, but more importantly, it has immeasurably improved the lives of captive animals.

FIGURE 9
Example of a traditional, nonenriched zoo habitat. This cage will house this siamang mated pair for years, perhaps decades. As their young are successively raised to maturity (about 6 years of age), they are placed in other zoos.

FIGURE 10
An enriched, indoor habitat for silver leaf eating monkeys at the Bronx Zoo's Asian Jungle World exhibit in New York.

Within the captive habitats, through information obtained from free-ranging studies, environments can be further enriched. Most especially, the animals can be kept engaged and stimulated by providing challenges in food-searching and object manipulation (the latter particularly important in chimpanzees).

FIGURE 11
A chimpanzee using a tool for removing termites, shown here at Gombe National Park.

FIGURE 12
A captive chimpanzee (at the Oakland Zoo) using the same termiting technique.

187

FIGURE 13

Chimpanzee at San Francisco Zoo inspects a barrel for food (honey or mustard). The chimp at left is holding a twig used for probing through holes. Captive chimps may spend hours engaged in such activities.

FIGURE 14

A chimpanzee at the Sacramento, California Zoo, also using a tool in the same manner as free-ranging animals.

HOMINID ORIGINS

CHAPTER 10

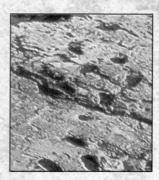

INTRODUCTION

In the three preceding chapters we have seen that humans are members of the primate order, and, more specifically, belong to the family, Hominidae (more colloquially referred to as "the hominids"). What, however, are the most distinctive features of our family, and—more to the present point—to about what date can we trace the origin of the hominids? In this and the next chapter we take up these questions by relating the history and interpretation of abundant and exciting finds from the African continent.

DEFINITION OF HOMINID

If any of the early hominoid fossils from the Miocene (discussed in Chapter 7) were to be defined as a *hominid*, the definition, necessarily, would have to be a dental one. Teeth and jaws are mostly what have been discovered from the Miocene in the period prior to 5 mya. However, dentition is not the only way to describe the special attributes of our particular evolutionary radiation and is certainly not the most distinctive of its later stages. Modern humans and our hominid ancestors are distinguished from our closest living relatives (the great apes) by more obvious features than relative jaw and tooth size. For example, scientists have pointed to such other hominid characteristics as large brain size, bipedal locomotion, and toolmaking behavior as being most significant in defining what makes a hominid a hominid. In this chapter, we will discuss all three of these distinctive attributes, but first we address the hominid toolmaking capacity.

Biocultural Evolution: Humans as Toolmakers

Although other primates do occasionally make tools (see Chapter 9), only hominids depend on culture for their survival. We and our hominid ancestors alone have the ability to "impose arbitrary form on the environment" (Holloway, 1969). For example, chimps who use termite sticks have a direct and immediate relationship with the raw material and purpose of the tool. Such is not the case in most human cultural behavior, which usually involves several steps, often quite arbitrarily removed from direct environmental context.

We are defining culture primarily as a mental process. The human mind (presumably the minds of at least some earlier hominids as well) has the unique capacity to *create* symbols. Humans, of course, also have the capacity to manipulate their environments in infinitely more complex ways than other animals. The simple human invention of a water-tight container, such as a hollowed-out gourd or an ostrich egg, is several orders of magnitude more complex than macaque or chimp "cultural" behavior.

Culture as a complex adaptive strategy has become central to human evolution and has acted as a potent selective force to mold our anatomical form over the last several million years. In the archeological record, early cultural behavior is seen as the preserved remains of stone implements, traces of a uniquely hominid activity. "The shaping of stone according to even the simplest plan is beyond the behavior of any ape or monkey" (Washburn, 1971, p. 105). Thus, when we find stone tools made to a standardized pattern, we know we have found a behavioral indicator of a hominid—and *only* hominid—adaptation. We are justified, then, in defining hominids as habitual toolmakers, *culturally dependent* animals, distinct in this respect from all other primates.

PALEOANTHROPOLOGY AS A MULTIDISCIPLINARY SCIENCE

In order to understand human evolution adequately, we need a broad base of information. The task of recovering and interpreting all the clues left by early hominids is the work of the paleoanthropologist. Paleoanthropology is defined as "the science of the study of early humans." As such, it is a diverse *multidisciplinary* pursuit seeking to reconstruct every bit of possible information concerning the dating, structure, behavior, and ecology of our hominid ancestors. In just the last few years, the study of early hominids has marshalled the specialized skills of many diverse scientific disciplines. Included primarily in this growing and exciting adventure are the geologist, archeologist, physical anthropologist, and paleoecologist. (See Table 10-1.)

The geologist, usually working with an anthropologist (often an archeologist), does the initial survey in order to locate potential early hominid sites. Many sophisticated techniques can contribute to this search, including aerial and satellite photography. Paleontologists may also be involved in this early search, for they can help find fossil beds containing faunal remains (where conditions are favorable for the preservation of such specimens as ancient pigs or baboons, conditions may also be favorable for the preservation of hominid remains). In addition, paleontologists can—through comparison with faunal sequences elsewhere—give quick estimates of the approximate age of sites without having to wait for the expensive and time-consuming **chronometric** analyses. In this way, fossil beds of the "right" geologic ages (that is, where hominid finds are most likely) can be identified.

CHRONOMETRIC *Chrono*: time *metric*: measure A dating technique that gives an estimate in actual number of years.

TABLE 10-1 Subdisciplines of Paleoanthropology		
PHYSICAL SCIENCES	**BIOLOGICAL SCIENCES**	**SOCIAL SCIENCES**
Geology	Physical anthropology	Archeology
Stratigraphy	Ecology	Cultural anthropology
Petrology (rocks, minerals)	Paleontology (fossil animals	Ethnography
Pedology (soils)	Palynology (fossil pollen)	Psychology
Geophysics	Primatology	Ethnoarcheology
Chemistry		
Geomorphology		
Taphonomy*		

*Taphonomy (*taphos*: dead) is the study of how bones and other materials come to be buried in the earth and preserved as fossils. A taphonomist studies such phenomena as the processes of sedimentation, action of streams, preservation properties of bone, and carnivore disturbance factors.

ARTIFACTS Traces of hominid behavior. Very old ones are usually made of stone.

Once potential areas of early hominid sites have been located, much more extensive surveying begins. At this point, the archeologists take over the search for hominid traces. We do not necessarily have to find the fossilized remains of early hominids (which will always be rare) to know they consistently occupied an ancient land surface. Behavioral clues, or **artifacts**, also inform us directly and unambiguously about early

FIGURE 10-1 Excavations in progress at Olduvai. This site is more than 1 million years old. It was located when a hominid ulna (arm bone) was found eroding out of the side of the gorge. Many artifacts and broken bones of other animals were also found at this site.

hominid occupation. Modifying rocks according to a consistent plan, or simply carrying them over fairly long distances, are behaviors characteristic of no other animal but a hominid. Therefore, when we see such behavioral evidence at a site, we know that hominids were once present there.

DATING METHODS

One of the key essentials of paleoanthropology is placing sites and fossils into a chronological framework. In other words, we want to know how old they are. How, then, do we date sites—or, more precisely, the geological strata in which sites are found? The question is both reasonable and important, so let us examine the dating techniques used by paleontologists, geologists, and paleoanthropologists.

Scientists use two kinds of dating for this purpose: relative and chronometric (which is also known as *absolute dating*). Relative dating methods tell you that something is older, or younger, than something else, but not how much. If, for example, a fossil cranium was found at a depth of 50 feet, and another cranium at 70 feet at the same site, we usually assume the cranium at 70 feet is older. We may not know the date (in years) of either one, but we would be able to infer a *relative* sequence. This method of dating is called **stratigraphy** and was one of the first techniques to be used by scholars working with the vast expanses of geologic time. Stratigraphy is based upon the law of superposition, which states that a lower stratum (layer) is older than a higher stratum. Given the fact that much of the earth's crust has been laid down by layer after layer of sedimentary rock, stratigraphy has been a valuable tool in reconstructing the history of earth and life on it.

STRATIGRAPHY Sequential layering of deposits.

Stratigraphic dating does, however, have a number of potential problems. Earth disturbances, such as volcanic activity, river action, and faulting may shift the strata or materials in them, and the chronology may thus be difficult or impossible to reconstruct. Furthermore, given the widely different rates of accumulation, the elapsed time of any stratum cannot be determined with much accuracy.

Another method of relative dating is *fluorine analysis*, which applies only to bone. Bones in the earth are exposed to seepage of groundwater that usually contains some fluorine. The longer a bone lies buried, the more fluorine it would incorporate during fossilization. Therefore, bones deposited at the same time in the same location should contain the same amount of fluorine.

The use of this technique by Professor Oakley of the British Museum in the early 1950s exposed the Piltdown hoax by demonstrating that the human skull was considerably older than the jaw ostensibly found with it (Weiner, 1955). Lying in the same location, the jaw and skull should have absorbed approximately the same quantity of fluorine. But the skull contained significantly more, meaning that, if it came from the same site, it had been deposited considerably earlier. Or, the two elements never really belonged together at all. The discrepancy of fluorine content led Oakley and others to a much closer examination of the bones, and they found that the jaw was not that of a hominid at all, but one of a juvenile orangutan! Clearly, then, someone had planted it at Piltdown, but who was the devious forger? To this day, no one knows for sure.

Unfortunately, fluorine is useful only with bones from the same location. Due to the differing concentration in groundwater, accumulation rates will vary from place to place. Also, some groundwater may not contain any fluorine. For these reasons, comparing fossils from different localities using fluorine analysis is impossible.

In both these techniques, stratigraphy and fluorine analysis, the age of the stratum or objects within them is impossible to calibrate. To determine age as precisely as possible, scientists have developed a variety of chronometric techniques, many based on the phenomenon of radioactive decay. The theory is quite simple: Certain radioactive isotopes of elements are unstable, disintegrate, and form an isotopic variant of another element. Since the rate of disintegration follows a predictable mathematical pattern, the radioactive material forms an accurate geologic clock. By measuring the amount of disintegration in a particular sample, techniques have been devised for dating the immense age of the earth (and moon rocks) as well as for material only a few hundred years old. Several techniques have been employed for a number of years and are now quite well known.

An important chronometric technique used in paleoanthropological research involves potassium 40 (^{40}K)—which produces argon 40 (^{40}Ar)—with a half-life of 1.3 billion years. That is, half the ^{40}K isotope changes to ^{40}Ar in 1.3 billion years. In another 1.3 billion years, half the remaining ^{40}K would be converted. Known as the K/Ar, or potassium-argon method, this procedure has been extensively used in dating materials in the 1 to 5 million year range, especially in East Africa. Organic material, such as bone, cannot be measured, but the rock matrix in which the fossilized bone is found can be.

Strata that provide the best samples for K/Ar are those that have been heated to an extremely high temperature, such as that generated by volcanic activity. When the sedimentary material is in a molten state, argon 40, a gas, is driven off. As the material cools and solidifies, potassium (^{40}K) continues to break down to ^{40}Ar, but now the gas is physically trapped inside the cooling material. In order to date the geologic material, it is reheated and the escaping gas is then measured. Potassium-argon has been used for dating very old events—such as the age of the earth—as well as those less than 100,000 years old (Dalrymple, 1972).

Another well-known chronometric technique popular with archeologists involves carbon 14 (^{14}C) with a half-life of 5730 years. This method has been used to date material as recent as a few hundred years and can be extended as far back as 75,000 years, although the probability of error rises rapidly after 40,000 years. The physical basis of this technique is also *radiometric*; that is, it is tied to the measurement of radioactive decay of an isotope (^{14}C) into another, stable, form (^{14}N and a beta particle). (See Fig. 10-2.) Radiocarbon dating has proven especially relevant for calibrating the latter stages of human evolution, including the Neandertals and the appearance of modern *Homo sapiens* (see Chapter 13).

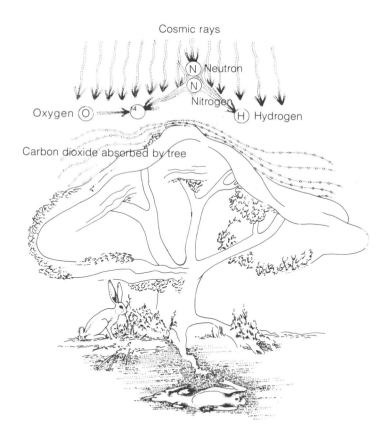

Cosmic rays

N Neutron

N

Nitrogen

Oxygen O → ^{14} H Hydrogen

Carbon dioxide absorbed by tree

FIGURE 10-2 Carbon-14 dating. Cosmic rays bombard the upper atmosphere, producing neutrons. When these collide with nitrogen, small amounts of ^{14}C are produced. The ^{14}C combines with oxygen to form carbon dioxide. The carbon dioxide-containing ^{14}C is absorbed by plants, and eventually animals feeding on the plants add ^{14}C to their bodies. When the plant or animal dies, it ceases to absorb ^{14}C and the ^{14}C changes back to nitrogen at a regular rate.

Other methods have also proven useful in dating early hominid sites. For example, *fission-track dating* is a chronometric technique that works on the basis of the regular fissioning of uranium atoms. When certain types of crystalline rocks are observed microscopically, the "tracks" left by the fission events can be counted, and an approximate age thus calibrated. *Bio-stratigraphy* is another relative technique based on fairly regular changes seen in the dentition and other anatomical structures in such groups as pigs, rodents, and baboons. This technique has proven helpful in cross-correlating the ages of various sites in both South and East Africa. A final type of dating, called *paleomagnetism*, is based on the shifting nature of the earth's geomagnetic pole. Although now oriented northward, the geomagnetic pole is known to have shifted several times in the past, and at times was oriented to the south. By examining magnetically charged particles encased in rock, geologists can determine the orientation of these ancient "compasses." One cannot derive a date in years from this particular technique, but it is used to "double-check" potassium-argon and fission-track determinations.

In fact, many of the techniques just discussed are used together to provide *independent* checks for dating important early hominid sites. Each technique has a degree of error, and only by *cross-correlating* the results can paleoanthropologists feel confident regarding chronological placement of the fossil and archeological remains they discover. This point is of highest importance, for a firm chronology forms the basis for making sound evolutionary interpretations (as discussed in the next chapter).

THE EAST AFRICAN RIFT VALLEY

Stretching along a trough of more than 1200 miles that extends through Ethiopia, Kenya, and Tanzania from the Red Sea in the north to the Serengeti Plain in the south is the eastern branch of the Great Rift Valley of Africa. This massive geological feature has been associated with mountain building, faulting, and vulcanism over the last several million years.

Because of these gigantic earth movements, earlier sediments that would otherwise have remained deeply buried were literally thrown to the surface, where they became exposed to the trained eye of the paleoanthropologist. Such movements have revealed Miocene beds in western Kenya, along the shores of Lake Victoria, where abundant remains of early hominoids have been found. In addition, Pliocene and Pleistocene sediments are also exposed all along the Rift Valley, and paleoanthropologists have in recent years made the most of this unique opportunity. These remains, ranging in time from early in the Pliocene and covering the first half of the Pleistocene (*circa* 4–1 mya) are generally simply referred to as **Plio-Pleistocene**.

More than exposing normally hidden deposits, rifting has stimulated volcanic activity, which in turn has provided the means of chronometrically dating (by potassium-argon and fission-track) many sites in East Africa. Unlike the other Plio-Pleistocene sites, located in South Africa, those along the Rift Valley are *datable* and have thus yielded much crucial information relevant to the precise chronology of early hominid evolution.

EAST AFRICAN HOMINID SITES

Earliest Traces

Between the later Miocene and the early Pliocene (from about 8 million until 4 million years ago) there currently is a gap in our knowledge. Little relevant fossil evidence has been recovered from this time period, but paleoanthropologists are well aware of two potentially productive areas in Kenya. These areas, each associated with a drainage system of a large lake within the Rift (Lake Baringo and Lake Turkana), are of the appropriate age and, in addition, have sediments that in many cases were highly favorable for fossilization. (See Figs. 10-3 and 10-5.)

Thus far, only a very few bits and pieces of individuals have been found. Prior to 4 mya none of these remains can definitely be attributed to the Hominidae, but can only generally be characterized as "hominoid." Nevertheless, given the reasonable likelihood of further discoveries, the

PLIO-PLEISTOCENE The time period including the Pliocene and the first half of the Pleistocene. For early hominids, currently covers the range 4–1 mya.

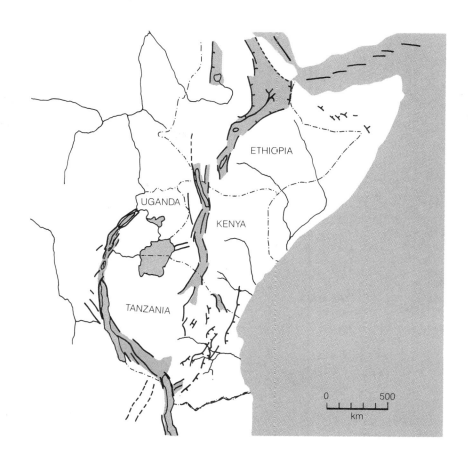

FIGURE 10-3 The East African Rift Valley system.

search goes on. In addition to knowing the best places to look, paleoanthropologists must also rely on some good luck. And, with a bit of luck, we surely will be able to begin to fill that vexing 4-million-year gap. Moreover, as shown below, the Turkana Basin has proven to be the most productive region in all of Africa for yielding hominid remains from the latter part of the Plio-Pleistocene (2.5–1.0 mya).

Laetoli

Located in northern Tanzania, Laetoli has yielded the oldest definitely confirmed *assemblage* (that is, a whole group) of early hominids. With numerous volcanic sediments in the vicinity, accurate K/Ar testing is possible and provides a date of 3.50–3.75 mya for this site.

Since systematic fossil recovery began in 1974 at Laetoli, 23 fossil hominid individuals have been found, consisting almost exclusively of jaws and teeth. In February, 1978, Mary Leakey announced a remarkable discovery at Laetoli: fossilized footprints embossed into an ancient volcanic bed more than 3.5 mya! Literally thousands of footprints have been found at this remarkable site, representing more than 20 different types of animals (Pliocene elephants, pigs, giraffes, antelopes, hyenas, and an abundance of hares). Several hominid footprints have also been found, including a trail more than 75 feet long, made by at least two, and perhaps three, individuals (Leakey and Hay, 1979). (See Fig. 10-4.)

Such discoveries of well-preserved hominid footprints are extremely important in furthering our understanding of human evolution. For the first time, we can make *definite* statements regarding locomotory pattern and stature of early hominids. Initial analysis of these early hominid footprints compared to modern humans suggests a stature of about 4 feet, 9 inches for the larger individual and 4 feet, 1 inch for the smaller individual, who made the trails seen in Fig. 10-4 (White, 1980). Studies of these impression patterns clearly show that the mode of locomotion of these hominids was fully bipedal and, further, *very* similar to modern humans (Day and Wickens, 1980). As we will discuss shortly, the development of **bipedal locomotion** is the most important defining characteristic of early hominid evolution. Some researchers, however, have concluded that these early hominids were not bipedal in quite the same way that modern humans are. From detailed comparisons with modern humans, estimates of step length, cadence, and speed of walking

BIPEDAL LOCOMOTION Walking habitually on two legs. Among primates, distinctive only of hominids. The most characteristic adaptive feature of the *entire* hominid line.

FIGURE 10-4 Laetoli hominid footprint trail, northern Tanzania. The trail on the left was made by one individual; the one on the right seems to have been formed by two individuals, the second stepping in the footprints of the first.

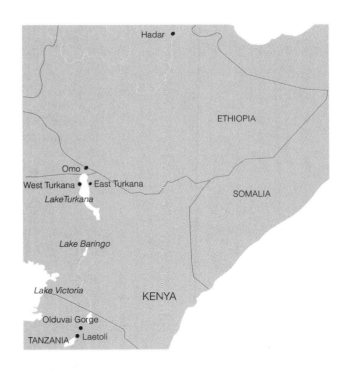

FIGURE 10-5 Early hominid localities in East Africa.

have been ascertained, indicating the Laetoli hominids were moving in a "strolling" fashion with a short stride (Chateris, et al., 1981).

Hadar (Ha-Dar') (Afar Triangle)

Potentially one of the most exciting areas for future research in East Africa is the Afar Triangle of northeastern Ethiopia, where the Red Sea, Rift Valley, and Gulf of Aden all intersect. A joint American-French team led by Don Johanson and the French paleontologist Maurice Taieb began intensive field work in this area in 1973. Concentrating on a 42 km² area in the central Afar, called the Hadar, paleoanthropologists have found remarkably well-preserved, extremely thick geological beds. Initial K/Ar dating suggested an age of up to 3.6 million years for the older hominid fossils and 2.5 million years for the upper beds. These dates must be considered provisional until corroborated by other techniques and additional laboratories.

In fact, there is considerable debate regarding the dates of the earlier beds at the Hadar. Many researchers, pointing to correlation of specific volcanic events (i.e., eruptions) as well as paleomagnetic and biostratigraphic data, have "shaved" up to 400,000 years from the 3.6 million year determination (thus yielding an estimate of 3.2 million years).

However, opinion still varies. The proposed correlation of the volcanic materials across northeastern Africa is not accepted by all researchers (e.g., Aronson, et al., 1983). Moreover, the bio-stratigraphy is also subject to differing interpretations (White, 1983). A 400,000-year discrepancy may not seem all that important, but it is a most significant time period (10 percent of the total known time range of hominids). To form a consistent theory of exactly what was occurring in the Plio-Pleistocene, we need precise chronological controls. The chronologies, however, often take years to sort out. Most crucially, cross-correlations between different dating techniques (K/Ar, fission-track, bio-stratigraphy, paleomagnetism) must be determined.

Due to the excellent preservation conditions in the once-lakeside environment at Hadar, an outstanding collection of fossilized bones has been discovered. Among the fossil remains, at least 35 hominid individuals (up to a maximum of as many as 65) have been discovered (Johanson and Taieb, 1980).

Two extraordinary discoveries at Hadar are most noteworthy. In 1974, a partial skeleton was found eroding out of a hillside. This skeleton is scientifically designated AL-288-1, but is usually simply called Lucy (after a popular Beatles' song). Representing more than 40 percent of a skeleton, it is one of the two most complete individuals recovered in the entire time period prior to 100,000 years ago.

The second find came to light in 1975 at AL (Afar Locality) 333. Johanson and his amazed crew found dozens of fossilized hominid bones scattered along a hillside. The bones represent at least 13 individuals, including 4 infants. Possibly members of one social unit, this group has been argued to have perhaps all died at the same time, thus representing a "catastrophic" assemblage (White and Johanson, 1989). However, the precise deposition of this site has not yet been completely explained, so this assertion must be viewed as quite tentative (in geological terms, an "instant" could represent many decades or centuries).

FIGURE 10-6 "Lucy," a partial hominid skeleton. Discovered at the Hadar in 1974.

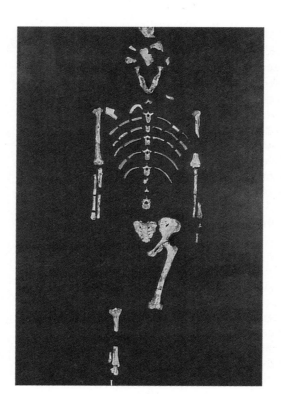

Omo (Oh'-moh)

The thickest and most continuous Plio-Pleistocene sequence in East Africa comes from the Omo River Basin in southern Ethiopia, just north of Lake Turkana. This site was also worked jointly by French and American scientists with F. Clark Howell of the University of California, Berkeley, leading the American team.

Total deposits at the Omo are more than one-half mile thick, and the area surveyed extends over more than 80 square miles. These exceedingly thick sediments are composed largely of lake and river deposits, but more than 100 volcanic ash deposits have also been recognized. These ash deposits provide an excellent basis for K/Ar determinations. This technique, supported by bio-stratigraphy and paleomagnetism, has placed the hominid-bearing levels at the Omo between 2.9 and 1.0 mya.

A fantastically rich paleontological sample, more than 40,000 mammalian specimens alone, has been recovered from the rich Omo deposits. This site, with its well-documented chronology and huge paleontological sequence, has become the basis for extrapolation to other East African sites, as well as hominid localities in South Africa. Hominid discoveries at the Omo come from 87 different localities and include mostly isolated teeth.

East Lake Turkana (Tur-kahn'-ah)

Under the direction of Richard Leakey and, for several years, the late Glynn Isaac, research in this vast arid area in northern Kenya has yielded the richest assemblage of Plio-Pleistocene hominids from the African continent. The current total exceeds 150 hominid specimens, probably representing at least 100 individuals. Among this fine sample are included several complete skulls, many jaws, and an assortment of postcranial bones. Moreover, next to Olduvai Gorge (discussed below), sites on the east side of Lake Turkana have produced the most information concerning the behavior of early hominids.

For several years, the dating of the geological beds in the East Turkana area were disputed. However, after considerable testing and retesting and cross-correlation of a variety of different dating techniques, a consensus was reached: most of the hominid-bearing levels at East Turkana are approximately 1.8 million years old. In addition, there are beds apparently considerably older which thus far have provided a few fragments of *very* early hominids dating back to 3.3 million years (Kimbel, 1988).

West Lake Turkana

Across the lake from the fossil beds discussed above are other deposits that recently have yielded new and very exciting discoveries. In 1984, on the west side of Lake Turkana, a nearly complete skeleton of a 1.6 million-year-old *Homo erectus* adolescent was found (see Chap. 12), and the following year a well-preserved 2.5 million-year-old skull was also found. This latter find—"the black skull"—is a most important discovery and has caused a major re-evaluation of Plio-Pleistocene hominid evolution. (See Chapter 11.)

Olduvai Gorge (Ohl'-doo-vye)

Located in the Serengeti Plain of northern Tanzania, Olduvai is a steep-sided valley resembling a miniature version of the Grand Canyon. (Indeed, the geological processes that formed the gorge are similar to what happened in the formation of the Grand Canyon.) Following millions of years of accumulation of several hundred feet of geological strata, faulting occurred about 70,000 years ago to the east of Olduvai. As a result, a gradient was established, and a rapidly flowing river proceeded to cut the gorge.

Olduvai today is thus a deep ravine cut into the almost mile-high grassland plateau of East Africa, and extends more than 25 miles in total length—potentially including hundreds of early hominid localities. Climatically, the semi-arid pattern with scrub vegetation observable today is thought to parallel conditions over most of the last 2 million years.

Since the 1930s, when they first worked there, Olduvai came to be identified with the Leakeys, Louis and his wife Mary, two of the key founders of modern paleoanthropology. Louis, through coverage in *National Geographic* and on television, became more famous than any other paleoanthropologist of his generation. Although occupied with lecture tours, fund raising, and directing research at the Centre for Prehistory in Nairobi, Louis Leakey continued to make periodic trips to Olduvai up until his death in 1972. Mary Leakey, for over 40 years, was responsible for directing archeological excavations at Olduvai (and later, Laetoli) and was instrumental in many of the most exciting discoveries. She re-

FIGURE 10-7 View of the main gorge at Olduvai. Note the clear sequence of geological beds. The discontinuity to the right is a major fault line.

tired from active field work in 1983 and today continues her writing and research from her home outside Nairobi.

The greatest contribution Olduvai has made to paleoanthropological research is the establishment of an extremely well documented and correlated *sequence* of geological, paleontological, archeological, and hominid remains over the last 2 million years. At the very foundation of all paleoanthropological research is a well-established geological picture, and at Olduvai, owing to four decades of work, this picture is understood in minute detail. Paleontological evidence of fossilized animal bones also has been retrieved in great abundance. More than 150 species of extinct animals have been recognized, and careful analysis of these remains has yielded voluminous information concerning the ecological conditions of early hominid habitats.

The archeological sequence at Olduvai is also extremely well-documented. Due to Mary Leakey's meticulous excavations and analyses, a more complete picture of the behavior of early hominids has emerged from Olduvai than from any other locality.

Finally, remains of several fossilized hominids have been found at Olduvai, ranging in time from the earliest occupation levels (*circa* 1.85 mya) to fairly recent *Homo sapiens*. Of the more than 40 individuals represented, many are quite fragmentary, but a few (including four skulls and a nearly complete foot) are excellently preserved. While the center of hominid discoveries has now shifted to other areas of East Africa, it was the initial discovery by Mary Leakey in 1959 of the "Zinj" (a robust australopithecine) skull that focused the world's attention on this remarkably rich area. This famous discovery provides an excellent example of how financial ramifications directly result from well-publicized hominid discoveries. Prior to 1959, the Leakeys had worked sporadically at Olduvai for almost three decades on a financial shoestring. During this time, they made marvelous paleontological and archeological discoveries, but there was little support for much-needed large-scale excavation. However, following the discovery of "Zinj," the National Geographic Society funded the research, and within the next year more earth was moved than in the previous thirty. Ongoing work at Olduvai has yielded yet further hominid finds, with a partial skeleton being discovered by researchers from the Institute of Human Origins in 1987.

SOUTH AFRICAN SITES

Earliest Discoveries

The first quarter of this century saw the discipline of paleoanthropology in its scientific infancy. Informed opinions considered the likely origins of the human family to be in Asia, where fossil forms of a primitive kind of *Homo* had been found in Indonesia in the 1890s. Europe was also considered a center of hominid evolution, for spectacular discoveries there of archaic *Homo sapiens* (including the famous Neandertals) and millions of stone tools had come to light, particularly in the early decades of this century.

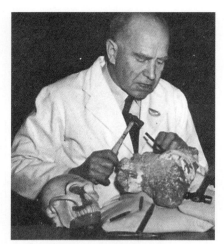

FIGURE 10-8 Dr. Raymond Dart, shown working in his laboratory.

ENDOCAST A solid impression of the inside of the skull, often preserving details relating to the size and surface features of the brain.

Few scholars would have given much credence to Darwin's prediction:

> In each region of the world the living mammals are closely related to the extinct species of the same region. It is, therefore, probable that Africa was formally inhabited by extinct apes closely allied to the gorilla and chimpanzee, and as these two species are now man's nearest allies, it is somewhat more probable that our early progenitors lived on the African continent than elsewhere. (Darwin, *The Descent of Man*, 1871).

Moreover, it would be many more decades before the East African discoveries (discussed above) would come to light. It was in such an atmosphere of preconceived biases that the discoveries of a young Australian-born anatomist were to jolt the foundations of the scientific community in the 1920s. Raymond Dart arrived in South Africa in 1923 at the age of 30 to take up a teaching position in Johannesburg. Fresh from his evolutionary-oriented training in England, Dart had developed a keen interest in human evolution. Consequently, he was well-prepared when startling new evidence began to appear at his very doorstep.

The first clue came in 1924 when Dart received a shipment of fossils from the commercial limeworks quarry at Taung (200 miles southwest of Johannesburg). He immediately recognized something that was quite unusual, a natural **endocast** of the inside of a braincase of a higher primate. The endocast fit into another limestone block containing the fossilized front portion of the skull, face, and lower jaw. However, these were difficult to see clearly, for the bone was hardened into a cemented limestone matrix. Dart patiently chiseled away for weeks, later describing the task: "No diamond cutter ever worked more lovingly or with such care on a precious jewel—nor, I am sure, with such inadequate tools. But on the seventy-third day, December 23, the rock parted. I could view the face from the front, although the right side was still imbedded. . . . What emerged was a baby's face, an infant with a full set of milk teeth and its permanent molars just in the process of erupting. I doubt if there was any

FIGURE 10-9 (*a*) The Taung child discovered in 1924. The endocast is in back with the fossilized bone mandible and face in front. (*b*) Taung. Location of the initial australopithecine discovery.

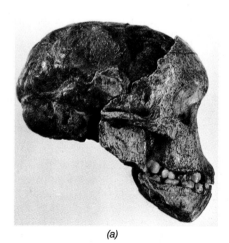

(a)

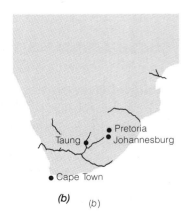

(b)

parent prouder of his offspring than I was of my Taung baby on that Christmas" (Dart, 1959, p. 10).

As indicated by the formation and eruption of teeth, the Taung child was probably about 3 to 4 years of age. Interestingly, the rate of development of this and many other Plio-Pleistocene hominids was more like that of apes than modern *Homo* (Bromage and Dean, 1985). Dart's initial impression that this form was a hominoid was confirmed when he could observe the face and teeth more clearly. However, as it turned out, it took considerably more effort before the teeth could be seen completely, since Dart worked for 4 years to separate the upper and lower jaws.

But Dart was convinced long before he had an unimpeded view of the dentition that this discovery was a remarkable one, an early hominoid from South Africa. The question was, what kind of hominoid? Dart realized it was extremely improbable that this specimen could have been a forest ape, for South Africa has had a relatively dry climate for millions of years. Even though the climate at Taung may not have been as dry as Dart initially speculated (Butzer, 1974), it was still a very unlikely spot to find an ape!

If not an ape, then, what was it? Features of the skull and teeth of this small child held clues that Dart seized upon almost immediately. The entrance of the spinal column into the brain (the *foramen magnum* at the base of the skull) was further forward in the Taung skull than in modern great apes, though not as much as in modern humans. From this fact Dart concluded that the head was balanced *above* the spine, indicating erect posture. In addition, the slant of the forehead was not as receding as in apes, the milk canines were exceedingly small, and the newly erupted permanent molars were very large, broad teeth. In all these respects, the Taung fossil was more akin to hominids than to apes. There was, however, a disturbing feature that was to confuse many scientists for several years: the brain was quite small. More recent studies have estimated the Taung child's brain size at approximately 405 cm^3 (which translates to a full adult estimate of 440 cm^3), not very large (for a hominid) when compared to modern great apes, as the following tabulation shows (after Tobias, 1971; 1983):

	RANGE (CM^3)	MEAN (CM^3)
Chimpanzee	282–500	394
Gorilla	340–752	506
Orang	276–540	411

As the tabulation indicates, the estimated cranial capacity of the Taung fossil falls within the range of modern great apes, and gorillas actually *average* about 10 percent greater. It must, however, be remembered that gorillas are very large animals, whereas the Taung specimen derives from a population where adults may have averaged less than 60 pounds. Since brain size is partially correlated with body size, comparing such differently sized animals is unjustified. A more meaningful comparison would be with the bonobo (*Pan paniscus*), whose body weight is comparable. Bonobos have adult cranial capacities averaging 356 cm^3 for males and 329 cm³ for females, and thus the Taung child, versus a *comparably sized* ape, displays a 25 percent increase in cranial capacity.

Despite the relatively small size of the brain, Dart saw that it was no ape. Details preserved on the endocast seemed to indicate that the association areas of the parietal lobes were more expanded than in any ape. However, more recent reexamination of the Taung specimen has shown the sulcal (folding) pattern is actually quite like African great apes (Falk, 1980; 1983). We must emphasize that attempts to discern the precise patterns of the "bumps and folds" in ancient endocasts is no easy feat, and thus "paleoneurology" is open to considerable speculation. Perhaps, then, it is no surprise that the other leading expert in this field (Ralph Holloway) disagrees with the conclusions noted above (Falk's), and, alternatively, argues the Taung endocast is more hominidlike.

Realizing the immense importance of his findings, Dart promptly reported them in the British scientific weekly *Nature* on February 7, 1925. A bold venture, since Dart, only 32, was presumptuously proposing a whole new view of human evolution. The small-brained Taung child was christened by Dart **Australopithecus africanus** (southern ape of Africa), which he saw as a kind of halfway "missing link" between modern apes and humans. This concept of a single "missing link" was a fallacious one, but Dart correctly emphasized the hominidlike features of the fossil.

Not all scientists were ready for such a theory from such an "unlikely" place. Hence, Dart's report was received with indifference, disbelief, and even caustic scorn. Dart realized that more complete remains were needed. The skeptical world would not accept the evidence of one partial immature individual, no matter how suggestive the clues. Clearly, more fossil evidence was needed, particularly adult crania (since these would show more diagnostic features). Not an experienced fossil hunter himself, Dart sought further assistance in the search for more **australopithecines** (the colloquial name referring to members of the genus *Australopithecus*).

South African Hominids Aplenty

Soon after publication of his controversial theories, Dart found a strong ally in Dr. Robert Broom. A Scottish physician and part-time paleontologist, Broom's credentials as a fossil hunter had been established earlier with his highly successful paleontological work on mammal-like reptiles in South Africa.

Although interested, Broom was unable to participate actively in the search for additional australopithecines until 1936. Very soon thereafter, however, he began to meet with incredible success. From two of Dart's students Broom learned of another commercial limeworks site called **Sterkfontein**, not far from Johannesburg. Here, as at Taung, the quarrying involved blasting out large sections with dynamite, leaving piles of debris that often contained fossils. A limitation with such deposits, however, is that chronometric dating techniques do not apply, and the best that can be done is to extrapolate other techniques (biostratigraphy and paleomagnetism) back to East Africa, where there is an

AUSTRALOPITHECUS AFRICANUS
(os-tral-oh-pith'-e-kus) (af-ri-kan'-us)

AUSTRALOPITHECINES (os-tral-oh-pith'-e-seens) **The colloquial term referring to members of genus** *Australopithecus.*

STERKFONTEIN (sterk'-fon-tane)

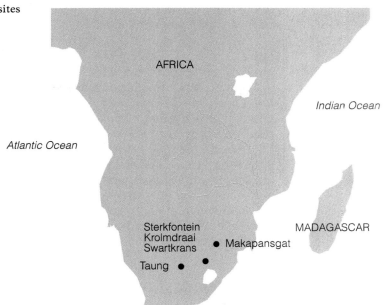

FIGURE 10-10 Australopithecine sites in South Africa.

established chronology. Indeed, it is important to remember that *all* the assigned ages for South African hominid sites are rather rough estimates, with the best current guess placing the Plio-Pleistocene hominids in the 3–1 million-year range.

Broom had found exactly what he was looking for—an adult cranium—at Sterkfontein just a few months after becoming actively involved in the search. Such remarkable fortune was not the end of Broom's luck, for in 1938 he learned of another australopithecine site at **Kromdraai**, about one mile from Sterkfontein. Following World War II (in 1948), Broom discovered **Swartkrans** in the same vicinity, and this site has turned out to be the most productive in southern Africa. A final australopithecine site, **Makapansgat**, was excavated in 1947 by Dart, who returned to the fossil-discovery stage after an absence of almost twenty years.

KROMDRAAI (kromm′-dry)

SWARTKRANS (swart′-krannz)

MAKAPANSGAT (mack-ah-pans′-gat)

Numerous extremely important discoveries came from these additional sites, discoveries that would ultimately swing the tide of opinion to the thoughts Dart first expressed in 1925. Particularly important was a nearly perfect skull and a nearly complete pelvis, both discovered at Sterkfontein in 1947. As the number of discoveries accumulated, it became increasingly difficult to simply write off the australopithecines as "aberrant apes."

By the early 1950s, the path was completely cleared for the nearly unanimous acceptance of the australopithecines as early hominids. With this acceptance also came the necessary recognition that hominid brains had their greatest expansion *after* earlier changes in teeth and locomotory systems. In other words, the rate of change in one functional system of the body varies from that in other systems, thus displaying a mode of change called **mosaic evolution**.

Today the search for further early hominid fossils continues in South Africa, and Sterkfontein, Kromdraai, Swartkrans, and Makapansgat have all been reopened for further excavation. Indeed, in the last few years, more than 150 additional specimens have been found at Sterkfontein alone. In addition, numerous important new discoveries have been made at Swartkrans. The total South African Plio-Pleistocene hominid sample is thus most significant, with more than 1500 specimens (counting isolated teeth) representing probably at least 200 individuals.

From an evolutionary point of view, the most significant remains are those from the australopithecine pelvis, which now includes portions of nine os coxae (hip bones). (See Figs. 10-11 and 10-12.) Remains of the pelvis are so important because, better than any other area of the body, this structure displays the unique requirements of a bipedal animal, such as modern humans *and* our hominid forbears.

THE BIPEDAL ADAPTATION

As we discussed in Chapter 7, there is a general tendency in all primates for erect body posture. However, of all living primates, efficient bipedalism as the primary form of locomotion is seen *only* in hominids.

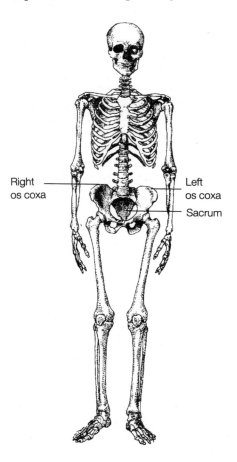

FIGURE 10-11 The human pelvis. Various elements shown on a modern skeleton.

Right os coxa

Left os coxa

Sacrum

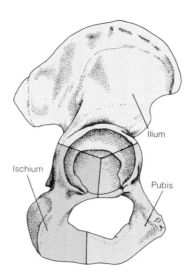

FIGURE 10-12 The human os coxa. Composed of three bones (right side shown).

Ilium

Ischium

Pubis

Functionally, the human mode of locomotion is most clearly shown in our striding gait, where weight is alternately placed on a single fully extended hindlimb. This highly derived mode of locomotion has developed to a point where energy levels are used to near peak efficiency. Such is not the case in nonhuman primates, who move bipedally with hips and knees bent and maintain balance with difficulty.

From a survey of our close primate relatives, it is apparent that, while still in the trees, our ancestors were adapted to a fair amount of upper-body erectness. Prosimians, monkeys, and apes all spend considerable time sitting while feeding, grooming, or sleeping. Presumably, our earliest hominid ancestors also displayed similar behavior. What caused these forms to come to the ground and embark on a unique way of life that would eventually lead to humans is still a mystery. Perhaps, natural selection favored some Miocene hominoid coming occasionally to the ground to forage on the forest floor or forest fringe. In any case, once it was on the ground and away from the trees, bipedal locomotion *could* become a tremendous advantage.

First of all, bipedal locomotion freed the hands for carrying objects and for making and using tools. Such early cultural developments then had an even more positive impact on further speeding the development of yet more efficient bipedalism—once again emphasizing the dual role of biocultural evolution. In addition, in the bipedal stance, animals have a wider view of the surrounding countryside, and in open terrain early spotting of predators would be of critical importance. Also, bipedal locomotion is an efficient means of covering long distances, useful perhaps in finding food to gather or scavenge and to locate water. Later (perhaps much later) in human evolution bipedalism would be highly advantageous in systematic hunting.

Our mode of locomotion is quite extraordinary, involving as it does a unique kind of activity in which "the body, step by step, teeters on the edge of catastrophe" (Napier, 1967, p. 56). The problem is to maintain balance on the "stance" leg while the "swing" leg is off the ground. In fact,

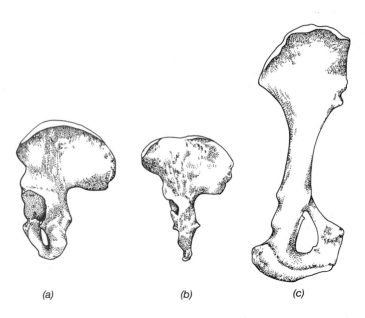

FIGURE 10-13 Os Coxae. (*a*) *Homo sapiens*; (*b*) australopithecine (Sts. 14); (*c*) chimpanzee. Note especially the length and breadth of the iliac blade.

during normal walking, both feet are simultaneously on the ground only about 25 percent of the time (and even less so, as speed of locomotion increases).

In order to maintain a stable center of balance in this complex form of locomotion, many drastic structural/functional alterations are demanded in the basic primate quadrupedal pattern. Functionally, the foot must be altered to act as a stable support instead of a grasping appendage. When we walk, our foot is used like a prop, landing on the heel and pushing off the toes, particularly the big toe. The lower limb must also be remodeled to allow full extension of the knee and to allow the legs to track closely to each other, thus keeping the center of support under the body. Finally, significant change must occur in the pelvis to permit efficient weight transfer from the upper body to the legs.

The major structural changes that are required for bipedalism are all seen in australopithecines in East and South Africa. In the pelvis, the blade (ilium) is shortened top to bottom, thus permitting more stable weight transfer. In addition, as compared to a quadruped, the pelvis is bent backwards and downwards; in this altered biomechanical position, the action of several key muscles is altered. There are further structural changes displayed by australopithecine anatomy that indicate efficient bipedalism, and, of course, there are the beautifully preserved footprints from Laetoli unequivocally showing a bipedal adaptation.

SUMMARY

In this chapter, we have discussed the background information concerning the earliest known evidence of the hominid line. The first evidence of hominids comes from sites in East and South Africa during the Plio-Pleistocene. In East Africa, especially, the discoveries in recent years have been quite spectacular, providing scientists with a wealth of new information. From a multidisciplinary approach, paleoanthropology has attempted to correlate these remains using geological, ecological, and archeological perspectives. Moreover, the opportunity to apply varied dating techniques, again most especially in East Africa, has proven most crucial in establishing a firm chronology for the early stages of hominid evolution.

Only very fragmentary evidence of the *earliest* stages of hominoid/hominid diversification are presently evident from localities in Kenya. However, abundant evidence is now known from the period after 4 mya (and up to about 1 mya). From this period, six localities in East Africa are highlighted (Laetoli, Hadar, Omo, East Turkana, West Turkana, and Olduvai Gorge). In addition, five other localities in South Africa (Taung, Sterkfontein, Makapansgat, Kromdraai, and Swartkrans) are also discussed.

While not providing the most complete or the most comprehensive information, South Africa (through the work of Dart and Broom) provided the *first* insights into early hominid emergence. Moreover, ongoing work in southern Africa continues to contribute to our picture of this crucial period.

Early hominids differ considerably from modern *Homo sapiens*. They are considerably smaller-brained, and at the same time, larger-toothed. However, they all show the distinctive hominid adaptation for *bipedal locomotion*. In the next chapter, we will discuss the different Plio-Pleistocene hominid forms and the varied evolutionary interpretations they continue to engender.

QUESTIONS FOR REVIEW

1. What kinds of cultural remains do archaeologists recover and why are they important in understanding human evolution?
2. Why is paleoanthropology called a multidisciplinary science? What are its most important components?
3. Discuss what is meant by *relative* compared to *chronometric* dating.
4. Why is more than one dating technique required to establish the chronology of an early hominid locality? Discuss using an example.
5. Why is it so significant that the East African Plio-Pleistocene sites are all found along the Rift Valley?
6. Compare and contrast two East African Plio-Pleistocene sites for the kinds of evidence discovered.
7. What led Dart to conclude that the Taung specimen was *not* an ape?
8. Why is skeletal evidence of the lower limb so important in defining early hominids?
9. What are the major structural alterations (from a quadrupedal pattern) required for efficient bipedalism?
10. Were the australopithecines bipedal? If so, what does this infer about them?

EARLY HOMINIDS: ORGANIZATION AND INTERPRETATION

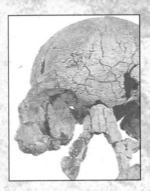

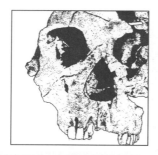

CHAPTER 11

INTRODUCTION

From the time period between 4 and 1 mya, East and South Africa have thus far yielded close to 500 hominid individuals. This huge collection of material (much of it in well-dated contexts) has allowed paleoanthropologists to formulate and reformulate their interpretations of human evolution. At present, it appears that at least four groups (which we will refer to as "sets") of hominids are distinguished in Africa during the Plio-Pleistocene. The first of these sets was distinctly earlier and more primitive, while the others appear somewhat later; moreover, two lineages apparently survived beyond 2 mya and lived contemporaneously for another one million years.

SET I. EARLY PRIMITIVE AUSTRALOPITHECINES (*A. AFARENSIS*)

Prior to 4 mya, the fossil hominid (or "hominoid") remains from East Africa (which is all there are anywhere) are extremely scrappy, represented by only a handful of specimens. It is not until 4–3 mya that we get the first *definite* collection of hominid fossils. These crucial remains come primarily from two East African sites explored within the last 20 years: Laetoli in northern Tanzania and Hadar in northeastern Ethiopia. From these two sites together, several hundred hominid specimens have been recovered, representing a minimum of 60 individuals and perhaps close to 100. In addition, there are of course those fascinating footprints from Laetoli. Finally, there are a few bits and pieces also from this same time period, probably belonging to the same group from East Turkana (lower beds) and from the Omo.

First discovered at Hadar and Laetoli in 1973 and 1974, respectively, *Australopithecus afarensis* was not formally named until 1978. As might be expected with the announcement of a new species, not all opinion has been in agreement. What exactly is *A. afarensis*? Without question, it is more primitive than the other australopithecine material from East or South Africa (discussed below). In fact, *A. afarensis* is the most primitive of any definite hominid form thus far found. By "primitive," we mean that *A. afarensis* is less evolved in any particular direction than seen in later species of *Australopithecus* or in *Homo*. That is to say,

FIGURE 11-1 *Australopithecus afarensis* maxilla, AL-200-1a, from Hadar, Ethiopia. (Note the parallel tooth rows and large canines.)

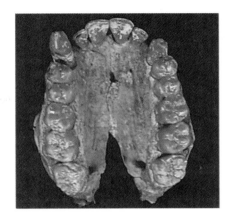

A. afarensis shares more primitive features with early homin*oids* and with living apes than is true of later homin*ids*, who display more derived characteristics.

For example, the teeth are quite primitive. The canines are often large, pointed teeth that slightly overlap; the first lower premolar is compressed; and the tooth rows are parallel or even slightly convergent (see Fig. 11-1). The pieces of the crania that are preserved also display several primitive hominoid characteristics. Cranial capacity estimates for *afarensis* show a mixed pattern when compared to later hominids. A provisional estimate for the one partially complete cranium (see Fig. 11-2)—apparently a large individual—gives a figure of 500 cm^3, but another, even more fragmentary cranium is apparently quite a bit smaller and has been estimated at about 375 cm^3 (Holloway, 1983). Thus, for some individuals (males?), *afarensis* is well within the range of other australopithecine species, but others (females?) may be significantly smaller.

FIGURE 11-2 Comparison of hominoid crania. (*a*) Human; (*b*) *Australopithecus afarensis* composite cranium assembled from three individuals—AL 333-45, 200-1a, and 400-1a; (*c*) chimpanzee.

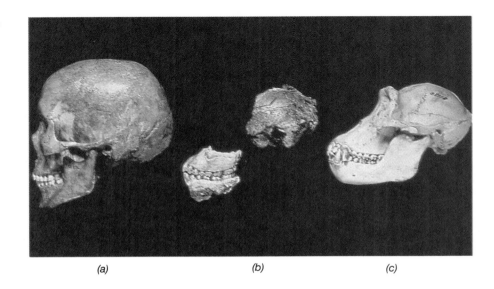

(a)   (b)   (c)

However, a conclusive depiction of *afarensis* cranial size cannot be attained at this time, owing to the poor preservation of cranial elements. Certainly, however, *afarensis* was small-brained, perhaps the smallest (on average) of any known hominid.

Conversely, an abundance of postcranial pieces have been found, most notably the Lucy skeleton from Hadar. Initial impressions suggest the upper limbs are long relative to the lower ones (also a primitive hominoid condition). In addition, the wrist, hand, and foot bones show several differences from modern humans (Susman et al., 1985). From these remains, stature can be fairly confidently estimated: *A. afarensis* was a short hominid, Lucy perhaps attaining a height of only 3½ feet. However, Lucy, as suggested from the pelvis, is generally thought to have been a female, and there is also evidence at Hadar as well as Laetoli of larger individuals. The most economical interpretation explaining this variation is that *A. afarensis* was quite sexually dimorphic—the larger individuals are male and the smaller, such as Lucy, are female. Estimates of male stature can be approximated from the larger footprints at Laetoli, implying a height of about 5 feet. If we accept this interpretation, *A. afarensis* was a very *sexually dimorphic* form. In fact, for overall body size, this species may have been as dimorphic as *any* living primate (i.e., as much as gorillas, orangs, or baboons).

What is most interesting about *A. afarensis* is the distinctive physical morphology it displays. In a majority of dental and cranial features, *A. afarensis* is clearly more primitive than are later hominids. This should not come as too great a surprise, since *A. afarensis* is 1 million years older than most other East African finds and perhaps 0.5–0.7 million years older than the oldest South African hominid. In fact, from the neck up, *A. afarensis* is so primitive that, without any evidence from the limb skeleton, one would be hard-pressed to call it a hominid at all (although the back teeth are derived like hominids).

What makes *A. afarensis* a hominid? The answer is revealed by its manner of locomotion. From the abundant limb bones recovered from Hadar and those beautiful footprints from Laetoli, we know unequivocally that *afarensis* walked bipedally. At the same time, some researchers have suggested that *afarensis* may still have been spending considerable time in the trees, where they found safe sleeping sites as well as some food.

SET II. LATER AUSTRALOPITHECINES—"ROBUST" FORMS (*A. AETHIOPICUS, A. BOISEI, A. ROBUSTUS*)

In the time period following 2.5 mya, later and more derived representatives of *Australopithecus* are found in both South and East Africa. Among them is a distinctive group that has popularly been known for some time as "robust" australopithecines. By "robust" it was meant that these forms, as compared to other australopithecines, were larger in body size. However, recent, more controlled studies (Jungers, 1988; McHenry, 1988) have shown that all species of *Australopithecus* overlapped consid-

TABLE 11-1	Estimated Body Weights for *Australopithecus* Species					
	AVERAGE WEIGHT[1]		AVERAGE WEIGHT[2]		RANGE[2]	
	lb	kg	lb	kg	lb	kg
A. afarensis	111.6	50.6	112.4	51.0	67.0–149.2	30.4–67.7
A. africanus	100.3	45.5	101.4	46.0	72.8–127.0	33.0–57.6
A. robustus	105.2	47.7	108.0	49.0	81.8–126.8	37.1–57.5
A. boisei	101.6	46.1	108.5	49.2	72.8–152.8	33.0–69.3

[1]After McHenry, 1988.
[2]After Jungers, 1988.

erably in body size. Table 11-1 shows the averages and projected ranges of body weights for the four australopithecine species for which adequate postcranial material has been found. As can be seen, none of the species differs much from the others in *average* weight, but all show dramatic intraspecific variation—presumably due to sexual dimorphism.

As a result of these new weight estimates, many researchers have either dropped the term "robust" (along with its opposite, "gracile") or present it in quotation marks to emphasize its conditional application. We believe the term "robust" can be used in this latter sense, as it still emphasizes important differences in scaling of craniodental traits. In other words, even if they are not larger overall, robust forms are clearly more robust in the skull and dentition.

The earliest representative of this robust group (or **clade**) comes from northern Kenya on the west side of Lake Turkana. A complete

CLADE A group of species sharing a common ancestor and distinct from other groups.

FIGURE 11-3 The "black skull" WT-17,000, discovered at West Lake Turkana in 1985. This specimen is provisionally assigned to *Australopithecus aethiopicus.*

cranium (WT-17,000—the "black skull") was unearthed there in 1985 and has proven to be a most important discovery. The skull, with a cranial capacity of only 410 cm³, has the smallest definitely determined cranial capacity of any hominid yet found. In addition, this fossil shows other primitive traits, quite reminiscent of *A. afarensis*. For example, there is a compound (joined) crest in the back of the skull, the upper face projects considerably, and the upper dental row converges in back (Kimbel, 1988).

What makes the black skull so fascinating, however, is that mixed with this array of primitive traits are a host of derived ones linking it to other members of the robust group (including a broad face, a very large palate, and a large area for back teeth). This mosaic of features neatly places skull 17,000 between earlier *afarensis* on the one hand and the later more robust species on the other. Because of this distinct pattern of morphology, the black skull has been assigned to a new species, *Australopithecus aethiopicus*.

Around 2 mya, different varieties of even more derived members of the robust lineage were on the scene in both East and South Africa. In East Africa, as well documented at Olduvai and east Turkana, robust australopithecines have relatively small cranial capacities (ranging from 510 to 530 cm³) and very large, broad faces with massive back teeth and jaws. Louis Leakey originally named the initial discovery of this form "Zinjanthropus," but paleoanthropologists now usually refer to the East African robust variety as *Australopithecus boisei*.

In addition, there are also numerous finds of robust australopithecines in South Africa at Kromdraai and most especially at Swartkrans. Like their East African cousins, the South African robust forms also have small cranial capacities, large broad faces, and very large premolars and molars (though not as massive as in East Africa). Owing to the dental proportions, as well as important differences in facial architecture (Rak, 1983), most researchers agree that there is a species-level difference between the East African robust variety (*A. boisei*) on the one hand and the South African group (*A. robustus*) on the other.

Despite these differences, all members of the robust lineage appear to be specialized for a diet of hard food items, such as seeds, nuts, and bark. Another assumption that has persisted for many years concerns the toolmaking capabilities of robust forms. Put rather bluntly, most paleoanthropologists have depicted robust forms as lacking in intellectual capabilities. However, new evidence from Swartkrans in South Africa has led Randall Susman (1988) to conclude otherwise. He suggests that robust australopithecines (*A. robustus*) found at this site had fine manipulative abilities, and thus could well have been the maker of the stone tools also found at Swartkrans. Complicating the issue further, in addition to robust australopithecines at Swartkrans, another hominid (*Homo*) is also represented (albeit in small numbers). So precisely *who* was responsible for the stone tools we find at Swartkrans (or in East Africa at Olduvai or East Turkana) is still largely a matter of conjecture (Klein, 1989).

SET III. LATER AUSTRALOPITHECINES—"GRACILE" FORMS (A. AFRICANUS)

Another variety of australopithecine (also small-brained, but not as large-toothed as the robust varieties) is known from Africa. However, while the robust lineage is represented in both East and South Africa, the smaller-toothed form (*A. africanus*) is known only from the southern part of the continent. First named *A. africanus* by Dart for the single individual at Taung (see Chapter 10), this australopithecine is also found at Makapansgat and Sterkfontein.

Traditionally, it had been thought there was significant variation in body size between the "robust" and "gracile" forms. However, as we showed in Table 11-1, there is not much difference in body size among any of the australopithecine species. In fact, most of the differences between "gracile" and "robust" are found in the face and dentition.

The facial structure of the graciles is more lightly built and somewhat more dish-shaped compared to the vertical configuration seen in robust specimens. The most distinctive difference observed between the two forms is in the dentition. Compared to modern humans, they both have relatively large teeth, manifested most clearly in the posterior tooth row (premolars and molars). Robust forms emphasize this trend to an extreme degree, with the huge back teeth crowding the front teeth into a small portion of the jaw. Conversely, the graciles have proportionately larger front teeth (incisors and canines) compared to the size of their back teeth. These differences in the relative proportions of the teeth and jaws best define a gracile, as compared to a robust form. In fact, most of the differences in face and skull shape noted above can be directly attributed to contrasting jaw function in the two forms.

SET IV. EARLY *HOMO* (*H. HABILIS*, *H. SPECIES INDETERMINATE*?)

The first hint that another hominid was living contemporaneously in Africa with australopithecines came at Olduvai in the early 1960s. Louis Leakey named a new form of hominid *Homo habilis*, based on remains found in beds about the same age as "Zinj." Unfortunately, the fossils at Olduvai attributable to this **taxon** are all fragmentary or distorted. More complete remains, discovered later at East Lake Turkana, would prove pivotal in establishing the validity of this species.

The naming of this fossil material as *Homo habilis* (handy man) was meaningful from two perspectives. Firstly, Leakey inferred that members of this group were the Olduvai toolmakers. You will recall, however, that some researchers have suggested that robust australopithecines could also have been making tools. Secondly, by calling this group *Homo*, Leakey was arguing for at least *two separate branches* of hominid evolution in the Plio-Pleistocene. Clearly, only one could then be on the line

TAXON (pl. taxa) A population (or group of populations) that is judged to be sufficiently distinct and is thus assigned to a separate category (such as genus or species).

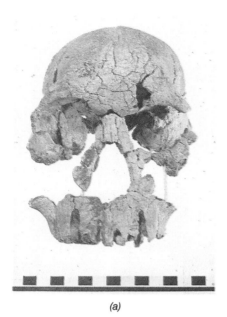
(a)

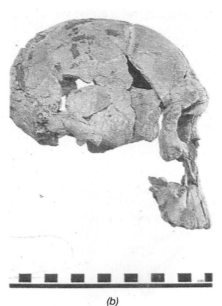
(b)

FIGURE 11-4 A nearly complete "early *Homo*" skull from East Lake Turkana (KNM-ER 1470). One of the most important single fossil hominid discoveries from East Africa. (*a*) Frontal view; (*b*) lateral view. Usually referred to as *Homo habilis.*

leading to modern humans, and Leakey was thus guessing he had found the more likely ancestor.

The most immediately obvious feature distinguishing the *habilis* material from the australopithecines is cranial size. For all the measurable *habilis* skulls, the estimated average cranial capacity is 631 cm³ compared to 520 cm³ for all measurable robust australopithecines and 442 cm³ for graciles (McHenry, 1988). *Habilis*, therefore, shows an average increase in cranial size of 21 percent and 43 percent, respectively, over both forms of australopithecine. In addition, some researchers have pointed to differences in dental proportions and aspects of the limb skeleton.

Early members of the genus *Homo* have also been found in South Africa, apparently there too living contemporaneously with australopithecines. At both Sterkfontein and Swartkrans, fragmentary remains of an early form of *Homo* have been recognized. However, some of these remains are still controversial in that, while most experts agree they belong in the genus *Homo,* there is still considerable disagreement whether they should be included in the species *habilis.* In addition, a newly discovered very partial skeleton from Olduvai Gorge (OH 62) is extremely small-statured (less than 4 feet, probably) and has several primitive aspects of limb proportions (Johanson et al., 1987).

Even more troublesome are two crania from East Turkana that do not fit neatly with other *habilis* specimens from this site. Some experts contend that *all* of these individuals from South and East Africa can be included within a broad intraspecific umbrella that assumes a high level of sexual dimorphism. Others (Lieberman, et al., 1988) are not as convinced, and would thus argue for at least two species of early *Homo* (*habilis* and *sp. indet.*—which signifies "species indeterminate").

On the basis of current evidence, we can reasonably postulate that one or more species of early *Homo* was present in Africa by at least 2 mya, developing in parallel with at least one line of australopithecine. These two hominid lines lived "side-by-side" for at least one million years, after which the australopithecine lineage apparently disappears forever. At the same time, most probably the *habilis* line was emerging into a later form, *Homo erectus*, which in turn developed into *Homo sapiens*.

INTERPRETATIONS: WHAT DOES IT ALL MEAN?

By this time, it may seem anthropologists have an almost perverse fascination in finding small scraps buried in the ground and then assigning them confusing numbers and taxonomic labels impossible to remember. We must realize that the collection of the basic fossil data is the foundation of human evolutionary research. Without fossils, all our theories and speculation would be completely hollow. Several ongoing paleoanthropological projects are now collecting additional data in an attempt to answer some of the more perplexing questions about our evolutionary history.

The numbering of specimens is an attempt to keep the designations neutral and to make reference to each specimen as clear as possible. The formal naming of forms as *Australopithecus* or *Homo* should come much later, since it involves lengthy interpretations. The assigning of genus and species names to hominid fossils is more than just a convenience; when we attach a particular label, such as *A. boisei*, to a particular specimen, we should be fully aware of the biological implications of such an interpretation. (See Chapter 7.)

From the time that fossil sites are first located to the eventual interpretation of hominid evolutionary events, several steps are necessary. Ideally, they should follow a logical order, for if interpretations are made too hastily, they can confuse important issues for years. A reasonable sequence is:

1. selection and surveying of sites
2. excavation of sites; recovery of fossil hominids
3. designation of individual remains with specimen numbers for clear reference
4. detailed study and description of fossils
5. comparison with other fossil material—in chronological framework if possible
6. comparison of fossil material with known ranges of variation in closely related groups of living primates
7. assigning taxonomic names to fossil material

The task of interpretation is still not complete, for what we want to know in the long run is what happened to the population(s) represented by the fossil remains. Indeed, in the process of eventually determining those populations that are our most likely antecedents, we may conclude some hominids represent evolutionary side branches. If this conclusion is accurate, they necessarily must have gone extinct. It is both interesting and relevant to us as hominids to try to find out what influenced some earlier members of our family to continue evolving while others died out.

CONTINUING UNCERTAINTIES—TAXONOMIC ISSUES

As previously discussed, paleoanthropologists are crucially concerned with making biological interpretations of variation found in the hominid fossil record. Most especially, researchers endeavor to assign extinct forms to particular genera and species. We saw (in Chapter 7) that for the diverse array of Miocene hominoids, the evolutionary picture is especially complex. As new finds accumulate, there persists continued uncertainty even as to family assignment, to say nothing of genus and species!

For the Plio-Pleistocene, the situation is considerably clearer. First of all, there is a larger fossil sample from a more restricted geographical area (South and East Africa) and from a more concentrated time period (spanning 3 million years, from 4–1 mya). Secondly, more complete specimens exist (for example, "Lucy"), and we thus have good evidence from most parts of the body. Accordingly, there is considerable consensus on several basic aspects of evolutionary development during the Plio-Pleistocene. Firstly, researchers agree unanimously that these forms are hominids (members of the family, Hominidae). Secondly, and as support for the first point, all these forms are seen as well-adapted bipeds. Moreover, researchers agree as to genus-level assignments for most of the forms (although some disagreement exists regarding how to group the robust australopithecines).

As for species-level designations, little consensus can be found. Indeed, as new fossils have been discovered (e.g., the black skull, OH 62), the picture seems to muddy further. Once again, we have a complex evolutionary process. In attempts to deal with it, we impose varying degrees of simplicity. In so doing, we hope to understand evolutionary processes more clearly—not just for introductory students, but for professional paleoanthropologists and textbook authors as well! Nevertheless, evolution is not necessarily a simple process, and thus disputes are bound to arise, especially in making such fine-tuned interpretations as species-level designations.

We discuss below some ongoing topics of interest and occasional disagreement among paleoanthropologists. You should realize that such continued debate is at the heart of scientific endeavor; indeed, it provides a major stimulus for further research.

Here, we raise questions regarding three areas of taxonomic interpretation. In general, there is still reasonably strong agreement on these points, and we follow the current consensus as reflected in recent publications (Fleagle, 1988; Grine, 1988a; Klein, 1989).

(1) Is *Australopithecus afarensis* one species? Some paleoanthropologists think that what has been described as a single species (especially pertaining to the large, diverse Hadar sample) actually represents at least two separate species. However, it is clear that australopithecine species were highly variable, and thus the pattern seen at Hadar may represent a single, highly dimorphic species. Most scholars accept this latter interpretation, and it is best, for the moment, to follow the more conservative view. As a matter of good paleontological practice, it is desir-

able not to overly "split" fossil samples until compelling evidence is presented.

(2) How many australopithecine genera are there? Several years ago a plethora of generic terms was suggested by Robert Broom and others. However, in the 1960s and 1970s, most researchers agreed to "lump" all these forms into *Australopithecus*. With the discovery of early members of the genus *Homo* in the 1960s, and its general recognition in the 1970s, most reseachers also recognized the presence of our genus in the Plio-Pleistocene as well.

In the last few years, an increasing tendency has arisen to resplit some of the australopithecines. With the recognition that the robust group (*aethiopicus*, *boisei*, *robustus*) forms an evolutionary distinct lineage (clade), many researchers (Howell, 1988; Grine, 1988) have argued that the generic term "Paranthropus" should be used to set these robust forms apart from *Australopithecus* (now used in the strict sense). We thus would have *Paranthropus aethiopicus*, *Paranthropus boisei*, and *Paranthropus robustus* as contrasted to *Australopithecus afarensis* and *Australopithecus africanus*.

We agree that a good case can be made for this genus-level distinction, given the evolutionary uniqueness of the robust clade. However, *for closely related taxa*, such as we are dealing with here, this type of interpretation is largely arbitrary. (See Chapter 7.) As the single genus *Australopithecus* has been used in the wider sense for three decades (to include all robust forms), and as it simplifies terminology, we follow the current consensus and continue the more traditional usage—*Australopithecus*—for all small-brained, large-toothed Plio-Pleistocene hominids (including all five recognized species: *A. afarensis*, *A. aethiopicus*, *A. africanus*, *A. boisei*, and *A. robustus*).

(3) How many species of early *Homo* existed? Here is another species-level type of interpretation that is unlikely soon to be resolved. Whether we find resolution or not, the *form* of the conflicting views is instructive. Of course, the key issue is evaluating variation as *intra-* or *inter*specific. Those who would view all the non-australopithecine African hominids (*circa* 2.5–1.6 mya) as one species point out that all Plio-Pleistocene hominid species show extreme intraspecific variation. Much of this variation is assumed to reflect dramatic sexual dimorphism. These scholars are thus reasonably comfortable in referring to all this material as *Homo habilis*. Other researchers, however, see too much variation to accept just one species, even a very dimorphic one. Systematic comparison with the most dimorphic living primate (gorillas) shows that what is called *H. habilis* differ amongst themselves more than do male and female gorillas. Consequently we have an added complication: Must we now consider another early species of genus *Homo in addition* to *habilis*? Several researchers (for example, Lieberman, et al., 1987) believe there is no alternative, but as yet do not agree on a new name (and refer to it as, "*Homo, species indeterminate*"). The recent discovery of a partial skeleton at Olduvai Gorge does not help resolve the issue. This specimen is a very small individual, and thus presumably a female. How much sexual di-

morphism did *H. habilis* display? Were males two to three times (on average) the size of females? We do not know the answers to these questions, but their framing in biological terms as intra- versus interspecific variation and the use of contemporary primate models provide the basis for ongoing discussion.

Another problem with the so-called "early *Homo*" fossil sample is that it overlaps in time with the earliest appearance of *Homo erectus* (discussed in Chapter 12). As a result, several specimens of what has been labeled "early *Homo*" (or *H. habilis*) may actually belong to *H. erectus*. At about 1.6 mya, *H. erectus* apparently replaced earlier members of the genus *Homo* quite rapidly. (In fact, the time range for the *habilis* specimens thus far discovered spans just 200,000 years.) At sites (especially East Turkana and Swartkrans) where fragmentary traces of this replacement process are evident, it poses a major challenge to distinguish exactly what is "*habilis*" and what is "*erectus*."

PUTTING IT ALL TOGETHER

The interpretation of our evolutionary past in terms of which fossils are related to other fossils and how they are related to us is usually shown diagrammatically in the form of a **phylogeny**. Such a diagram is a family tree of fossil evolution. This kind of interpretation is the eventual goal of evolutionary studies, but it is the *final* goal only after adequate data are available to understand what is going on.

Even though hominid fossil evidence has accumulated in great abundance, the fact that so much of the material has been discovered fairly recently makes any firm judgment concerning the precise route of human evolution premature. However, paleoanthropologists are certainly not deterred from making their "best guesses," and thus diverse speculative theories have abounded in recent years. Until the existing fossil evidence has been adequately studied, to say nothing of new finds, such speculative theories must be viewed with a critical eye.

Below we present several phylogenies representing different and, in many cases, opposing views of hominid evolution. We suggest that you do not attempt to memorize them, for they all could be out of date by the time you read this book. It will prove more profitable to look at each one and assess the biological implications involved (for example, the number of different lines suggested, where the divergence points are placed, which species are seen as ancestral to others). Also, note which groups are placed on the main line of human evolution leading to *Homo sapiens* and which are placed on extinct side branches.

In Fig. 11-5, we present several of these recent hypotheses that attempt to explain early human evolution. All these schemes postdate 1979, when *A. afarensis* was first suggested as the likely common ancestor of later hominids (Johanson and White, 1979). Since the early 1980s, most paleoanthropologists have accepted this view. One exception is shown in Phylogeny B (after Senut and Tardieu, 1985), but this view—based on the premise that what is called *A. afarensis* is actually more than one species—has not been generally supported (see above).

PHYLOGENY A depiction of evolutionary lines of descent. A "family tree."

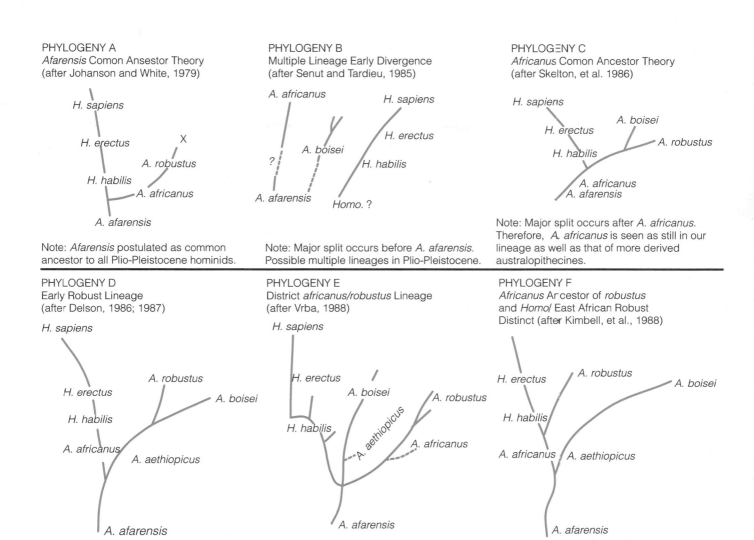

PHYLOGENY A
Afarensis Comon Ansestor Theory
(after Johanson and White, 1979)

Note: *Afarensis* postulated as common ancestor to all Plio-Pleistocene hominids.

PHYLOGENY B
Multiple Lineage Early Divergence
(after Senut and Tardieu, 1985)

Note: Major split occurs before *A. afarensis*. Possible multiple lineages in Plio-Pleistocene.

PHYLOGENY C
Africanus Comon Ancestor Theory
(after Skelton, et al. 1986)

Note: Major split occurs after *A. africanus*. Therefore, *A. africanus* is seen as still in our lineage as well as that of more derived australopithecines.

PHYLOGENY D
Early Robust Lineage
(after Delson, 1986; 1987)

PHYLOGENY E
District *africanus/robustus* Lineage
(after Vrba, 1988)

PHYLOGENY F
Africanus Arcestor of *robustus* and *Homo/* East African Robust Distinct (after Kimbell, et al., 1988)

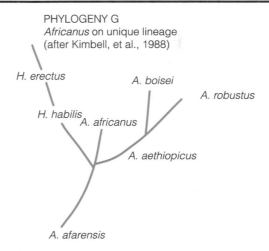

PHYLOGENY G
Africanus on unique lineage
(after Kimbell, et al., 1988)

FIGURE 11-5 Phylogenies of hominid evolution.

We have not included evolutionary schemes prior to 1979, as they do not account for the crucial discoveries at Laetoli and Hadar of *Australopithecus afarensis*. These now outdated models frequently postulated *A. africanus* as the common ancestor of later australopithecines *and* genus *Homo*. In modified form, this view is still continued in some respects. (See Phylogeny C.) Indeed, probably the most intractable problem for interpretation of early hominid evolution involves what to do with *A. africanus*. Carefully look at the different evolutionary reconstructions to see how various researchers deal with this still complicated issue.

SUMMARY

In East and South Africa during the better part of this century, a vast collection of early hominids has been gathered, a collection totaling more than 500 individuals (and thousands of specimens). While considerable evolutionary change occurred during the Plio-Pleistocene (approximately 3 million years are covered in this chapter), all forms were clearly hominid, as shown by their bipedal adaptation. The time range for this hominid material extends back to nearly 4 million years in East Africa, with the earliest and most primitive hominid now recognized: *Australopithecus afarensis*.

Later hominids of a robust lineage are known in East Africa (*A. aethiopicus*, *A. boisei*) and South Africa (*A. robustus*). These forms seem to appear on the scene about 2.5 mya and disappear by 1 mya.

In addition, a smaller-toothed (but not necessarily smaller-bodied) "gracile" australopithecine variety is known exclusively from South Africa, beginning at a time range perhaps as early as 2.5 mya. However, as noted in Chapter 10, dating control in South Africa is most tenuous; thus, we cannot be very certain of any of the dates for South African hominids.

Finally, best known again in East Africa (but also found in South Africa), a larger-brained and smaller-toothed variety is also present by 2 mya. This species, called *Homo habilis*, is thought by most paleoanthropologists to be closer to our ancestry than the later varieties of australopithecines.

However, drawing precise lines of evolutionary relationship (phylogenies) is not currently possible. Given the current state of knowledge, there are several equally supportable phylogenies. In fact, in a recent publication, three leading researchers (Bill Kimbel, Tim White, and Don Johanson, 1988) make this point; moreover, they note that of four possible phylogenetic reconstructions (resembling Phylogenies D, E, F, and G in Fig. 11-5), they have not reached agreement among themselves as to which is the most likely.

Thus, it can be said there is considerable consensus regarding the broad outlines of early hominid evolution. But a complete understanding is not yet at hand. Such is the stuff of science!

QUESTIONS FOR REVIEW

1. What are the different types of robust australopithecines that have been discovered? Why are they called "robust?"
2. How do robust australopithecines compare with other australopithecines?
3. What does the contemporaneous appearance of genus *Homo* (i.e., at the same time as some australopithecines) imply?
4. What did Louis Leakey imply by using the specific name "habilis?"
5. Discuss two taxonomic issues concerning early hominids. Try to give support for alternative positions.
6. What is a phylogeny? Construct one for early hominids (4–1 mya). Make sure you can describe what conclusions your scheme makes.
7. Discuss at least two alternative ways that *A. africanus* is currently incorporated into phylogenetic schemes.

HOMO ERECTUS

CHAPTER 12

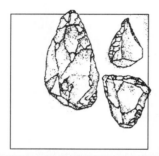

INTRODUCTION

In preceding chapters, we introduced the earliest known hominids: australopithecines and early *Homo (H. habilis)* of the Plio-Pleistocene. We discussed at some length the confusion surrounding them, and the number of species or lineages and their nomenclature. In this chapter, we continue the account of human evolution with the appearance of another species—*Homo erectus*. Unlike earlier hominids, who lived mainly in the Pliocene and the early Pleistocene, *Homo erectus* emerged in the Lower Pleistocene and lived well into the Middle Pleistocene. In our discussion of *H. erectus*, therefore, it will be helpful to give a brief background of the Pleistocene.

THE PLEISTOCENE (1.8 mya–10,000 ya)

The Pleistocene, better known as the "ice age," is the last epoch of geological history prior to the Recent. In the Northern Hemisphere, the Pleistocene has been characterized—over the last million years—by periodic advances of massive ice sheets (glaciers). While some schemes have attempted to distinguish four major glacial advances (with three interglaciations), particularly as applied to Europe, correlation between areas has proven nearly impossible.

The Pleistocene, which lasted almost 2 million years, was an important age in hominid evolutionary history. During this epoch, *Homo erectus* appears, and because of increased brain size and toolmaking abilities, this hominid has sometimes been called the first human. By the end of the Pleistocene, modern humans had long since appeared, dependence on culture as the human way of life had dramatically increased, and domestication of plants and animals—one of the great cultural revolutions of human history—was either about to commence or had already been developed. With this background of Pleistocene history, let us examine more closely the hominid who shaped the foundation for the evolution of our own species.

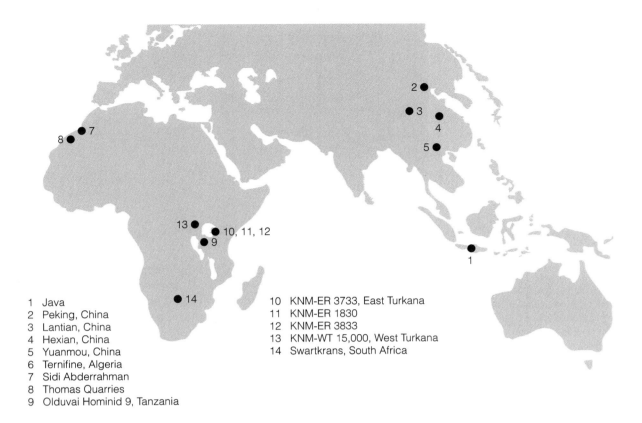

1 Java
2 Peking, China
3 Lantian, China
4 Hexian, China
5 Yuanmou, China
6 Ternifine, Algeria
7 Sidi Abderrahman
8 Thomas Quarries
9 Olduvai Hominid 9, Tanzania

10 KNM-ER 3733, East Turkana
11 KNM-ER 1830
12 KNM-ER 3833
13 KNM-WT 15,000, West Turkana
14 Swartkrans, South Africa

HOMO ERECTUS

From the available evidence, it appears that *H. erectus* evolved in Africa from *H. habilis* (or possibly another species of early *Homo*) about 1.8 or 1.7 mya. *H. erectus* populations apparently remained in East Africa until about one million years ago, when they disbursed to other regions of Africa as well as Asia.* It is in Asia where most *erectus* fossils have been found, especially in China and Java. Interestingly, their physical form and life style endured for about for about 1½ million years, until after 500,000 years ago, by which time archaic *sapiens* had appeared.

Morphologically, *H. erectus* was intermediate between earlier hominids and modern humans. *Erectus* was taller and larger-brained than earlier hominids, but shorter† (on average) and smaller-brained than *H. sapiens*. In short, in many physical and cultural traits, *H. erectus* falls into an evolutionary middle stage between the older and more recent forms. The cranial capacity of *H. erectus* ranges widely from 775 to 1225 cm³, with a mean of 1020 cm³. In terms of averages, the skull of *erec-*

FIGURE 12-1 A partial listing of *Homo erectus* sites. *H. erectus* inhabited areas of Europe, Africa, and Asia, a much wider distribution than australopithecines.

---

*Europe is another possibility, but remains of *H. erectus* have apparently not been found in Europe.
†One find—KNM-WT 15000) of a 12-year-old *H. erectus* boy—suggests *erectus* may have been as tall (perhaps taller) than *H. sapiens*.

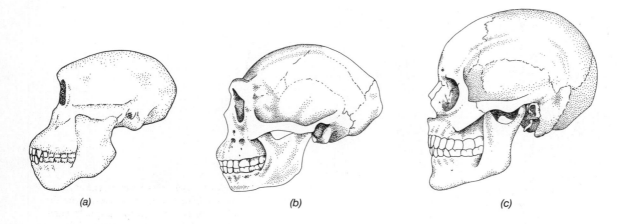

(a)   (b)   (c)

FIGURE 12-2 (a) *Australopithecus (afarensis)*; (b) *H. erectus* (Peking); (c) *H. sapiens* (anatomically modern). Note the changes in prognathism, ascending ramus, slope of foreheads, vault height, and development of occiput. (Not to scale.)

ALVEOLAR Tooth-bearing portion of the upper jaw.

tus is roughly twice the size of *Australopithecus*, 50 percent larger than *H. habilis*, and 75 percent as large as *H. sapiens*.

The *erectus* skull presents a number of notable features (Fig. 12-3). It is flatter than *H. sapiens*, apparently due to a smaller brain; a remarkably heavy brow ridge (supraorbital torus, Fig. 12-4) rides over the eye orbits, and at the back of the skull the occipital bone tapers like a rounded cone and also displays a torus. The face projects slightly, the upper jaw more so (**alveolar** prognathism), and the lower jaw lacks a projecting chin. Cheek teeth, especially molars, smaller than those of earlier hominids but larger than *H. sapiens'*, are characteristic of *erectus*.

From the rear, we can see an important feature that distinguishes a *H. erectus* skull: a pentagonal shape, with maximum breadth at or near the base (Fig. 12-5). In later hominids, maximum breadth is higher up on the skull.

FIGURE 12-3 *H. erectus* cranium.

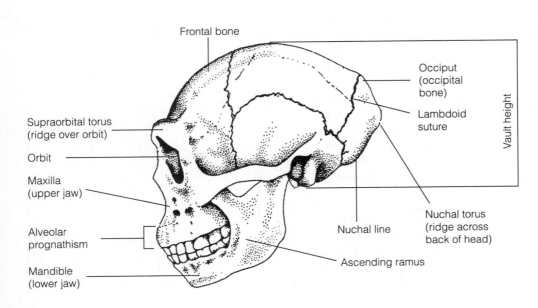

Frontal bone

Occiput (occipital bone)

Lambdoid suture

Vault height

Supraorbital torus (ridge over orbit)

Orbit

Maxilla (upper jaw)

Alveolar prognathism

Mandible (lower jaw)

Nuchal line

Nuchal torus (ridge across back of head)

Ascending ramus

FIGURE 12-4 *H. erectus* (Peking Man). From this view, the supraorbital torus, low vault of the skull, nuchal torus, and angled occiput can be clearly seen.

Sangiran 17

FIGURE 12-5 Craniogram showing outline from an occipital view; note the widest area in figure on right is toward base of skull giving a pentagonal form.

Two dental traits associated with *H. erectus* individuals are shovel-shaped incisors and taurodontism. The back of the incisors resembles a tiny scoop or coal shovel. Taurodontism refers to an enlarged pulp cavity, an advantage in some species that rely on tough, difficult-to-chew food items. In the postcranial skeleton, *H. erectus* also displays some differences from anatomically moderns. "Nonetheless, the functional locomotor capabilities appear to have been generally similar to adaptations in *H. sapiens* for habitual erect posture and efficient striding bipedal gait" (Howell, 1978).

ASIA

Java

FIGURE 12-6 Eugene Dubois.

The first scientist to deliberately design a research plan that would take him from the lab to where the fossil bones were buried, was Eugene Dubois, a Dutch anatomist (Fig. 12-6). Up until this time (late nineteenth century), embryology and comparative anatomy were considered the proper method of studying humans and their ancestry, and the research was done in the laboratory. Dubois changed all this.

At the University of Amsterdam, Dubois prepared for a medical degree. However, he soon lost interest in becoming a practicing physician and turned to his real interest, natural science. Upon graduation, Dubois accepted the position of assistant to his anatomy professor. After six years of research and teaching, he decided to leave the university. He joined the Royal Dutch Indies Army as a medical officer, and sailed to Sumatra in southeast Asia in 1887.

After several years of research in Sumatra, Dubois started working in Java in June, 1890. Finding the banks of the Solo River to be the most productive area, he concentrated his work there, near the town of Trinil. In October, 1891, the men working for Dubois unearthed a skullcap that was to become famous around the world. Dubois named it *Pithecanthropus erectus*—erect apeman. (The name was later changed to *Homo*

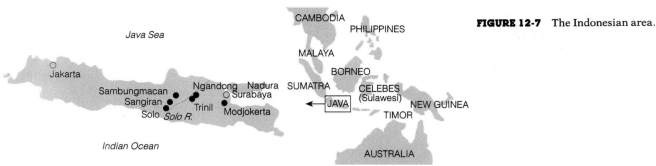

FIGURE 12-7 The Indonesian area.

CAMBODIA
PHILIPPINES
MALAYA
BORNEO
SUMATRA
CELEBES (Sulawesi)
NEW GUINEA
JAVA
TIMOR
AUSTRALIA

Java Sea
Jakarta
Sambungmacan
Sangiran
Solo *Solo R.*
Ngandong Nadura
Trinil
Modjokerta
Surabaya
Indian Ocean

erectus erectus.) A femur was recovered about fifteen yards upstream in what Dubois claimed was the same level as the skullcap (Fig. 12-8). When he examined it, Dubois discerned at once that it resembled a human femur belonging to an individual with upright posture. He assumed the skullcap (with a cranial capacity of just over 900 cm³) and the femur belonged to the same individual.

After studying these discoveries for a few years, Dubois startled the world in 1894 with a paper entitled "*Pithecanthropus erectus*, a Human Transitional Form from Java." Dubois' theory that his find was a transitional form between apes and humans met with devastating opposition from the majority of scientists. Dubois returned to Europe in 1895 and, hurt by the criticism, locked the bones in a trunk, and turned his research in other directions.

Despite the scientific opposition to Dubois' find, the skullcap has long been accepted by paleoanthropologists as legitimate, and dated as Middle Pleistocene, somewhere in the vicinity of 800,000 years ago. However, whether the femur and the skullcap belonged to the same individual is debatable. The femur may even be that of a modern!

The search for ancient humans in Java did not end with Dubois. Others, notably a younger paleontologist, G. H. R. von Koenigswald, took up the task in the 1930s, and the search continues.

Many of the skulls—from Sangiran and Sambungmacan, dated later than the Dubois Trinil skullcap—tend to be larger than the Dubois skullcap, in the 1000+ cm³ range. It has been suggested that the larger

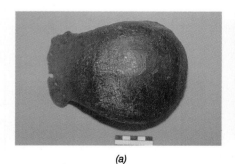

(a)

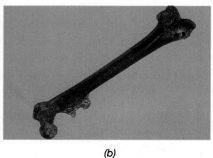

(b)

FIGURE 12-8 Skullcap (*Pithecanthropus* I, found by Eugene Dubois). Femur, also found by Dubois, led him to name this form *Pithecanthropus erectus*, now known as *H. erectus*. The abnormal spur of bone on the femur is known as an *exostosis*. It has no bearing on the identification of the femur.

TABLE 12-1 Java Hominidae (*H. erectus*)*

PLEISTOCENE	DESIGNATION AND OTHER NAMES	SITE	MATERIAL	CRANIAL CAPACITY (CM³)
Upper ?Middle	*H. soloensis* Ngandong Man Solo Man	Ngandong	skull bones, tibia At least 12 individuals	Range: 1150–1300
Middle or Upper	*H. modjokertensis* Perning 1	Perning	Infant calvarium	650
Middle	S12† P7	Sangiran	skull cap	1004
Middle	S17 P8	Sangiran	cranium	Estimated: 1059, 1125
Middle	Sambungmacan 1	Sambungmacan	skull cap	1035
Middle	Tr2	Trinil	skull cap	Estimates: 850–940
Middle	S2	Sangiran	skull cap	Estimates: 775–813
Middle	S6 Meganthropus paleojavanicus	Sangiran	partial right mandible	
Lower	S4 *P. robustus*	Sangiran	calvarial fragments	900
Lower	S5, S9 *P. dubius*	Sangiran	right mandibles	

*Lower and Middle Pleistocene (not to scale).
†S = Sangiran; P = *Pithecanthropus*.

size of the later skulls reflects an evolutionary trend toward *H. sapiens*; other experts, however, do not believe the increase is significant (Rightmire, 1990).

One group of Java skulls, at one time placed in their own species as *H. soloensis* (Fig. 12-9), is now generally known as Ngandong, after the site along the Solo River where they were found. In cranial capacity, they tend to be larger, over 1200 cm³, than most of the other Java skulls; also, they share some traits with early *sapiens*, including Neandertals. This raises the question of what lineage they belong to—early (archaic) *sapiens* or *H. erectus*?—often a problem when a fossil displays a mosaic of features. At present the designation *H. erectus* is favored.

FIGURE 12-9 (*a*) Laternal view of Solo skull; (*b*) rear view of Solo skull.

(a)

(b)

Java *erectus* forms lived on that island apparently for more than half a million years. Evidence of their behavior is sparse since few stone artifacts have been found. Possibly, perishable material such as bamboo or other kinds of wood were used, which may explain the dearth of artifacts.

Java may have been the earliest Asian home of *H. erectus*, but *erectus* populations were also dispersed in other regions of Asia, especially China. The most famous fossils, known in the West as Peking Man, were the first *Homo erectus* remains recognized in China.

CHINA

Zhoukoudian

Europeans had known for a long time that "dragon bones," so important to the Chinese for their healing and aphrodisiac powers, were actually mammal bones. In 1917, the Geological Survey of China resolved to find the dragon bone sites, and mounted an expedition in an area that appeared promising. The survey decided on an abandoned limestone quarry (actually a cave) at Zhoukoudian (Fig. 12-10), a village about 30

FIGURE 12-10 Zhoukoudian Cave. Grid on wall drawn for purposes of excavation.

miles southwest of Beijing, then known as Peking. Excavations were begun and, while many mammal bones were found, except for two teeth, no other human materials were discovered.

Dr. Davidson Black (Fig. 12-11), professor of anatomy at Peking Union Medical College, inspired by the discovery of the teeth, decided to become involved in the search for human remains. Black studied the teeth for 2 years and then announced they represented a new hominid species, *Sinanthropus pekinensis*, the Chinese man from Peking. In 1929, Black obtained funds to establish the Cenozoic Research Laboratory for the study of Cenozoic geology and paleontology.

In the same year a young Chinese geologist named W. C. Pei (who took over the direction of the excavation) discovered, on December 1, one of the most remarkable hominid skulls ever recovered up to that time. Pei brought the skull to Dr. Black, but because it was embedded in hard limestone, it took Black 4 months of hard, steady work to free it from its tough matrix. The result was worth the labor since the skull, that of a juvenile, was thick, low, and relatively small, but in Black's mind there was no doubt of its identity—it was human.

FIGURE 12-11 Dr. Davidson Black.

The response to the discovery, quite unlike that which greeted Dubois almost 40 years earlier, was immediate and enthusiastically favorable. The Zhoukoudian skull, known widely as Peking Man, became famous the world over.

Work at Locality 1, as this part of the cave is known, continued. Dr. Black, whose health was not robust, maintained a killing schedule and succumbed to a heart attack in 1934. Black was succeeded by Dr. Franz Weidenrich, a distinguished anatomist (Fig. 12-12), well known for his work on European fossil hominids. Excavations at Zhoukoudian ended in 1937, with Japan's invasion of China, but work at the Cenozoic Research Lab continued.

As relations between the United States and Japan deteriorated, Weidenreich decided to remove the fossil material to the United States, to prevent it from falling into Japanese hands. The bones were packed in cartons and arrangements were made for the U.S. Marine Corps to take the bones with them when they left Beijing to return to the States. The bones, however, never reached the United States and have never been found. No one to this day knows (or is not telling) what happened to them, and their location remains a mystery.

The bone assemblage at Zhoukoudian consists of six almost complete skulls, many bone fragments and teeth, the most and best from any *H. erectus* locality. Physically, Zhoukoudian possesses typical *erectus* characteristics. There are the fore and aft bulges, the skull is keeled by a sagittal ridge (Fig. 12-13), the face protrudes, the upper jaw is prognathic, the incisors are shoveled, and molars contain large pulp cavities. Like the Java forms, the skull is vintage *H. erectus*, showing its greatest breadth near the bottom. These similarities have persuaded taxonomists that the correct name for Zhoukoudian, now generally accepted, is *Homo erectus pekinensis*.

What mainly distinguishes Chinese from Javanese hominids is cranial capacity. Java hominids average 900 cm³; Chinese, 1088 cm³. The difference might be due to the more recent age of the Chinese fossils (roughly 500–250 thousand years ago). The larger Zhoukoudian skull is reflected

FIGURE 12-12 Dr. Franz Weidenreich.

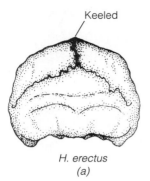

Keeled

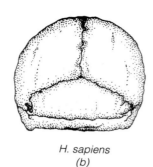

H. erectus
(a)

H. sapiens
(b)

FIGURE 12-13 (a) The keeled skull of *H. erectus*; (b) the skull of *H. sapiens* which does not show keeling.

BURIN A chisel-like stone tool used for engraving on horn, wood, and ivory; characteristic of the Upper Paleolithic.

FIGURE 12-14 Zhoukoudian (reconstructed cranium). (a) Frontal view; (b) lateral view; (c) rear view. The widest part of the skull is toward the bottom. The keeled effect can be seen in (a) and (c).

in a higher vault (Fig. 12-14), a higher forehead, and a longer and broader cranium. Zhoukoudian represents a later period in *erectus* evolution. With greater dependence on culture and selective pressures associated with that dependence, brain size may well have increased.

More than 100,000 artifacts were recovered from this site that was apparently occupied for almost 250,000 years. Chinese scientists Wu and Lin (1983) divided the site, on the basis of tool size, into three cultural stages, dating from 460 to 230 thousand years ago. Tools were large and made of soft stone in the earliest stage, and improved in the third stage to smaller tools made of a better quality stone.

Common tools at the site are choppers and chopping tools, but retouched flakes are also present, fashioned into scrapers, points, **burins**, and awls (Fig. 12-15). Burins have a chisel-like end and are usually used for engraving, such as the artwork shown in Fig. 13-42 (p. 277), or for utilitarian purposes. Awls are used for piercing, possibly for making holes in hide, in order to secure clothes to the body. Handaxes, abundant in Europe and Africa, were absent from Zhoukoudian.

Antler fragments were found, which have led to hypothesizing that horn may have been used as a material tool source. However, such tools have not been discovered. Hominid skulls, consisting mainly of brain cases (lacking facial and basal bones), suggest several intriguing possibilities: (a) use of the brain case as a drinking bowl; (b) mutilation of

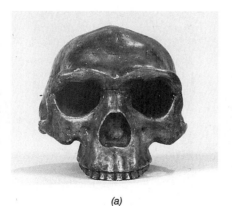

(a)

(b)

(c)

FIGURE 12-15 Chinese tools. (Adapted from Wu and Olsen)

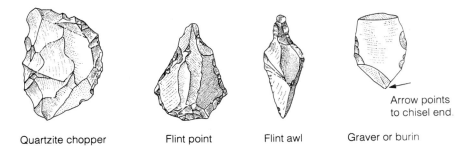

Quartzite chopper   Flint point   Flint awl   Graver or burin

Arrow points to chisel end.

the skull in order to remove the brain for eating; or (c) use of the skull as some sort of trophy or possibly in some ritualistic way. However, none of these views can currently be supported by evidence. (See Fig. 12-16.)

The way of life at Zhoukoudian has been traditionally (this evidence has also been questioned) described as consisting of hunters who killed deer, horses, and other animals, and foragers who gathered fruits, berries, ostrich eggs, and so on. They may have killed and eaten other *H. erectus* individuals, although the practice of cannibalism is doubted by many scholars. Some of the animal bones appear burned, implying cooking skills and fire use.

Could Zhoukoudian *erectus* speak? Their hunting and technological skills suggest they may have possessed some kind of symbolic communication. However, this is a subject on which experts differ, and a study of the endocranium does not give an unequivocal answer. Did they wear

FIGURE 12-16 Cannibalism at Zhoukoudian? The area around the foramen magnum appears to have been cut away—in order to remove the brain? Or was the base of the skull gnawed away by hyenas? (Photo of cast.)

FIGURE 12-17 Fossil and archeological sites of *H. erectus* in China.

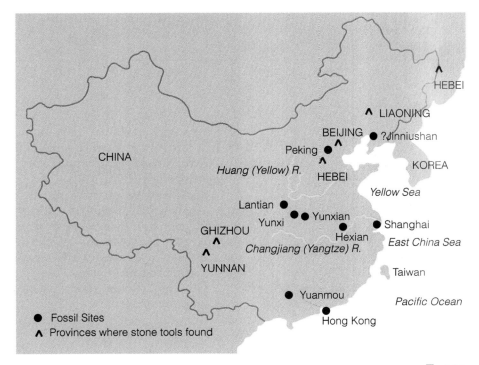

TABLE 12-2 *H. erectus* Fossils of China

DESIGNATION	SITE	AGE[a] PLEISTOCENE YEARS	MATERIAL	CRANIAL CAPACITY (CM³)
Jinniushan	Jinnu Mt., near Yingou	280,000	Incomplete skeleton, including calvarium	1400
Hexian	Longtandong Cave, Anhui	Middle 280–240,000	calvarium, skull frag., mandible frag., isolated teeth	1025
Zhoukoudian	Zhoukoudian Cave, Beijing	Middle 460–230,000[b]	5 adult crania, skull frags., facial bones, isolated teeth, 40+ individuals	1015–1225; avg: 1088
Yunxi	Bailongdong Cave, Hubei	Middle ?500,000	isolated teeth	
Yunxian	Longgudong Cave, Hubei	Middle ?500,000	isolated teeth	
Yuanmou	Shangnabang	Middle 600–500,000	upper central incisors	
Lantian	Chenjiawo, Lantian	Middle 650,000	mandible	
Lantian	Gongwangling, Lantian	Middle 800–750,000	calvarium, facial bones	780

Sources: Wu and Dong (1985); Lisowski (1984); Pope (1984); *Atlas of Primitive Man in China* (1980).

[a]These are best estimates—authorities differ.

[b]In a recent study of dating methods used in China, Aigner (1986) questions the long duration attributed to Zhoukoudian Locality I. She believes it is "mid-Middle Pleistocene," can be equated with the Holstein interglacial of Europe, and did not last more than 100,000 years.

clothing? Perhaps, since they manufactured awls. How long did they live? Studies of the fossil remains reveal that almost 40% of the bones belong to individuals under the age of 14, and only 2.6% are estimated in the 50 to 60 age group (Jia, 1975).

The Zhoukoudian culture described above has been challenged by archeologists (Binford and Stone, 1986a, 1986b) who contend that Zhoukoudian hominids were scavengers, not hunters. They also question the use of fire by *H. erectus* (except in the later phases of occupation). The so-called ash layers found in the cave (cited as evidence of fire) were not, they claim, produced by fire.

Although Zhoukoudian is China's best-known hominid fossil, and more work has been done at Zhoukoudian than any Chinese site, there are other hominids worth noting. Remains of two females were discovered at sites near Lantian, in central China. One of the remains, a partial cranium, may be the oldest Chinese hominid fossil yet found. A cranium from Hexian in eastern China, dated at 200,000 years ago, displays several *sapiens* features. Two incisors from Yuanmou County, northern China, have been suggested as the earliest remains of *H. erectus* in China. They have been dated as early as 1.7 mya and as recent as 500,000 years ago. The dates remain controversial.

We do not wish to leave the impression that Zhoukoudian Cave provides the only evidence for the way early humans lived in China. There are, in fact, many archeological sites, some as old or older than Zhoukoudian. Early stone tools have been found in widely separated provinces throughout China. Work at Zhoukoudian continues under the sponsorship of the Institute of Vertebrate Palaeontology and Palaeoanthropology (IVPP) of China. (See Fig. 12-17.)

EAST AFRICA

Since 1959, with the discovery of "Zinj," East Africa has become the El Dorado of the search for ancient humans. A prodigious quantity of fossil hominid remains, many of them australopithecines, have been recovered, and an increasing number of *Homo* specimens have been excavated in recent years.

The remains of *Homo erectus* come from East African locales (see map, Fig. 12-18) of Olduvai Gorge, Tanzania, and Lake Turkana, Kenya. Bodo, from Ethiopia, once classified as *H. erectus*, more likely belongs with archaic *sapiens*.

FIGURE 12-18 *H. erectus* sites in East Africa.

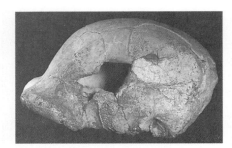

FIGURE 12-19   OH 9.

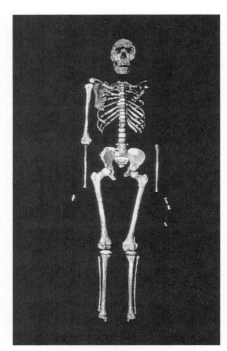

FIGURE 12-20   KMW-WT 15000. The most complete and oldest *H. erectus* yet found.

Olduvai

As far back as 1960, Dr. Louis Leakey unearthed a skull, Olduvai Hominid (OH) 9 (Fig. 12-19), which he identified as *H. erectus*. OH 9, who lived more than a million years ago, has a surprisingly massive cranium with the largest cranial capacity (1067 cm³) of all early *erectus* specimens.

Also from Olduvai is a partial skull, OH 12, which resembles OH 9 but is much younger, in the .83–.62 million year range. It is smaller, probably reflecting a case of sexual dimorphism.

Lake Turkana

Some 400 miles north of Olduvai Gorge, on the northern boundary of Kenya, is a finger lake, Lake Turkana. (See Fig. 12-18.) Explored by Richard Leakey and his colleagues since 1969, the eastern shore of the lake has been a virtual gold mine of australopithecines, *Homo habilis*, and a few *H. erectus* remains.

Several fossils, possibly belonging to *H. erectus*, were found at Koobi Fora on the east side of Lake Turkana, dated from about 1.8 to 1.0 mya. These fossils, with significantly smaller cranial capacity, are older than the Olduvai *erectus*.

In August of 1984, Kamoya Kimeu, the excavation team leader, with his uncanny knack for finding fossils, lived up to his reputation by discovering a small piece of skull near Richard Leakey's base camp on the *west* side of Lake Turkana. Leakey and his colleague, Alan Walker of Johns Hopkins University, excavated the site (known as Nariokotome) in 1984 and 1985.

The dig was a smashing success. The workers unearthed the most complete *H. erectus* yet found. Known properly as KNM-WT 15000,* this all but complete skeleton includes facial bones and most of the postcranial bones, a rare event indeed for *erectus*, since these bones are scarce at other *H. erectus* sites. (See Fig. 12-20.)

Another remarkable feature of the find is its age. The dating is based on the chronometric dates of the geologic formation in which the site is located and is set at about 1.6 million years. The fossil is that of a boy about 12 years old, estimated to have been 5 feet 5 inches tall. Had he grown to maturity, his estimated height may have reached 6 feet, taller than *H. erectus* was heretofore thought to be. Tentatively, the cranial capacity is estimated at 900 cm³. The postcranial bones appear to be quite similar, though not identical, to modern humans.

South Africa

The evidence for *H. erectus* in South Africa is unclear. A crushed mandible found at Swartkrans is placed in the *erectus* taxon by some scientists; other researchers, however, disagree. A crushed mandible does not lend itself to decisive conclusions.

---

*WT is the symbol for West Turkana; that is, the west side of the lake. The east side of the lake is symboled as ER, East Rudolf, the former name of the lake.

TABLE 12-3 *H. erectus*, East Africa

SITE/AGE	DESIGNATION	MATERIAL	CRANIAL CAPACITY (CM³)	DISCOVERED[c] (DATE)
Olduvai[a]				
Tanzania				
Bed IV	OH 23	Mandible fragments		1968
	OH 2	2 vault fragments		1935
	OH 12	Cranial fragments		1962
	OH 22	Right half of mandible		1968
	OH 28	Pelvic bone, femur shaft		1970
Bed III	OH 51	Left side of mandible		1974
1.2 my	OH 9	Calvarium	1067	1960
Lake Turkana[b]				
Koobi Fora, Turkana, Kenya				
1.65 my	KNM-ER 3883	Braincase, some facial bones	800	1974
1.5–1.4 my	KNM-ER 730	Mandible lacking right side		1970–1980
1.7 my	KNM-ER 1808	Skeletal and cranial elements		1973
1.5 my	KNM-ER 3733	Well-preserved crania	850	1974
West Turkana				
Nariokotome				
1.6 my	KNM-WT 15000	Almost complete skeleton	900	1984

[a]Louis Leakey and Mary Leakey were directors of excavations at Olduvai when these finds were made.
[b]Richard Leakey is director of excavations at Lake Turkana.

North Africa

H. erectus appears to have originated in East Africa close to 2 million years ago. We find them, the first hominids to leave Africa, in Java and China, about 500,000 years ago. As much as a million years ago, on their way to the Far East, some groups of *H. erectus* may have detoured west. Their remains, found in Algeria and Morocco (Fig. 12-21), consist mainly of lower jaws (Fig. 12-22) and some portions of skulls tentatively dated from 700 to 500 thousand years ago.

FIGURE 12-21 *Homo erectus* sites in North Africa.

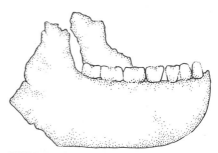

FIGURE 12-22 Ternifine (Tighenif), a mandible from Algeria, North Africa. Note the robustness of the jaw.

Europe

Until recently, a half dozen or so European fossil remains were considered to be *H. erectus*. However, it seems that *erectus* did not make it to Europe. This may seem strange since we find *erectus* in northwest Africa, just across the Strait of Gibraltar. The European fossils, once assigned to *H. erectus*,* share derived traits with *H. sapiens*, and are now designated as archaic *sapiens*. They are discussed in the next chapter.

HUMAN EMERGENCE: *AUSTRALOPITHECUS* TO *HOMO ERECTUS*

Evolution of *H. Erectus*

Surveying hominid events of the Lower and Middle Pleistocene, we see the disappearance of australopithecines and early *Homo (H. habilis)* and the appearance of *H. erectus* populations that expand their habitat beyond African boundaries. When we examine *H. erectus*, we find the course of human evolution changing in several directions: *physical, technological,* and *social.*

Physical Anatomically, *H. erectus* is notably similar to modern human populations. The femur/pelvis complex may not be identical to ours, but their erect walking stride would be very much like our own. Their legs were longer than their arms, and their stature falls within the range of modern populations. In Asia, their height was around 5 feet 5 inches, but the 12-year-old boy from Lake Turkana would probably have been a six-footer had he lived until maturity. The overriding difference between *H. erectus* and moderns is the skull, which, of course, is the residence of

---

*Some paleoanthropologists argue that early European archaics (discussed in the next chapter) belong in the taxon *H. erectus*.

the brain. The *erectus* brain was about one-third smaller than the average today, and brain size affected the skull structure. Smaller cranial size, lower vault, and widest breadth toward the bottom of the skull (see Fig. 12-14c) are most likely due to a smaller and differently proportioned brain.

Technological   Scholars have noted the remarkable stasis of the physical and cultural characteristics of *H. erectus* populations, which seemed to have changed so little in about 1.5 million years of existence. Nevertheless, there were some modifications in the physical traits we have mentioned, as well as in the cultural.

Compared to earlier hominids, brain expansion may have enabled *H. erectus* to develop a more sophisticated tool kit, especially a core worked on both sides, called a *biface* (known widely as a handaxe) (Fig. 12-23). The biface has a flatter core than the roundish earlier pebble tool. This change enabled the toolmaker to shape straighter and sharper edges into a more efficient implement. The handaxe belongs to the **Acheulian** tradition and became standardized as the basic *H. erectus* all-purpose tool, with some modification, for more than a million years. It served to cut, scrape, pound, dig, and more—a most useful tool that has been found in Europe, Africa, parts of Asia, and one that has also been used by early *sapiens*.

Like members of their species elsewhere, *H. erectus* in China manufactured choppers and chopping tools. And like other *erectus* toolmakers, they fashioned scrapers and other small tools but did not produce bifaces (handaxes). Also introduced by *H. erectus*, especially in Africa, was the cleaver (Fig. 12-24), perhaps used in butchering—the chopping and breaking of bones of large animals.

Social   One of the fascinating qualities of *H. erectus* was a penchant for travel. From the relatively close confines of East Africa, *erectus* became a world traveler, and by the time *H. sapiens* appears, one million years later, *H. erectus* had trekked to distant points of the earth. Moving north from East Africa, *erectus* could have chosen several directions. One was eastward over the land bridge that, at the time, joined East Africa to the Arabian Peninsula (Fig. 12-25).

The life of hunters/scavengers is nomadic, and the woodland and savanna that covered the southern tier of Asia bordering the Indian Ocean, from East Africa to Southeast Asia, would have been an excellent environment for *H. erectus*, for these areas are similar to the econiche of early African *erectus*.

Why did *H. erectus* leave "home"? We will never know for certain, but there were climatic and geographic changes that may have been responsible. It was a time of heavy precipitation, which fell as snow in the Northern Hemisphere and created the great glaciers of Europe and North America. In tropical areas, heavy rainfall produced rivers, lakes, and new grasslands. With additional food sources available, a population increase may have led splinter groups to seek their own areas.

If the new groups succeeded, other small groups may have eventually budded off these, and so the process would have continued as *erectus*

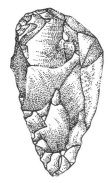

FIGURE 12-23   Acheulian biface ("handaxe").

ACHEULIAN   The culture period, or stone tool industry, of the Middle and part of the Lower Pleistocene; characterized by the handaxe.

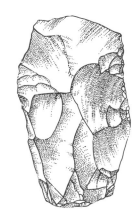

FIGURE 12-24   Acheulian cleaver. The flat edge of the cleaver distinguishes it from the handaxes and cleavers.

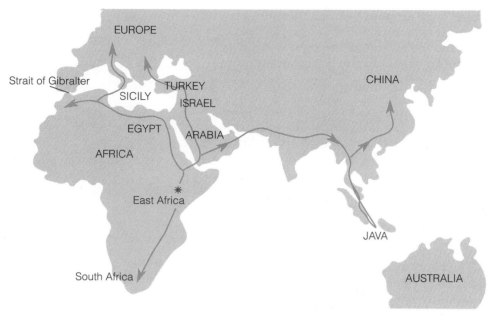

FIGURE 12-25 The *H. erectus* expansion. Assuming *H. erectus* originated in East Africa, the map illustrates emigration routes to northwest Africa, eastern Asia, and probably South Africa.

moved farther and farther away from their ancestral home, ultimately reaching northwest Africa to the west and Java and China to the east.

We have discussed several aspects of *H. erectus*. What is of most interest to paleoanthropologists are the subtle physical changes that occurred in the 1.5 million years of their existence. From a biocultural and evolutionary point of view, can these modifications from preceding hominids be explained?

Many of the scenarios explaining *Homo erectus* evolution (including some we have discussed here) focus upon dietary adaptations. In point of fact, we do not know what *H. erectus* ate. *If* in later *erectus* times, meat became a more regular component of the diet, this dietary shift certainly could have affected dental proportions and cranial architecture. In addition, cultural modifications, such as more efficient cutting, grinding, and pounding tools may have rendered vegetable materials as well as meat more easily chewed. Finally, many archeologists think *H. erectus* may well have been the first hominid to *cook* food—an extremely important cultural innovation, since it makes a wide variety of foods much easier both to chew and digest. Of course, as we mentioned, there is still considerable debate whether *Homo erectus* really used fire at all.

When we look back at the evolution of *H. erectus*, we realize how significant were this early human's achievements toward **hominization**. For example, it was *H. erectus* who

HOMINIZATION The process of becoming human.

1. Increased in body size with more efficient bipedalism than earlier hominids
2. Embraced culture wholeheartedly as a strategy of adaptation
3. May have used fire extensively
4. Became a more efficient scavenger and perhaps hunter

5. Probably established some sort of social organization, such as family and band

6. Possessed a brain that reshaped and increased in size to within *sapiens* range

In short, it was *H. erectus*, committed to bipedalism and a cultural way of life, who transformed hominid evolution to human evolution.

SUMMARY

Homo erectus lived from about 1.8 million years ago to about 200,000 years ago, a period of 1.5 million years. The first finds were made by Dubois in Java, and later discoveries came from China and Africa.

Differences from australopithecines are significant in *H. erectus*: a larger and reproportioned brain, taller stature, and changes in facial structure and skull buttressing. The long period of *erectus* existence was marked by a remarkably uniform technology over space and time. Nevertheless, *H. erectus* introduced more sophisticated tools and probably new forms of food processing, using tools and probably fire as well. They were also able to migrate to different environments and successfully adapt to new conditions.

Apparently originating in East Africa, *H. erectus* migrated in several directions—to south and northwest Africa, and then east to Java and China. The evidence from China, especially Zhoukoudian, infers an *erectus* way of life that included hunting and the controlling of fire, but anthropologists are not in complete agreement about this interpretation.

It is generally assumed that *erectus* evolved to *sapiens* since many fossils (discussed in the next chapter) display both *erectus* and *sapiens* features. There remain questions concerning the behavior and evolution of *H. erectus* (e.g., Did they hunt? Did they control fire? Was evolution to *H. sapiens* gradual or rapid?).

QUESTIONS FOR REVIEW

1. What was the effect of Pleistocene weather on *H. erectus*?

2. Describe *H. erectus*. How is *H. erectus* anatomically different from australopithecines? From *H. sapiens*?

3. What evidence indicates that the *erectus'* brain is smaller than the *sapiens'* brain?

4. What are the significant features of the cultural life of *H. erectus*?

5. What were the contributions of Eugene Dubois to paleoanthropology?

6. Why do you think the Beijing *erectus* was enthusiastically accepted, whereas Java was not?

7. What tools did *H. erectus* introduce? How were they used?

8. Dates of fossils are frequently mentioned in the text. Why do you think fossil dates are important?

9. What is the *H. erectus* evidence from Africa? What questions of human evolution does the evidence raise?

10. Summarize the evolutionary events (physical and cultural) of the *H. erectus* period.
11. Cite as many reasons as you can why KNM-WT 15000 is important.
12. Can you suggest any reasons why the earliest remains of *H. erectus* have come from East Africa?
13. *H. erectus* migrated to various points in Africa and vast distances to east Asia. What does this tell you about this species?
14. Why do we "owe" so much to *H. erectus*?

HOMO SAPIENS

CHAPTER 13

INTRODUCTION

We noted in Chapter 12 that *H. erectus* was present in Africa more than 1.5 mya. About a million years later, *H. erectus* could also be found in Java and China. We also noted that *H. erectus* probably migrated to Europe, since a number of fossils that display both *erectus* and *sapiens* features have been excavated in Europe, as well as in Africa, China, and Java.

These forms, for the most part, fall into the domain of the latter half of the Middle Pleistocene, from about 400 to 130 kya,* and are often referred to as archaic *sapiens*, early *sapiens*, or transitional forms. The term *sapiens* applies since the appearance of *sapiens* traits suggests an evolutionary trend toward the *sapiens* stage. Because it appears they are evolving toward anatomically modern human beings, but have not yet attained that stage of grace, we shall list them as archaic *sapiens*. For the purpose of organizing the material that covers these several hundred thousand years, we will divide archaic *sapiens* into categories of early archaics and Neandertals.

In this chapter, then, we shall examine the course of human evolution in the Middle Pleistocene and Upper Pleistocene. The chapter is divided into two basic parts: archaic *sapiens* and *H. sapiens sapiens* (a.m.s.).† This scheme is somewhat simplistic given the problems of classifying evolving hominids, but it will serve as an adequate device for dealing with the emergence of the *H. sapiens sapiens* grade of human evolution.

ARCHAIC FORMS: ARCHAIC *SAPIENS*

Modifications in the direction of a *sapiens* stage by early archaics are reflected in: brain expansion; increased upper skull (parietal) breadth (the base portion of the skull is no longer the widest area) and, therefore, the rear view of the skull is no longer pentagonal; decrease in size of molars and, generally, an increase in size of anterior teeth; and usually a decrease in cranial and postcranial robusticity.

---

*kya stands for "thousand years ago." The symbol *k* is commonly used for thousand.

†Anatomically modern *sapiens* is abbreviated as a.m.s.

FIGURE 13-1 Sites of archaic *sapiens*, including Neandertals.

Archaic *sapiens* are found on three continents: Africa, Asia, and Europe (Fig. 13-1). In Europe, the well-known Neandertals are included in this category.

Africa

Sapiens characteristics can be seen in fossils found at several African sites (Fig. 13-2). In a shallow Broken Hill mine shaft at Kabwe, Zambia, south Africa, were a complete cranium (Fig. 13-3b) and other cranial and post-cranial material belonging to several individuals, dated in the neighborhood of 130 kya. Broken Hill (or Kabwe) displays a mosaic of older traits (e.g., a massive supraorbital torus—see Fig. 13-3) and later traits (e.g., cranial capacity of 1230 cm³, which is significantly beyond the *erectus* av-

FIGURE 13-2 Sites of African archaic *sapiens*.

FIGURE 13-3 (*a*) Broken Hill (Rhodesian Man), Kabwe. Note very heavy supraorbital torus. (*b*) Photograph of original.

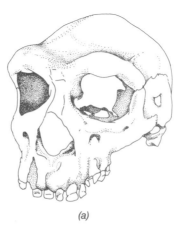

(a)

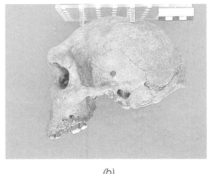

(b)

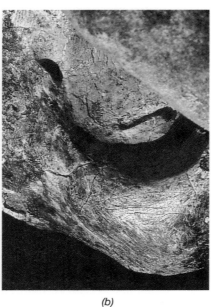

(a)   (b)

FIGURE 13-4 (*a*) Bodo. An early archaic *sapiens* from Africa. (*b*) View from above. Note the cutmarks on the floor of the eye orbit and on the cheekbones. (Courtesy of Tim White)

erage). Also from South Africa and resembling Broken Hill in some features is Elandsfontein (Saldanha), from the southernmost end of the continent.

Discovered in 1976 in northeast Ethiopia, in the general area where Lucy was found (see Chapter 10), is an incomplete cranium, Bodo (Fig. 13-4a, b), dating from the Middle Pleistocene. Like Broken Hill, the Bodo skull is a mosaic of *H. erectus* and more modern features. Hippopotamus bones at the site were associated with Acheulian tools (Fig. 13-5), suggesting that the Bodo population butchered the animals (Fig. 13-6) they scavenged or hunted. It also appears that Bodo was scalped! When Professor Tim White of the University of California, Berkeley, examined the skull, he found 17 cutmark areas around the orbits and on the upper sides of the skull. White believes these marks suggest patterned intentional defleshing with a stone tool. If so, this specimen would represent the earliest solid evidence for deliberate scalping (White, 1986).

These finds in Africa raise questions: Were the people represented by these skulls related? What was the relationship of the earlier *erectus* populations from East and South Africa with the later archaic *sapiens* forms?

(a)   (b)   (c)   (d)

FIGURE 13-5 Small tools of Acheulian industry. (*a*) Side scraper; (*b*) point; (*c*) end scraper; (*d*) burin.

FIGURE 13-6 A Middle Pleistocene butchering site at Olorgesaile, Kenya, excavated by Louis Leakey who had the catwalk built for observers.

Asia

Like their counterparts in Europe and Africa, Chinese archaic *sapiens* (see map, Fig. 13-7) that date from about 260 to 100 kya, also display both older and more recent characters. Of the China archaics, Dali (Fig. 13-8) is the most complete skull. Despite its relatively small cranial capacity of 1120 cm³, it is clearly an archaic *sapiens*. Material from four other sites also reflect the mosaic of both species. These include Changyang, Ixujiayao, Maba, and an almost complete skeleton from Jinniushan (Yingkou), which has a surprising cranial capacity of 1335 cm³.

Chinese anthropologists believe that evolution in China proceeded from *H. erectus* to archaic *sapiens* to anatomically moderns. That such re-

FIGURE 13-7 Sites of Chinese archaic *sapiens*.

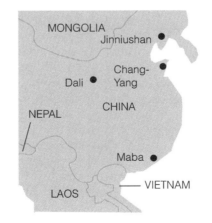

FIGURE 13-8 Dali. A good example of Chinese archaic *sapiens*.

FIGURE 13-9 Map of European early archaic *sapiens*.

gional evolution occurred in many areas of the world or, alternatively, that anatomically modern migrants from Africa displaced local populations, is the subject of a major ongoing debate in paleoanthropology. This important controversy will be discussed later in the chapter.

India

In 1982, a partial skull that dated in the 100 kya range was discovered in the Narmada Valley, central India. Associated with this fossil were Acheulian handaxes, cleavers, flakes, and choppers (Kennedy, 1990).

Europe

H. erectus may have once roamed the fields of Europe, but there are no fossils that unequivocally prove it. The earliest hominids found in Europe, like their contemporaries in Africa and Asia, already possess features resembling both *erectus* and *sapiens*. Furthermore, some of these archaic *sapiens* may have been ancestral to Neandertals, since both share a number of somewhat similar characters.

European forms, from roughly 500 to 130 kya (most dates are not certain) may be separated into earlier and later archaics (see Table 13-1). They differ from one another in their mix of *erectus* and *sapiens* traits: some are more *erectus*, others more *sapiens*, but all are considered to be archaic *sapiens*. Remains have been found in England, France, Germany, Spain, Hungary, and Greece.

Resemblances to *H. erectus* may be seen in the robusticity of the mandible (Fig. 13-10), thick cranial bones, thick occipital bone, pro-

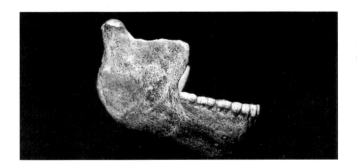

FIGURE 13-10 Cast of Mauer jaw found near Heidelberg. Note the very wide ascending ramus and overall robusticity of the mandible.

nounced occipital torus, heavy supraorbital torus, and receding frontal bone. *Sapiens* features (Fig. 13-11) reflect a tendency for thinner bones, a rounder occipital bone, and a larger cranial capacity; in some cases, Neandertal traits are also seen.

MIDDLE PLEISTOCENE EVOLUTION

Like the *erectus* mix in Africa and Asia, the fossils from Europe exhibit a mosaic of traits characteristic of both species. It is important to note that the fossils from each continent differ; that is, the mosaic Chinese forms are not the same as those from Africa or Europe which, in turn, are not the same as each other.

FIGURE 13-11 The Petralona skull, an early archaic *sapiens* from Greece.

TABLE 13-1 European Archaic *Sapiens*			
NAME	**LOCATION**	**DATE (KY)**	**CRANIAL CAPACITY (CM³)**
Earlier archaics			
Arago	France	about 400	1050–1150
Atapuerca	Spain	350–200	—
Bilzingsleben	Germany	425–200	—
Mauer	Germany	500+	—
Petralona	Greece	?500	1320
Vérteszöllös	Hungary	?210–160	larger than *erectus*
Later archaics			
Biache	France	200–160	1200
La Chaise	France	200–150	—
Montmaurin	France	190–130	—
Steinheim	Germany	300–250	1100–1200 (?female)
Swanscombe	England	300	1325 (estimate)

Convex side scraper   Point

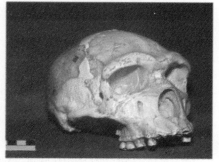

Convergent scraper   Levallois flake

FIGURE 13-12 Mousterian flake tools (after Bordes).

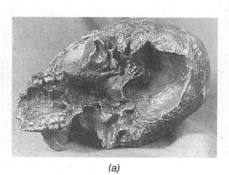

FIGURE 13-13 Partial Arago skull, an early archaic.

Compared to *H. erectus*, archaic physical changes are not dramatic. There is, however, a definite increase in brain size, a critical change reflected in a higher vault, and a change in the shape of the skull from pentagonal to globular, which may be seen from a rear view. It is interesting to note that, in Europe, the changes move toward a Neandertal *sapiens* style, whereas in Africa and Asia, changes move toward modern *sapiens*.

MIDDLE PLEISTOCENE CULTURE

The Acheulian technology of *H. erectus* persevered for more than a million years in the Lower and Middle Pleistocene, with relatively little change until near the end of the period, when it became slightly more sophisticated. The handaxe, absent in China in the Lower Pleistocene, remains absent in the Middle Pleistocene, and choppers and chopping tools continue to be the basic tools. Bone, a very useful tool material, was not used much by archaic *sapiens*. Flake tools (Fig. 13-12) similar to those of the earlier era persisted, although perhaps in greater variety. Archaic *sapiens* in Africa and Europe invented a method—the Levallois technique—(see p. 267) for controlling flake size and shape. This was no mean feat and suggests that archaic cognitive abilities, compared to those of *H. erectus*, had improved.

Archaic *sapiens* continued to live both in caves and open-air sites, and may have increased their use of caves. Questions have been raised, which are still unanswered, concerning the ability of archaic *sapiens* to control fire. Did they actually *make* fire, or did they simply use fire from natural sources, such as brush fire?

As an example of early *sapiens* culture, an episode of life in Middle Pleistocene France is taken from the reconstruction of Terra Amata by archeologists Henry and Marie-Antoinette de Lumley (1969).

Terra Amata

In the city of Nice (see map, Fig. 13-15) on the French Riviera, bulldozers exposed a sandy deposit containing paleolithic implements during the

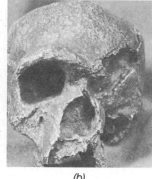

(a)   (b)

FIGURE 13-14 Cast of Steinheim skull. (*a*) Basal view, showing how the foramen magnum was enlarged, apparently for removal of the brain—for dietary or ritualistic purposes; (*b*) frontal view showing warped skull.

FIGURE 13-15 The site of Terra Amata.

construction of luxury apartments in 1965. The de Lumleys, who were monitoring the construction, persuaded the builders to halt operations and then, with their crew, excavated deposits 70 feet deep. They uncovered a series of strata that disclosed signs of Würm, Riss, and Mindel glacial and interglacial periods.

Reconstructing the culture of Terra Amata, the de Lumleys found that the Terra Amatans built temporary oval-shaped huts (Fig. 13-16), using heavy stones to brace the walls. Inside the hut the living floor consisted of a thick bed of organic matter and ash, interrupted by imprints (post holes) left by posts that supported the roof. In the center of the hut was a hearth a foot or two in diameter (Fig. 13-17).

The daily activity of the inhabitants consisted of gathering plants, hunting small and large game,* collecting sea food, and manufacturing tools. Animal bones at the site include those of birds, turtles, rabbits, and rodents, but bones of large animals, such as deer, elephant, wild boar, ibex, rhinoceros, and wild ox, were more plentiful. In addition to meat,

---

*We have already noted that some archeologists have challenged the assumption that early hominids systematically hunted (see Chap. 12).

FIGURE 13-16 Shelter at Terra Amata. Evidence of habitation at Terra Amata enabled de Lumley to reconstruct what a hut might have looked like. (Courtesy California Academy of Sciences)

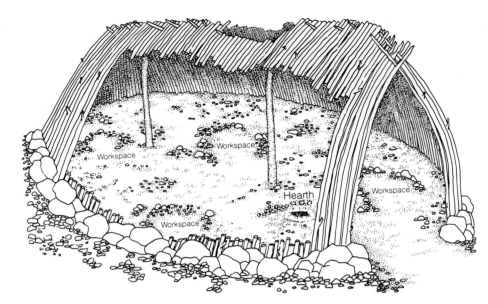

FIGURE 13-17 Cutaway of Terra Amata hut. Note the hearth, the workspaces where people sat making tools, the poles that supported the roof, and the stones at the base of the hut supporting the sides. (Adapted from de Lumley, 1969)

there is evidence these early Europeans gathered shellfish from the Mediterranean Sea.

Artifacts from the site consisted mainly of stone tools of the Acheulean industry: chopping tools, bifaces, cleavers, several kinds of scrapers and flakes, projectile points, and pebble tools. The scrapers were probably used in meat processing and the choppers in butchering. Projectile points suggest a throwing weapon, such as a spear or lance.

Terra Amata was a temporary camp set up for a few days in late spring or summer. As summer ended, winds covered the camp with a layer of sand, which was then packed down by winter rains. When the hunters returned the following year, they again built their huts in the same place, on the outlines of the previous year, and the entire process was repeated.

NEANDERTALS (125–30 KYA)

Despite their apparent disappearance about 30 kya, Neandertals continue to haunt the best-laid theories of paleoanthropologists. They fit into the general scheme of human evolution, and yet they are misfits. Classified as *H. sapiens*, they were like us, and yet different. It is not an easy task to put them in their place!

These troublesome hunters are the cavemen of cartoonists—they are usually depicted walking about with bent knees, dragging a club in one hand and a woman by her hair in the other. They are described as brutish, dwarfish, apelike, and obviously of little intelligence, an image more than somewhat exaggerated.

While cartoonists' license is not to be denied, the fact remains that Neandertals walked as upright as any of us, and, if they dragged clubs

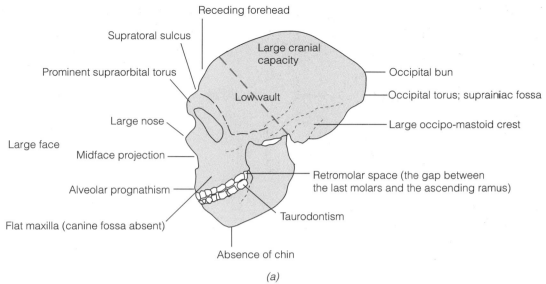

(a)

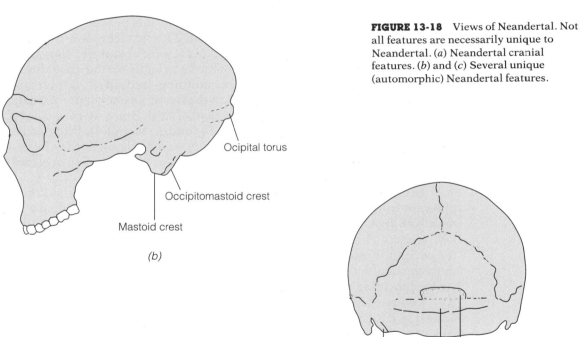

(b)

FIGURE 13-18 Views of Neandertal. Not all features are necessarily unique to Neandertal. (a) Neandertal cranial features. (b) and (c) Several unique (automorphic) Neandertal features.

(c)

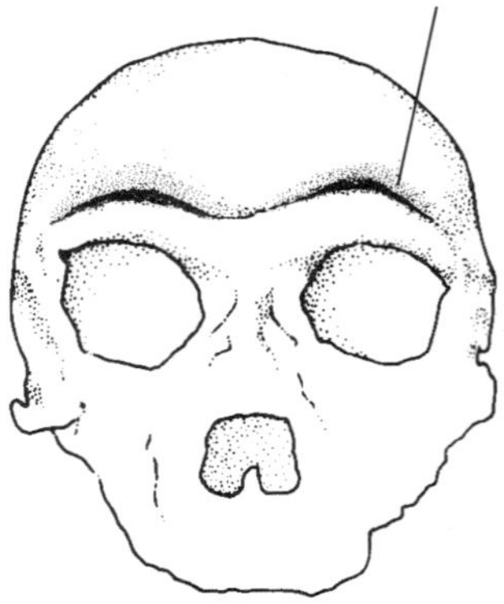

Arched
supraorbital
torus

FIGURE 13-19 The arched browridges of Neandertal.

MOUSTERIAN A culture period, or stone tool industry, of the Middle Paleolithic, usually associated with Neandertals. Characterized mainly by stone flakes.

and women, there is not the slightest evidence of it. Nor were they dwarfish or apelike. Also, in the light of twentieth-century human behavior, we should be careful whom we call brutish.

As far as intelligence is concerned, Neandertals produced excellent **Mousterian** implements and, in fact, invented a new technique, the disc-core technique (Campbell, 1976). Neandertals were also clever enough to cope with the intensely cold weather of the last glacial period. In addition to open sites, they lived in caves, wore clothing, built fires, gathered in settlements (some of which extended to the Arctic Ocean), hafted* some of their tools, and hunted with a good deal of skill. Since there was very little vegetable food available on the cold tundra, Neandertals had to be very skillful hunters in order to survive by subsisting off herds of reindeer, woolly rhinoceros, and mammoth. Finally, the brain size of Neandertals is within the range of moderns.

Other physical traits set Neandertals apart as a unique population different from moderns, from their contemporaries in Africa and eastern Asia, and from their European predecessors. Their skull is large, long, low, and bulging at the sides. At the rear of the skull, a bun protrudes, but the occiput is rounded without the *erectus* angulation. The forehead rises more vertically than *erectus*, and the browridges arch over the orbits instead of forming a straight bar (Fig. 13-19).

Compared to moderns, the Neandertal face stands out. It projects, almost as if it were pulled forward. Usually associated with this feature is lack of a chin. The anterior teeth tended to be larger, possibly because they were used as tools, and the posterior teeth were smaller. Postcranially, Neandertals were very robust, barrelchested, and powerfully muscled.

We have stressed the physical differences between Neandertal and moderns, but aside from their muscularity, and skull and face, there was not a great deal of disparity between "them and us."

---

*A haft is a handle of a weapon or tool.

UPPER PLEISTOCENE

With the onset of a warm period (the Riss-Würm interglacial), about 125 kya (Fig. 13-20), we encounter the complex situation of the Neandertals. For some 85,000 years, Neandertals lived in Europe and western Asia, and their comings and goings have raised more questions and controversies than perhaps any other hominid group.

There are several basic questions to bear in mind as we examine the Neandertal event more closely. Whatever happened to them? Did they evolve to anatomically modern humans? Did they merge with their anatomically modern contemporaries? Did they become extinct because they could not compete successfully with their modern neighbors? Or do they still exist in some remote areas as a Bigfoot or Yeti? (We may as well point out there is no worthwhile evidence for such survivors despite the sensational accounts that appear in the magazines at the supermarket checkstands.) In considering these and other questions, we shall start at the beginning.

NEANDERTAL BEGINNINGS

Neandertal takes its name from the Neander Valley near Dusseldorf, Germany. In 1856, workmen quarrying limestone caves in the valley blew up the entrance of one of the caves and came across fossilized bones. These bones were given to the local high school natural science teacher, Johann Karl Fuhlrott, who believed the bones were those of an ancient human. Others disagreed, and the fate of Neandertal Man, as the bones were

Years ago	Temperature C W	Stratigraphy
10.000		Late I
13.000		
20.000		
25.000		
29.000		Middle II
40.000		
50.000		
60.000		Early II
65.000		
75.000		

FIGURE 13-20 The Würm glaciation. During a glacial period, such as the Würm, the temperature—and the presence of ice—varies. The 65,000 years of the Würm were not simply one long cold period.

FIGURE 13-21 European Neandertal sites.

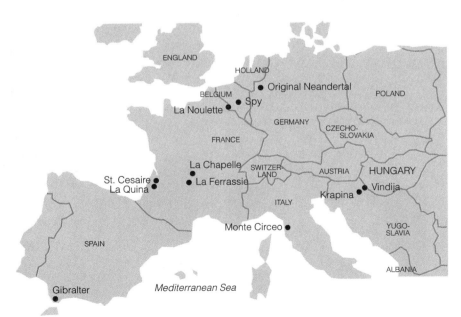

FIGURE 13-22 Map of La Chapelle site.

named, hung in the balance for years until later finds were discovered. Additional fossils not only proved Fulhrott correct, but more importantly, they brought home the shocking realization that a form of human different from nineteenth-century Europeans had, in fact, existed.

The discovery, in 1908, of La Chapelle-aux-Saints settled the issue of fossil hominid existence once and for all.

La Chapelle-aux-Saints

One of the most important Neandertal discoveries was made in 1908 at La Chapelle-aux-Saints (Fig. 13-22), in Correze in southwestern France. Found in a Mousterian cultural layer was a nearly complete human skeleton. The body had been deliberately buried in a shallow grave and fixed in a ritual position, a bison leg placed on its chest, and the trench filled with flint tools and broken animal bones.* The position of the body suggests respect for the dead, and the tools included with the body may very well indicate a belief in an afterlife, where such implements could be used.

The skull of this male, who was at least 40 years of age, is very large, with a cranial capacity of 1620 cm³. Although the skull exhibited typical Neandertal features, La Chapelle was not a typical Neandertal, but a very robust male. Other Neandertal specimens are not as extreme, and some show traits that come close to moderns. One of the mandibles found with another Neandertal, Monte Circeo (Fig. 13-23), from Italy, had a chin, as was also the case with La Quina, from France. Also from France is La Ferrassie (Fig. 13-24), who was not as robust as La Chapelle, the frontal bone is less sloping, and the chin less receding. (See Table 13-2 for a list of European Neandertals.)

---

*That Neandertals buried their dead has been challenged, but the challenge has been counterchallenged, and majority opinion continues to favor deliberate burial.

FIGURE 13-23 (a) Cast, La Chapelle-aux-Saints. Note the occipital bun, facial and alveolar prognathism, low vault, and lack of chin; (b) photo of actual calvarium; (c) Monte Circeo, a more typical Neandertal. Supraorbital torus displays Neandertal traits but the occipital area is more modern.

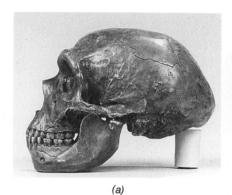

(a)

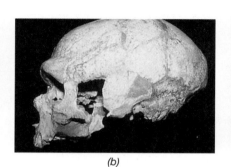

(b)

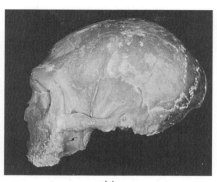

(c)

TABLE 13-2 Partial List of European Neandertals*†

SITE	YEAR FOUND	HUMAN REMAINS	ARCHEOLOGICAL PERIOD	DATE
Šipka, Czechoslovakia	1880	Part of a child's chin	Mousterian	Podhradem (interstadial, 32–28 kya)
Ochoz, Czechoslovakia	1905 1964	Lower jaw, molar, and post-cranial fragments of an adult	Mousterian	Early Würm
Ganovce, Czechoslovakia	1926 1955	Cranial fragments	Mousterian	Riss-Würm
Subalyuk, Hungary	1932	Lower jaw and postcranial bones of an adult; child's cranium	Mousterian	Early Würm
Sala, Czechoslovakia	1961	Frontal bone of skull	None	Upper Pleistocene
Kulna, Czechoslovakia	1965	Skull bones and teeth	Mousterian	38.6 kya 45.6 kya
Taubach, Germany	1887	Teeth	Middle Paleolithic	None
Wildscheuer, Germany	1953	Cranial fragments	Mousterian	Early Würm
Salzgitter-Lebenstedt, Germany	1956	Cranial bones	Mousterian	55.6 kya
Baco Kiro, Bulgaria	?	Very fragmentary portions	Aurignacian (?)	43.0 kya

(Above portion of table adapted from Smith, 1984, pp. 142–143.)

Forbes Quarry, Gibraltar	1848 1928	Adult skull, child's skull fragments	Levallois-Mousterian	Early Würm
Spy, Belgium	1886	2 skeletons	Mousterian	Early Würm
Le Moustier, France	1908	Adolescent skeleton	Mousterian	Early Würm

*In addition to those mentioned in text.

†This table is intended to give the student some idea of the finds of ongoing paleoanthropological European research. New finds continue to be excavated, adding to the evidence and history of Neandertal evolution.

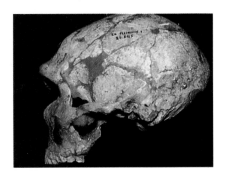

FIGURE 13-24 La Ferrassie. A more typical Neandertal. Mandible (not shown) has a chin.

NEANDERTALS MEET MODERNS

The most recent of Western European Neandertals comes from St. Cesaire (Fig. 13-25), southwestern France, and is dated about 37–35 kya. The bones were recovered from a bed of discarded chipped blades, handaxes, and other stone tools of a type called *Chatelperronian*, a tool industry of the Upper Paleolithic (see chart, below) that is associated with Neandertals.

Anatomically modern humans were living in Western Europe by about 35 kya or earlier; therefore, for perhaps several thousand years, anatomically moderns and Neandertals were living "side by side"! This circumstance raises some intriguing questions: How did these two groups interact? Was Neandertals relationship with moderns (taller, more gracile groups) a peaceful, cooperative one between equals, or was it violent? The evidence does not tell us, but if the history of the past several thousand years is applied, the association was violent and stratified—a superior and inferior relationship, with the culturally superior group vanquishing the inferior.

Whatever the quality of the relationship might be, when two groups come into contact, invariably there is a diffusion of material objects. Nonmaterial elements such as ideas, values, beliefs, and customs also ordinarily (although not necessarily) diffuse from the more to the less sophisticated population.

Evidence from a number of French sites (Harrold, 1989) indicates that Neandertals did indeed borrow technological methods and tools,

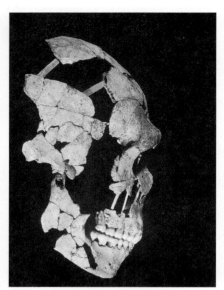

FIGURE 13-25 St. Cesaire, the "last" Neandertal.

		GLACIAL	PALEOLITHIC	EUROPEAN CULTURE PERIODS	HOMINIDAE	
UPPER PLEISTOCENE	10,000					
	20,000	Late	20,000 – 25,000	Magdalenian Solutrean Gravettian Aurignacian/ Perigordian Chatelperronian	N E A N D E R T A L S	M O D E R N S
	30,000	W Ü R M	Upper Paleolithic			
	40,000	Middle				
	50,000			Mousterian		
		Early	Middle Paleolithic			
	75,000					
		Riss-Würm		Levalloisian		
	100,000	(interglacial)				
				Acheulian		
	125,000					

such as blades, from the moderns and modified their own Mousterian tools, creating a new industry, the Chatelperronian.

However, the *concept* of diffusion does not tell us the *how* of diffusion. Did the Neandertals trade, steal, or battle for what they acquired? Did the moderns peacefully teach their technology to their neighbors? Did the two groups cooperate in hunting, exchange tall tales around a campfire, or did they fear and hunt each other with intent to kill? Did the two groups interbreed—trade mates, for example—and, over a period of time, did the Neandertals become assimilated into the modern population? Or, as we asked before, did moderns annihilate Neandertals and terminate their existence?* There is yet another interesting question. Since the Neandertals borrowed technology from the moderns, how did they communicate? Was it done with some sort of language—vocal? sign? (See symbolism, p. 268.)

Although Western European Neandertals are the best known and are considered the standard measure of Neandertal identification, there are significant finds in Central Europe, especially Krapina and Vindija in Yugoslavia. Krapina consists mostly of fragments and may represent at least 20 individuals—men, women, and children. It is also important as a burial site, one of the oldest (70 kya) on record.

Vindija, about 30 miles from Krapina, is dated at about 42 kya. Specimens appear in the lower levels with features that approach the morphology of early south-central modern *sapiens*, but the overall pattern is definitely Neandertal. However, these modified Neandertal features may also be seen as an evolutionary trend toward modern *sapiens*.

Western Asia

Israel   There are several well-known Neandertal sites in Israel. (See map, Fig. 13-26.) Two of them were discovered in Mt. Carmel caves near Haifa. Tabun (Fig. 13-27), one of the first Neandertal finds in the Near East, has been dated somewhere between 40–70 kya or older. A partial skeleton, missing the skull and lower limbs, about 60 ky old, was recently found in the Kebara Cave, close to Tabun. A complete Kebara pelvis, slightly larger than moderns, supports what has long been believed: that Neandertal locomotion and posture were not significantly different from our own.

Some thirty miles east of Mt. Carmel, in a cave near Lake Kinerett (Sea of Galilee), a crushed skeleton and other skeletal material, known as Amud (Fig. 13-28), were found. The dating is unclear, perhaps in the 40–30 kya range.†

---

*For a fictionalized account of the confrontation of Neandertals and anatomically modern humans, read Nobel prizewinner William Golding's excellent novel, *The Inheritors*. There are also several movies depicting this subject. Another popular novel featuring this motif is Jean M. Auel's *Clan of the Cave Bear*.

†Research was recently renewed at the Amud site by the Institute of Human Origins, Berkeley, California. It is hoped that new finds will provide evidence for a more accurate site date.

(Detail of map at right)

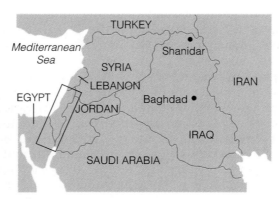

FIGURE 13-26 Near Eastern Neandertal sites.

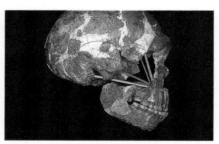

FIGURE 13-27 Tabun. Neandertal from Israel. The supraorbital torus and facial prognathism are similar to Western European Neandertals. Note the lack of occipital bunning.

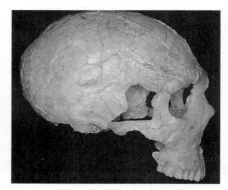

FIGURE 13-28 Amud. Neandertal from Israel. Less robust than western European Neandertals, with some features of early moderns.

Iraq A remarkable site, located in the Zagros Mountains in northeastern Iraq, is Shanidar Cave, where partial skeletons of nine individuals—male and female—were found; four of them deliberately buried. One of the men (Fig. 13-29) suffered a crushing injury that affected the right side of his body, especially his right arm, which was atrophied (it may have been amputated at the elbow which, if true, is the first evidence of deliberate human surgery). Another individual was deliberately buried, and flowers may have been placed on his grave at the time of death. It is interesting that these Levant (Near East) Neandertals are less robust than the European Neandertals.

Central Asia

Uzbekistan About 1,600 miles east of Shanidar in Uzbekistan, in a cave at Teshik-Tash, we find a deliberate burial of a 9-year-old boy surrounded by five pairs of wild goat horns, suggesting a burial ritual.

Asian Neandertals are a bit of a mystery: the dating for some of the fossils is still uncertain, the relationship to early a.m.s is not entirely clear, and their origin—Africa? Western Europe? Eastern Europe?—remains unsettled.

At the present time, it appears there was an eastern movement of European Neandertals as the fourth major glaciation advanced southward. Facing a cooling environment, Neandertals may have migrated eastward, reaching what is now known as Israel. The eastward movement continued to Iraq and ultimately to central Asia. Although the relationship between Neandertals and early moderns is still being debated, the Mt. Carmel cave dwellers Tabun and Kebara (or their forbears) may have lived "next door" to the Mt. Carmel cave inhabited by an early modern, Skhūl (p. 273).

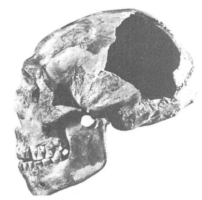

FIGURE 13-29   Shanidar 1.

MIDDLE PALEOLITHIC CULTURE

Neandertals   Neandertals who lived in the culture period known as the Middle Paleolithic are usually associated with the Mousterian tool industry. In the early Würm, Mousterian culture extended from the Atlantic Ocean across Europe and North Africa to (what has been known as) the Soviet Union, Israel, east to Uzbekistan, and perhaps China.

Technology   Mousterian people specialized in the production of flake tools based on the Levallois method, a prepared core technique that originated perhaps as much as 200 kya. A chunk of flint was chipped all the way round and on top, resembling a turtle form, and was then rapped on the side to produce a flake ready for use (Fig. 13-30).

FIGURE 13-30   The Levallois method.

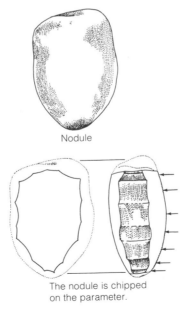

Nodule

The nodule is chipped on the parameter.

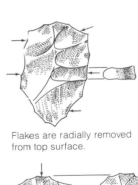

Flakes are radially removed from top surface.

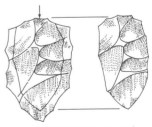

A final blow at one end removes a large flake.

Neandertals improved on the Levallois technique by inventing a method of obtaining a flake each time they struck the edge of the core. They then trimmed (retouched) the flake into various forms such as scrapers, points, knives, and so on.

Neandertal craftspeople elaborated and diversified traditional methods and may have developed specialized tools for skin and meat preparation, hunting, woodworking, and perhaps hafting. They may also have used new materials, such as antler and bone, and their technological achievements may have laid the basis for the remarkable changes by the moderns who followed them.

Settlements Neandertals lived in a variety of open sites, caves, rock shelters, and shelters they erected. Evidence for life in caves is abundant, and Mousterians must have occupied them extensively. Windbreaks of poles and skin were probably erected at the cave mouth for protection against the weather. Fire was also in general use by this time, of course, and no doubt was used for cooking, warmth, and keeping dangerous animals at bay.

Symbolism It has been suggested by some that, although Neandertals were capable of speech (symbolic vocal language), they were limited by the physical structure of their throats. The recent discovery of Kebara, at Israel's Mt. Carmel, included a hyoid bone (Fig. 13-31)—a bone that is important to speech and located in the throat. Analysis showed this bone to be very similar to that of moderns. The discovery of the bone has led several paleoanthropologists to propose a reanalysis of Neandertals' ability to speak (Arensburg et al., 1989).

An important innovation of the Middle Paleolithic is deliberate burial. A remarkable burial at La Ferrassie (France) looks like a family cemetery where the presumed parents, five children, and an infant are buried (Fig. 13-32). In the Guattari Cave, Monte Circeo (near Rome), a partially crushed skull was placed in the center of a circle of stones. There were also burials at Shanidar, Kebara, and elsewhere in the Middle Paleolithic.

Some scholars believe that Neandertal burials were accompanied by some sort of ritual as suggested, for example, by stones surrounding the skull in the Guattari Cave; however, this is very difficult to prove. That Neandertals intentionally buried their dead tells us they may have had a more human attitude toward death than their predecessors, or an awareness of their distinctiveness from other living things, that they were something more than simply animals.

In our discussion of Shanidar, it was pointed out that one of the adult male skeletons showed evidence of serious injuries, and that he possibly survived his wounds and suffering only because of special care given him. It has been suggested (although we will never know for certain) that a social structure existed with values of cooperation and concern for others, indicating a sense of compassion toward members of one's group or kin.

Another Neandertal innovation is a form of ornamentation or the beginnings of artistic expression. Drilled animal teeth, drilled bone, in-

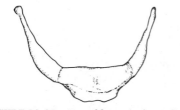

FIGURE 13-31 Hyoid bone (enlarged). The bone plays a significant role in articulating sounds (and in interpretation of Neandertal ability to speak).

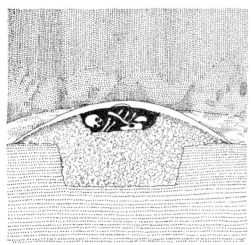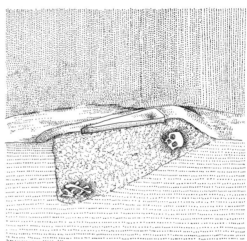

FIGURE 13-32 La Ferrassie burial.

cised bone, and pierced bone have been found at Neandertal sites. This may be a form of art, ornamentation, or symbols; it is difficult to say, but it conveys the impression that Neandertals were moving toward a non-utilitarian use of materials.

Economy Neandertals were successful hunters. They also gathered berries, nuts, and other plants, as the evidence found at various sites indicates. It is also assumed that, in the freezing weather of the fourth glacial, Neandertals wore clothing, and they may have developed methods of curing skins.

Africa

In Africa, the Eurasian Middle Paleolithic is referred to as the Middle Stone Age (MSA) and, in many ways, is similar to its Eurasian counterpart. For example, the main technological industry in Africa also is the Mousterian.

At the beginning of the last interglacial, about 120 kya, the climate began to change, and different ecological regions appeared. Adapting to new econiches, regional cultures developed different toolmaking techniques and manufactured localized types of tools using materials available in their regions. Hunting strategies varied depending on the type of game available and on the butchering and processing techniques. An African innovation may have been the use of paint, since ochre-stained scrapers and other hematite-stained tools have been found.

LATE ARCHAIC OR EARLY MODERNS

When fossil material displays a mosaic of early and recent features, the classification largely becomes a matter of interpretation. This is the case for a number of African fossils (Table 13-3) that are listed by some paleo-

TABLE 13-3 African Moderns*

NAME/COUNTRY	DATE (KYA)	MATERIAL
Dar-es-Soltan, Morocco	Uncertain	Adult young; adult calotte; teeth, limb bones, phalanges
Afalou, Algeria	12–8	Over 50 individuals; skeletons, male, female, children; blades, scrapers, burins
Kom Ombo, Egypt	13	Calvaria, adult male frontal and other cranial parts
Elmenteita, Kenya	10	Adults and juveniles: crania and cranial bones; skeletons
Lukenya Hill, Kenya	17	Adult frontal and parietal, probably male
Naivasha, Kenya	11	Adult female, over 50, cranium mandible, long bones
Lothagam Hill, Kenya	9–6	Remains of nearly 30 individuals, skeletons and various skeletal bones
Gamble's Cave, Kenya	8	Cranium; cranial bones, mandibles, limb bones; skeleton
Asselar, Mali	7	Adult male and postcranial skeleton
Taforalt, Morocco	11	Skeleton; cranium; skeleton fragments; remains of 180 adults, 6 adolescents, 97–100 children
Hmatjes River, South Africa	10.5	18 individuals of both sexes and varying ages
Wadi Halfa, Sudan	15	Mandible
Ishango, Zaire	9	Many cranial and postcranial bones
Kalemba, Zambia	15	Several crania; mandibles; vertebrae; postcranial fragments; both sexes, varying ages
Leopard's Hill, Zambia	16.7	Occipital and parietal
Mumbwa, Zambia	20	Several calvaria; cranium, mandible, limb bones

*In addition to those included in text.

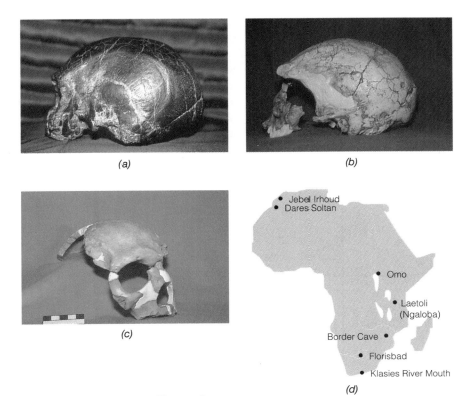

FIGURE 13-33 Examples of later African archaic *sapiens*. (*a*) Eliye Springs, West Turkana, Kenya, East Africa; (*b*) Laetoli 18, south of Olduvai Gorge, Tanzania, East Africa; (*c*) Florisbad, Orange Free State, South Africa; (*d*) Map of late archaics.

(a)

(b)

(c)

(d)

anthropologists as later archaics, and by others as anatomically modern. We have placed them among the later archaics, but they may just as well have been listed as anatomically moderns. They are found in South Africa, East Africa, and North Africa. (See map, Fig. 13-33.)

The dates of all these late archaics or early moderns fall in the range of 150–50 kya, although not all dates are radiometric. Morphologically, these specimens vary in their similarity to moderns. Some of them appear more archaic than modern; others, more modern than archaic. The late archaics may be considered transitional between archaics and moderns, or as premoderns; that is, ancestors of anatomically moderns. None of the African archaics can be considered Neandertals. Neandertals are a Eurasian phenomenon, and are not found in either Africa or eastern Asia.

HOMO SAPIENS SAPIENS (ANATOMICALLY MODERN HUMANS)

We now arrive at the appearance of our subspecies. As we are evolutionarily "so close to home," it is understandable that considerable debate has arisen concerning the origin of anatomically modern humans. Of the several models proposed, three will be discussed: (1) Afro-European *sapiens*; (2) Recent African Evolution; and (3) Multiregional Evolution.

According to the Afro-European *sapiens* hypothesis (Bräuer, 1984), early archaic *sapiens* in Africa evolved to later archaics, from whom arose modern humans around 100 kya. Because of climatic and environmental conditions, they migrated out of Africa and entered the Near East and

THE FAR SIDE   By GARY LARSON

© Chronicle Features, 1983

"Neanderthals, Neanderthals! Can't make fire!
Can't make spear! Nyah, nyah, nyah . . .!"

Europe. The moderns and local populations interbred, with the gene flow from moderns becoming the dominant morphological component.

The Recent African Evolution hypothesis (Stringer et al., 1984) resembles the preceding model with some differences. Modern humans evolved in Africa somewhat earlier (200 kya to 100 kya) and represented a biological speciation event. They migrated out of Africa to Eurasia, Europe, and the Far East, completely *displacing* local archaic populations—without interbreeding, since they were a different species.

In both these models, moderns originated in Africa between 200 and 100 kya, and migrated from Africa to Europe and Asia, displacing local populations. The third model, the Multiregional Evolution Model (Wolpoff, 1984) takes quite a different position, especially regarding the notion of displacement.

The Wolpoff model proposes that the evolutionary appearance of moderns occurred a number of times in various regions of the world. Moreover, evolution of these regional populations was *continuous* from archaic *sapiens* to *H. sapiens sapiens*. Thus, evolution from archaic to modern occurred separately in regional areas of the world at roughly the same time.

To support their argument, advocates of the Recent African Evolution (Single-Origin) hypothesis cite the so-called "Garden of Eden" study. Molecular biologist Rebecca L. Cann and colleagues (1987) developed a scenario in which moderns originated in Africa about 200 kya and then migrated out of Africa to other areas of the world about 135 kya, at the earliest.

The molecular biologists' research relied on their analysis of mitochondrial DNA (mtDNA) to calculate the date of origin for anatomically moderns, as well as their migration from Africa. Mitochondria are tiny organelles found in the cell, outside the nucleus. They contain a set of DNA, dissimilar from nuclear DNA, inherited *only through the mother*. (The ovum carries mitochondria; the sperm does not.) Thus, mtDNA lacks the gene shuffle that occurs in the meiotic recombination of nuclear DNA.

Gathering samples of mtDNA from individuals (using placentas, which is fetal tissue), whose ancestors lived in Africa, Asia, Europe, Australia, and New Guinea, the biologists postulated a genetic pattern (which they called a type) for each area. They then compared the diversity of the various patterns.

They found the greatest variation among Africans and therefore the oldest—the longer the time, the greater the accumulation of variations. They also found that the African variants contained only African mtDNA, whereas those from other areas all included at least one African component, which must have come from Africa. Therefore, there must have been a migration from Africa to other areas of the world. By counting the number of genetic mutations, and applying the rate of mutation, Cann et al. reached a date for the origin of anatomical moderns: between 285 and 143 kya, averaging out at about 200 kya.

Not all scientists agree with this scenario. The rate of mutations may be incorrect and, therefore, the date of the migration out of Africa would be incorrect. Also, gene flow outside of Africa could upset the direct inheritance of the African maternal line.

The supporters of the Multiregional (Multi-Origin) Model fault the single-origin hypothesis because, they insist, presentday humans resemble the archaics of *their* region, not African archaics. None of these hypotheses has yet gained acceptance, and both debate and research continue.

We cannot at present resolve the question of modern origin, but it appears likely that the first anatomically modern humans appeared in sub-Saharan Africa before 100 kya. It is difficult to assign a more specific date since dating is a problem (with most reliant material beyond the range of radiocarbon dating (see p. 194). Even then, there is the problem of correctly identifying the fossil bones. Occasionally, this decision is straightforward, but it is awkward when a skull exhibits a mosaic of traits—should it be considered an archaic, for example, or a modern?

Africa

The problem of dating and identification occurs with several African fossils. We noted earlier that a number of fossils in Africa are referred to as late archaic or early modern. Some paleoanthropologists believe that several of these (e.g., Klasies River Mouth) are definitely anatomically modern, despite their early dates (over 100 ky). Other researchers are not certain and await further evidence.

Aside from these early forms—assuming the dates are correct—there are many a.m.s from widespread areas of Africa dated at 10 ky or less (see Table 13-3).

Asia

Israel Early Israelis (Fig. 13-34) possess a number of archaic traits, but their overall configuration places them in the a.m. category. Although quite robust, their skulls and postcranial bones are more gracile than archaic *sapiens*. The occiput is rounded, vault higher, supraorbital torus reduced, chin has a definite eminence, midfacial and facial prognathism is reduced (although alveolar prognathism is accented), anterior teeth are smaller, and leg bones are more gracile.

Working out an evolutionary sequence in Israel is troublesome, because the moderns—Skhūl and Qafzeh—(Fig. 13-36) have been given dates of 90 ky. Neandertals in Israel (Tabun, Kebara) have been dated in the 50–70 ky range. Assuming the dates are valid, moderns would have preceded Neandertals! Migration may be a possible explanation. Moderns may have migrated into Israel, probably from Africa, before Neandertals emigrated from Europe. If this were so, we again face the situation of two physically different peoples confronting one another.

China The sites of early moderns in China can be seen in Fig. 13-37. The dating of these fossils is probably late Pleistocene, and the fossils display a mixture of archaic and modern features. Archaic traits include the su-

FIGURE 13-34 Early modern sites in Israel.

FIGURE 13-35 (*a*) Mt. Carmel, south of Haifa, Israel; (*b*) the Skhūl cave at Mt. Carmel.

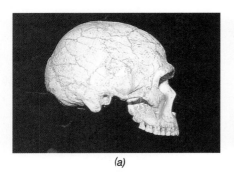

(a)

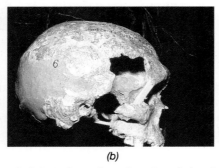

(b)

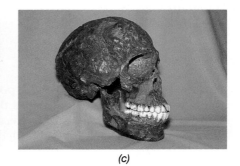

(c)

FIGURE 13-36 (*a*) Skhūl 5; (*b*) Qafzeh 6; (*c*) Quafzeh 9. Early moderns from Israel, dated at about 90 ky. Modified archaic traits are visible.

FIGURE 13-37 Upper Pleistocene Chinese sites.

FIGURE 13-38 Map of several Australian *H. sapiens sapiens* sites, and one from Java.

FIGURE 13-39 Mungo I, lateral view. The frontal bone reflects the gracile character of the skull. Less robust.

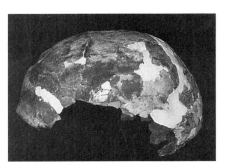

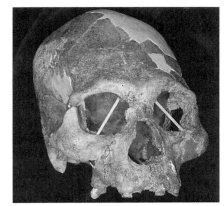

FIGURE 13-40 Kow Swamp 5. Note the greater robusticity of this skull compared with Mungo.

praorbital torus and the occipital area, but the lack of facial prognathism is a modern feature.

Sri Lanka   The earliest modern remains in Asia have been discovered in southern Sri Lanka and have been dated at 28,500 years (Kennedy and Deraniyagala, 1989).

Australia

In order to enter Australia, modern humans must have developed water transport by 40 kya, since there is evidence of human habitation in Australia (Fig. 13-38) at about that date. The earliest fossils are from Lake Mungo (Fig. 13-39), dated to at least 30 kya. They are rather gracile, with only moderate development of the supraorbital torus.

A more robust form, Kow Swamp (Fig. 13-40), with a bulging forehead, thick bones, heavy supraorbital torus, and so on, is dated at 10 kya. The morphological differences between Kow Swamp and Lake Mungo

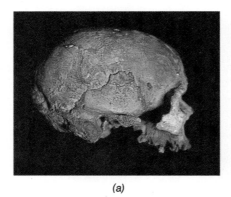

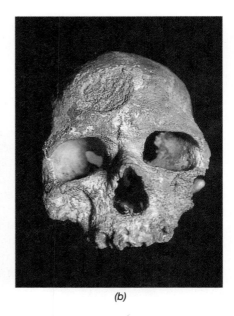

FIGURE 13-41 Cro-Magnon 1. Modern traits are quite clear. (*a*) Lateral view; (*b*) frontal view. (Courtesy of David Frayer)

(a)

(b)

have been attributed to two separate incursions into Australia. Others, however, have suggested that deliberate cranial deformation* of Kow Swamp peoples may explain their rugged skulls.

Europe

Western Europe This area and its fossils have received the most paleo-anthropological and archeological attention, one of the reasons being serendipity. Many of the scholars interested in this kind of research happened to live in Western Europe, and the southern region of France happened to be a fossil gold mine. A great deal of information was gathered, and numerous hypotheses of human evolution, based on these data, were proposed.

Unfortunately, the data were too localized, and the hypotheses and theories had to be discarded when discoveries were made elsewhere, especially in Africa. Nevertheless, Western Europe has contributed many fossils and artifacts of the Upper Paleolithic and is still the best source for fossil humans and their culture for this period.

The most famous of Western European *sapiens* is unquestionably Cro-Magnon, a site in southern France. Dated at about 25 kya, the Cro-Magnons were not the earliest moderns of Europe. The three male skulls reflect a mixture of modern and archaic traits. The oldest individual, known as the "Old Man" (Fig. 13-41), was the most gracile of the males. Even more gracile, and most modern looking, is the female skull, a situation which may reflect sexual dimorphism.

---

*Cranial deformation has been practiced for many years in various parts of the world.

Central Europe Central Europe has also been a source of many modern fossil finds. At several sites it appears that some fossils display Neandertal and modern features, which supports the local continuity (from Neandertal to modern) hypothesis. Such was the case at Vindija (p. 265).

Professor Fred Smith offers another example of local continuity from Mladeč of Czechoslovakia. Four of the five skulls possess a prominent supraorbital torus and other reduced features. These, says Smith, "are clearly modern *H. sapiens* in morphology and not specifically Neandertal-like in a single feature" (Smith, 1984, p. 174).

In Central Europe we find a situation in which older moderns are more robust and exhibit more archaic characteristics. Later moderns continue with archaic traits, but there is a definite trend toward gracilization. This trend presents support for local continuity from archaic to modern; however, there remains opposition to this model by those who believe the modern traits came from African migrations.

HUMAN ACHIEVEMENT IN THE UPPER PALEOLITHIC

About 50 kya, a warming trend of several thousand years partially melted the glacial ice, leaving, in Eurasia (the source of our best evidence), a vast area of treeless country covered with lakes, marshes, and many varieties of vegetation. This environment served as an enormous pasture for herbivorous animals and carnivores that fed off the herbivores. The tundra, stretching from Spain into the Russian steppes, was a hunter's paradise.

New tools were invented for coping with large and possibly dangerous animals. The last stage of the Upper Paleolithic, known in Europe as the Magdalenean, was a spectacular period of technological innovation. The spear thrower, or atlatl (Fig. 13-42), extended the hunter's arm, thus enabling him to throw a spear with greater penetrating force. For fishing in rivers, the barbed harpoon was a clever example of the craftperson's

FIGURE 13-42 Magdalenian tools. During this last period of the Upper Paleolithic, early human artistic expression reached its greatest height. Note the carving on the tools.

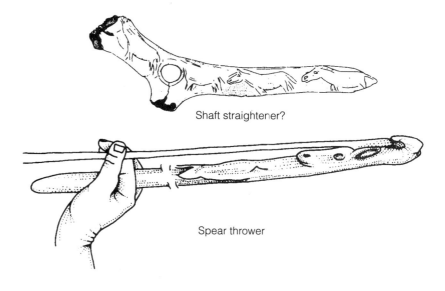

Shaft straightener?

Spear thrower

FIGURE 13-43 The punch blade technique.

skill. It is possible that the bow and arrow may have come into use during this period.

The introduction of the punch technique (Fig. 13-43) provided blank cores that could be fashioned into burins (Fig. 13-44), for working wood, bone, and antler; into borers, for drilling holes in skins, bones, and shells; and into blades with serrated or notched edges for scraping wooden shafts into a variety of tools. Recent evidence from sub-Saharan Africa also shows that great strides were being made in technological innovations there at the same time.

Large herds of reindeer roamed the tundra along with mammoths, bisons, horses, and a host of smaller animals that served as a bountiful source of food. It was a time of affluence, and the Magdaleneans spread out over Europe, living in caves and open-air camps, and building large shelters. During this period, Western Europe (or perhaps Africa) achieved the highest density of population in human history up to that time.

Hunters in Europe continued, as one of their hunting techniques, the practice of driving animals into bogs and swamps, where they could easily be dispatched and butchered.* Food was so abundant that overkill may have been responsible for the extinction of some Pleistocene species.

The **Upper Paleolithic** [known in Africa as the Late Stone Age (LSA)] was a technological age and, in its way, is comparable to the past hundred years of our own time. In addition to their reputation as hunters and tool innovators, Western Europeans of the Upper Paleolithic are even better known for their art, especially their extraordinary cave art done in southern France and northern Spain.

*This technique was also used by North American Indians.

Burin

FIGURE 13-44 Burin, a kind of chisel.

FIGURE 13-45 Solutrean blade. This is the best-known work of the Solutrean tradition of the Upper Paleolithic. Solutrean stone work is considered the best of the Upper Paleolithic.

(a)

(b)

Interest in art can be seen throughout the Upper Paleolithic. Fine sculpture has been excavated in several European areas. Tools and handles were often engraved with admirable and realistic animal carvings and sculptured figurines. Female figurines, known as Venuses were sculpted, and appear to be modeled after actual women. Other figurines may seem grotesque with sexual characteristics exaggerated, perhaps to symbolize fertility or for other ritual purposes (Fig. 13-46).

Already early in the Upper Paleolithic, cave wall art was in full display, and sculpture in the round achieved surprising grace and style. In Lascaux Cave of southern France, immense wild bulls dominate what is called the Great Hall of Bulls, and horses, deer, and other animals adorn the walls in black, red, and yellow. The age of art continued and, arguably, reached its pinnacle in the last Upper Paleolithic stage, the Magdalenean. In a cave at Altamira in northern Spain, superb portrayals of bison in red and black, are painted on walls and ceiling (Fig. 13-47). The cave is a cornucopia of beautiful art whose meaning has never been satisfactorily explained. It could have been ritualistic, religious, magical, a form of visual communication, or art for the sake of its beauty.

FIGURE 13-46 (*a*) Venus of Brassempouy; (*b*) Venus of Willendorf. Upper Paleolithic artists in Europe were capable of figurative or symbolic expression (Willendorf, in which fertility may be significant) and realism (Brassempouy illustrates a woman's head in an essentially natural way).

FIGURE 13-47 Cave painting. A fine painting of a bison bellowing.

Most of our knowledge of the Upper Paleolithic stems from European studies. There were similar changes in other parts of the world, but they have yet to be as thoroughly examined.

In Africa, microliths (thumbnail-sized stone flakes hafted to make knives, saws, etc.) and blades characterize Late Stone Age technology. Personal adornment items also come into use at this time. Bone beads and shell and stone pendants have a wide distribution, and ochre and other coloring materials may have been used for painting the body or decorating clothing. Rock art of the Late Stone Age is known from many areas of sub-Saharan Africa.

Core tools in Australia were used for procuring wood and shaping such implements as throwing sticks. More than 20 kya, Australians had begun grinding stone axe heads, the first ever made anywhere, and a few thousand years later ground stone mortars, pestles, grinders, and grinding slabs had become established. These stone tools suggest the gathering of seeds, roots, and vegetables, and probably made possible at least a semisedentary lifestyle.

The early Australians buried their dead, and some were ceremoniously cremated and then buried, a practice maintained by Aborigines through the last century. They also produced a rock art, and red ochre was used to decorate artifacts, walls, and bodies of the living. Bone beads were another decorative and, perhaps, ceremonial item.

FIGURE 13-48 *H. sapiens sapiens* sites. Note that anatomically moderns inhabit all continents. Only better known fossils are listed.

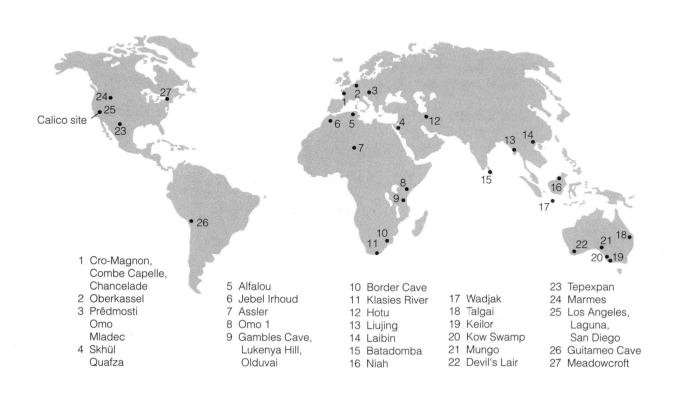

Calico site

1 Cro-Magnon,
   Combe Capelle,
   Chancelade
2 Oberkassel
3 Prêdmosti
   Omo
   Mladec
4 Skhül
   Quafza

5 Alfalou
6 Jebel Irhoud
7 Assler
8 Omo 1
9 Gambles Cave,
   Lukenya Hill,
   Olduvai

10 Border Cave
11 Klasies River
12 Hotu
13 Liujing
14 Laibin
15 Batadomba
16 Niah

17 Wadjak
18 Talgai
19 Keilor
20 Kow Swamp
21 Mungo
22 Devil's Lair

23 Tepexpan
24 Marmes
25 Los Angeles,
    Laguna,
    San Diego
26 Guitameo Cave
27 Meadowcroft

FIGURE 13-49 Major types of North American Paleo-Indian projectile points: (*a*) Clovis, (*b*) Folsom, (*c*) Plano, (*d*) Dalton. (Courtesy of William Turnbaugh)

(a)　　(b)　　(c)　　(d)

THE NEW WORLD

By 30 kya, northeast Asia was inhabited by anatomically modern humans. They hunted large herbivores using stone- and bone-tipped weapons and probably domesticated dogs. Their tailored skin clothing, shelters made from animal hides, and the use of fire helped them survive in this cold and barren environment. It is very likely they were the ancestors of American Indians.

During the last glaciation, much of the northern latitudes were covered by vast sheets of ice for thousands of years at a time. Water frozen in the glaciers lowered sea levels of the world more than 300 feet, exposing and forming a land bridge called Beringia, which was about 1300 miles wide from north to south. The land bridge served as an extension of northeast Asia to North America, and people moving into it for its available resources eventually entered Alaska. The date of entry into the New World is still a major archeological issue. Archeologists are divided into two groups: those who believe the date was about 12,500 years ago, and those who believe it was much earlier.

This dynamic age was doomed, or so it appears, with the climatic changes of about 10 kya. As the glaciers retreated and the temperature slowly rose, animals, plants, and humans were seriously affected. Because traditional prey animals and easy-to-process food were depleted or disappeared altogether, other means of obtaining food were sought.

Grinding hard seeds or roots became important, and as familiarity with vegetation increased, domestication of plants and animals developed. When dependence on domestication became critical, permanent settlements, new technology, and more complex social organization appeared.

Anatomically moderns evolved before the Late Pleistocene, but it was during this period that they developed the physical form we see today.

SUMMARY OF UPPER PALEOLITHIC

As we look back at the Late Pleistocene (Upper Paleolithic, Late Stone Age), we can see it as the culmination of several million years of biocultural evolution. Cultural evolution continued with the appearance of early archaic *sapiens* and moved a bit faster with later archaic *sapiens*. Neandertals in Eurasia, and their contemporaries elsewhere, added ceremonial burials, rituals, technological innovations, and much more.

Building on the existing culture, Late Pleistocene populations attained sophisticated cultural and material heights in a seemingly short burst of exciting creativity in Europe. Such technological changes also occurred on other continents, but it is in the caves of Western Europe where its display is most spectacular.

Paleo-Indians, the earliest people of the New World, hunted big game, such as mammoths, with spears or lances, and about 10 kya were succeeded by hunters who pursued the giant long-horned bison. With the disappearance of the giant bison, hunters switched their efforts to the smaller bison (*Bison bison occidentalis*). A popular bison-hunting method involved stampeding bison into arroyo cul-de-sacs or over cliffs.

Perhaps Paleo-Indians overhunted the large game, or perhaps the end of the Ice Age created adverse ecological conditions; in any case, about 10 kya large game was becoming extinct. Hunting remained an important source of food, but more emphasis was being placed on foraging. In many areas, fish and shellfish also became items in the diet. During this period, new technologies developed that produced fishing gear, traps, baskets and other containers, and composite weapons, such as harpoons and the throwing board, or atlatl (Fig. 13-50).

Food collection evolved into food production in the New World about 9 kya, but only a few animals were domesticated, practically none of economic significance. Farming became a substantial food source in sections of North America, the dry highlands of Mexico, and western South America.

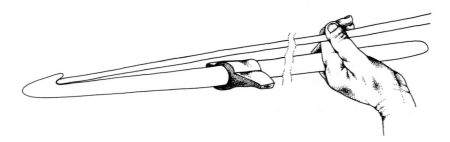

FIGURE 13-50 Use of the *atlatl*, or spearthrower, with a stone weight for balance.

SUMMARY

Archaic *sapiens*, apparently evolving from *H. erectus*, display a mosaic of *erectus* and *sapiens* characteristics. In Europe and western Asia, Neandertals appear about 125 kya. Other varieties of archaic *sapiens* are also present in Africa and China, and in both cases may have led to a.m. humans without a Neandertal phase. Neandertals introduced technological innovations, new settlement patterns, and new methods of obtaining food. They also practiced some forms of religious rituals. Recent research suggests Neandertals may have been capable of articulated speech.

The date and location of the appearance of the first a.m. human beings are being fiercely debated at present. One side claims anatomical moderns evolved in Africa more than 100 kya and then, migrating out of Africa, completely displaced archaic *sapiens* in the rest of the world. The "Garden of Eden" hypothesis, based on molecular biological research with mtDNA, supports this position. The other side maintains that, in various geographic regions of the world, local groups of archaic *sapiens* evolved to anatomical moderns with no (or perhaps some) African migration.

In the Late Pleistocene, new technological, ritualistic, and artistic developments appear at a more rapid rate. Various forms of art are practiced on all continents, but the most sophisticated artistic achievements are seen in the caves of Western Europe.

Modern human reached Australia 40 kya or earlier. Entry into the New World was made by people from northeast Asia, over the land bridge that is now the Bering Strait, at least 12.5 kya.

All anatomically modern populations were hunters, but climatic changes may have altered conditions, so that new sources of food were required. An emphasis on collecting plant food led to farming in many world areas.

QUESTIONS FOR REVIEW

1. What physical traits characterize archaic *sapiens* as *sapiens*?
2. How do archaic *sapiens* differ from modern humans?
3. Why are Neandertals so well known to the general public?
4. What innovations did Neandertals produce?
5. It has been said that La Chapelle was one of the most important Neandertal discoveries. Explain why La Chapelle does, or does not, deserve this attention.
6. St. Cesaire is dated at about 35 kya. From a social point of view, what is the significance of this?
7. Discuss the question of single source vs. multiple sources of *H. sapiens sapiens*. Which hypothesis do you think makes more sense? Explain.
8. Describe the Neandertal lifestyle. Why do you believe it was a (good) (poor) time to live?
9. Consider the people of Terra Amata and *H. erectus*. What "progress" (if any) was made by the Terra Amatans?

10. What is the significance of anatomical moderns evolving in Africa more than 100 kya?
11. What is the "Garden of Eden" hypothesis?
12. Why is mtDNA so important to this hypothesis?
13. Australia is quite close to Java and China; why was it inhabited so much later?
14. How does the New World fit into the history of a.m. humans?
15. In what ways was Upper Paleolithic inferior/superior to Middle Paleolithic culture?
16. Can you suggest any biological influences in the culture of early moderns? Any cultural effects on their morphology?

PALEOPATHOLOGY: DISEASES AND INJURIES OF BONE

An important branch of physical anthropology includes studies of injuries and disease processes in ancient human populations. In most cases, experts in this field (called *paleopathology*) work exclusively with dry, skeletonized specimens. Occasionally, however, under unusual circumstances, soft tissues—such as skin, hair, cartilage, or even internal organs—may also be preserved. For example, artificial mummification was practiced in ancient Egypt and Chile, and natural mummification may also occur in extremely dry climates (such as in the American Southwest and parts of North Africa).

In addition, in permanently wet environments such as bogs, where bacterial action is forestalled, soft tissues can endure. For example, there are the famous bog bodies discovered in Denmark and England. In such circumstances, preservation may be quite extraordinary. Indeed, from a 10,000-year-old bog in Florida, remains of a human brain were identified—and DNA from it was cloned and partially mapped! Finally, under permanently frozen conditions, soft tissue preservation may also be facilitated, as attested by the well-publicized 1991 discovery of a 5000-year-old man found in a glacier in the Austrian Alps.

FIGURE 1
Naturally mummified tissue on a cranium from Nubia (part of the modern country of the Sudan), c. 700–1400 A.D.

One major category of pathological process that leaves its mark on bone is trauma. Injuries in ancient human populations may be manifested in the skeleton as fractures (which frequently are well-healed), dislocations, or wounds (for example, from projectile points).

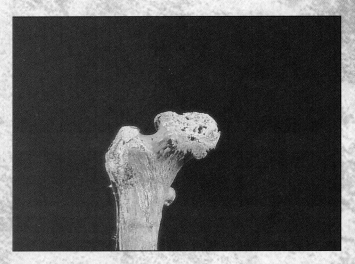

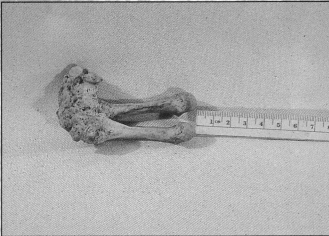

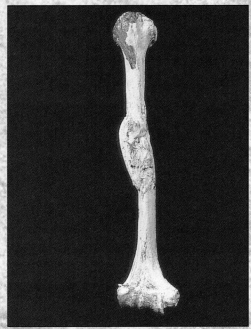

FIGURE 2 (above)
Flattened, deformed head of femur, possibly resulting from a traumatic hip dislocation. 50+ year-old female, from Nubia.

FIGURE 3 (above right)
Fused right hand, including all carpals and two metacarpals. This reaction probably resulted from a severe fall, which also fractured both left and right forearms. Male, 30 to 35 years old, Central California, c. 500–1500 A.D.

FIGURE 4 (right)
Healing fracture of humerus (upper arm bone). Note the large fracture callus at midshaft.

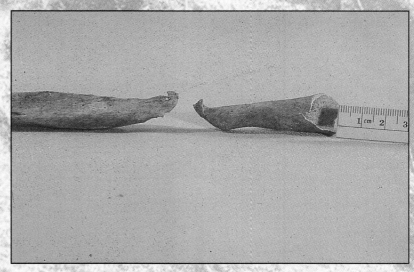

FIGURE 5
Healed, but ununited, fracture of radius (forearm bone). The bone ends would have been joined by fibrous tissue and probably continued to function well. Male, 35 to 44 years old, Central California.

FIGURE 6
Embedded piece of obsidian projectile point in a lumbar vertebra. The portion being held was found with burial and may have been retained during life in soft tissue (muscle?). The injury shows some healing. Male, 25 to 40 years old, Central California.

FIGURE 7
Cutmarks on the back of a human cranium associated with an inflammation (roughened area). There are also several other cutmarks on the skull. The incisions (which are healed) may have been part of a surgical procedure to relieve the scalp inflammation. Alternatively, the inflammation may have resulted from the procedure (a partial scalping?). Female, 19 to 30 years old, Central California.

FIGURE 8
Bullet wound in a tibia (lower leg bone).
This individual was wounded during the
Civil War. (Specimen from the National
Museum of Health and Medicine, Armed
Forces Institute of Pathology.)

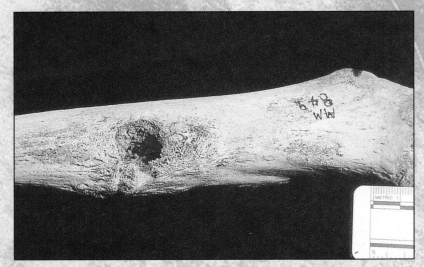

FIGURE 9
A portion of a femur (thigh bone) that was
removed during an amputation. In fact,
the leg was partially amputated at one
level (arrow), but the wound became
infected, and a second amputation
became necessary. This individual was a
Union soldier wounded in 1862. He died
12 days after the second operation.
(Specimen AFIP 1002793 from the
National Museum of Health and
Medicine, Armed Forces Institute of
Pathology.)

Another category of skeletal abnormalities include those that are *congenital* (present at birth) and *hereditary* (genetically inherited). Rarely in skeletal collections are severe hereditary maladies (such as dwarfism) clearly diagnostic. More commonly, modifications are subtle, and probably asymptomatic (that is, not producing symptoms).

Bone tumors are another category of bone pathology. Fairly commonly, small benign tumors are apparent on the cranium or peripheral to the knee joint. These tumors are usually asymptomatic.

Much more rarely, malignant, life-threatening conditions can reliably be diagnosed from skeletal remains (such conditions as lung or colon cancer usually kill the person *before* the skeleton becomes involved).

FIGURE 10
Unfused portion along the midline of a sacrum (termed, "spina bifida occulta"), a fairly common, asymptomatic condition. Male, 16 to 18 years old, Central California.

FIGURE 12
Numerous lesions of the cranium (such erosive lesions were also found in other bones). Probably the result of a disseminated (metastasized) cancer, possibly originating from the breast.

FIGURE 11
Small benign tumor at distal end (knee) of femur. Male, 30 to 39 years old, Central California.

A very common condition seen in all skeletal populations is degenerative arthritis. Bone changes are most visible around the margins of vertebral body surfaces or are either peripheral to the margins or are on the articular surfaces of appendicular joints (such as the knee).

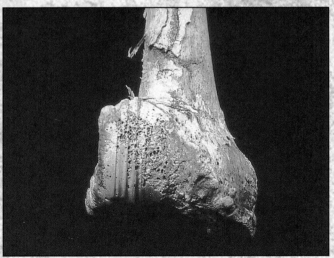

FIGURE 13 (above)
Severe bony lipping around the margins of two lumbar vertebrae.

FIGURE 14 (above right)
Partially collapsed and fused lumbar vertebrae. Female, 30 + years old, Central California.

FIGURE 15 (right)
Extreme degenerative arthritis of a knee joint in an adult female from Nubia. Paleopathologists have speculated that such degeneration may result from activities that produce repeated, severe functional stress.

In common conditions, such as arthritis (which are seen in all human groups) the most informative approach is to compare *frequencies* of involvement in different populations. Such an approach is called *paleo-epidemiology*, and is best controlled when the study samples are partitioned by sex and age (the latter is especially important in age-correlated diseases, such as arthritis).

FIGURE 16

Bar graph showing incidence of involvement of vertebral body arthritis (osteophytosis) controlling for age and sex. The frequencies shown here are for a Medieval Nubian population, and such information can be used in comparison with data from other groups.

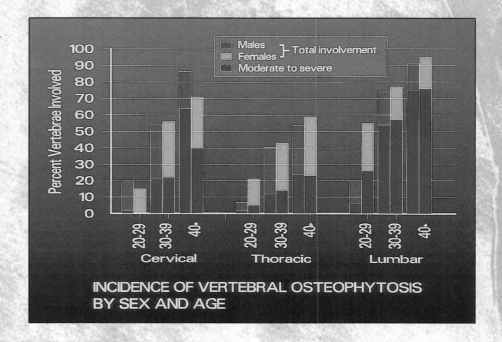

INCIDENCE OF VERTEBRAL OSTEOPHYTOSIS BY SEX AND AGE

As we discussed in Chapter 14, infectious disease has become among the most significant selective factors acting on human populations, especially over the last few thousand years. Evidence of such diseases as syphilis, tuberculosis, and osteomyelitis occasionally produce bone reaction. Interpretation of such processes in skeletons from varied geographical and chronological contexts provides some of the best biological data regarding the history of significant human diseases.

Infection from parasites (such as intestinal worms) and/or nutritional deficiencies can stimulate metabolic changes and thus abnormal bone turnover. Such conditions may be apparent in the skeleton as extra, poor-quality bone, or in other areas where bone has been abnormally reduced (especially seen on the roofs of the eye orbits).

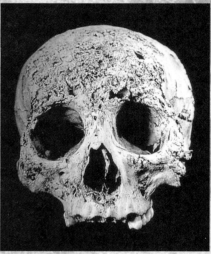

FIGURE 17 (left)
A partial cranium (seen from above) also showing diagnostic reactive changes typical of syphilis. This case is documented from the nineteenth century, with the patient known to have died of tertiary syphilis. (Specimen AFIP 1002814 from the National Museum of Health and Medicine, Armed Forces Institute of Pathology.)

FIGURE 18 (upper right)
Extreme reaction in a cranium diagnostic of syphilis (although other possibilities must be considered). Alaskan Eskimo.

FIGURE 19 (lower left)
Probable case of tuberculosis, as seen in the thoracic vertebrae. Note the highly erosive lesions. In fact, as the disease progresses, the entire vertebra can collapse (as occurred in this individual— second element from the bottom), producing a severe forward angulation of the spine. Pueblo Bonito, New Mexico.

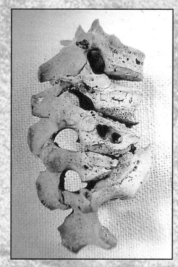

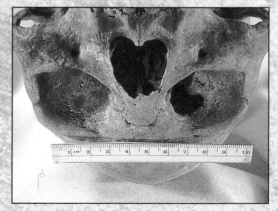

FIGURE 20
Reactive, porous bone in eye orbits. Such a process in some geographic regions (especially the United States Southwest) is thought to result oftentimes from iron deficiency anemia. Here, in a Central California Indian, the cause is unknown (but probably related to some metabolic abnormality— possibly secondary to some infection). The condition was still active at the time of death. Male, 31 to 40 years old, Central California.

Probably the most common types of skeletal disease seen in ancient human groups are abnormalities of the dentition. In some groups, owing to abrasive diets (and perhaps using the teeth as tools), severe wear is seen throughout the dentition.

Other types of dental lesions include caries (popularly called "cavities"), abscesses, loss of teeth (with resorbed sockets and loss of bone in the jaws), and improperly erupted teeth.

FIGURE 21
Severe dental wear in the upper jaw. There is almost no enamel left on most of the teeth. Male, 30+ years old, Central California.

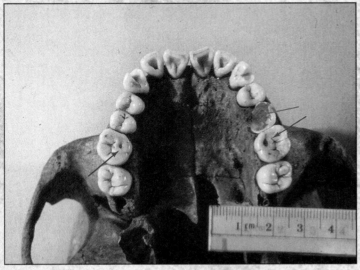

FIGURE 22
Caries are apparent on the first molars (blue arrows). Also, note there is a retained milk (deciduous) tooth on the left side of jaw (red arrow), and, consequently, the adult premolar never erupted. Female, Central California.

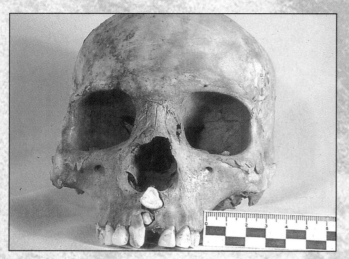

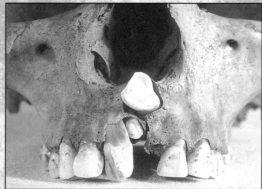

FIGURE 23 (above left)
Malerupted teeth in a young female (20 to 24 years old) from Central California. The left central incisor is seen below the nasal aperture. Note the considerable inflammatory reaction around the face.

FIGURE 24 (above right)
Close-up of specimen in Figure 23. This individual had a developmental defect that led to the improperly aligned teeth (with inflammation secondary to the dental problems).

FIGURE 25 (right)
Severe abscess in the upper jaw of a California Indian. Despite the degree of bone reaction, such lesions can be asymptomatic. Male, 31 to 40 years old.

The techniques developed by paleopathologists in studying ancient human skeletal remains can also be used in the study of nonhuman primate skeletons. For example, deceased chimps from Gombe National Park have been cleaned of soft tissues, and their skeletons have revealed a variety of fascinating details about these animals (information that can be correlated with the wealth of behavioral data collected by Jane Goodall).

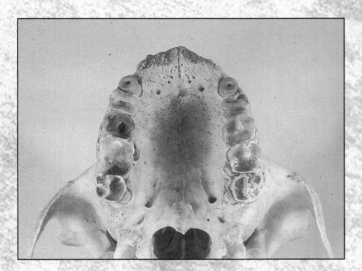

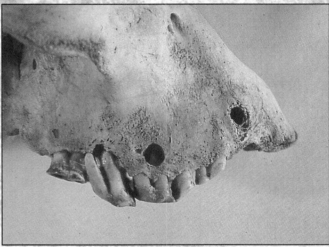

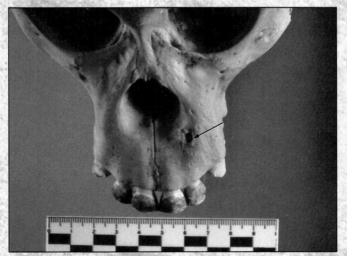

FIGURE 26 (above left)
Severe dental wear in adult female, Flo, from Gombe National Park (estimated at 40 + years at the time of death).

FIGURE 27 (above right)
Multiple dental abscesses in Flo's upper jaw, probably secondary to extreme wear (illustrated in Figure 26).

FIGURE 28 (left)
Healed bite wound (arrow) in the young adult chimpanzee, MacDee, aged 13, from Gombe National Park. Such evidence of interpersonal violence at Gombe (presumably the bite was from another chimp) corroborates behavioral observations.

LESSONS FROM THE PAST, LESSONS FOR THE FUTURE

CHAPTER 14

Homo sapiens is one product of 4 billion years of evolution. Our species is but one of millions living today, and we—in *some* significant ways—have come to dominate this planet (indeed, in many instances, to the detriment of other life forms). We thus frequently think of the human species as the true masters of the world. However, what will be the fate of *Homo sapiens*? Will our species continue to thrive? And, if so, what kind of world will our descendants face? The study of evolution, specifically human evolution, offers insights from the past that can help illuminate the future.

THE BIOLOGICAL CONTINUUM

Many cultures, including those of Western Europe and the United States, have traditionally viewed humanity as separate from nature. This separatist view may well have come about with the domestication of plants and animals some 10,000 years ago. Although this statement is speculative, it is worthwhile to note that many, and perhaps most, hunter-gatherers viewed themselves as *part* of the natural world in which they lived.

As we have emphasized, the biological view is that humans are animals and, more specifically, primates. Like all life forms on earth, our very existence is based in the molecule DNA. As all living forms share this *same* genetic foundation, it can be argued most economically that all life has evolved from a common ancestor. The biological continuum of genetic function runs from bacteria through humans—a fact put to excellent advantage in recombinant DNA research (where human genes are transplanted into bacteria, which then act as "biochemical factories," producing human proteins, such as insulin).

As mentioned, the continuum can be most obviously seen in our primate relatives. Chimpanzees and gorillas share with humans a very similar anatomy. Moreover, there are numerous behavioral similarities, as well as shared emotional and psychological needs. At an even more basic level, the chromosomes and protein sequences in these three hominoids are also extremely similar. At the most basic level of all, chimpanzee and human DNA are *more than 98% identical*. This similarity is so pronounced in fact, that many scientists advocate placing humans and chimpanzees (gorillas, as well) in the same genus (i.e., *Homo*).

BIOLOGICAL DIVERSITY

As noted above, we have come to regard our species as the masters of the planet. In Western cultures, this view has been reinforced by the conventionally held Old Testament assertion that humans shall have dominion over the animals.* Moreover, there is the prevailing view that nature represents an array of resources that exists primarily to be exploited for the betterment of humankind. This view is as widely held today, unfortunately, as ever before. More than merely being anthropocentric, such a view bespeaks a misplaced, unjustified arrogance.

By most standards, *Homo sapiens* is currently a successful organism. There are currently more than 5.3 billion human beings living on this planet. Each one of these 5,300,000,000 individuals comprises upwards of 20 trillion cells. Nevertheless, we and all other multicellular organisms contribute but a small fraction of all the cells on the planet—the vast majority of which are bacteria. Thus, if we see life ultimately as a competition among reproducing organisms, bacteria are the winners, hands down.

Bacteria then, by most standards, could be viewed as the dominant life form on this planet. However, even when only considering multicellular animals, there are some further lessons in evolutionary humility. As mammals, we are members of a group numbering about 4,000 species—indeed, a category of life on the decline over the last several million years. Looking even more specifically, as primates, we see ourselves belonging to a grouping that today numbers not even 200 species (and is also probably declining since its peak several million years ago). Compare these species numbers with those estimated for insects—some 15,000,000! Number of species (as an indicator of biological diversity) is as good a barometer of evolutionary success as any other. By this standard, humans (and our close relatives) could hardly be seen as the most successful of species.

Evolutionary success can also be gauged by species longevity. Fossil evidence indicates *Homo sapiens* has been on the scene for at least 200,000 years, and perhaps as long as 400,000 years. Such time spans, seen through the perspective of a human lifetime, may seem enormous. But consider this: our immediate predecessor, *Homo erectus*, had a species longevity of about 1.5 million years. In other words, we as a species would need to exist another million years simply to match *Homo*

---

*The *Old Testament*, in *Genesis*, actually presents two separate versions; the second conveys a quite different meaning: that humans are to have "stewardship" over the animals.

erectus! If such considerations as these are not humbling enough, remember that some sharks and turtles have thrived basically unchanged structurally for 400 million years!

HUMANS AND THE IMPACT OF CULTURE

As you have seen, humans are the product of biocultural evolution, and it is impossible to overstate the importance of culture in the biological evolution of our species. The earliest hominids used tools, probably in much the same manner as do modern chimpanzees. In turn, such tool use selected for greater neurological complexity (and problem solving ability), which in turn permitted the development of an increasingly complex tool kit. As a result of the feedback produced by this interaction of biology and culture, *Homo sapiens* became the large-brained species we are today. In a sense, then, humans have the unique ability to say, "We have created ourselves."

Because humans increasingly came to use culture as a means of adapting to the natural environment, physical anthropologists view culture as an adaptive strategy. Stone tools, temporary shelters, animal products (including animal skin clothing), and the use of fire, all permitted earlier populations to expand from the tropics and to exploit resources in regions previously unavailable to them. In fact, it was culture that enabled humans to become more successful as time passed.

For most of human history, technology remained simple, and the rate of culture change was slow. Indeed, humans enjoyed what could be termed a "comfortable" relationship with this unique adaptive strategy. However, as technologies became more complex, and especially when humans began to settle down as agriculturalists, their relationship with culture became more complicated and, over time, less and less comfortable.

Early groups of hunter-gatherers suffered few if any ill effects from their means of adapting. Moreover, early cultural practices had little negative impact upon the natural environment, at least on a global scale. (This is not to say, however, that impacts were not felt locally.)

Many scientists, in fact, believe that several large mammalian species were pushed toward extinction by massive overhunting by earlier human populations, particularly near the end of the Pleistocene, some 10,000 years ago. In North America, at least 57 mammalian species became extinct, including the mammoth, mastadon, giant ground sloth, the saber-toothed cat, several large rodents, and numerous ungulates or grazing animals (Lewin, 1986; Simmons, 1989). Although climate change (warming) was undoubtedly a factor in these Pleistocene extinctions, big game hunting by humans may also have been important.

In Eurasia, losses included the woolly mammoth, woolly rhinoceros, the giant Irish elk, and several carnivores. Although it can never be known for certain, it appears likely that overhunting was responsible for at least some of the late Pleistocene extinctions. This scenario may be especially true for the New World. Although there is some dispute as to when humans first entered North America from Asia, it is certain they were firmly established by at least 12,000 years ago (and probably earlier).

Although we have no direct evidence that early American big game hunters contributed to extinctions, we do have evidence of what can happen to indigenous species when new areas are colonized by humans for the first time. Within just a few centuries of human occupation of New Zealand, the Moa, a large flightless bird, was exterminated. Madagascar serves as a similar example. In the last one thousand years, after the arrival of permanent human settlement, 14 species of lemurs, in addition to other mammalian and bird species, have become extinct (Jolly, 1985; Napier and Napier, 1985). One such species was *Megaladapis*, which weighed an estimated 300 pounds (Fleagle, 1988)!

Hunter-gatherer groups for whom we have ethnographic evidence differed in their views regarding conservation of prey species. In some cases, it was believed that overhunting would anger deities. Others (some Great Basin Indians, for example) killed large numbers only every several years, allowing populations of game species, such as antelope, time to replenish. Still others avoided killing pregnant females, or were conscientious about using all parts of the body to avoid waste. Nevertheless, there were some groups, such as the Hadza of the Pacific Northwest Coast, who appear not to have been especially concerned with conservation.

Moreover, hunting techniques were frequently incompatible with conservation. Prior to domestication of the horse (or its availability in the New World), the only effective way to hunt large herd animals was to organize game drives. In some cases, fire was used to drive stampeding animals into blind canyons or human-made "corrals." Other times, bison in particular were driven over cliffs or into *arroyos* (narrow, deep gullies). Unfortunately, this practice often led to waste, as more animals might be killed than could be utilized (even though it was common practice to store dried meats for future use). Moreover, there might be so many animals that it was impossible to retrieve those at the bottom of the pile.

The Olsen-Chubbuck site in eastern Colorado is a bison kill site where, in one hunt some 10,000 years ago, 190 bison (*Bison occidentalis*) were driven into an arroyo. (This species, approximately 25 percent larger than the familiar *Bison bison*, is believed to have become extinct approximately 7000 years ago.) Of the 190 animals killed, 170 (90 percent) were partially or completely butchered (Wheat, 1972). The 20 complete skeletons of those left unbutchered were found at the bottom of the arroyo where they would have been virtually inaccessible.

Although excess numbers of herd animals were often killed by humans, the evidence from the Olsen-Chubbuck site indicates such was not always the case. However, it is true that once hunter-gatherer groups came into contact with European agricultural and/or industrial cultures, practices changed. One example of changing practices is seen in the devastation of some animal populations, such as the beaver, in North America. Because of the fur trade in the first half of the nineteenth century, the beaver was decimated on the Great Plains and became extinct in the central Rocky Mountains (Simmons, 1989). Although the fur trade was initiated by white Europeans, such trading firms as the Hudson's Bay Company relied heavily upon pelts traded to them by Indians in exchange for other goods, such as alcohol.

From the archeological record, it appears that around 15,000 years ago, partly due to climate change and the extinction of many of the large-bodied prey species, some human groups began to settle down, abandoning their nomadic lives. Moreover, by about 10,000 years ago (and probably earlier), some peoples had learned that by keeping domestic animals and growing vegetable crops, they had more abundant and reliable food supplies. The domestication of plants and animals is seen as one of the major events in human history, an event that ultimately was to have far-reaching and serious consequences for the entire planet.

Keeping domesticated plants and animals requires a settled way of life, and increased sedentism, combined with more reliable food sources, led to increased population growth. Viewed from the perspective of late twentieth-century humans living in an industrialized society, it might seem that adopting a settled lifestyle would lead to better health and nutrition. Yet, scientists believe that health and nutrition among hunter-gatherers was, in fact, quite good compared to that of humans living in early settlements; for with settled lifestyle comes increased exposure to infectious disease.

Hunter-gatherers typically stayed in an area for a short period of time. Therefore, their exposure to such disease-carrying organisms as mosquitos (which are attracted to human settlements and refuse accumulations) was less than for people living in permanent settlements. Over time, inhabitants of densely settled areas were increasingly challenged by a wide range of infectious diseases. These diseases (smallpox, bubonic plague, and malaria, to name a few) claimed many victims as humans came to live in communities of ever-increasing size. Such communities permitted disease organisms to exploit the numerous hosts that were present in relatively crowded conditions. In addition, these communities created favorable living conditions for many disease-carrying organisms. Domesticated animals, sewage, garbage, stored grain, and thatched roofs, all serve as habitats for fleas, mosquitos, and rats. Consequently, there was an increase in human exposure to numerous infectious conditions, which previously had not been of great importance. Moreover, close association with domesticated animals and animal products exposed humans to such infectious conditions as tuberculosis. And, in large settlements (towns and cities), some diseases were able to establish a permanent foothold and became **endemic**, meaning that at all times there were some infected individuals in the population. In fact, endemic disease is one important result of humans living together in large numbers.

It can justifiably be said that increased exposure to infectious disease was one of the earliest alterations in the harmonious relationship between humans and cultural innovation. Furthermore, infectious disease has been and continues to be a powerful selective force acting upon human populations over time to produce phenotypic variations (e.g., the relationship between malaria and sickle-cell hemoglobin).

ENDEMIC Pertains to the continued presence, at least in some individuals, of a disease in a population.

Early agriculturalists, for whom we have only crude population estimates, probably numbered a few million, worldwide. At this level, population density was still exceedingly low, but human activity was already beginning to have an impact upon the land. It was during the **Neolithic**, for example, that once-forested Britain was cleared of most of its trees.

The human strategy has always been to exploit natural resources. Indeed, all living organisms must effectively exploit their habitat, or perish. However, for nonhuman species, resources are usually renewable. But if an overpopulated species decimates the resource base upon which it depends, it too will suffer a potentially massive die-off. (Remember what Malthus said about population size being limited by the availability of resources.) Eventually, however, resource populations are renewed, thus permitting increased numbers of exploiters once again. The checks on population size imposed by limited resources establish a balance between predator and prey populations, and ultimately, the future of both species depends upon continuous renewal.

Unfortunately, humans began to exploit, and increasingly depend upon, nonrenewable resources. Forests can be viewed as renewable resources, provided they are given the opportunity for regrowth. However, in many areas, forest clearing was virtually complete and followed by overgrazing and soil erosion. Therefore, in those areas, trees became a *nonrenewable* resource, perhaps the first resource to have this distinction.

However, given relatively small population size, even by the time of the ancient Greeks and Romans, human impact on ecosystems still remained a localized, not a global, phenomenon. Nevertheless, these impacts were significant. Much of what is now desert in the Middle East is the direct legacy of overgrazing (mostly by goats) and subsequent erosion over the last few thousand years. Moreover, the civilizations of ancient Greece and Rome did their part in clearing much of the land throughout the Mediterranean. The fact that Greece today is largely treeless is due to the activities of its human inhabitants over 2000 years ago! It has even been suggested that the decline of the Greek and Roman civilizations was in part the result of environmental degradation in the form of pollution, and the exhaustion and loss of precious topsoil (Ehrlich and Ehrlich, 1990).

Destruction of natural resources in the past has also had severe consequences for other parts of the world as well. The 1990 typhoon and severe flooding that killed over 100,000 people in Bangladesh was partly due to deforestation of regions in the Himalayas of northern India. There is also evidence that continued erosion and flooding in China is partly the result of deforestation that occurred in the past. Lastly, many scientists have long speculated that the collapse of the Maya civilization of southern Mexico around 1000 years ago was due to overcultivation of land and depletion of nutrient-poor tropical soils.

Archaeologists can provide many examples of what humans have done wrong in the past. But, just as importantly, archaeologists are also able to provide us with positive examples from earlier cultures, innovative techniques that, for all our modern wisdom, we still have yet to match. For example, in the Andean highlands of South America, soil is

NEOLITHIC The terms applied to the period during which humans began to domesticate plants and animals. The Neolithic is also associated with increased sedentism.

very poor and subject to erosion. Agricultural peoples living in the region today (in Bolivia and Peru), even with considerable input from modern technology, still can barely scrape together a meager existence. Yet, such unrelenting poverty was not always the case in this part of the world. The Inca ancestors of these peoples, 500 years ago, reaped enormous wealth from this same land and built from it one of the largest, best organized, empires in the world. How did they do it?

Asking this very question led archeologist Craig Erickson to seek an answer. By examining Inca agricultural fields, terracing, and irrigation, he was able to extrapolate the ancient techniques and duplicate many of the same methods. This was no mere academic exercise, however, for the next step was to *teach* these methods to the modern farmers. As a result, crop yields have vastly improved, with less environmental damage, with less use of fertilizer, and at less cost than before!

CULTURAL DIVERSITY— A TREASURE RAPIDLY DISAPPEARING

Much of the vast cultural knowledge accumulated over the millennia resides among the native peoples of the world. Highly specific information regarding edible plants as well as valuable medicinal sources has traditionally been known by elders, healers, etc., of many cultures. It is thought that Western science and medicine could still learn a great deal from these peoples, especially regarding the remarkable curative powers of some plants. (Western scientists only recently isolated a compound in the bark of yew trees that proved to be a very effective treatment for certain forms of cancer.) Moreover, there is growing concern that by destroying the rain forests we are losing untold compounds, that could prove invaluable in treating numerous diseases, including AIDS.

Unfortunately, much medical knowledge and herbal lore used for millennia is rapidly vanishing as traditional cultures, developed over thousands of years, are swallowed in the rush toward urbanization in the developing world. In many tropical areas, not only are the traditional cultures disappearing, but the entire habitat is being obliterated, including the animals and plants of which we in the "developed" world still know so little.

COULD THE HUMAN SPECIES BECOME EXTINCT?

An obvious answer to this question is yes. After all, *eventually* there will be no sun, and ultimately (in a few billion years) no earth, so all life here will cease to exist. Of course, science fiction writers have long-envisioned wide-ranging colonization of the galaxy by interstellar voyagers from earth. *Perhaps* such a circumstance will come about. Certainly, on this planet, we are the only species with the ability to envision our possible fate and with the cultural capacity to do something about it.

However, it is only through such cultural/technological means that, over the long term, we as a species have a chance to endure. There are no *biological* guarantees. Most species that have existed on this planet have long since died out. Such could be the expected fate for all living forms as well.

Evolution, as commonly rendered in nature programs on television, in popular books, etc., presents a misleading picture. We often are told that *species* are "adapting, so to survive." An accurate understanding of evolutionary processes shows such statements to be nonsense. Life forms, through the central process of natural selection, compete *as individuals*. Their success in such competition is measured solely by their individual abilities to reproduce. Life forms, in following this biological imperative, may indeed prove to be individually successful, but, at the same time, may be contributing to a situation highly detrimental to the species. For example, it is through such maximization of individual reproductive success that overpopulation occurs. Severe overexploitation of resources, a population "crash," and even complete extinction may then ensue. No matter. The individual organism obviously cannot foresee such a calamity, and will, accordingly, act to maximize its own success—regardless of the ultimate effects on the species.

Humans, as we will discuss shortly, are in the midst of an explosive population increase. An increase of this magnitude is by no means unique, although it is probably unprecedented in such a large animal (and certainly in one so environmentally "hungry"). Another biological lesson shows we are but part of an integrated ecological system. As we expand so rapidly (and appear so successful in the short term) we cannot predict the potential negative effects of this very "success" for the long term.

It is clear, then, that all life forms *can* become extinct, even hominids. Robust australopithecines are sometimes depicted as overly specialized, rather dimwitted vegetarians. Yet, they were highly successful hominids in their own right and *may* have had significant cognitive and cultural capacities. One thing we know for certain, they as a group endured for at least 1.5 million years. In the end, however, they vanished. As hominids, we can learn from such evolutionary history—if we choose to use this knowledge. To ignore the past condemns us not just to darkness, but to oblivion.

THE PRESENT CRISIS: OUR CULTURAL HERITAGE?

It would be difficult to escape the media attention given today to environmental problems. At some level, everyone is aware that problems exist. Unfortunately, it seems that few are aware of how truly serious the situation is, and even fewer still are prepared to do anything about it.

If one had to point to one single challenge facing humanity, a problem to which virtually all others are tied, it would have to be population growth. We currently are trapped in a destructive cycle of our own devising. Population size has increased in our own species as we have increased our ability to produce food surpluses. As population size increases, more and more land is converted to crops, pasture, and construction, providing more opportunities for yet more humans. Additionally, through the medical advances of the twentieth century, we have reduced mortality at both ends of the life cycle. Thus, fewer people die in childhood and, having survived to adulthood, they live longer than ever before. Although these medical advances are unquestionably beneficial to individuals (who has not benefited from medical technology?), it is also clear that there are significant detrimental consequences to the species.

Population size, if left unchecked, increases exponentially; that is, as a function of some percent, like interest in a bank account. Currently, human population increases worldwide, at an annual rate of about 1.8%. Although this figure may not seem too startling at first, it deserves some examination. In addition, it is useful to discuss doubling time, or the amount of time it takes for a population to double in size.

As we have already shown, scientists estimate that around 10,000 years ago, only about 5 million people inhabited the earth (not even half as many as live in Los Angeles or New York City today). By A.D. 1650 there were perhaps 500 million and by 1800, one billion. In other words, in the 8350 years from 10,000 years ago until 1650, population size doubled seven and a half times. But, from 1650 to 1800 it doubled again, which means that doubling time had been reduced to only 150 years (Ehrlich and Ehrlich, 1990).

Dates and associated population estimates up to the present are as follows: 1930s—2 billion; mid 1960s—3 billion; mid 1980s—4 billion; present—5.3 billion. Moreover, by the end of this century, we are expected to add another billion people. Current estimates indicate that we have a doubling time of only 39 years, and thus by the year 2030, world population will be 10.6 billion people! In fact, in the 37 years between 1950 and 1987 world population *did* double from 2 to 4 billion. Put another way, we add 95 million people worldwide a year, or 1000 every 6 seconds (Ehrlich and Ehrlich, 1990)!

The rate of growth is not equally distributed among all nations. Although the world's rate of increase has ranged from 1.7% to 2.1% since the 1950s (Ehrlich and Ehrlich, 1990), it is the developing countries that share most of the burden. During the 1980s, the population of Kenya grew at a rate of a little over 4% per year, while India added a million per month, and 36,000 babies were born every day in Latin America.

You might logically ask, "Can we make technological changes sufficient to feed all these people? If so, is there enough land for housing, crop cultivation, and grazing? Can we develop enough of the earth's surface to satisfy our needs and still nave any left for other species?" The most likely answer to the first two questions is, "Probably for a while, but eventually no." The answer to the last is definitely "no."

With increases in numbers come greater demands that necessitate further consumption of nonrenewable resources. At the same time, activities involved in the production of goods and services produce waste and pollution, all of which leads to further environmental degradation.

Consider for a moment the fact that the energy used for human activities is derived from the burning of fossil fuels such as oil and coal (nonrenewable resources). The burning of fossil fuels increases the amount of carbon dioxide emitted into the atmosphere and this, in turn, traps heat. Increased production of carbon dioxide and other "green-house gases" such as, for example, methane and chlorofluorocarbons (CFCs), is of growing concern to many in the scientific community who anticipate possibly dramatic climate change in the form of "global warming." Environmentalists have stated fears that we are already seeing the effects of global warming as evidenced by the fact that the 1980s were the hottest decade on record. Others state that we do not currently have enough data to be certain that the heat and drought of the last decade represent nothing other than cyclical change.

Regardless of who is correct, the need for concern cannot be overstated. An increase in the mean annual temperature worldwide of even one or two degrees Fahrenheit could result in melting of the polar caps, with subsequent flooding of coastal areas, loss of agricultural lands to desert, dramatic changes in weather patterns, and extinctions of animals and plant species.

In no place can the devastating and rapid effects of environmental degradation be seen more clearly than in the tropical rain forests of the world. These once-immense and incredibly diverse habitats contain more varied forms of life than any other ecosystem. For example, one study conducted in Borneo identified 700 species of trees in just 10 separate 1-hectare (2.5 acres) areas. This is approximately the number of tree species in all of North America (Lewin, 1986). Researchers currently record at least 100 newly discovered plant species a year from Madagascar and the Andes, while estimating at least another 50,000 have yet to be found (Lewin, 1986). Yet, the rush toward modernization, urbanization, and technological "progress" all put these wondrous environments in imminent danger. So rapid, in fact, is the current pace of destruction that, if you are now in your twenties, most of what is left of tropical forests will be obliterated during your lifetime.

Deforestation, both in the tropics and North America, also has the potential to contribute to global warming, for we are reducing the number of trees available to absorb carbon dioxide. Moreover, in the tropics, trees are burned as land is cleared, a practice that releases carbon dioxide contained within vegetation into the atmosphere. In fact, an estimated 20 percent of all carbon dioxide emissions are accounted for by the burning of the Amazon rain forest alone (Ehrlich and Ehrlich, 1990). As a sobering note, Friends of the Earth, an environmental organization, recently reported to the press that 1991 may be the worst year yet for destruction of Brazil's Atlantic Forest. According to their estimates, between 50,000 and 80,000 fires were burning in this critical area at any given time during October of 1991.

As pointed out earlier, another major concern is the growing hole in the earth's ozone layer. Essentially, ozone is a form of oxygen, and the ozone layer filters ultraviolet radiation, thus acting to protect the earth from ultraviolet B (UV-B) radiation which, in turn, damages DNA, thus leading to skin cancer. Scientists believe that the well-publicized hole in the ozone layer above Antarctica has been caused primarily by CFCs used as aerosal propellants, solvents, refrigerants, and as components of styrofoam products. (CFCs release chlorine into the atmosphere and the chlorine binds to oxygen molecules, thus breaking down atmospheric ozone.)

Unfortunately, scientists do not know the full extent of damage to the ozone layer, but it now appears to be greater than was thought only a few years ago. Estimates place the loss above the United States at approximately two to three percent (Ehrlich and Ehrlich, 1990). Moreover, it is not known how much more damage will occur even if all CFC use were discontinued today. (The largest manufacturer of CFCs in the United States recently pledged to stop all CFC manufacture by 1997.) What is known is that, with ozone depletion, skin cancer rates will increase, as will associated mortality. Currently there are approximately 600,000 cases of skin cancer per year in the United States, with 9000 deaths. With continued ozone depletion, the United States Environmental Protection Agency estimates these figures could double in the next 40 years. Even more sobering, it is also suspected that terrestrial life on earth is not possible without an ozone layer.

Steps are being taken to correct some of the almost insurmountable problems facing humankind. Automobile manufacturers are working to develop more fuel-efficient automobiles. In fact, one Japanese company has just begun to market a car that is said to get 60 to 65 miles per gallon of gasoline. Alternative fuels using alcohol for automobiles are also being used with success in the United States, and manufacturers continue to experiment with electrically powered cars.

International agreements, including one signed by eighty nations (including the United States) in 1989, are now in place to end production of CFCs by the year 2000. This agreement, signed in Helsinki, Finland, also established a fund to help poor nations develop alternatives to CFC use.

Sadly, the one all-important problem facing humans today—population growth—is not being effectively addressed. Governmental restrictions on family size are abhorrent to most people and fly in the face of traditional views, regardless of nationality. For this reason, politicians rarely address the issue. Even in China, where very coercive tactics have been employed to enforce the one child per family rule, the goal of zero population growth has not been achieved. Moreover, opposition to abortion, particularly in the United States, has severely limited funding for family planning programs in developing countries.

These massive problems (and we have scarcely touched upon the subject) bespeak an adaptive strategy gone awry. Indeed, it would seem that we no longer enjoy a harmonious relationship with culture. Instead, culture has become the environment in which we live, and every day that environment becomes increasingly hostile. All one need do is look at the very air we breathe to realize we have overstepped our limits.

What can be done? Are these problems we have created amenable to human solution? Perhaps, but any objective assessment of the future offers little room for optimism. The declining quality of the air, the hole in the ozone layer, the possible greenhouse effect, the reduced amounts of arable land, and the accumulation of refuse already seem catastrophic problems in a world of 5.3 billion people. How well does the world *now* cope with feeding, housing, and educating its inhabitants? What quality of life do the majority of the world's people enjoy right now? What kind of world have we wrought for the other organisms that share our planet, as many are steadily isolated into fragments of what were once large habitats? If these concerns are not currently overwhelming enough, what kind of world will we see in 40 years when the world's population will number over 10 billion?

In recent years, it would seem that environmental concerns are becoming more widely discussed. World leaders now frequently pay lip service to preserving the environment. All this is well and good, but the real test of any policy will be the willingness of the world's population to sacrifice *now*—for rewards that will not become apparent for perhaps several decades.

If there is any real chance at all of reversing current trends, *everyone* will have to sacrifice. In the developing world, family planning must universally be adopted to halt population expansion. Most cultures are so constructed, however, as to make such behavioral change very difficult (perhaps impossible).

Sacrifice on the part of the developing world alone would not be adequate to stem the tide. It is entirely too easy and convenient for a North American to point, for example, at residents of Bangladesh and to demand they control reproduction (it runs 2 to 3 times that of the United States). But consider this: The average American uses an estimated 400 times the resources consumed by a resident of Bangladesh (Ehrlich and Ehrlich, 1990)! The United States alone produces 25 to 30 percent of all carbon dioxide emissions into the atmosphere. Clearly, much of the responsibility for current problems rests squarely upon the shoulders of the industrialized west.

In addition to population containment, the developed nations (most especially, the United States) must get along using far fewer resources. In order to accomplish any meaningful reduction in our wasteful habits, major behavioral changes and personal sacrifice will be required. For example, private automobile transportation (especially with only one passenger) and large, single-family dwellings are luxuries we enjoy, but they are luxuries the planet can ill afford. In addition, the dogs, cats, horses, and other pets we so prize are enormously costly in terms of resources (land to grow grain to feed the livestock to feed the pets). Must we then give up our pets as well? We could also ask: Wouldn't it be less costly to reduce our dietary intake of meat and grow grain to feed people directly?

Who is prepared to make the sacrifices that are required? Whence will the leadership come? It is fine to have "environmental" presidents and politicians, but the measure of leadership does not derive from being photographed at scenic locations while mouthing environmentally correct phrases. The planet is already in critical condition and there is no time left for indecision. Either we, as members of the species *Homo sapiens*, find the courage to make dramatic personal sacrifices, or we are doomed to suffer the unspeakable consequences of our own folly.

Studies of human evolution have much to contribute to our understanding of how we, as a single species, came to exert such control over the destiny of our planet. It is a truly phenomenal story of how a small apelike creature walking on two feet across the African savanna challenged nature by learning to make stone tools. From these humble beginnings came large-brained humans who, instead of stone tools, have telecommunications satellites, computers, and nuclear arsenals at their fingertips. The human story is indeed unique and wonderful. Our two feet have carried us, not only across the plains of Africa, but onto the polar caps, the ocean floor, and even across the surface of the moon! Surely, if we can accomplish so much in so short a time, we can act responsibly to preserve our lovely home and all the wondrous creatures who share it with us.

ATLAS OF PRIMATE SKELETAL ANATOMY

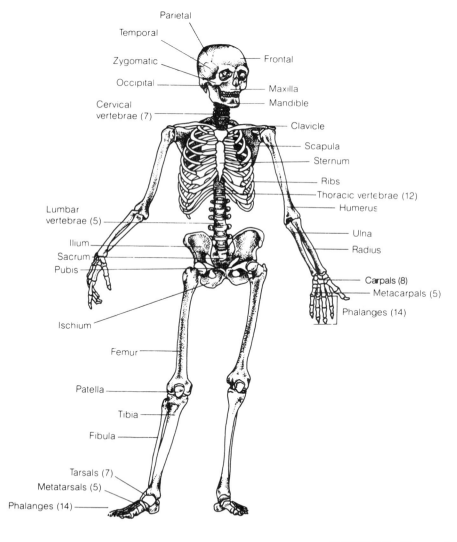

FIGURE A-1 Human skeleton (*Homo sapiens*)—bipedal hominid.

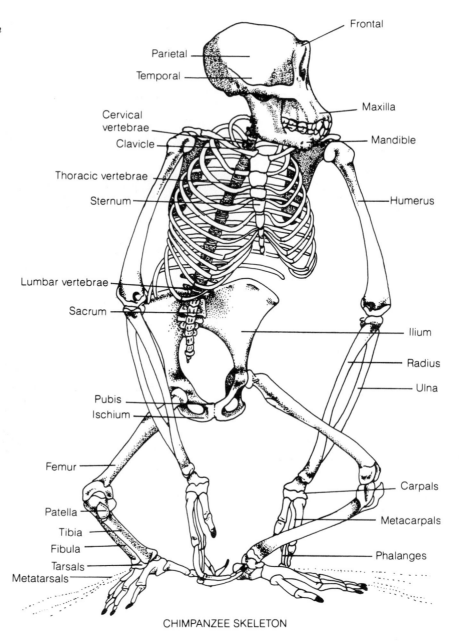

FIGURE A-2 Chimpanzee skeleton (*Pan troglodytes*) A knuckle-walking pongid.

Frontal

Parietal

Temporal

Maxilla

Cervical vertebrae

Mandible

Clavicle

Thoracic vertebrae

Sternum

Humerus

Lumbar vertebrae

Sacrum

Ilium

Radius

Ulna

Pubis

Ischium

Femur

Carpals

Patella

Metacarpals

Tibia

Fibula

Phalanges

Tarsals

Metatarsals

CHIMPANZEE SKELETON

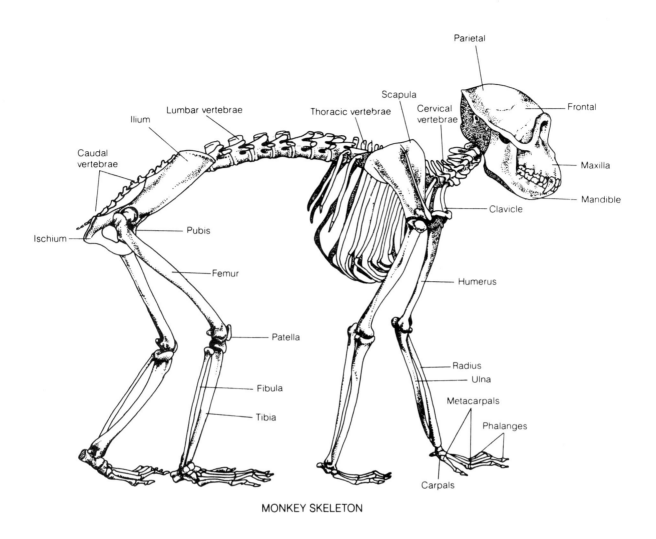

MONKEY SKELETON

FIGURE A-3 Monkey skeleton (rhesus macaque; *Macaca mulatta*)—A typical quadrupedal primate.

FIGURE A-4 Human cranium.

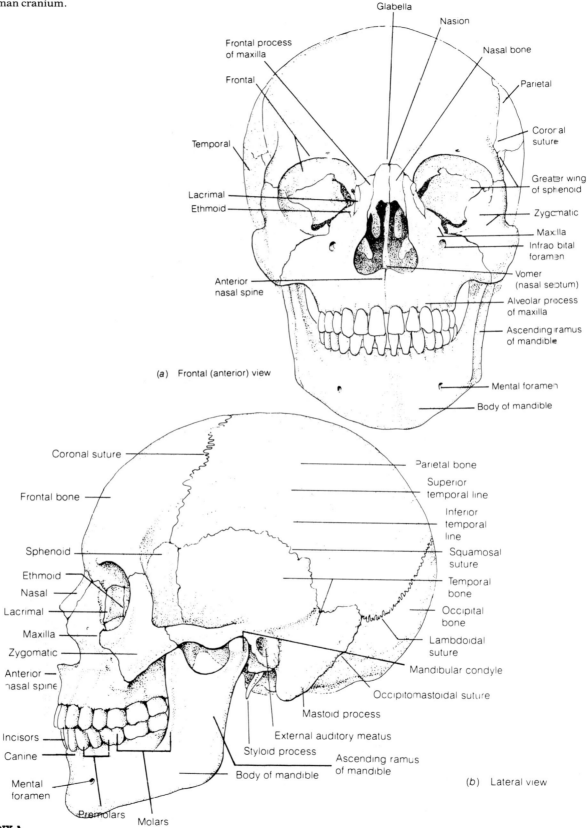

Glabella

Nasion

Nasal bone

Frontal process
of maxilla

Frontal

Parietal

Coronal
suture

Temporal

Greater wing
of sphenoid

Lacrimal

Zygomatic

Ethmoid

Maxilla

Infraorbital
foramen

Vomer
(nasal septum)

Anterior
nasal spine

Alveolar process
of maxilla

Ascending ramus
of mandible

(a) Frontal (anterior) view

Mental foramen

Body of mandible

Coronal suture

Parietal bone

Frontal bone

Superior
temporal line

Inferior
temporal
line

Sphenoid

Ethmoid

Squamosal
suture

Nasal

Temporal
bone

Lacrimal

Maxilla

Occipital
bone

Zygomatic

Lambdoidal
suture

Anterior
nasal spine

Mandibular condyle

Occipitomastoidal suture

Incisors

Mastoid process

Canine

External auditory meatus

Styloid process

Mental
foramen

Ascending ramus
of mandible

Body of mandible

(b) Lateral view

Premolars   Molars

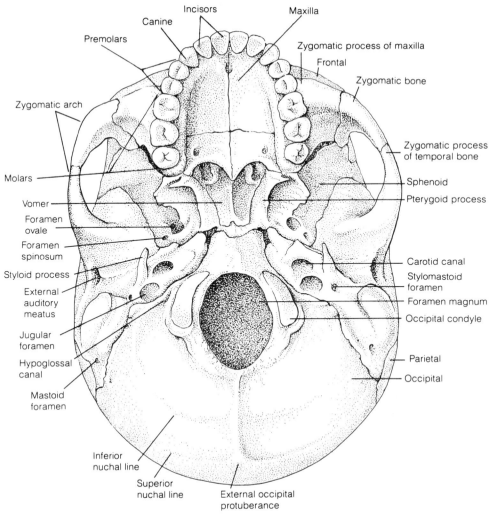

(c) Basilar View

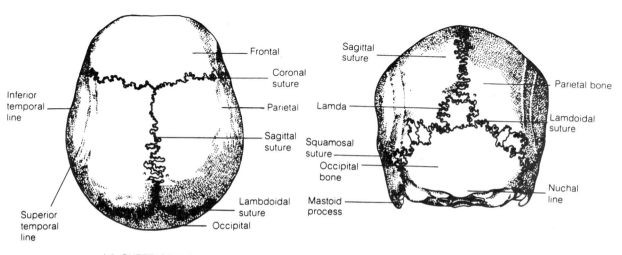

(d) SUPERIOR VIEW

(e) REAR VIEW

FIGURE A-5 Gorilla crania.

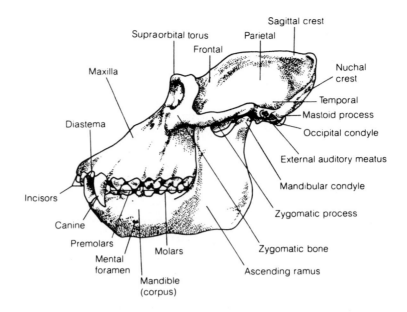

(a) MALE

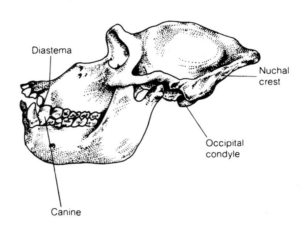

(b) FEMALE

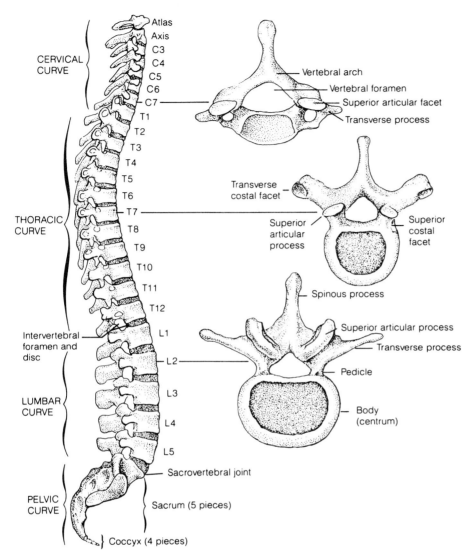

Human vertebral column (lateral view) and representative views of selected cervical, thoracic, and lumbar vertebrae (superior views).

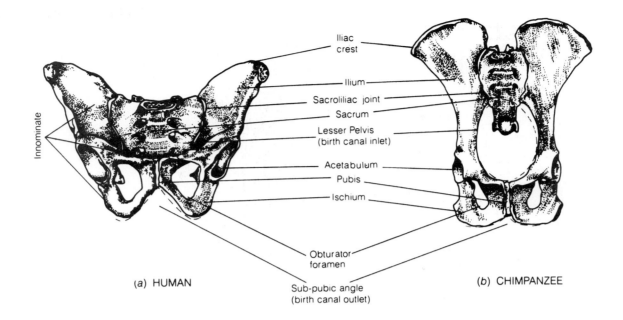

FIGURE A-7 Pelvic girdles.

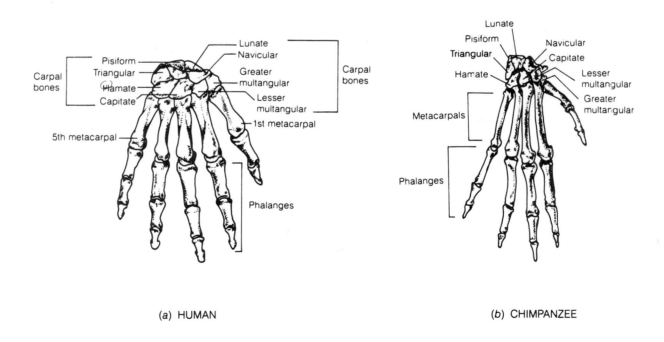

FIGURE A-8 Hand anatomy.

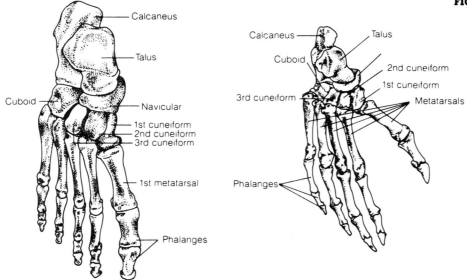

FIGURE A-9 Foot (pedal) anatomy.

Calcaneus

Talus

Cuboid

Navicular

1st cuneiform
2nd cuneiform
3rd cuneiform

1st metatarsal

Phalanges

(a) Human (dorsal view)

Calcaneus — Talus
Cuboid
2nd cuneiform
1st cuneiform
3rd cuneiform — Metatarsals

Phalanges

(c) Chimpanzee

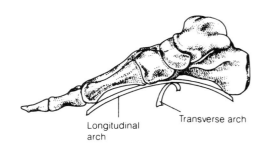

Transverse arch

Longitudinal
arch

(b) Human (medial view)

FORENSIC ANTHROPOLOGY*

It is a fascinating and startling fact that there are hundreds of millions of humans buried around this planet, and often their bones come to light for one reason or another. Indeed, thousands of skeletons have been excavated and are now curated in various natural history and anthropology museums. Skeletal biologists (also called *human osteologists*) are often asked to assist in unearthing these human remains and to perform various specialized analyses on them when prehistoric or, occasionally, historic burial sites are excavated.

Many situations occur in which forensic anthropologists are called upon by the police and other law enforcement agencies to assist in identification by using their knowledge of skeletal biology. Usually, the anthropologist is called upon to provide clues as to the personal identity of a deceased individual or individuals (through analysis of partially skeletalized remains), but is also occasionally asked to perform other tasks. Some examples of these tasks are: to identify skeletal trauma, match remains from a suspected scene of a crime with the corpus delecti, sort human from nonhuman remains, and, sometimes, to either compare a photograph to a living person, or to compare two photographs to determine the identity of the persons pictured. A few case reports will better illustrate the types of problems encountered by a forensic anthropologist. These are based on actual cases, and will be resolved for you at the end of this section.

Case 1: An old plane crash was discovered in the remote mountains of Colorado, and skeletal material was still inside. How many people are represented by this skeletal material, and who were they?

Case 2: A skeleton was discovered by a farmer while plowing his fields before planting. He contacted the local sheriff, who wondered if a past homicide victim could have been buried there.

Case 3: A building has exploded because of a natural gas leak, and five people are thought to have been inside at the time of the explosion and

---

*This appendix was written by Diane France and Robert Jurmain, with special thanks to George Gill for his contributions.

fire. These individuals were: a 23-year-old female and a 24-year-old female, both with no children, a 32-year-old female with three children, a 53-year-old male and a 54-year-old male. As these remains were almost completely skeletonized, how could they be identified?

Case 4: A very old photograph that bore a striking resemblance to Abraham Lincoln was discovered in the attic of an old house. Tests could be performed by other forensic specialists (questioned documents examiners, for example) to determine the age of the photographic paper, etc., and, of course, these would aid in discounting a fraudulent claim; but the photograph could still be of the correct age and be of a person other than Lincoln.

The first three cases must begin with a determination of the species represented by the remains. If the bones are not human, the forensic anthropologist's role is usually over, but if they are human, the work has just begun. Even if the police have an idea of who is represented by these remains, the specialist usually begins the investigation with a determination of the basic features: sex, age, race, stature, skeletal pathology, and notation of idiosyncrasies that could aid in final identification (such as healed fractures, prosthetic devices, and so on).

SEXING THE SKELETON

Several evolutionary factors have helped us to be able to identify sex in the human skeleton. The pelvic girdles in quadrupeds do not differ greatly between males and females of a species, but in humans the birth canal had a tendency to become smaller with bipedalism. This problem was compounded by the human newborn, whose head was relatively larger than the newborns of other animals, so throughout our evolution modifications were selected for in the female pelvic girdle relating to proportionately larger birth outlets, and these modifications aid in the determination of sex today. This sexual dimorphism (difference in morphology between the sexes) is most reliably diagnosed in the pelvic girdle, as shown below (see Figures 1 and 2).

 **FIGURE B-1**   Male pelvic girdle.

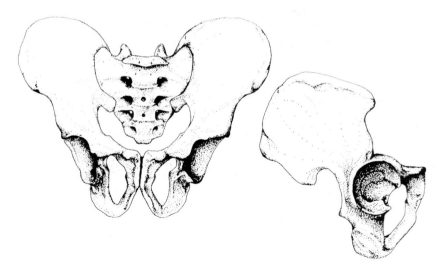

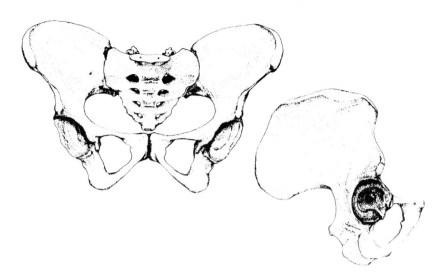

FIGURE B-2 Female pelvic girdle.

PELVIC GIRDLE	TYPICAL MALE	TYPICAL FEMALE
Subpubic angle	Less than 90 degrees	More than 90 degrees
Pubic shape	Triangular	Rectangular
Subpubic angle shape (see also Phenice, 1969)	Convex	Concave
Greater sciatic notch	Less than 68 degrees	More than 68 degrees
Sacrum	Smaller and more curved	Larger and straighter

In addition, humans display types of sexual dimorphism also common to most other animals: Males are usually larger and have more rugged areas for muscle attachments than do females of the same species. However, in order to utilize this size difference in sex determination, the researcher must be able to identify the population from which the skeleton was taken, as whole populations differ in skeletal size and robusticity. For instance, Asian Indians are much smaller and more gracile than Australian Aborigines.

After the pelvis, the cranium is the area of the skeleton most commonly used for sex determination. Some of these traits are listed below (see Figure 3).

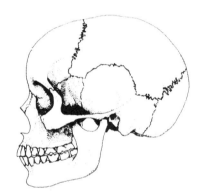
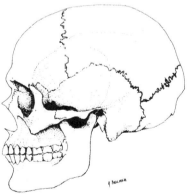

FIGURE B-3 Cranium and mandible: female (top); male (bottom).

CRANIUM	TYPICAL MALE	TYPICAL FEMALE
Muscle attachment areas (mastoid process, etc.)	More pronounced	Less pronounced
Supraorbital torus (brow ridges)	More pronounced	Less pronounced
Frontal bone	Slanting	Globular
Supraorbital rim (in eye orbit)	Rounded	Sharp
Palate	Deep	Shallow

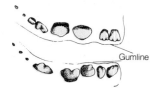

(a) Birth: The crowns for all the deciduous (milk) teeth (shown in color) are present; no roots, however, have yet formed.

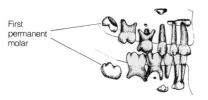

(b) 2 years: All deciduous teeth (shown in color) are erupted; the first permanent molar and permanent incisors have crowns (unerupted) formed, but no roots.

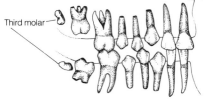

(c) 12 years: All permanent teeth are erupted except the third molar (wisdom tooth).

FIGURE B-4 Skeletal age: dental development.

Other bones of the body also show secondary sex characteristics, but are often less reliable than those of the cranium, as heavy muscle use affects the size and ruggedness of the muscle attachments, which can then sometimes change the diagnosis of sex. Areas probably not as affected by muscle use are:

Suprascapular notch on scapula	Often present	Often absent
Femur: angle of neck to shaft	Smaller angle	Greater angle

The standards discussed here are for adult skeletons; sexing techniques for pre-adolescents are not as yet widely used.

DETERMINATION OF AGE

During growth, the skeleton and dentition undergo regular changes that allow the determination of age at death. The age determination in individuals under about 20 years centers on deciduous (baby) and permanent dentition eruption times, on the appearance of ossification centers, and on the fusion of the separate ends of long bones to bone shafts.

Dental Eruption

The determination of the ages at which the deciduous and permanent dentition erupts is useful in identifying age to approximately 15 years. The third molar (wisdom tooth) erupts after this time, but is so variable in age of eruption (if it erupts at all) that it is not a very reliable age indicator. (See Fig. B-4.)

Bone Growth

Postcranial bones are preceded by a cartilage model that is gradually replaced by bone, both in the primary growth centers (the diaphyses) and in the secondary centers (the ends of the bones, or epiphyses). The initial ossification centers are, of course, very small, and are only rarely encountered by a forensic anthropologist. The bone continues to grow until the epiphyses fuse to the diaphyses. Because this fusion occurs at different times in different bones, the age of an individual can be determined by which epiphyses have fused and which have not (see Figs. 5 and 6). The characteristic undulating appearance of the unfused surfaces of bone helps differentiate it from the mature long bone (smooth) or merely a broken end of a bone (sharp and jagged).

Females mature more quickly than males, so usually 1 to 2 years must be subtracted from the previous ages for female skeletons.

Once a person has reached physiological maturity (by the early 20s), the determination of age becomes more difficult. Several techniques are used, including the progressive, regular changes in the pubic symphyseal face (the most common technique), in the sternal ends of the ribs, in the auricular surface of the ilium, in ectocranial (outside the cranium) and

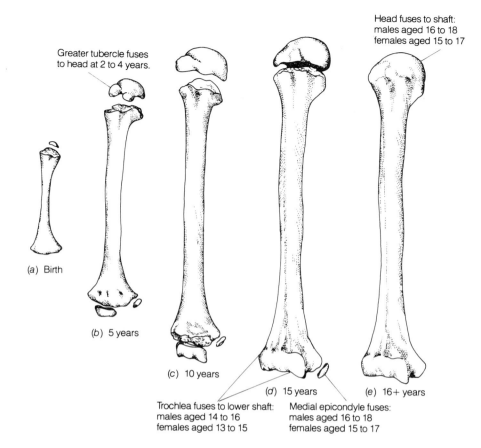

Greater tubercle fuses to head at 2 to 4 years.

Head fuses to shaft:
males aged 16 to 18
females aged 15 to 17

(a) Birth

(b) 5 years

(c) 10 years

(d) 15 years

(e) 16+ years

Trochlea fuses to lower shaft:
males aged 14 to 16
females aged 13 to 15

Medial epicondyle fuses:
males aged 16 to 18
females aged 15 to 17

FIGURE B-5 Skeletal age: epiphyseal union in the humerus. Some regions of the humerus exhibit some of the earliest fusion centers in the body, while others are among the latest to complete fusion (not until late adolescence).

endocranial (inside the cranium) suture closures, and in cellular changes determined by microscopic examination of the cross section of various long bones. In addition, degenerative changes, including arthritis and osteoporosis, can aid in the determination of relative age, but should not be used by themselves to determine age, as injury and certain diseases can cause changes that mimic old age in bones.

Pubic Symphyseal Face: The pubic symphyseal face in the young (Fig. 8) is characterized by a billowing surface, (with ridges and furrows) such as seen on a normal epiphysis, but undergoes regular metamorphosis from age 18 onwards. Figure 9 shows a symphyseal face typical of an age in the mid-30s, with a more finely grained face and perhaps still containing remnants of the ridge and furrow system. Figure 10 is typical of an age in the early 60s, with bony outgrowths often developing on the outer rims of the symphyseal face. The first technique was developed by T. W. Todd (1920, 1921) utilizing dissection room cadavers. McKern and Stewart (1957) developed a technique using American males killed in the Korean War. Both of the samples from which these systems were derived have limitations in that the dissection room sample used by Todd is based on individuals of uncertain age (Brooks, 1985, 1986) and the Korean War

FIGURE B-6 Distal femur.

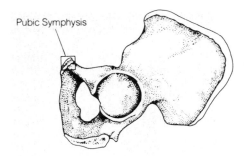

(a) Position of the pubic symphysis. This area of the pelvis shows systematic changes progressively throughout adult life. Two of these stages are shown in (b) and (c).

(b) Age: 21. The face of the symphysis shows the typical "billowed" appearance of a young joint; no rim present.

(c) Age: mid-50s. The face is mostly flat, with a distinct rim formed around most of the periphery.

FIGURE B-7 Skeletal age: Remodeling of the pubic symphysis.

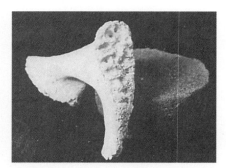

FIGURE B-8 Pubic symphysis face typical of an age in the late teens or early twenties.

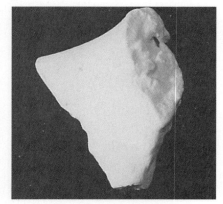

FIGURE B-9 Pubic symphysis face typical of an age in the mid-thirties.

Dead sample is predominantly young Caucasoid males, with few individuals over age 35.

Recently a system has been developed by J. M. Suchey, D. Katz, and S. T. Brooks based on a large sample ($n = 739$) of males for whom legal documentation of age is provided by death certificates. This autopsy room sample should be more representative of the general population than past samples. The majority of the males were born either in the United States or Mexico. This sample was taken at autopsies involving homicides, suicides, accidents, or unexpected natural deaths.

DETERMINATION OF RACE

When an anthropologist is asked to help in the identification of a parcel of bones, part of that identification must include a statement as to probable race, because society includes race as a part of the personal identity. Racial identification is often difficult, however, as most of the morphological characteristics we use to distinguish race follow a continuum; that is, one trait is more often, but not exclusively, associated with one race. Even skin color, the most noticeable of characteristics, cannot adequately categorize all individuals, for there are dark-skinned Caucasoids and Mongoloids (disregarding the effects of tanning), and light-skinned Negroids. In fact, it can be said that for many traits, there is more variation *within* races than *between* races. (See Chapter 5.)

The races of the world have been divided in different ways in history, but many anthropologists today identify five or six basic groups: Mongoloids (including Japanese, Chinese, and North, Central, and South American Indians), Negroids (including African and American Blacks), Caucasoids (including Europeans, and other people with European ancestry, West Asians, Asian Indians, and some North American peoples), Australoids (Australian Aborigines), and Polynesians. This is not by any means a complete classification scheme, nor is it the only classification scheme used by physical anthropologists today.

The chart below lists some of the differences we usually see in the skulls of three races common to the Western Hemisphere (most of the currently important differences used in the identification of race occurs in the skulls). (See also Brues, 1977; Krogman, 1962; Stewart, 1979; Bass, 1987; and Gill, 1986).

FEATURE	NEGROID	CAUCASOID	MONGOLOID
Central incisors (cross section) (Dahlberg, 1951)	Blade	Rarely shoveled	Shoveled
Cranial shape[a]	Dolicocranic (long)	Mesocranic (medium)	Brachycranic (round)
Nasal root (top of nasal bridge)	Wide, rounded	Narrow, pinched	Medium tented
Nasal aperture[b]	Platyrrhiny (wide)	Leptorrhiny (narrow)	Mesorrhiny (medium)
Zygomatic bone	Medium	Retreating	Projecting
External auditory meatus (ear opening)	Round	Round	Oval
Facial shape	Prognathic (lower face projects forward)	Orthognathic (lower face nonprojecting)	Medium

FIGURE B-10 Pubic symphysis face typical of an age in the early sixties.

In addition to the standard measurements, indices, and observations discussed here, further methods using skull and face measurements have been developed to aid in race determination. The most widely used of these is a *discriminant function* method (using a set of formulae), and was developed by Giles and Elliot (1962) for distinguishing Blacks, Caucasoids, and American Indians. Measurements are taken on the cranium of each adult, plugged into the formulae, and the final values plotted on a graph. It must be pointed out that, first, sex must be established (the formulae vary for males and females) and, secondly, the method is devised to answer only a limited question ("Is the cranium from a Black, from a Caucasoid, or from an American Indian?"). The discriminant func-

[a] The cranial shape is obtained from the Cranial Index, calculated from:

$$\frac{\text{Cranial breadth}}{\text{Cranial length}} \times 100$$

Up to 75 = dolicocrany
75–79.9 = mesocrany
80–84.9 = brachycrany
85 and up = hyperbrachycrany
(Bass, 1987)

[b] The nasal aperture shape is obtained from the Nasal Index:

$$\frac{\text{Nasal breadth}}{\text{Nasal height}} \times 100$$

Up to 47.9 = Leptorrhiny
48–52.9 = Mesorrhiny
53 and up = Platyrrhiny
(Bass, 1987)

tion method itself helps address the first point (sex) since the technique has also been used to devise a formula for sex determination (from a few of the same measurements). The problem with this method is not so much the need to determine sex first, or the fact that it answers a limited question (since most skulls on this continent come from Blacks, Caucasoids, or American Indians), but rather it relates to its accuracy. Particularly regarding American Indian specimens from the western United States, the percentage of correct ascertainment is quite low (Birkby, 1966; Gill, 1986). The sexing formula has proven quite accurate, however.

A new metric method developed by Gill and Hughes (Gill et al., 1988) appears to be much more accurate in race determination than the widely used Giles-Elliot approach. With six measurements (and three indices from them), it defines the amount of projection of the mid-face (which is extreme among the sharp-featured Caucasoids). The method does require a specialized (and rather rare) caliper, but is quite reliable in sorting Caucasoids from members of all other populations (in approximately 90 percent of cases). This method is also mathematically simple, and can be performed quickly in an autopsy setting. However, it cannot address the problem of sorting Mongoloids from Blacks, since their mid-facial projections are similar.

So, even today, with many new techniques and extensive use of the computer, race determination remains a challenging and somewhat subjective area. It requires the simultaneous use of many approaches rather than any single "foolproof" method. "By definition, race is quantitative

FIGURE B-11 Estimating stature: measuring the length of the femur.

FEMUR LENGTH (mm)*	STATURE	
	cm	inches
452	169	66
456	170	66
461	171	67
465	172	67
469	173	68

*Note: Data drawn from White males with known statures at time of death.

[no sharp boundaries]. Perfection can never be attained in defining or diagnosing a condition that does not even exist in absolute form" (Gill, 1986: 156).

ESTIMATION OF STATURE

Formulae for stature reconstruction in unidentified individuals have been developed by measuring the long bones of deceased individuals of known stature (Trotter and Gleser, 1952; Genoves, 1967). As is true of any statistical approximation of a population, these formulae are applied most reliably to the samples from which they are derived, though they may also be used on wider populations represented by these samples. Because these formulae were derived for each sex of various racial groups, the sex and race of the unknown individual must be known before these formulae can be reliably applied.

RESOLUTION OF THE CASE STUDIES

Case 1:   Even though the remains were burned, at least two individuals were identified as the pilot and friend who had filed the initial flight plan. It had been suspected at the time of the crash that at least one more person had been aboard, but there was no evidence to support that claim.

Case 2:   The skeleton was human, and was determined to be that of an American Indian male. Although often remains of this kind in these circumstances are automatically diagnosed as an archeological burial, the rapid decay rates of flesh and bone in many areas of the United States and other countries will cause the remains to look ancient in a very short time; thus, a forensic anthropologist must be alert to this possibility. In this case, however, further circumstantial evidence suggested that this was archeological, in that a projectile point was found in the tibia at the knee.

Cases of this kind are useful in disputes between American Indian groups in land and resource ownership, for, in increasing numbers, the tribal affinity of remains can be determined. Human identification in these circumstances has far-reaching ramifications.

Case 3:   As noted in the introduction, the ages of two of the females and two of the males were very similar to each other, so that even with the determination of sex and age, the identity of these very fragmentary remains was not easily determined. The 32-year-old female was identified by age determination of the pubic symphysis, and by the evidence on the pelvis that she had had children. There was evidence of at least two other women aside from the 32-year-old female, but because the stature of these other women was very similar, the identification was only tentative. Completely reliable identification was not possible, and it was noted only that there was no evidence that those women were *not* present in the building. The identification of the men was similarly difficult, as they again were about the same age. In addition, though one of the men had a surgical staple in his right knee, which would ordinarily have been evidence for identification, that area of the body was not recovered for either individual. One of the men, however, was over 6 feet tall, while the other was around 5 feet 8 inches tall. Stature reconstruction using the femur, and premortem and postmortem x-rays of the pelvic region of the men were ultimately used for the identification.

Case 4: Dr. Ellis Kerley (1984) determined, by comparing many features of a known Lincoln photograph to this photograph, that this was of a person other than our sixteenth president.

PHOTO SUPERIMPOSITION

Employed when a probable identification has been made, the technique of photo superimposition has been used in many cases lately, including the famous case of the identification of the Nazi war-criminal Josef Mengele (presented at the Annual Meeting of the American Academy of Forensic Sciences in New Orleans in 1986). In this and other cases, the skull (or large portions of the skull) are superimposed onto photographs of the known individual. If enough landmarks fall on the same position on the skull *and* on the photograph, the researcher is satisfied that he has made the correct identification. (Note: this technique could also have been used to reinforce the decision made in some of the cases outlined above.)

FACIAL RECONSTRUCTION IN HUMAN IDENTIFICATION*

Facial reconstruction (also termed *facial reproduction*) is a process used when other identification procedures (including fingerprints and dental matches) have been unsuccessful. Two different methods of producing a face on the skull are employed: a portrait of the individual using clues from the bones of the face; and a more direct, three-dimensional method of applying clay to the skull (or to a plaster cast of the skull). These techniques employ both science and art: The physical anthropologist discovers the age, sex, and race of the skull, but there is no direct evidence from bone that indicates the eye color, hair color and style, lip form, or degree of wrinkling or fleshiness in the individual. Therefore, there is a great deal of subjectivity in the rendering of the finished product; an exact reproduction is not expected, only a general likeness.

The following photographs show a facial reproduction taking shape. Erasers or blocks of clay marking tissue depths (arrived at experimentally from cadavers) are commonly glued to the skull. Clay strips,

---

*Contributed by Diane France and Sandra C. Mays, Supervisor, Crime Laboratory Section, Wyoming State Crime Laboratory. Stages of reconstruction are from both authors; finished reconstruction by Sandra Mays.

graduated to the various tissue depths, then "fill in the dots" between erasers, and the face is "fleshed out." The eyes, nose, lips, and sometimes ears are then fashioned according to various guidelines, and a wig is usually added.

Figures i and j show the reproduction of a Caucasoid female, over 60 years old. The first figure shows a nearly complete reproduction, but without the effects of aging, while Figure j is the finished product, including the features characteristic of a woman of that age.

FIGURE B-12   Facial reconstruction from a skull.

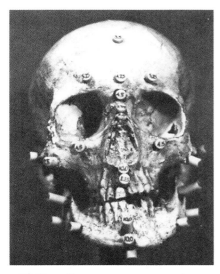

FIGURE a   Erasers precut to experimentally determined tissue depths are glued to skull.

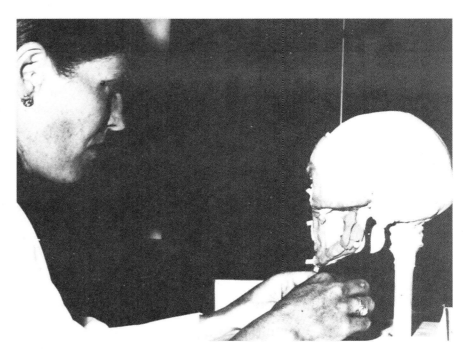

FIGURE b   Sandra Mays applies strips of clay between erasers, graduated to eraser depths.

FIGURES c and d Strips of clay connect erasers and clay is added to "flesh out" the face.

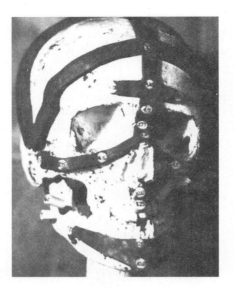
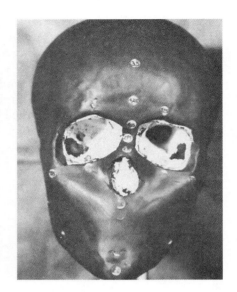

FIGURES e and f A nose and lips are added and refined.

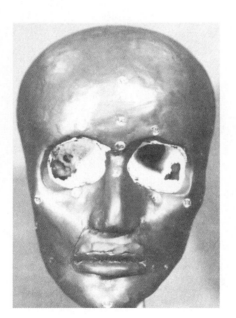
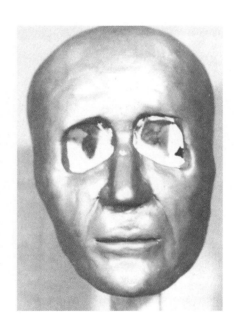

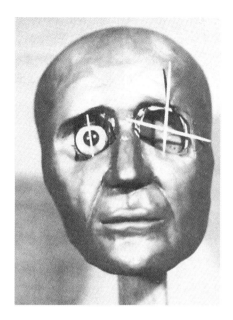

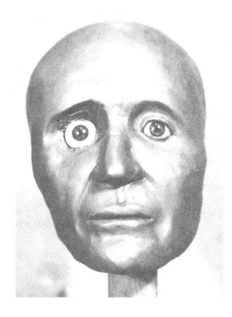

FIGURES g and h Glass (or plastic) eyes are placed into orbits and eyelids are fashioned.

FIGURES i and j Completed reproduction. (i) Before adding aging features. (j) After "aging" the face to correspond with aging indicators ascertained from other parts of the skeleton.

GLOSSARY

Acheulian The culture period, or stone tool industry, of the middle and part of the lower Pleistocene; characterized by the handaxe.

Adaptation An evolutionary shift in a population in response to environmental change; the result of natural selection.

Adaptive niche The whole way of life of an organism: where it lives, what it eats, how it gets food, and so forth.

Adaptive radiation The relatively rapid expansion and diversification of an evolving group of organisms as they adapt to new niches.

Affiliative Pertaining to associations between individuals. Affiliative behaviors—such as grooming—reinforce bonds between individuals.

Allele An alternate form of a gene. Alleles occur at the same locus on homologous chromosomes and govern the same trait; however, their action results in different expressions of the trait.

Alveolar Tooth-bearing portion of the upper jaw.

Amino acids Small molecules that are the components of proteins.

Analogies Similarities between organisms based strictly on common function with no assumed common evolutionary descent.

Anthropoid The suborder of primates including New World monkeys, Old World monkeys, apes, and humans.

Anthropology anthropos: man; logos: science, study of.

Arboreal Tree-living.

Arboreal hypothesis The traditional view that primate characteristics can be explained as a consequence of primate diversification into arboreal habitats.

Artifacts Traces of hominid behavior. Very old ones are usually made of stone.

Australopithecines The colloquial term referring to members of genus *Australopithecus*.

Autonomic Physiological responses that are not under voluntary control of the individual. The release of adrenaline when frightened is an example of an autonomic response.

Autosomes All chromosomes except the sex chromosomes.

Balanced polymorphism The maintenance of two or more alleles in a population due to the selective advantage of the heterozygote.

Binocular stereoscopic vision Vision where visual fields overlap and sensory input is sent from each eye to both sides of the brain. Seen typically in primates.

Biocultural The interaction of biological and cultural factors. An approach to the study of human evolution and behavior that stresses the influence of each of these aspects and their reciprocating effects on one another.

Biological continuum When expressions of phenomenon continuously grade into one another so that there are no discrete categories, they are said to exist on a continuum. Color is such a phenomenon. The term *biological continuum* refers to the fact that biological organisms are related through common ancestry and that behaviors and traits seen in one species are also seen in others to varying degrees.

Biological determinism The concept that various aspects of behavior (e.g., intelligence, values, morals) are governed by biological factors (genes). The inaccurate association of various behavioral attributes with certain biological traits, such as skin color.

Bipedalism (bipedality) Walking on two feet as among hominids and some other animals.

Bipedal locomotion Walking habitually on two legs. Among primates, distinctive only of hominids. The most characteristic adaptive feature of the *entire* hominid line.

Brachycephalic Having a broad head or a skull in which the width is 80 percent or more of the length.

Breeding isolates Populations that are clearly isolated either geographically and/or socially from other groups.

Burin A chisellike stone tool used for engraving on horn, wood, and ivory; characteristic of the upper Paleolithic.

Centromere The constricted portion of a chromosome. After replication, the two strands of a double-stranded chromosome are joined at the centromere.

Cerebrum The outer portions of the brain; in vertebrates, divided into right and left hemispheres.

Change in allele frequency The microevolutionary definition of evolution.

Chordata (Chordates) The phylum of the Animal Kingdom that includes vertebrates.

Chromosomes Discrete structures composed of DNA and protein found only in the nuclei of cells. Chromosomes are only visible under magnification during certain stages of cell division. Each species is characterized by a specific number of chromosomes.

Chronometric A dating technique that gives an estimate in actual number of years.

Clade A group of species sharing a common ancestor and distinct from other groups.

Classification The ordering of organisms into categories, such as phyla, orders, families, to show evolutionary relationship.

Codominance Refers to the expression of two alleles in heterozygotes. In this situation, neither is dominant nor recessive so that both influence the phenotype.

Codons The triplets of messenger RNA bases that refer to a specific amino acid during protein synthesis.

Complementary Refers to the specific manner in which DNA bases bond to one another. Complementary base pairing allows for accurate DNA replication.

Core area The portion of a home range containing the highest concentration of resources. The core area is protected against intruders and is therefore also considered the territory.

Cosmology The study of the creation of the universe and the laws that govern it.

Cultural relativism The view that differences in attitudes, values, and other social attributes that exist between populations are due to cultural variations not biological variation.

Culture The set of rules, standards, and norms shared by members of a society; transmitted by learning, and responsible for the behavior of those members.

Cusps The elevated portions (bumps) on the chewing surfaces of premolar and molar teeth.

Cytoplasm The portion of the cell contained within the cell membrane, excluding the nucleus. The cytoplasm consists of a semifluid material and contains numerous structures involved with cell function.

Deoxyribonucleic acid (DNA) The double-stranded molecule that contains the genetic code. DNA is a main component of chromosomes.

Derived Relating to a character state that reflects a more specific evolutionary line, and thus more informative of precise evolutionary relationships.

Displays Stereotyped behaviors that serve to communicate emotional states. Displays are most often associated with reproductive or agonistic behavior.

Diurnal Active during the day.

Dolicocephalic Having a long, narrow head. A skull in which the width is less than 75 percent of the length.

Dominance hierarchies Systems of social organization whereby individuals within a group are ranked relative to one another. Higher-ranking individuals have greater access to preferred food items and mating partners than lower-ranking individuals. Dominance hierarchies are frequently referred to as "pecking orders."

Dominant A trait governed by an allele that can be expressed in the presence of another, different allele (i.e., in heterozygotes). Dominant alleles prevent the expression of recessive alleles in heterozygotes.

Ecological Pertaining to the relationship between organisms and all aspects of their environment.

Ecological niche Specific environmental setting to which an organism is adapted.

Empirical Derived from or depending on experience or experiment.

Endemic Pertains to the continued presence, at least in some individuals, of a disease in a population.

Endocast A solid impression of the inside of the skull, often preserving details relating to the size and surface features of the brain.

Endogamy Mating within the population.

Enzymes Enzymes are specialized proteins that initiate and direct chemical reactions in the body.

Epochs A category of the geological time scale; a subdivision of period. In the Cenozoic, epochs include: Paleocene, Eocene, Oligocene, Miocene, Pliocene (from the Tertiary) and the Pleistocene and Recent (from the Quaternary).

Estrus Period of sexual receptivity of female mammals; correlated with ovulation.

Ethnography The study of surviving nonliterate societies. (Literate societies may also be studied.)

Eugenics The science of race improvement through forced sterilization of members of some groups and encouraged reproduction among others. An overly simplified, often racist view—now discredited.

Evolutionary trend An overall characteristic of an evolving lineage, such as the primates. Useful in helping to categorize them as compared to other lineages (i.e., other placental mammals).

Exogamy Mating outside the population.

Forensic Pertaining to courts of law. In anthropology, the use of anthropology in questions of law.

Frugivorous Having a diet composed primarily of fruit.

Gametes Reproductive cells (eggs and sperm in animals) developed from precursor cells in ovaries and testes.

Gene A gene is a sequence of DNA bases that specifies the order of amino acids in an entire protein or, in some cases, a portion of a protein. A gene may be made up of hundreds or thousands of DNA bases.

Gene pool The total complement of genes in a population.

Genetic equilibrium The mathematical relationship expressing—under ideal conditions—the predicted distribution of genes in a population; the central theorem of population genetics.

Genetics The branch of science that deals with the inheritance of biological characteristics.

Genotype The genetic makeup of an individual. *Genotype* can refer to an organism's entire genetic makeup, or to the alleles at a particular locus.

Genus A group of closely related species (e.g., *Homo*, *Pan*).

Geological Time Scale The organization of earth history into eras, epochs, and periods. Commonly used by geologists and paleoanthropologists.

Grooming Picking through fur to remove dirt, parasites, and other materials that may be present. Social grooming is common among primates and reinforces social relationships.

Heterozygous Having different alleles at the same locus on both members of a pair of homologous chromosomes.

Holism Viewing the whole in terms of an integrated system; cultural and ecological systems as wholes.

Hominidae From *homo* (man) and the suffix *dae*, indicating the group humans belong to.

Hominids Popular form of Hominidae, the family to which modern humans belong. Includes all bipedal hominoids back to the divergence from African great apes.

Hominization The process of becoming human.

Hominoid Apes and humans and all extinct forms, back to the time of divergence from Old World monkeys.

Homologies Similarities between organisms based on descent from a common ancestor.

Homologous Refers to members of chromosome pairs. Homologous chromosomes carry genes that govern the same traits. During meiosis, homologous chromosomes pair and exchange segments of DNA. They are alike with regard to size and position of the centromere.

Homozygous Having the same allele at the same locus on both members of a pair of homologous chromosomes.

Hormones Proteins produced by specialized cells that travel to other parts of the body where they influence chemical reactions.

Human evolution Physical changes over time leading to anatomically modern human beings.

Human variation Physical differences among humans.

Hybrid Offspring of mixed ancestry; a heterozygote.

Hypothesis Unproved theory. A theory is a statement with some confirmation.

Intraspecific Within-species. Refers to variation seen within the same species.

Interspecific Between-species. Refers to variation *beyond* that seen within the same species to include additional aspects seen between two different species.

Ischial callosities Patches of tough, hard skin on the rear ends of Old World monkeys and chimpanzees.

K-selected (k-selection) Adaptive strategy whereby individuals produce relatively few offspring in whom they invest increased parental care. Although only a few infants are born, chances of survival are increased for each individual because of parental investments in time and energy. Examples of nonprimate k-selected species are birds and wild canids (i.e., wolves, coyotes, and wild dogs).

Lactating (lactation) The production and secretion of milk by the mammary glands.

Large-bodied hominoid Those hominoids including "great" apes (orang, chimp, gorilla) and hominids, as well as all ancestral forms back to the time of divergence from small-bodied hominoids (i.e., the gibbon lineage).

Macroevolution Large-scale evolutionary changes that require many hundreds of generations and are usually only detectable palentologically (in the fossil record).

Meiosis Cell division in specialized cells in ovaries and testes. Meiosis involves two divisions and results in four daughter cells, each containing only half the original number of chromosomes. These cells can develop into gametes.

Messenger RNA A form of RNA that is assembled on one sequence (one strand) of DNA bases. It carries the DNA code to the ribosome during protein synthesis.

Metazoa Multicellular animals. A major division of the Animal Kingdom.

Microevolution Small-scale evolutionary changes that occur over the span of a few generations, and, therefore, can be seen in living populations.

Midline An anatomical term referring to a hypothetical line that divides the body into right and left halves.

Migration The exchange of alleles between populations (also called gene flow).

Mitosis Simple cell division or the process by which somatic cells divide to produce two identical daughter cells.

Monogenism The theory that all human races are descendants of one pair (Adam and Eve).

Mosaic evolution A pattern of evolutionary change in which functional systems within the body evolve at different rates.

Mousterian A culture period, or stone tool industry, of the Middle Paleolithic, usually associated with Neandertals. Characterized mainly by stone flakes.

Mutation A change in DNA. Technically, "mutation" refers to changes in DNA bases as well as changes in chromosome number and/or structure.

Natural selection The differential reproductive success of some genotypes compared to others (relative to specific environments).

Neocortex The outer (cellular) portion of the cerebrum, which has expanded through evolution, particularly in primates, and most especially in humans. The neocortex is associated with higher mental function.

Neolithic The terms applied to the period during which humans began to domesticate plants and animals. The Neolithic is also associated with increased sedentism.

Nocturnal Active at night.

Nucleotides Nucleotides are basic units of the DNA molecule composed of a sugar, a phosphate, and one of four DNA bases.

Nucleus A structure (organelle) found in all eukaryotic cells. The nucleus contains chromosomal DNA.

Old World anthropoid Anthropoids native to the Old World, including Old World monkeys, apes, and humans.

Osteology The study of bones.

Paleopathology The study of ancient diseases.

Paleospecies A species defined from fossil evidence, often covering a long time span.

Paradigm A cognitive construct or framework within which we explain phenomena. Paradigms shape our world view. They can change as the result of technological and intellectual innovation.

Phenotype The observable or detectable physical characteristics of an organism; the detectable expression of the genotype.

Phenotypic ratio The proportion of one phenotype to other phenotypes in a population. For example, Mendel observed that there were approximately three tall plants for every short plant in the F_2 generation. This is expressed as a phenotypic ratio of 3:1.

Phylogeny A depiction of evolutionary lines of descent. A "family tree."

Plio-Pleistocene The time period including the Pliocene and the first half of the Pleistocene. For early hominids, currently covers the range 4–1 mya.

Polyandry A mating system wherein a female continuously associates with more than one male (usually two or three) with whom she mates. This type of pattern is seen only in marmosets and tamarins.

Polygenic Refers to traits that are influenced by genes at two or more loci. Examples of such traits are stature, skin color, and IQ. Many polygenic traits are also influenced by environmental factors.

Polygenism The theory that human races are not all descended from Adam and Eve and therefore are not all members of the same species.

Polytypic Refers to species composed of several populations that differ from each other with regard to certain physical traits.

Population Within a species, the community of individuals where mates are usually found.

Prehensility Grasping, as by the hands and feet of primates.

Primates The order of mammals to which humans, apes, monkeys, and prosimians belong.

Primatologist Scientist who studies the evolution, anatomy, and behavior of primates. Usually trained as a physical anthropologist.

Primitive Relating to a character state that reflects an ancestral condition, and thus not diagnostic of those derived lineages usually branching later.

Principle of Independent Assortment The statement that the distribution of one pair of genes into gametes does not influence the distribution of another pair.

Principle of Segregation Genes occur in pairs (because chromosomes occur in pairs). During gamete production, the members of each gene pair separate so that each gamete contains one member of each pair. During fertilization, the full number of chromosomes is restored and members of gene pairs are reunited.

Prosimians Common form of Prosimii, a suborder of primates, composed of small primates such as lemurs and tarsiers.

Protein synthesis The assembly of chains of amino acids into functional protein molecules. The process is directed by chromosomal DNA.

Punctuated equilibrium The concept that evolutionary change proceeds through long periods of stasis, punctuated by rapid periods of change.

Quadrupedal (*quadrupedalism*) Using all four limbs to support the body during locomotion. The basic mammalian (and primate) form of locomotion.

Random genetic drift Shifts in allele frequency due to chance factors in small populations.

Recessive A trait that is not phenotypically expressed in heterozygotes. Also refers to the allele that governs the trait. In order for the trait to be expressed there must be two copies of the allele (i.e., the individual must be homozygous).

Recombination Also called *crossing-over*, recombination is the exchange of DNA between homologous chromosomes during meiosis.

Replicate To duplicate. The DNA molecule is able to make copies of itself.

Reproductive strategies The complex of behavioral patterns that contribute to individual reproductive success. The behaviors need not be deliberate, and they often vary considerably between male and female.

Rhinarium The moist, hairless pad at the end of the nose seen in most mammalian species. The rhinarium functions to enhance an animal's ability to smell.

Ribonucleic acid (RNA) A single-stranded molecule, similar in structure to DNA. The three types of RNA are essential to protein synthesis.

Ribosomes Structures composed of a specialized form of RNA and protein. Ribosomes are found in the cell's cytoplasm and they are essential to protein synthesis.

R-selected (r-selection) Adaptive strategy that emphasizes relatively large numbers of offspring and reduced parental care (compared to K-selected species). (The terms *K-selection and r-selection* are relative terms; i.e., mice are r-selected compared to primates, but compared to many fish species, they are K-selected.)

Ritualized Behaviors that are exaggerated and removed from their original context to communicate meaning. Mounting behaviors in macaques and baboons to express dominance is removed from its original context of reproduction.

Sex chromosomes The X and Y chromosomes.

Sexual dimorphism Differences in size or shape between males and females of the same species.

Shared derived Relating to specific character states shared in common between two forms and considered the *most* useful for making evolutionary interpretations.

Somatic cells Basically, all the cells in the body except those involved with reproduction.

Specialized A trait evolved for a specific function.

Speciation The process by which new species are produced from earlier ones. The most important mechanism of macroevolutionary change.

Species A population or group of populations living in the same econiche that can, or actually do, interbreed and produce fertile offspring.

Stratigraphy Sequential layering of deposits.

Substrates The surfaces over which an animal locomotes (e.g., ground, small branch, etc.).

Taxon (pl. taxa) A population (or group of populations) that is judged to be sufficiently distinct and is thus assigned to a separate category (such as genus or species).

Taxonomy The science of the classification or organisms, including the principles, procedures, and rules of classification.

Territories A group's or individual's territory is the area that will be aggressively protected against intrusion, particularly by other members of the same species.

Transfer RNA The type of RNA that binds to specific amino acids and transports them to the ribosome during protein synthesis.

Uniformitarianism A concept maintaining that the ancient changes in the earth's surface were caused by the same physical principles acting today. The earth's crust was formed slowly and gradually. Mountains, rivers, valleys, etc., were the result of purely natural forces such as erosion by wind, water, frost, ice, and rain. Although not originated by Charles Lyell, uniformitarianism is associated with him because he popularized it.

Upper Paleolithic A culture period noted for technological, artistic, and behavioral innovations. Also known for the widespread expansion of anatomically modern human beings. The Upper Paleolithic is usually dated from about 125–10 kya.

Variation Inherited differences among individuals.

Vertebrates Animals with bony backbones. Includes fishes, amphibians, reptiles, birds, and mammals.

Viviparous Giving birth to live young.

World view A literal translation from the German *Weltanschauung* (Welt: world; anschauung: view). A personal or group philosophy explaining history; a way of looking at the world.

Zygote A zygote is a cell formed by the union of an egg and a sperm cell. It contains the full complement of chromosomes (in humans, 46) and has the potential of developing into an entire organism.

BIBLIOGRAPHY

Altmann, Stuart A. and Jeanne Altmann
1970 *Baboon Ecology.* Chicago: University of Chicago Press.
Arensburg, B., L. A. Schepartz, A. M. Tiller, et al.
1990 "A Reappraisal of the Anatomical Basis for Speech in Middle Paleolithic Hominids." *American Journal of Physical Anthropology,* **83**(2):137–146.
Aronson, J. L., R. C. Walter, and M. Taieb
1983 "Correlation of Tulu Boi Tuff at Koobi Fora with the Sidi Hakoma Tuff at Hadar." *Nature,* **306**:209–210.
Avery, O. T., MacLeod, C. M., and McCarty, M.
1944 "Studies on the Chemical Nature of the Substance Inducing Transformation in Pneumococcal Types." *J. Expl. Med.,* **79**:137–158.

Bass, W. M.
1987 *Human Osteology: A Laboratory and Field Manual* (3rd Ed.). Columbia, Mo.: Missouri Archaeological Society Special Publication No. 2.
Bearder, Simon K.
1987 "Lorises, Bushbabies & Tarsiers: Diverse Societies in Solitary Foragers." *In*: Smuts, et al., q.v., pp. 11–24.
Binford, Lewis R. and Nancy M. Stone.
1986a "The Chinese Paleolithic: An Outsider's View." *AnthroQuest,* Fall 1986(1):14–20.

——— 1986b "Zhoukoudian: A Closer Look." *Current Anthropology,* **27**(5):453–475.
Birdsell, Joseph B.
1981 *Human Evolution.* (3d Ed.), Boston: Houghton Mifflin Co.
Birkby, W. H.
1966 "An Evaluation of Race and Sex Identification from Cranial Measurements," *American Journal of Physical Anthropology,* **24**:21–28.
Blumenbach, J. F.
1776 *De generis humani varietate nativa,* Göttingen, Germany. Trans. of later edition. *In: This Is Race.* E. W. Count (ed.), 1950. New York: Henry Schumann, pp. 25–39.
Bodmer, W. F. and L. L. Cavalli-Sforza
1976 *Genetics, Evolution, and Man.* San Francisco: W. H. Freeman and Company.
Brace, C. Loring and Frank B. Livingstone
1971 "On Creeping Jensenism," *In: Race and Intelligence,* C. L. Brace, G. R. Gamble and J. T. Bond (eds.), Anthropological Studies, No. 8, American Anthropological Association, Washington, D.C.
Brace, C. L. and Ashley Montagu
1977 *Human Evolution* (2nd Ed.). New York: Macmillan.
Bräuer, Günter
1984 "A Craniological Approach to the Origin of Anatomically Modern *Homo sapiens* in Africa and Implications for the Appearance of Modern Europeans." *In*: Smith and Spencer, q.v., 327–410.
Bromage, Timothy G. and Christopher Dean
1985 "Re-evaluation of the Age at Death of Immature Fossil Hominids." *Nature,* **317**:525–527.
Brooks, S. T.
1985 Personal Communication.

——— 1986 "Comments on 'Known' Age at Death Series." Presented in conjunction with "Skeletal Age Standards Derived from an Extensive Multi-Racial Sample of Modern Americans," by J. Suchey and D. Katz, at the Fifty-Fifth Annual Meeting of the American Association of Physical Anthropologists, Albuquerque, New Mexico.
Brown, T. M. and K. D. Rose
1987 "Patterns of Dental Evolution in Early Eocene Anaptomorphine Primates Comomyidael from the Bighorn Basin, Wyoming." *Journal of Paleontology,* **61**:1–62.
Brues, A. M.
1977 *People and Races.* New York: MacMillan Publishing Company.

——— 1990 *People and Races.* (2nd Ed.). Prospect Heights: Waveland Press.
Butzer, Karl W.
1974 "Paleoecology of South African Australopithecines: Taung Revisited." *Current Anthropology,* **15**:367–382.

Campbell, Bernard
1974 *Human Evolution.* Chicago: Aldine Publishing Co. (2nd Ed., 1985).
Cann, R. L., M. Stoneking and A. C. Wilson
1987 "Mitochondrial DNA and Human Evolution." *Nature,* **325**:31–36.

Carrol, Robert L.
1988　*Vertebrate Paleontology and Evolution*. New York: W. H. Freeman and Co.

Cartmill, Matt
1972　"Arboreal Adaptations and the Origin of the Order Primates." *In*: *The Functional and Evolutionary Biology of Primates*, R. H. Tuttle (ed.), Chicago: Aldine-Atherton, pp. 97–122.

―――
1974　"Rethinking Primate Origins." *Science*, **184**:436–443.

Charteris, J., J. C. Wali, and J. W. Nottrodt
1981　"Functional Reconstruction of Gait from Pliocene Hominid Footprints at Laetoli, Northern Tanzania." *Nature*, **290**:496–498.

Clark, W. E. Le Gros
1971　*The Antecedents of Man*. (3rd Ed.). New York: The New York Times Books.

Coon, Carleton
1962　*The Origin of Races*. New York: Alfred A. Knopf.

Dalrymple, G. B.
1972　"Geomagnetic Reversals and North American Glaciations." *In*: W. W. Bishop and J. A. Miller (eds.), *Calibration of Hominoid Evolution*. Edinburgh: Scottish Academic Press, pp. 303–329.

Dart, Raymond
1959　*Adventures with the Missing Link*. New York: Harper and Brothers.

Darwin, Charles
1859　*On the Origin of Species*. A Facsimile of the First Edition, Cambridge, Mass.: Harvard University Press (1964).

Darwin, Francis (ed.)
1950　*The Life and Letters of Charles Darwin*. New York: Henry Schuman.

Day, M. H. and E. H. Wickens
1980　"Laetoli Pliocene Hominid Footprints and Bipedalism." *Nature*, **286**:385–387.

Delson, Eric
1987　"Evolution and Palaeobiology of Robust *Australopithecus*." *Nature*, **327**:654–655.

Dene, H. T., M. Goodman and W. Prychodko
1976　"Immunodiffusion Evidence on the Phylogeny of the Primates." *In*: *Molecular Anthropology*, M. Goodman, R. E. Tashian and J. H. Tashian (eds.), New York: Plenum Press, pp. 171–195.

De Vore, I. and S. L. Washburn
1963　"Baboon Ecology & Human Evolution." *In*: *African Ecology and Human Evolution*, F. C. Howell and F. Bourlière (eds.). New York: Viking Fund Publication No. 36, pp. 335–367.

Dolhinow, P.
1977　"Normal Monkeys?" *American Scientist*, **65**:266.

Ehrlich, Paul R. and Anne H. Ehrlich
1990　*The Population Explosion*. New York: Simon & Schuster.

Falk, Dean
1983　"The Taung Endocast: A Reply to Holloway." *American Journal of Physical Anthropology*, **60**:479–489.

Fedigan, Linda M.
1982　*Primate Paradigms*. Montreal: Eden Press.

―――
1983　"Dominance and Reproductive Success in Primates." *Yearbook of Physical Anthropology*, **26**:91–129.

Fleagle, J. G.
1983　"Locomotor Adaptations of Oligocene and Miocene Hominoids and their Phyletic Implications." *In*: R. Ciochon and R. Corruccini (eds.), *New Interpretations of Ape and Human Ancestry*, New York: Plenum, pp. 301–324.

―――
1988　*Primate Adaptation and Evolution*. New York: Academic Press.

Fossey, Dian
1981　"The Imperiled Mountain Gorilla." *National Geographic*, **159**(4):501–523.

―――
1983　*Gorillas in the Mist*. Boston: Houghton-Mifflin.

Froelich, J. W.
1970　"Migration and Plasticity of Physique in the Japanese-Americans of Hawaii." *American Journal of Physical Anthropology*, **32**:429.

Fouts, Roger S., D. H. Fouts and T. T. van Cantfort
1989　"The Infant Loulis Learns Signs from Cross-Fostered Chimpanzees." *In*: R. Gardner, et al., q.v., pp. 280–292.

Galdikas, Biruté M.
1979　"Orangutan Adaptation at Tanjung Puting Reserve: Mating and Ecology." *In*: *The Great Apes*, D. A. Hamburg and E. R. McCown (eds.), Menlo Park, Ca.: The Benjamin/Cummings Publishing Co., pp. 195–233.

Gardner, R. Allen, B. T. Gardner and T. T. van Cantfort (eds.)
1989　*Teaching Sign Language to Chimpanzees*. Albany: State University of New York Press.

Garn, Stanley
1965　*Human Races*. (2nd Ed.). Springfield, Ill.: Charles C Thomas. (3rd Ed., 1971.)

Gates, R. R.
1948　*Human Ancestry*. Cambridge: Harvard Univ. Press, p. 367.

Genovés, S.
1967　"Proportionality of Long Bones and Their Relation to Stature among Mesoamericans," *American Journal of Physical Anthropology*, **26**:67–78.

Gingerich, P. D.
1985 "Species in the Fossil Record: Concepts, Trends, and Transitions." *Paleobiology*, **11**:27–41.
Goodall, Jane
1986 *The Chimpanzees of Gombe.* Cambridge: The Bellknap Press of Harvard University Press.
Gossett, Thomas F.
1963 *Race, the History of an Idea in America.* Dallas: Southern Methodist University Press.
Gould, Stephen Jay
1981 *The Mismeasure of Man.* New York: W. W. Norton.
Gould, S. J. and N. Eldredge
1977 "Punctuated Equilibria: the Tempo and Mode of Evolution Reconsidered." *Paleobiology*, **3**:115–151.
Gould, S. J. and R. Lewontin
1979 "The Spandrels of San Marco and the Panglossian Paradigm: A Critique of the Adaptionist Programme." *Proceedings of the Royal Society of London,*, **205**:581–598.
Greene, John C.
1981 *Science, Ideology, and World View.* Berkeley: University of California Press.
Grine, Frederick E. (ed.)
1988a *Evolutionary History of the "Robust" Australopithecines.* New York: Aldine de Gruyter.
1988b "New Craniodental Fossils of *Paranthropus* from the Swartkrans Formation and their Significance in "Robust" Australopithecine Evolution." *In*: Grine (ed.), q.v., pp. 223–243.

Harlow, Harry F.
1959 "Love in Infant Monkeys." *Scientific American*, **200**:68–74.
Harlow, Harry F., and Margaret K. Harlow
1961 "A Study of Animal Affection." *Natural History*, **70**:48–55.
Hartl, Daniel
1983 *Human Genetics.* New York: Harper and Row.
Holloway, Ralph L.
1969 "Culture: A Human Domain." *Current Anthropology*, **10**:395–407.

———
1983 "Cerebral Brain Endocast Pattern of *Australopithecus afarensis* Hominid." *Nature*, **303**:420–422.
Hooton, E. A.
1926 "Methods of Racial Analysis." *Science*, **63**:75–81.
Howell, F. Clark
1978 "Hominidae." *In*: *Evolution of African Mammals*, V. J. Maglio and H.B.S. Cooke (eds.), Cambridge: Harvard University Press, pp. 154–248.

———
1988 "Foreword." *In*: Grine (ed.), q.v., pp. xi–xv.
Howells, W. W.
1971 "The Meaning of Race." *In*: *The Biological and Social*

Meaning of Race, Richard H. Osborne (ed.), San Francisco: W. H. Freeman and Co., pp. 3–10.
Hrdy, Sarah Blaffer
1977 *The Langurs of Abu.* Cambridge, Mass.: Harvard University Press.
Humphries, Rolfe
1955 *Ovid Metamorphoses.* Bloomington: Indiana Univ. Press.

Jensen, Arthur
1980 *Bias in Mental Testing.* New York: The Free Press.
Jia, L. and Huang Weiwen
1990 *The Story of Peking Man.* New York: Oxford University Press.
Johanson, Donald, F. T. Masao, G. G. Eck, et al.
1987 "New Partial Skeleton of *Homo habilis* from Olduvai Gorge, Tanzania." *Nature*, **327**:205–209.
Johanson, Donald C. and Maurice Taieb
1980 "New Discoveries of Pliocene Hominids and Artifacts in Hadar." International Afar Research Expedition to Ethiopia (Fourth and Fifth Field Seasons, 1975–77). *Journal of Human Evolution*, **9**:582.
Jolly, Alison
1984 "The Puzzle of Female Feeding Priority." *In*: Meredith F. Small, q.v., pp. 197–215.

———
1985 *The Evolution of Primate Behavior.* (2nd Ed.), New York: Macmillan.
Jungers, W. L.
1988 "New Estimates of Body Size in Australopithecines." *In*: Grine (ed.), q.v., pp. 115–125.

Kan, Yuet Wai and Andrée M. Dozy
1980 "Evolution of the Hemoglobin S and C Genes in World Populations." *Science*, **209**:388–391.
Kennedy, Kenneth, A. R.
1990 "Narmada Man Fossil Skull from India." *American Journal of Physical Anthropology*, **31**:248–249.
Kennedy, Kenneth A. R. and S. U. Deraniyagala
1989 "Fossil Remains of 28,000-Year-Old Hominids from Sri Lanka." *Current Anthropology*, **30**:397–399.
Kimbel, William H.
1988 "Identification of a Partial Cranium of *Australopithecus afarensis* from the Koobi Fora Formation, Kenya." *Journal of Human Evolution*, **17**:647–656.
Kimbel, William H., Tim D. White and Donald C. Johanson
1988 "Implications of KNM-WT-17000 for the Evolution of 'Robust' *Australopithecus*." *In*: Grine (ed.), q.v., pp. 259–268.
Klein, R.
1989 *The Human Career. Human Biological and Cultural Origins.* Chicago: University of Chicago Press.
Klineberg, Otto
1935 *Race Differences.* New York: Harper and Brothers.

Krogman, W. M.
1962 *The Human Skeleton in Forensic Medicine.* Springfield, IL: C. C. Thomas.

Kummer, H.
1968 *Social Organization of Hamadryas Baboons.* Chicago: University of Chicago Press.

Leakey, M. D. and R. L. Hay
1979 "Pliocene Footprints in Laetolil Beds at Laetoli, Northern Tanzania." *Nature,* **278**:317–323.

Lerner, I. M. and W. J. Libby
1976 *Heredity, Evolution, and Society.* San Francisco: W. H. Freeman and Company.

Lewin, Roger
1986 "Damage to Tropical Forests, or Why Were There So Many Kinds of Animals?" *Science,* **234**:149–150.

Lewis, B.
1971 *Race and Color in Islam.* New York: Harper.

Lewontin, R. C.
1972 "The Apportionment of Human Diversity." *In: Evolutionary Biology* (Vol. 6), Th. Dobzhansky et al. (eds.), New York: Plenum, pp. 381–398.

Lieberman, Daniel, David R. Pilbeam and Bernard A. Wood
1988 "A Probalistic Approach to the Problem of Sexual Dimorphism in *Homo habilis*: A Comparison of KNM-ER-1470 and KNM-ER-1813." *Journal of Human Evolution,* **17**:503–511.

Livingstone, Frank B.
1964 "On the Nonexistence of Human Races." *In: Concept of Race,* A. Montagu (ed.), New York: The Free Press, pp. 46–60.

_____
1980 "Natural Selection and the Origin and Maintenance of Standard Genetic Marker Systems." *Yearbook of Physical Anthropology,* 1980, **23**:25–42.

Lyell, Charles
1830–33 *Principles of Geology,* 3 vols. Reprinted New York: Strecgert-Gafberm, 1869.

MacKinnon, J. and K. MacKinnon
1980 "The Behavior of Wild Spectral Tarsiers." *International Journal of Primatology,* 1:361–379.

Malthus, Thomas Robert
1914 *An Essay on the Principles of Population.* 2 volumes. Reprinted London: Everyman.

Masserman, J., S. Wechkin, and W. Terris
1964 " 'Altruistic' Behavior in Rhesus Monkeys." *American Journal of Psychiatry,* **121**:584–585.

Mayr, Ernst
1970 *Population, Species, and Evolution.* Cambridge: Harvard University Press.

McHenry, Henry
1988 "New Estimates of Body Weight in Early Hominids and their Significance to Encephalization and Megadontia in 'Robust' Australopithecines." *In:* Grine (ed.), q.v., pp. 133–148.

McKern, T. W. and T. D. Stewart
1957 "Skeletal Age Changes in Young American Males," Technical Report EP-45, Natick, MA: U.S. Quartermaster Research and Development Center.

Mittermeir, Russel A.
1982 "The World's Endangered Primates: An Introduction and a Case Study—The Monkeys of Brazil's Atlantic Forests." *In: Primates and the Tropical Rain Forest,* Proceedings, California Institute of Technology, World Wildlife Fund—U.S., pp. 11–22.

Mittermeir, R. A. and D. Cheney
1987 "Conservation of Primates in their Habitats." *In:* Smuts, et al., (eds.), q.v., pp. 477–496.

Molnar, Stephen
1983 *Human Variation. Races, Types, and Ethnic Groups* (2nd Ed.). Englewood Cliffs: Prentice-Hall.

Mourant, A. E., A. C. Kopec and K. Domaniewoke-Sobczak
1976 *The Distribution of Human Blood Groups and Other Polymorphisms.* London: Oxford University Press.

Napier, John
1967 "The Antiquity of Human Walking." *Scientific American,* **216**:56–66.

Napier, J. R. and P. H. Napier
1985 *The Natural History of the Primates.* London: British Museum (Natural History).

Proctor, Robert
1988 "From Anthropologie to Rassenkunde." *In:* George W. Stocking, q.v., pp. 138–179.

Pulliam, M. R. and T. Caraco
1984 "Living in Groups: Is There An Optimal Group Size?" *In: Behavioural Ecology: An Evolutionary Approach* (2nd Ed.), J. R. Krebs and N. B. Davies (eds.). Sunderland, Mass.: Sinauer Associates.

Rak, Y.
1983 *The Australopithecine Face.* New York: Academic Press.

Richard, A. F. and S. R. Schulman
1982 "Sociobiology: Primate Field Studies." *Annual Reviews of Anthropology,* **11**:231–255.

Rightmire, G. Philip
1990 *The Evolution of* Homo erectus. New York: Cambridge University Press.

Romer, Alfred S.
1959 *The Vertebrate Story.* Chicago: University of Chicago Press.

Rose, K. D.
1991 "Species Recognition in Eocene Primates." *American Journal of Physical Anthropology,* Supplement 12, p. 153.

Rumbaugh, D. M.
1977 *Language Learning by a Chimpanzee: The Lana Project.* New York: Academic Press.

Schaller, George B.
1963 *The Mountain Gorilla*. Chicago: University of Chicago Press.
Scheller, Richard H. and Richard Axel
1984 "How Genes Control Innate Behavior." *Scientific American*, **250**:54–63.
Senut, Brigette and Christine Tardieu
1985 "Functional Aspects of Plio-Pleistocene Hominid Limb Bones: Implications for Taxonomy and Phylogeny." *In*: E. Delson (ed.), q.v., pp. 193–201.
Simmons, J. G.
1989 *Changing the Face of the Earth*. Oxford: Basil Blackwell Ltd.
Skelton, R. R., H. M. McHenry and G. M. Drawhorn
1986 "Phylogenetic Analysis of Early Hominids." *Current Anthropology*, **27**:1–43; **27**:361–365.
Small, Meredith F. (ed.)
1984 *Female Primates. Studies by Women Primatologists*. Monographs in Primatology, Volume 4. New York: Alan R. Liss.
Smith, Fred H.
1984 "Fossil Hominids from the Upper Pleistocene of Central Europe and the Origin of Modern Europeans." *In*: Smith and Spencer, q.v., pp. 187–209.
Smith, Fred H. and Frank Spencer (eds.)
1984 *The Origins of Moderns*. New York: Alan R. Liss, Inc.
Smuts, Barbara B., Dorothy L. Cheney, Robert M. Seyfarth, et al. (eds.)
1987 *Primate Societies*. Chicago: University of Chicago Press.
Stammbach, Edward
1987 "Desert, Forest and Mountain Baboons: Multilevel Societies." *In*: Smuts et al., (eds.), q.v., pp. 112–120.
Stewart, T. D.
1979 *Essentials of Forensic Anthropology: Especially as Developed in the United States*. Springfield, IL: C. C. Thomas.
Stocking, George W., Jr. (ed.)
1988 *Bones, Bodies, Behavior. History of Anthropology*, vol. 5. Madison: The University of Wisconsin Press.
Stringer, C. B., J. J. Hublin and B. Vandermeersch
1984 "The Origin of Anatomically Modern Humans in Western Europe." *In*: Smith and Spencer, q.v., pp. 51–135.
Struhsaker, Thomas T. and Lysa Leland
1979 "Socioecology of Five Sympatric Monkey Species in the Kibale Forest, Uganda." *Advances in the Study of Behavior*, Vol. 9. New York: Academic Press, pp. 159–229.
——
1987 "Colobines: Infanticide by Adult Males." *In*: Smuts, et al. (eds.), q.v., pp. 83–97.
Sugiyama, Y.
1965 "Short History of the Ecological and Sociological Studies on Non-Human Primates in Japan." *Primates*, **6**:457–460.

Sugiyama, Yukimaru and Jeremy Koman
1979 "Tool-Using and -Making Behavior in Wild Chimpanzees at Bossou, Guinea." *Primates*, **20**:513–524.
Sumner, D. R., M. E. Morbeck and J. Lobick
1987 "Age-Related Bone Loss in Female Gombe Chimpanzees." *American Journal of Physical Anthropology*, **72**:259.
Susman, Randall L.
1988 "New Postcranial Remains from Swartkrans and their Bearing on the Functional Morphology and Behavior of *Paranthropus robustus*." *In*: Grine (ed.), q.v., pp. 149–172.
Susman, Randall L., Jack T. Stern and William L. Jungers
1985 "Locomotor Adaptations in the Hadar Hominids." *In*: E. Delson (ed.), q.v., pp. 184–192.
Szalay, Frederick S. and Eric Delson
1979 *Evolutionary History of the Primates*. New York: Academic Press.

Tobias, Phillip
1971 *The Brain in Hominid Evolution*. New York: Columbia University Press.
Todd, T. W.
1920–21 "Age Changes in the Pubic Bone," *American Journal of Physical Anthropology*, **3**:285–334; **4**:1–70.
Trotter, M. and G. C. Gleser
1952 "Estimation of Stature from Long Bones of American Whites and Negroes," *American Journal of Physical Anthropology*, **10**:463–514.
Tuttle, Russel H.
1990 "Apes of the World." *American Scientist*, **78**:115–125.

Vrba, E. S.
1988 "Late Pliocene Climatic Events and Hominid Evolution." *In*: F. Grine (ed.), q.v., pp. 405–426.

de Waal, Frans
1982 *Chimpanzee Politics*. London: Jonathan Cape.
——
1987 "Tension Regulation and Nonreproductive Functions of Sex in Captive Bonobos (*Pan paniscus*)." *National Geographic Research*, **3**:318–335.
——
1989 *Peacemaking Among Primates*. Cambridge: Harvard University Press.
de Waal Malefijt, Annemarie
1974 *Images of Man. A History of Anthropological Thought*. New York: Alfred A. Knopf.
Washburn, Sherwood L.
1971 "The Study of Human Evolution." *In*: *Background for Man: Readings in Physical Anthropology*, P. Dolhinow and V. Sarich (eds.). Boston: Little, Brown, pp. 82–121.

Watson, J. D. and F. H. C. Crick
1953a *Nature* **171**:737–738.

_____

1953b *Nature* **171**:964.

Weiner, J. S.
1955 *The Piltdown Forgery*. London: Oxford University Press.

Wheat, Joe Ben
1972 "The Olsen-Chubbuck Site; A Paleo-Indian Bison Kill." *American Antiquity*, **37**:1–180.

White, T. D.
1986 "Cut Marks on the Bodo Cranium: A Case of Prehistoric Defleshing." *American Journal of Physical Anthropology*, **69**(4):503–509.

White, Tim D. and Donald C. Johanson
1989 "The Hominid Composition of Afar Locality 333: Some Preliminary Observations." *Hominidae*, Proceedings of the 2nd International Congress of Human Paleontology, Milan: Editoriale Jaca Book, pp. 97–101.

Williams, Robert C.
1985 "HLA II: The Emergence of the Molecular Model for the Major Histocompatibility Complex." *Yearbook of Physical Anthropology*, **28**:79–95.

Wolpoff, Milford, Wu Xin Chi, and Alan G. Thorne
1984 "Modern *Homo sapiens* Origins." *In*: Smith and Spencer (eds.), q.v., pp. 411–483.

Wrangham, R. W.
1980 "An Ecological Model of Female-Bonded Primate Groups." *Behaviour*, **75**:262–300.

_____

1987 "Evolution of Social Structure." *In*: Smuts et al. (eds.), q.v., pp. 282–296.

Wu, Rukang and S. Lin
1983 "Peking Man." *Scientific American*, **248**(6):86–94.

INDEX